Exile: The Writer's Experience

UNIVERSITY OF NORTH CAROLINA
STUDIES IN THE GERMANIC LANGUAGES
AND LITERATURES

Initiated by RICHARD JENTE (1949–1952), established by F. E. COENEN (1952–1968),
continued by SIEGFRIED MEWS (1968–1980)

RICHARD H. LAWSON, Editor

Publication Committee: Department of Germanic Languages

83 FLORA KIMMICH. *Sonnets of Catharina von Greiffenberg: Methods of Composition.* 1975. Pp. x, 132.

84 HERBERT W. REICHERT. *Friedrich Nietzsche's Impact on Modern German Literature.* 1975. Pp. xxii, 129.

85 JAMES C. O'FLAHERTY, TIMOTHY F. SELLNER, ROBERT M. HELM, EDS. *Studies in Nietzsche and the Classical Tradition.* 2nd ed. 1979. Pp. xviii, 278.

86 ALAN P. COTTRELL. *Goethe's* Faust. *Seven Essays.* 1976. Pp. xvi, 143.

87 HUGO BEKKER. *Friedrich von Hausen. Inquiries into His Poetry.* 1977. Pp. x, 159.

88 H. G. HUETTICH. *Theater in the Planned Society: Contemporary Drama in the German Democratic Republic in Its Historical, Political, and Cultural Context.* 1978. Pp. xvi, 174.

89 DONALD G. DAVIAU, ED. *The Letters of Arthur Schnitzler to Hermann Bahr.* 1978. Pp. xii, 183.

90 KARL EUGENE WEBB. *Rainer Maria Rilke and* Jugendstil: *Affinities, Influences, Adaptations.* 1978. Pp. x, 137.

91 LELAND R. PHELPS AND A. TILO ALT, EDS. *Creative Encounter. Festschrift for Herman Salinger.* 1978. Pp. xxii, 181.

92 PETER BAULAND. *Gerhart Hauptmann's* Before Daybreak. *Translation and Introduction.* 1978. Pp. xxiv, 87.

93 MEREDITH LEE. *Studies in Goethe's Lyric Cycles.* 1978. Pp. xii, 191.

94 JOHN M. ELLIS. *Heinrich von Kleist. Studies in the Character and Meaning of His Writings.* 1979. Pp. xx, 194.

95 GORDON BIRRELL. *The Boundless Present. Space and Time in the Literary Fairy Tales of Novalis and Tieck.* 1979. Pp. x, 163.

96 G. RONALD MURPHY. *Brecht and The Bible. A Study of Religious Nihilism and Human Weakness in Brecht's Drama of Mortality and the City.* 1980. Pp. xi, 107.

97 ERHARD FRIEDRICHSMEYER. *Die satirische Kurzprosa Heinrich Bölls.* 1981. Pp. xiv, 223.

98 MARILYN J. BLACKWELL, ED. *Structures of Influence: A Comparative Approach to August Strindberg,* 1981. Pp. xiv, 308.

99 JOHN M. SPALEK, ROBERT F. BELL, EDS. *Exile: The Writer's Experience.* 1982. Pp. xxiii, 370.

For other volumes in the "Studies" see page 369.

Send orders to: (U.S. and Canada)
The University of North Carolina Press, P.O. Box 2288
Chapel Hill, N.C. 27514
(All other countries) Feffer and Simons, Inc., 100 Park Avenue, New York, N.Y. 10017

Number Ninety-Nine
University of
North Carolina
Studies in the
Germanic Languages
and Literatures

Exile: The Writer's Experience

Edited by John M. Spalek
and Robert F. Bell

The University of North Carolina Press Chapel Hill 1982

© 1982 The University of North Carolina Press

All rights reserved

Manufactured in the United States of America

ISBN 0-8078-8099-X

Library of Congress Cataloging in Publication Data

Main entry under title:

Exile : the writer's experience.

　(University of North Carolina studies in the Germanic
languages and literatures ; no. 99)

　Includes bibliographical references and index.

　1. German literature—20th century—History and
criticism—Addresses, essays, lectures. 2. German
literature in foreign countries—Addresses, essays,
lectures. I. Spalek, John M. II. Bell, Robert F.,
1937–　　　III. Series.

PT405.E9133　　　830　　　81-7502

ISBN 0-8078-8099-X　　　AACR2

Contents

Acknowledgments

The editors wish to express their appreciation to the following persons who made valuable suggestions in the course of the preparation of the manuscript: Adrienne Ash, Robert M. Browning, Karl S. Guthke, and Thomas R. Hansen. A special word of thanks is due to Joseph P. Strelka for his advice in the early stages of the composition of the volume.

The editors also wish to thank the following journals for permission to publish the following articles: *Brecht Heute /Brecht Today* for the article by Guy Stern; *Literatur und Kritik* for the article by Robert Kauf; *Colloquia Germanica* for the article by Dieter Sevin; the Francke Verlag for the article by Joseph P. Strelka. The editors would like to stress that all the articles previously published have been revised for the purposes of this publication.

Quotations from published poems by Bertolt Brecht are printed with the permission of Eyre Methuen, and quotations from poems by Nelly Sachs are published with the permission of Farrar, Straus and Giroux.

The photoready copy of this book was prepared for offset by Marcella Curtright, Carson, California.

Introduction

Much of twentieth-century literature, especially from the European continent, has been written in exile. That such literature can be of the highest quality is implicit in the stature of Thomas Mann, Nelly Sachs, Ramón Sender, Rafael Alberti, Witold Gombrowicz, Czeslaw Milosz, Vladimir Nabokov, Alexander Solzhenitsyn, and E. M. Cioran. Although writing in exile has a long and distinguished history (Ovid, Dante, Victor Hugo, Heinrich Heine, Adam Mickiewicz), the phenomenon of a national literature in exile seems to be a distinct product of the twentieth century. In fact, the waves of exile literature in this century coincide roughly with the chronological order of political upheavals and consequent emigration of writers from Russia, Germany, Austria, Czechoslovakia, Spain, Poland, the Baltic countries and, most recently, from the German Democratic Republic. Totalitarian political systems of both the right and the left have forced the intellectual opposition into emigration from which many have chosen never to return. Exile literature thus emerges as an ancient phenomenon that has acquired new importance as a result of the political developments of the last sixty years.

The term "exile" is used here to define mainly writers and intellectuals--spokesmen of culture--whose professional tool is their language and whose aim is to preserve and develop the cultural tradition they represent. German literature was "in exile" from 1933 to 1945, and involved hundreds, even thousands of professionally active journalists, critics, dramatists, script writers, novelists, poets, and others who earned their living by the pen.

The repressive measures instituted by the new National Socialist regime against its opponents after 30 January 1933 brought a mass exodus that depleted not only the literary, but also the entire cultural elite of Germany. The best talent in all the arts and sciences was either expelled for racial or political reasons, or chose to leave the country in protest against repression. Five years after the Nazi accession to power in Germany, the artistic and scientific establishment of Austria and Czechoslovakia--the latter with many German-speaking and German-educated individuals among its population--suffered the same fate when their respective countries were annexed by Hitler.

The exodus of the nineteen-thirties (1933-38) was not offset on a comparable scale after 1945 by a return of the exiles to Europe. The disruption of personal and professional life caused by the National Socialist regime, the defeat of Nazi Germany and the accompanying physical devastation of the country, as well as the division of Germany-- all of these factors deterred the majority of those who might have returned. It is thus misleading, even if correct, to say that the German exile spanned the years 1933-45, because to do so conceals a salient feature of the situation: exiled writers, with relatively few exceptions, did not return to Germany after the war, but chose instead to remain in their adopted homelands. Sidney Rosenfeld's essay is an illustration of the fact that German writing in exile continues even today.

The devastating consequences of the writers' exodus for Germany's literary development were paralleled, if not exceeded, by the depletion of numerous other professions after 1933 (natural and social scientists, artists, intellectuals). This exodus has turned into a permanent loss for German cultural life. The international prestige of German physics and film-making, for example, has only lately begun to recover from the loss of over one hundred important physicists and an equal number of film professionals: producers, directors, script-writers, actors, and technicians. An even more dramatic illustration is the permanent departure of nearly four hundred clinical and experimental psychologists and psychiatrists (Erik Erikson, Erich Fromm, Max Wertheimer, Wolfgang Köhler, Wilhelm Reich, Kurt Lewin). We can cite similar examples for such fields as music, art history, mathematics, economics, biochemistry, and political science, areas in which the German contribution has been seminal. But it was in the literary life in exile, where issues of immediate cultural importance focusing on aesthetics, intellectual history, and philosophy were argued, that the endurance of the German humanistic tradition was tested.

Hence it is fitting that the *writer* in exile is most often regarded as the exile per se. The quality that gives him this representative status is the tool of his trade: his native language, which he cannot abandon without simultaneously surrendering his identity with the culture he represents. The problem of identity does not affect a mathematician, an architect, or a painter in the same way. Their tools and means of communication are much more easily understood and do not require the labor of "translation." Thus we justifiably speak of "literature in exile" while we do not speak in the same sense of "mathematics in exile."

The most salient characteristic of exile literature is its inexorable involvement, whether directly or in disguise, with the political situation that caused it, and practically all the essays in this volume bear this out. This political involvement manifests itself in a wide range of writing: from polemical essays attacking specific issues (frequently showing a justifiable propagandistic bias) to novels analyzing more general phenomena such as the origins of dictatorship, techniques of oppression and persecution, political myopia, and intellectual or moral irresponsibility on the part of a nation --depicted in a manner that unmistakably reflects parallels with contemporary events (see in particular the discussion by Joseph P. Strelka of the novels of Thomas Mann, Hermann Broch, and Joseph Roth). More specifically, however, German exiled writers provide us with a description of life and conditions in Nazi Germany--either in contemporary, realistic settings (Anna Seghers, Lion Feuchtwanger), or by suggesting a parallel in historical disguise (Hermann Broch, Joseph Roth). It bears repeating that those authors who left Nazi Germany felt that they alone could expose the true character of the regime that had expelled them. The writers of the so-called "Inner Emigration" were, of course, subject to strict censorship and not free to be explicit in their criticism. A typical example of the technique of the Inner Emigration is Ernst Jünger's story *Auf den Marmorklippen*, 1939 [*On the Marble Cliffs*],[1] an allegorical depiction of the struggle between a seductive and ruthless power and those who attempt to resist its advance.

As might be expected, exile literature also abounds in descriptions of life in exile. These range from direct autobiographical narratives to what seem involuntary reflections in works otherwise not dealing with the theme of exile (see in particular the essay by Guy Stern). The most direct descriptions of exile are the collections of letters, the numerous autobiographies and autobiographical novels, such as Leonhard Frank's *Links wo das Herz ist*, 1952 [*Heart on the Left*].[2] The magnitude of the forced emigration of the thirties and its impact on the individual is evident from the nearly four hundred autobiographies published so far. There are several possible reasons for this phenomenon. The attempt on the part of exiles to rescue their lives and accomplishments from oblivion--a danger more real than imaginary --is among the most important. In addition, the motive of self-justification to posterity must not be overlooked. Beyond these more personal reasons, the autobiographies represent an attempt to continue a tradition through difficult times. Yet a word of caution as to the documentary value of these first-hand accounts is in order: they are often highly subjective and their "facts" must be compared to other accounts and historical documents before being accepted.

INTRODUCTION

There are several critical perspectives from which German exile literature has been examined and reviewed: (1) One critical approach--most characteristic of the initial stage of exile research--has been to see this body of literature as the legitimate heir to the German humanistic tradition and Judeo-Christian heritage. This view has also stressed the unity and common character of exile literature. In the forefront of this group has been Walter A. Berendsohn, whose groundbreaking book *Die humanistische Front*, 1946 [*Humanistic Front*][3] set the tone and the argument for those who see exile literature as the expression of Western humanistic values.

(2) The most controversial critical method is the one based upon a priori political assumptions about a work and its author. Most, though not all, evaluations employing this approach come from the German Democratic Republic, for instance Klaus Jarmatz,[4] Wolfgang Kiessling,[5] and Werner Mittenzwei.[6] Proceeding from an avowedly Marxist viewpoint, such critics judge a work according to its reputed ideological orientation, supporting their conclusions with assumptions about the political sympathies of the writer. The controversy centers, in this case, on a definition of antifascist literature. Simply stated, German exile literature, though tacitly conceived in opposition to National Socialism, is not regarded as deserving the name of "antifascist" unless it conforms to a Marxist view of the historical process. This narrow definition excludes many writers from the ranks of the antifascists, such as the conservative opponents of Hitler, writers of moderate Social Democratic persuasion, and the non-Marxist Jews. To restrict the label antifascist to a group of ideologically aligned writers is obviously too narrow a definition to be useful. Some of the most trenchant exposés of the Nazis were written by non-Marxists, and some of the culturally most conservative exiles became vocal opponents of Hitler through their literature as well as their political activity (Thomas Mann, Hermann Broch, Franz Werfel). In short, the criteria for determining an antifascist attitude of the writers cannot be deduced from their social or political status but rather from the intensity of vision in the individual works.

(3) A third and, for literary scholarship, perhaps the most important critical approach has to do with the literary expression of the writer's experience, that is, with the question to what extent the exile experience affected the writer's style and means of expression. It is generally acknowledged that this approach is still in its developing stages, and that the study of exile literature up to now has been emphasizing history, political content, ideological commitment, and biography.

The study of exile literature as literature would be concerned with the preferred use of certain genres and themes, and the importance of motifs, symbols, and structural characteristics. Such studies can take two forms: either the intensive study of individual works, or a synthesizing approach using a literary genre, such as the historical novel or the *Novelle*. There are already a number of studies of individual works in existence, for instance Otto F. Best's article on Leonhard Frank in *Deutsche Exilliteratur* ,[7] the essays by Manfred Durzak and Erna Moore on Elias Canetti and Friedrich Torberg in *Protest--Form--Tradition* ,[8] and the study by Guy Stern about Brecht's *Galileo* in this volume. Some initial attempts to deal with literary genres are the essays by Theodore Ziolkowski on the sonnet in exile,[9] the article by James Rolleston on the *novella* in this volume, and the dissertation by Bruce M. Broerman on the historical novel.[10]

The approach to the study of exile literature as literature can also utilize two more approaches: the diachronic approach, that is, the study of exile experience in literature throughout history, and the synchronic approach, that is, the comparative study of exile literature in several languages in the twentieth century (German, Spanish, Polish, Russian, and Baltic countries). Werner Vordtriede's perceptive article on the typology of exile literature is an example of the former,[11] and John M. Spalek's essay, entitled "Literature in Exile: The Comparative Approach" could serve as an example of the latter.[12]

The third approach, outlined above, is perhaps best suited to ask the question that has been asked repeatedly in exile research: What is Exile Literature?

The present volume on exile as the experience of the writer attempts to give a more comprehensive presentation of this subject in English than earlier studies had done. Not counting a growing number of American dissertations on German literature in exile, there have been four book-length studies published so far. The earliest is that of William K. Pfeiler (himself an émigré) on lyric poetry in exile (1957).[13] The second is Robert E. Cazden's book about the free German press in exile (published in 1970, but written several years earlier).[14] The remaining two are recent works: One is a study of anti-Nazi writers in exile by Egbert Krispyn (1979),[15] and the other is *Protest--Form--Tradition* , edited by Joseph P. Strelka, Robert F. Bell, and Eugene Dobson. In addition, we may expect in the near future the publication of a basic survey of German literature in exile in the Twayne series by Thomas R. Hansen.

The number of studies written in German on the writers in exile is quite impressive, considering that research on the emigration of writers and intellectuals started in earnest only in the late nineteen-sixties. The most comprehensive published bibliography of secondary literature is contained in the recent study by Alexander Stephan (1979), and it lists several hundred publications.[16]

The critical literature on the German writers and intellectuals in exile, as well as that on scientists and political émigrés, can be divided into several phases: (1) During the nineteen-thirties, shortly after the Nazi take-over, there were numerous publications by émigré writers and intellectuals reflecting the various controversies and debates within the exile community.[17] During the same years, only five book-length works about German literature in exile were published (four by exiles themselves, and one by a Norwegian, Odd Eidem).[18] Walter Berendsohn's study, published in 1946, was also written before 1940.

(2) Between 1940 and 1947 several books were published; again, most were by exiles: Peter M. Lindt (1944); Walter P. Jacob (1946); Franz Carl Weiskopf (1947); and Richard Drews and Alfred Kantorowicz (1947).[19] These books were basically anthologies designed to reintroduce the German public to the writers who left the country after 1933. The book by Drews and Kantorowicz, entitled *Verboten und Verbrannt* [*Banned and Burned*] was the most widely distributed title.

(3) During the nineteen-fifties, research seems to have turned its attention to the political and academic emigration, with the possible exception of Pfeiler. The studies treating the political emigration were those by Erich Matthias (1953), Lewis J. Edinger (1956), and Walter A. Schmidt (1958), to mention the most important.[20] The emigration of academics was treated by Stephen Duggan and Betty Drury (1948); William Rex Crawford (1953); Donald P. Kent (1953); and Helge Pross (1955).[21] As with the studies done in the previous decades, a prominent share of the work was carried out by former émigrés themselves.

(4) The number of studies about exile literature begins to increase after 1960, the most important being the first edition of the bio-bibliographies of writers in exile by Wilhelm Sternfeld and Eva Tiedemann,[22] in which the term "literature in exile" is interpreted widely enough to include journalistic, political, historical, and autobiographical writings. The other significant publication is the volume by Egon Schwarz and Matthias Wegner (1964) consisting of selections from the writing of exiled authors and intellectuals with a connecting commentary by the editors.[23]

(5) The bulk of publications, especially on German literature in exile, occurred in the decade starting roughly in 1966 and continuing until about 1976. The impetus came from several directions. Starting in 1969, there has been a series of conferences devoted to German literature in exile, both in Europe and in the United States, the earliest being the first international conference in Stockholm, organized by Walter A. Berendsohn, the driving force behind exile research in the late sixties. Since 1969 there have been at least a dozen important symposia: University of Kentucky (1971), University of Wisconsin (1971), Washington University in St. Louis (1972), Copenhagen (1972), Akademie der Künste in West Berlin (1973), University of Alabama (1975), Vienna (1975), three successive conferences at the University of

South Carolina (1976, 1977, 1979), at the Reisensburg in West
Germany (1979), the Smithsonian Institution (1980), and the
University of California at Riverside (1980).[24]
Of seminal importance was also the exhibit on German
literature in exile organized by the Deutsche Bibliothek in
Frankfurt in 1965. The catalogue of this exhibit, a book of
over 300 pages, was published in 1966 and reissued two more
times.[25] This exhibit also stimulated numerous other exhibits that served to call the public's attention to the fact of
the anti-Nazi emigration of the thirties.
The most significant publications of the years 1966-76
are those by Matthias Wegner (1967), Klaus Jarmatz (1966),
Hans-Albert Walter (beginning in 1972), Manfred Durzak
(1973), Hans-Christoph Wächter (1973), Wolfgang Kiessling
(1973), and the two-part study edited by John M. Spalek and
Joseph Strelka on German writers in California (1976).[26]
(6) Judging from the publications that have appeared
since 1976, the present decade promises to be just as prolific as the preceding one. Among the most recent publications centering on literature in exile are those by Hans
Würzner about German literature in exile in the Netherlands
(1978); Werner Mittenzwei's study of exile in Switzerland
(1978); Lothar Schirmer's edition of papers about the theater
in exile (1979); Michael Winkler's anthology (1977); Ernst
Loewy's voluminous compilation (1979); Hanno Hardt's volume
(1979); and Alexander Stephan's basic introduction (1979).[27]
The main purpose of this volume is to offer the American reader a fairly comprehensive introduction to German
writing in exile. Though the essays treat only a select number of writers, the themes and problems, the experiences
described and analyzed in these essays are recurrent throughout German exile literature.
The volume includes twenty-four essays, five of which
present general surveys of the main literary genres in exile:
lyric poetry, the novel, the *Novelle*, and the drama. A
survey of journalistic writing--not often considered in a
strictly literary study--finds its rightful place in this context, for journalism must be considered vital to the literary
life of the émigrés. The essays on the genres examine, on
the one hand, the continuity of literary tradition and, on
the other, its transformation under the constraints of exile.
A survey of the genres reveals, furthermore, the extent to
which the historical novel predominated in the consciousness
of prose writers (Strelka, Sanger), and the degree to which
traditional literary forms reasserted their importance: for
example, the sonnet in lyric poetry (Ash, Kauf) and the
Novelle in prose fiction (Rolleston).
The introductory essays are followed by three studies
that offer comparative views and historical background material. Henri Paucker discusses the exile experience of the
writer in terms of the existentialist metaphor. His comments
illustrate the applicability of existentialist terminology to
the ethos of exile literature. The essays by Carol Paul-

INTRODUCTION

Merritt and Erich Frey (including the text of the Tolan Committee Hearing of 1943) treat the writers in the United States,
the country that became either the temporary asylum or the
permanent home of the largest number of refugees.   Paul
Merritt traces the gradual growth of receptivity on the part
of the liberal American press to the cause of exiles during
the nineteen-thirties.   Frey's essay and the appended text
show Thomas Mann in his role as the spokesman for the German exiles in the United States, and the essay sheds light
on the strictures to which the so-called "enemy aliens" in
this country, including many who fled Nazi Germany, were
subjected during the years of World War II.
        Herbert Lehnert's study on Thomas Mann and Bertolt
Brecht demonstrates that exiled writers and intellectuals seldom composed homogeneous groups, as the thesis of Berendsohn's "humanistische Front" seemed to suggest.   There were
profound political as well as personal differences that even
the common plight of exile and opposition could not elimi-
nate.
        The   individual   studies   devoted   to   Hermann   Broch,
Robert Musil, Joseph Roth, Ernst Waldinger, and Franz Werfel
will remind the reader of still another differentiation: that
of the exile's country of origin.   German literature in exile,
the term used to describe the literature written in German
between 1933 and 1945 outside of Germany, includes authors
not only from Germany proper but also from Austria, Czechoslovakia, and Hungary.
        The studies by Guy Stern, John Fuegi, Dieter Sevin,
and Susan Cernyak illustrate the peculiar situation of the
leftist writer in exile.   Fuegi explores the complex situation
of Brecht, the avowed left-wing writer, who ultimately settled
in the United States rather than in the Soviet Union, a seemingly natural ideological home.   Similarly, Dieter Sevin
traces the experiences of Plievier, who, after spending the
war years in Soviet Russia and returning to East Germany
after 1945, moved to West Germany in 1949.   Susan Cernyak's
essay on Anna Seghers, who spent her exile years in Mexico,
shows the curious insensitivity of this talented Marxist writer
to the plight of her race and the persecution it had to
endure.
        Lore Foltin's essay on Franz Werfel traces his change
of attitude toward the United States, an experience common
to a number of writers of his generation who sought refuge
from Hitler in this country.   Before 1933, it was rather characteristic of European intellectuals visiting the United States
to be either condescending or outright critical of the life
and culture in America.   Such books as those of Arthur Holitscher, Alfred Kerr, Egon Erwin Kisch, and Ernst Toller,[28]
usually the products of relatively short visits to this continent, emphasized the more sensational aspects of American
life: Prohibition, religious cults, crime, pragmatism, and
materialism.   Whether stated or implied, such accounts note

in the United States the lack of "culture" in a European sense. Franz Werfel's revised view of the United States describes this country as synonymous with democracy and liberty, and the same positive view of America can be found in the autobiographies and novels written by German exiles after 1945. It can be safely said that the affirmative view of the United States in the works of exiles is more than a response to a crisis; it remained permanent and enduring.

Several essays in this volume respond to a central question of exile research: Did the experience of exile have any substantial effect upon the subject matter in the literature of the émigrés? The essays by Ash, Rolleston, and Strelka answer this question in the affirmative, and Robert Kauf proves the hypothesis using the specific example of the poet Ernst Waldinger, for whom the experience of exile pervades life and art. Furthermore, Guy Stern's analysis of Brecht's *Leben des Galilei* [*Galileo*] discovers the theme of Brecht's own exile experience in an historical figure with symbolic dimensions for the modern era.

We hope that these essays will provide incentive to further investigation that may support or modify the findings presented here. But whether or not the critical opinions expressed here remain valid, one can assent to Lion Feuchtwanger's understated appraisal of German exile literature written in 1943: "All in all, literature in exile has stood the test fairly well. When the tide has passed and when we can again weigh with accurate balance what is good and what is not, posterity will find that, among the works of this period, those composed in exile will not be light in the scales."[29]

Notes

[1] Ernst Jünger, *Auf den Marmorklippen* (Hamburg: Hanseatische Verlagsanstalt, 1939). English version *On the Marble Cliffs*, trans. Stuart Hood (Norfolk, Conn.: New Directions, 1947).

[2] Leonhard Frank, *Links wo das Herz ist: Roman* (Munich: Nymphenburger Verlagshandlung, 1952); English version *Heart on the Left*, trans. Cyrus Brooks (London: A. Barker, 1954).

[3] Walter A. Berendsohn, *Die humanistische Front: Einführung in die deutsche Emigranten-Literatur; Erster Teil: von 1933 bis zum Kriegsausbruch 1939* (Zürich: Europa, 1946).

[4] Klaus Jarmatz, *Literatur im Exil* (Berlin: Dietz, 1966); Klaus Jarmatz and Simone Barck, eds., *Antifaschistische deutsche Literaturkritik 1933-1945* (Halle: Mitteldeutscher Verlag, 1980); and Klaus Jarmatz, Simone Barck, and

Peter Diezel, eds., *Exil in der UdSSR* (Leipzig: Philipp Reclam, 1980).

[5]Wolfgang Kiessling, *Alemania Libre in Mexiko*, 2 vols. (Berlin: Akademie-Verlag, 1974).

[6]Werner Mittenzwei, *Exil in der Schweiz* (Leipzig: Philipp Reclam, 1978).

[7]Otto F. Best, "Leonhard Frank," in *Deutsche Exilliteratur seit 1933: Band I, Kalifornien*, ed. John M. Spalek and Joseph Strelka (Berne: Francke, 1976), pp. 371-82.

[8]Manfred Durzak, "From Dialect-Play to Philosophical Parable: Elias Canetti in Exile"; and Erna Moore, "Friedrich Torberg's *Mein ist die Rache* As a Literary Work of Art," in *Protest--Form--Tradition: Essays on German Exile Literature*, ed. Joseph P. Strelka, Robert F. Bell, and Eugene Dobson (University: The University of Alabama Press, 1979), pp. 35-36 and 111-21.

[9]Theodore Ziolkowski, "Form als Protest: Das Sonett in der Literatur des Exils und der Inneren Emigration," in *Exil und innere Emigration: Third Wisconsin Workshop*, ed. Reinhold Grimm and Jost Hermand, Wissenschaftliche Paperbacks, Literaturwissenschaft, 17 (Frankfurt/M: Athenäum, 1971), pp. 153-72.

[10]Bruce M. Broerman, "The German Historical Novel in Exile after 1933," Diss. State University of New York at Albany 1976.

[11]Werner Vordtriede, "Vorläufige Gedanken zu einer Typologie der Exilliteratur," *Akzente*, 15, No. 6 (Dec. 1968), 556-75.

[12]John M. Spalek, "Literature in Exile: The Comparative Approach," in *Deutsches Exildrama und Exiltheater: Akten des Exilliteratur-Symposiums der University of South Carolina 1976*, ed. Wolfgang D. Elfe, James Hardin and Günther Holst, Jahrbuch für Internationale Germanistik, Reihe A: Kongressberichte, 3 (Berne: Peter Lang, 1977), pp. 14-26.

[13]William K. Pfeiler, *German Literature in Exile: The Concern of the Poets*, University of Nebraska Studies, N.S., No. 16 (Lincoln: University of Nebraska Press, 1957).

[14]Robert E. Cazden, *German Exile Literature in America 1933-50: A History of the Free German Press and Book Trade* (Chicago: American Library Association, 1970).

[15]Egbert Krispyn, *Anti-Nazi Writers in Exile* (Athens: The University of Georgia Press, 1978).

[16]Alexander Stephan, *Die deutsche Exilliteratur 1933-1955: Eine Einführung* (Munich: C. H. Beck, 1979).

[17]See, for instance, Dagmar E. Malone, "Die literarischen Kontroversen innerhalb der Exil-Literatur der dreissiger Jahre," Diss. University of Southern California 1970; *Die Expressionismusdebatte: Materialien zu einer marxistischen Realismuskonzeption*, ed. Hans-Jürgen Schmitt, edition suhrkamp, 646 (Frankfurt/M: Suhrkamp, 1973).

18 In chronological order: Wolf Franck, *Führer durch die deutsche Emigration*, Phoenix Bücher, 4 (Paris: Editions du Phénix, 1935); Erich Stern, *Die Emigration als psychologisches Problem* (Boulogne-sur-Seine: privately printed, 1937); Odd Eidem, *Diktere i Landflyktighet* (Oslo: Tiden Norsk Forlag; Copenhagen: Forlaget Fremad, 1937); Alfred Döblin, *Die deutsche Literatur (Im Ausland seit 1933): Ein Dialog zwischen Politik und Kunst*, Schriften zu dieser Zeit, 1 (Paris: Science et littérature, 1938); and the study by Berendsohn, see note 3.

19 Peter M. Lindt, *Schriftsteller im Exil: Zwei Jahre deutsche literarische Sendung am Rundfunk in New York* (New York: Willard, 1944); Walter P. Jacob, ed., *Theater: Sieben Jahre Freie Deutsche Bühne; Ein Brevier* (Buenos Aires: Editorial Jupiter, 1946); Franz Carl Weiskopf, *Unter fremden Himmeln: Ein Abriss der deutschen Literatur im Exil 1933-1947; Mit einem Anhang von Textproben aus Werken exilierter Schriftsteller* (Berlin: Dietz, 1947); and Richard Drews and Alfred Kantorowicz, eds., *Verboten und Verbrannt: Deutsche Literatur--12 Jahre unterdrückt* (Berlin and Munich: Heinz Ullstein/Helmut Kindler, 1947).

20 Erich Matthias, *Sozialdemokratie und Nation: Zur Ideengeschichte der sozialdemokratischen Emigration 1933-1938* (Stuttgart: Deutsche Verlagsanstalt, 1952); Lewis J. Edinger, *German Exile Politics: The Social Democratic Executive Committee in the Nazi Era* (Berkeley: University of California Press, 1956); and Walter A. Schmidt, *Damit Deutschland lebe: Ein Quellenwerk über den deutschen antifaschistischen Widerstandskampf, 1933-1945* (Berlin: Kongress-Verlag, 1958).

21 Stephen Duggan and Betty Drury, *The Rescue of Science and Learning: The Story of the Emergency Committee in Aid of Displaced Foreign Scholars* (New York: Macmillan, 1948); William Rex Crawford, ed., *The Cultural Migration: The European Scholar in America* (Philadelphia: University of Pennsylvania Press, 1953); Donald P. Kent, *The Refugee Intellectual: The Americanization of the Immigrants of 1933-1941* (New York: Columbia University Press, 1953); and Helge Pross, *Die deutsche akademische Emigration nach den Vereinigten Staaten 1933-1945*, introd. Franz L. Neumann (Berlin: Duncker und Humblot, 1955).

22 Wilhelm Sternfeld and Eva Tiedemann, eds., *Deutsche-Exil-literatur 1933-1945: Eine Bio-Bibliographie*, Veröffentlichungen der deutschen Akademie für Sprache und Dichtung Darmstadt, 29A (Heidelberg: Lambert Schneider, 1962). A second, revised and expanded edition appeared in 1970.

23 Egon Schwarz and Matthias Wegner, eds., *Verbannung: Aufzeichnungen deutscher Schriftsteller im Exil* (Hamburg: Christian Wegner, 1964).

INTRODUCTION

[24]The papers given at these conferences have either appeared in print or are about to be published. For the papers given at the Stockholm conference, see *Colloquia Germanica*, No. 1/2 (1971); the paper given by Helmut Müssener, entitled "Die deutschsprachige Emigration nach 1933--Aufgaben und Probleme ihrer Erforschung," was published in *Moderna Språk: Language Monographs*, No. 12 (1971). Several of the papers given at the Kentucky conference in 1971 were published separately. For the papers given at the conference at the University of Wisconsin in 1971, see note 9. The papers of the conference at Washington University in St. Louis, a sequel to the conference at Madison, were edited by Peter Uwe Hohendahl and Egon Schwarz, *Exil und Innere Emigration II: Internationale Tagung in St. Louis*, Wissenschaftliche Paperbacks, Literaturwissenschaft, 18 (Frankfurt/M: Athenäum, 1975). The proceedings of the Copenhagen conference were edited by Helmut Müssener and Gisela Sandquist, *Protokoll des II. internationalen Symposiums zur Erforschung des deutschsprachigen Exils nach 1933 in Kopenhagen 1972* (Stockholm: Deutsches Institut der Universität Stockholm, 1972). For the papers of the Alabama conference in 1975, see note 8. The proceedings of the conference in Vienna in 1975 are also available: *Österreicher im Exil 1934 bis 1945: Protokoll des Internationalen Symposiums zur Erforschung des österreichischen Exils von 1934 bis 1945*, ed. Dokumentationsarchiv des Österreichischen Widerstandes und Dokumentationsstelle für Neuere Österreichische Literatur (Vienna: Österreichischer Bundesverlag für Unterricht, Wissenschaft und Kunst, 1977). The papers of the symposium at the Akademie der Künste in Berlin in 1973 have also recently appeared: *Theater im Exil 1933-1945: Ein Symposium der Akademie der Künste*, ed. Lothar Schirmer (Berlin: Akademie der Künste, 1979). The papers of the first two South Carolina conferences have also been published. For the 1976 conference, see note 12. The papers of the 1977 symposium are: *Deutsche Exilliteratur/Literatur im Dritten Reich: Akten des II. Exilliteratur-Symposiums der University of South Carolina*, ed. Wolfgang Elfe, James Hardin, and Günther Holst, Jahrbuch für Internationale Germanistik, Reihe A: Kongressberichte, 5 (Berne: Peter Lang, 1979). The papers of the conferences at the Reisensburg in 1979, the Smithsonian Institution, and the University of California at Riverside (both 1980) are being prepared for publication.

[25]*Exil-Literatur 1933-1945: Ausstellung der Deutschen Bibliothek, Frankfurt am Main, Mai bis August 1965*, ed. Werner Berthold and Christa Wilhelmi, Sonderveröffentlichungen der Deutschen Bibliothek, 1 (Frankfurt/M: printed by Johannes Weisbecker, 1965); a second and a third revised edition appeared in 1966 and 1967, respectively.

[26]Matthias Wegner, *Exil und Literatur: Deutsche Schriftsteller im Ausland 1933-1945* (Frankfurt/M: Athe-

näum, 1967); a second revised edition appeared in 1969; Klaus Jarmatz, see note 4; Hans-Albert Walter, *Deutsche Exilliteratur 1933-1950* (Darmstadt: Luchterhand). Vols. I, II, and VII of Walter's series appeared in 1972 and 1974, respectively; in the meantime, it has changed publishers (Stuttgart: Metzler) and format. Manfred Durzak, ed., *Die deutsche Exilliteratur 1933-1945* (Stuttgart: Philipp Reclam, 1973); Hans-Christof Wächter, *Theater im Exil: Sozialgeschichte des deutschen Exiltheaters 1933 - 1945*. Mit einem Beitrag von Louis Naef: *Theater der deutschen Schweiz* (Munich: Hanser, 1973). For Wolfgang Kiessling and John M. Spalek and Joseph Strelka, see notes 5 and 7.

27 Hans Würzner, ed., *Zur deutschen Exilliteratur in den Niederlanden 1933-1940*, Amsterdamer Beiträge zur Neueren Germanistik, 6 (Amsterdam: Rodopi, 1978); Michael Winkler, ed., *Deutsche Literatur im Exil 1933-1945: Texte und Dokumente*, Universal-Bibliothek, 9865 (Stuttgart: Philipp Reclam, 1977); Ernst Loewy, in collaboration with Brigitte Grimm, Helga Nagel, and Felix Schneider, eds., *Exil: Literarische und politische Texte aus dem deutschen Exil 1933-1945* (Stuttgart: J. B. Metzler, 1979); Hanno Hardt, Elke Hilscher, and Winfried B. Lerg, eds., *Presse im Exil: Beiträge zur Kommunikationsgeschichte des Exils, 1933-45* (Munich: K. G. Saur, 1979). For the books by Mittenzwei, Schirmer, and Stephan, see notes 6, 24, and 16, respectively.

28 See Arthur Holitscher, *Amerika heute und morgen: Reiseerlebnisse* (Berlin: S. Fischer, 1912); Alfred Kerr, *Newyork und London: Stätten des Geschicks; Zwanzig Kapitel nach dem Weltkrieg* (Berlin: S. Fischer, 1923); and *Yankeeland: Eine Reise* (Berlin: R. Mosse, 1925); Egon Erwin Kisch, *Egon Erwin Kisch beehrt sich darzubieten: Paradies Amerika* (Berlin: E. Reiss, 1930); and Ernst Toller, *Quer Durch: Reisebilder und Reden* (Berlin: Gustav Kiepenheuer, 1930).

29 Lion Feuchtwanger, "The Working Problems of the Writer in Exile," in *Writers' Congress: The Proceedings of the Conference held in October 1943 under the sponsorship of the Hollywood Writers' Mobilization and the University of California* (Berkeley and Los Angeles: University of California Press, 1944), p. 349. The German text of this lecture is available in *Deutsche Literatur im Exil 1933-1945*, ed. Heinz Ludwig Arnold, Vol. I: *Dokumente* (Frankfurt/M: Athenäum Fischer Taschenbuch Verlag, 1974), pp. 238-42.

Exile: The Writer's Experience

Lyric Poetry in Exile

Adrienne Ash

> "This emigration--I have to say . . .
> somehow it's fascinating and enormously
> stimulating to be thrown totally on
> one's own, with a desk for a home."[1]

This is what Austrian poet Franz Theodor Csokor wrote of his adventure in exile. However, his experience was the exception. Poets, whether German, or Austrian, or Czech, usually felt not the exhilaration but only the oppression of exile with its attendant problems of physical subsistence and linguistic isolation. Some poets found asylum in distant parts of the world, such as Paul Zech in Argentina, Karl Wolfskehl in New Zealand, and Else Lasker-Schüler in Palestine, but most chose to remain closer to their homeland, taking up residence in Czechoslovakia, Switzerland, England, France, or Sweden. The poet in exile, unlike the novelist, exerted less influence upon a host culture and rarely received either artistic praise or criticism for his literary production. He existed in a cultural vacuum, neither exempt from nor responsible for participation in political or even aesthetic affairs of the adopted nation. And in a final state of severance, the majority of exiled poets never returned to Europe from their cultural limbo.

That the "prose mode" seemed eminently more inimical to the Nazi effort to redirect the cultural life of Germany, that poetry was essentially a more harmless, politically uncommitted literary form, was the theme of a famous letter of Thomas Mann to Eduard Korrodi:

> You say that not all literature, but mainly the novel, has gone into exile. That wouldn't be surprising. The pure poem--pure in the sense that it remains rather aloof from social and political problems, something the lyric has not always done--is governed by other laws

1

> than those of narrative prose . . . . The former grows
> and blooms, serene and undisturbed in sweet oblivion
> of the world.[2]

Although Thomas Mann here made the distinction between *poé-sie pure* and *poésie engagée*, he underestimated the indiscriminate measures of the National Socialist anti-aesthetes, who found pure lyric poetry at least as offensive as the most polemic political novels.   Second, he reveals an astonishing naiveté vis-à-vis his fellow émigrés who were lyricists.   A surprising number of lyricists were forced to emigrate, and the so-called "purists" of the lyric suffered perhaps most under the conditions of exile.   Unlike prose writers, they were less likely to find their work being translated (because less marketable); and unlike more topical poets, the viability and continuity of their poetic subjects were disoriented by exile.

Among all those lyricists who emigrated, there emerged three fairly distinct literary "generations."   The first, "older" generation was made up of those poets and writers born before the turn of the century, half or more of whom belonged to the early expressionist movement and its fringes. In the Kurt Pinthus anthology *Menschheitsdämmerung* [*Dawn of Mankind*] can be found the names of four poets of some literary stature: Johannes R. Becher, Else Lasker-Schüler, Franz Werfel, and Paul Zech.   Werfel and Lasker-Schüler attained some popularity and renown in exile, but in Werfel's case it was more for his novels, and in Lasker-Schüler's for the drama of her personality.

The second generation--poets who began to publish only in the 1920s--was a group composed of such diverse personalities as Oskar Maria Graf, Ernst Waldinger, and Theodor Kramer.   These poets were in their thirties and forties when exile began, and their heritage was George, Rilke, and expressionism, along with post-World War I socialist poetry. Exile for them came at a time when they were struggling for personal recognition and relevance in literature.   They were frustrated in exile and less in the limelight as a whole than the senior group.

The youngest generation is represented by those whose subsequent development as poets was undoubtedly altered by their uprooting.   Many of this generation, such as translator-poet-essayist Erich Fried, are still known today.   Some, such as Oskar Seidlin and Heinz Politzer, are known not for the poetry they wrote outside Germany, but for their work in literary criticism and theory.   Of those whose poetry has been recognized, at least by students of literature, Stephan Hermlin is one.   The only evidence one has for the intellectual survival of this young generation is the successes, such as Fried.   The question of how many burgeoning young poetic talents merely gave up their ambitions in exile and were never heard from again remains moot.

Departure for all exiles was only the beginning.   The major obstacle for any literary émigré was one of livelihood. Valiant efforts were made to publish German writers abroad and thus allow authors and poets a modicum of public access for their writing. The Aurora Press, founded in New York City by Wieland Herzfelde, was a Herculean effort to print exile literature.3   The publishing house of Emil Oprecht in Zürich, Switzerland, also made a good deal of exile lyric available, as did Barthold Fles Verlag, located, like the Aurora Press, in New York.   The Austrian P.E.N. Club in exile in Great Britain took care of its own, producing modest editions of Austrian émigrés Erich Fried and Richard Frieden-thal.   Poets in exile in the Soviet Union had unusually good fortune.   Johannes R. Becher, Erich Weinert, Hedda Zinner, and a fairly large group of leftist poets had three major presses at their service, and all three published great quan-tities of poetry in German.   Among newspapers, three periodi-cals in the West published poetry to a significant extent between 1933 and 1940.   *Das neue Tagebuch*, edited in Paris by Leopold Schwarzschild, found room in its pages for the poetry of Alfred Kerr, Max Hermann-Neisse, Walter Mehring, Berthold Viertel, Theodor Kramer, Paul Zech, Hans Sahl, and Alfred Wolfenstein.   The New York-based *Aufbau*, too, pub-lished so much poetry that Walter A. Berendsohn remarked in retrospect: "A comprehensive, rich, and stimulating anthology of German emigrants could be compiled from the pages of the *Aufbau* alone."4   As in book publishing, however, the Marx-ist press carried off the honors, at least in quantity: *Inter-nationale Literatur: Deutsche Blätter*, edited by Johan-nes R. Becher, and *Das Wort*, edited by Bertolt Brecht, Lion Feuchtwanger, and Willi Bredel, published more poetry in single years than other journals did in several.

The second major obstacle to continued poetic effort in exile was the simple contextual estrangement from language. Once poets had been forced to move away from German-speaking areas, this exclusion from the ritual of their own language and civilization, a sine qua non as it seemed for art, was the greatest problem.   Some felt that the agonizing step of translation had to be made, bringing with it a lost sound or rhyme here, an altered metaphor there.   Poet Karl Wolfskehl's letters register his concern about the imprecision of translation, itself a metaphor for the exile dilemma.5 There was no more desperate situation than the severance from what Wolfskehl mournfully eulogized as "the living word," and no topic was so thoroughly discussed in so many dialogues and lyrics from all quarters of emigration.

There was first the conscious longing for the mother tongue and an attempt to hold aloof from the impinging native speech.   Ernst Weiss wrote: "It is an ancient evil of emigration that language is, in effect, refrigerated.   At best it can be preserved."6   In actuality, it could not even be preserved.   The language of the "isolationist" poet tended toward reduction, whereas the language of those who tried to adapt, at least on a day-to-day basis, ran the increasing danger of contamination.   Such a situation was not without its humor.   This is Mascha Kaléko's satirical, and sympa-thetic, portrayal of a fellow émigré:

> Wenn unsereins se lengvitsch spricht,
> So geht er wie auf Eiern.
> Der Satzbau wackelt, und die grammar hinkt,
> Und wenn ihm etwa ein ti-ehtsch gelingt,
> Das ist ein Grund zum Feiern.
>
> ("Momentanaufnahme eines Zeitgenossen")[7]

There was also the problem of language's insinuating sounds. The rhythms of any language attract the poet's attention in particular, quite apart from vocabulary and "meaning." Lion Feuchtwanger writes: "It happens at some point to all of us, that a foreign phrase, a foreign cadence, pushes its way to the fore."[8] In the limbo between languages, the insinuating sounds and words become intrinsic. Theodor Kramer acknowledged and put this discovery to use: "roll-call," "camp," "jazz," "drink," "black-out," and other English expressions without German equivalents occur in much of his exile poetry.[9] Kramer thereby intensifies the presentation of an alien environment and thus of the split personality of the poet adrift.

Finally, the attempt to bridge the gap and learn the new language often failed. Jesse Thoor wrote from England: "I won't ever learn this language, or maybe only what sticks in my ear. As you know, I'm just a notorious, handicapped speaker of German."[10] Hugo von Hofmannsthal, in another time, described the attraction of a foreign tongue in more positive terms: "When we grow deaf to the beauty of our own language, a foreign tongue exerts an indescribable spell: we need only dip our wilted thoughts in it and they are rejuvenated like cut flowers that have been thrown into fresh water."[11] For exiles the expression of such hope was romantic and even unreal.

Carl Zuckmayer, an occasional author of poetry, also perceived, like Hofmannsthal, the advantages of a new language over the old one. In "Kleine Sprüche aus der Sprachverbannung" ["Little Verses by One Exiled from His Language"], written on the occasion of Thomas Mann's seventieth birthday, he wrote as much in earnest as in jest:

> Die fremde Sprache ist ein Scheidewasser.
> Sie ätzt hinweg, was überschüssig rankt.
> Zwar wird die Farbe blass und immer blässer—
> Jedoch die Form purgiert sich und erschlankt.[12]

For some writers, the answer was exactly this reduction and simplicity; at least they tried for it. Unfortunately, much exile poetry was what one might well judge to be the opposite: effulgent, verbose. Nonetheless, the ideal of trimming language close to the bone prefigured the so-called *Kahlschlag* ("clear cutting") of 1945.

Regardless of the course each poet chose, existence apart from what Feuchtwanger called the living current of the mother tongue was the greatest malaise of the poet-exile's life. There was a noticeable tendency to return to an era of "quieter" language. Here lay the comforting vocabulary of *Meer*, *Liebe*, *Sehnsucht* ("sea," "love," "longing"). The large proportion of poems dealing with abstract subject matter, the emotional tone, the use of archetypal images, are all a consequence of the reduced hold of the poet on the language.

Nature is one nexus of poetic spirit and inspiration, traditionally an exemplary world order toward which one might well have expected the poetry of emigration to turn. Although the use of natural imagery was no doubt tainted by association with what became known as inner emigration and notions of escapist art, a handful of poets were drawn to this genre. Whereas some poets focused attention upon the disintegration of humanism and poetry's inability to influence men's actions, Paul Zech explored the visual surface of the natural world with a kind of wonder and sense of intimacy that is surprising in its concentration, serenity, and optimism.

"I am not part of the new literary generation; I am nearly forty years old," wrote Zech in the autobiographical notes to the original edition of *Menschheitsdämmerung*.[13] In 1933 Zech was nearly sixty years old and imprisoned at Spandau. After his release in June of that year, he fled by way of Prague and Paris to South America, where he lived out his exile, primarily in Argentina. *Neue Welt: Verse der Emigration* [*New World: Verses of Exile*], his volume of exile poetry, was published in 1939 in Buenos Aires. The work is divided into three books: "Bei Nacht und Nebel" ["Under Cover of Darkness"], "Wanderschaft" ["On the Road"], and "Die argentinischen Sonnette." The first book consists primarily of quatrains; books two and three, of sonnets. Zech chose the sonnet form for a closed, sculptured description of his landscape, and his images are exotic and opulent. He was physically a vigorous man who undertook extensive travel in Latin America, and the broad dramatic vision of the poems reflects this. The "argentinische Sonnette" display Zech's immersion in the new world. His interest is that of painter, biologist, and archeologist as well as that of poet. "Ich will dir eine Wiesenlandschaft malen..." ["I will paint a meadow landscape for you"] is the beginning of one of his poems (no. X). As a visual artist, he is fascinated by landscape composition, especially in a rendering directly reminiscent of his expressionist period:

> Mit dem Geschaukel der verfilzten Rücken
> drehn sich die Horizonte meilenweit.
> In Pausen humpeln Bäume wie auf Krücken
> verloren durch die Herdenewigkeit.[14]

And the naturalist Zech is equally enchanted by the myriad species of plant and animal life. His exotic diction recalls Stefan George:

> . . . auch dieses Tal hat Eisenbahnen nie gesehn,
> sah nur gehäuft in flachen Silberschalen
> die purpurdunklen Wasserorchideen.

> Sah nur in Scharen, Raubgetier und Reiher,
> den schwarzen Ibis und den ockerbraunen Schwan.

> auf Weidenstümpfen manchmal schlägt die Leyer
> ein Pfau zu dem Gekrächz von Ara und Tucán.15

The "argentinische Sonnette" are long, wide, and lazy, embracing the reader in vast spaces and timelessness. They are the most expansive poems on the natural world written in exile and set themselves apart from the more confined lyric of political, urban exiles.

Reviewing the lyric on the natural world, one might speculate that the language of a "nature" poem, even one with philosophical excursions or metaphysical implications, might have been more secure and workable ground for an exiled poet: nature is not just German. Poetry reliant on political or social referents might, by definition, have been more disturbed. Whatever the case, relatively few exiled lyricists explored the natural order for poetic subject matter and view.

"All great exile writing is an attempt to rescue a tradition that has been interrupted," writes Werner Vordtriede.16 This is nowhere more the case than with three poets who were among the most eminent of literary exiles: Nelly Sachs, Else Lasker-Schüler, and Karl Wolfskehl. All three were deeply committed to their Judaic heritage. Exile provided an "objective correlative" for the history of the Jews, a history that is, as surely as any, a topos of literature. With each of these three, the attempt to rescue German literature was different in origin and execution.

Nelly Sachs lived seven years inside the Third Reich before it became necessary for her to flee to Sweden. There she remained until her death in 1970. In exile she wrote two volumes of poetry: *In den Wohnungen des Todes* [*In the Dwellings of Death*] and *Sternverdunkelung* [*Eclipse of the Stars*].17 The poems of *In den Wohnungen des Todes* were written in 1943-44, with full knowledge of the concentration camps, and drew on the mystical interpretation of scripture, the Kabbalah. The voice of the poems speaks with fervor, and the poems themselves are religious in the broadest sense. Of this work Hans Magnus Enzensberger writes: ". . . her book remains the only poetic testimony that can hold its own beside the dumfounding horror of the documentary reports."18 Experience, whether love, parting, wandering, or of loss of innocence, is evoked through imagery that engrosses and entangles, weaving an airy, but unbreakable web of mystery. The tradition that quickens these images adds both remoteness and immediacy. The poems move with grace and inexorability, full of pathos and, at the same time, full of stateliness:

> Wir Ungeborenen
> Schon beginnt die Sehnsucht an uns zu schaffen
> Die Ufer des Blutes weiten sich zu unserem Empfang . . .
> ("Chor der Ungeborenen")19

The pathos lies in yearning as the informing sense, and in the theme: the embryonic growth of being and its own vision of death. The stateliness lies in the psalm-like acoustic and

structural aspects of the verse. The verbal texture is created through fields of images and sounds:

> Der Sand in meinem löchrigen Schuh
> Das warst du... du... du...
> Male ich Sand der einmal Fleisch war –
> Oder Goldhaar – oder Schwarzhaar –
> Oder die Küsse und deine schmeichelnde Hand
> Sand male ich, Sand – Sand – Sand
>
> ("Die Malerin") [20]

> Windmühlen schlagen wie Stundenuhren
> Die Zeit; bis sie verlöscht die Spuren.
>
> ("Der Ruhelose") [21]

Brief quotations cannot do justice to the complex strands of
images that weave the fabric of the whole. The following
one is generated by the images of *Staub* ("dust"), *Sand*
("sand"): *staubverwandt* ("related to dust"), *Sehnsucht-
staub* ("yearning dust"), *Staubhügel* ("dust hill"), *Grab-
staub* ("grave dust"), *Staubkörner* ("grains of dust"), *Sand-
körner* ("grains of sand"), *Wüstensand* ("desert sand"). The
fascination aroused by Sachs's poetry cannot be summarized,
but the opening poem of the cycle, "O die Schornsteine" ["O
the Chimneys"] communicates the power of her verse, for
which she won the Nobel Prize:

> O die Schornsteine
> Auf den sinnreich erdachten Wohnungen des Todes,
> Als Israels Leib zog aufgelöst in Rauch
> Durch die Luft –
> Als Essenkehrer ihn ein Stern empfing
> Der schwarz wurde
> Oder war es ein Sonnenstrahl?

> O die Schornsteine!
> Freiheitswege für Jeremias und Hiobs Staub –
> Wer erdachte euch und baute Stein auf Stein
> Den Weg für Flüchtlinge aus Rauch?

> O die Wohnungen des Todes,
> Einladend hingerichtet
> Für den Wirt des Hauses, der sonst Gast war –
> O ihr Finger,
> Die Eingangsschwelle legend
> Wie ein Messer zwischen Leben und Tod –

> O ihr Schornsteine,
> O ihr Finger,
> Und Israels Leib im Rauch durch die Luft! [22]

This sequence is characteristic of her style: lingering musical themes, involving both variation and complete change,
yet actualizing as well the poetic process of recurrence.
Transformation as a theme and a structural principle endows
Sachs's poetry with movement and energy. The focal point,
as ever, is man's memory--his ability to re-know and re-

experience the past in the present, all of which lies at the
root of myth.   Without emotion for its own sake, the poems
reach rather for the essence of emotion: the knowledge that
all things pass away.   For Sachs, Hitler's Germany could be
viewed as a "fulfillment," in immediate and terrible terms,
of Jewish fate as sung from oldest time: thus her references
to images of age and aging, and to the eons of man's spiritual struggle.

Her major accomplishments in the light of exile poetry
are: (1) she uses free rhythms and strophe forms rather
than more formal structures, and (2) she creates a uniquely
harmonious poetry at a time when poetry seemed to abound
with references to its own incoherent state and to the chaos
of the world.

Else Lasker-Schüler was not particularly politically
minded and found it difficult both to be an exile and to
accept the fact of other exiles having fates similar to her
own.   She took exception to a world that changed.   The
tearing down of the past was nearly impossible for her.   The
poems of her much-praised exile volume *Mein blaues Klavier*
[*My Blue Piano*][23] are as brief as her mercurial moods and
as intense as the last years of her life.

Despite an earlier bohemian existence, her notoriety in
the Berlin cafés of the expressionist years, and her somewhat celebrated relationship to Kurt Hiller, Lasker-Schüler
came to write, by 1935, poetry that concerned itself with
traditional social values: mother and child ("Meine Mutter")
["My Mother"], love between man and woman (her many love
poems), the ties of family, the ties to God.   The moods of
her exile work were sorrow (*trüb*, "gloomy"; *trostlos*, "in-
consolable"; *Zweifel*, "doubt"; *Weinen*, "weeping"; *Sehnsucht*, "longing") and fear (*fürchten*, *schrecken*, "terrify";
bang, "fearful"; *Angst*, "anxiety"; *Grauen*, "horror").   Blue
was the prevalent color in her poems: *blauvertausendfacht*
("thousandfold blue"), "blau vor Paradies" ("Paradise blue"),
"mein blaues Klavier."   *Verzaubert* ("enchanted") was her
word for the essence of the ideal poem.   Her imagery reflected the magic she celebrated: *Kristall* ("crystal"),
Stiefkönigin ("step-queen"), *Träume* ("dreams"), *Bilder-
buch* ("picture book"), *Pharaonenwälder* ("Pharaoh's
woods"), *Mondfrau* ("moonwoman"), *Paläste* ("palaces").
Mein blaues Klavier is typical of Lasker-Schüler's internal
poetic landscape; it is an anguished world that is nonetheless colorful, imaginative, and wondrous:

> Ich habe zu Hause ein blaues Klavier
> Und kenne doch keine Note.
>
> Es steht im Dunkel der Kellertür,
> Seitdem die Welt verrohte.
>
> Es spielen Sternenhände vier
> – Die Mondfrau sang im Boote –
> Nun tanzen die Ratten im Geklirr.

> Zerbrochen ist die Klaviatür.....
> Ich beweine die blaue Tote.
>
> Ach liebe Engel öffnet mir
> - Ich ass vom bitteren Brote -
> Mir lebend schon die Himmelstür -
> Auch wider dem Verbote.
>   ("Mein blaues Klavier") [24]

Not only the shorter lyrics, but the extremely confessional nature of Lasker-Schüler's poems distinguish her work from that of other exiles, whose self-presence in poems tended toward group identification ("we exiled poets," "we Austrians," "we real Germans") rather than the self in isolation.   Most exile poetry tended to discredit fantasy, though not necessarily imagination, yet Lasker-Schüler wrote of her fantasies with such candor (indicated by the fact that her poems are always in the first person) that they became seductive fictions.   The way into her world is clearly stated: *Traum* ("dream") and *Nacht* ("night).   Thus what could have been the exploration of an esoteric, hermetic world turns into an accessible experience in poetry.

> Ich träume so fern dieser Erde
> Als ob ich gestorben wär
> Und nicht mehr verkörpert werde.
>   ("So lange ist es her.....") [25]

Nowhere in exile poetry is the topos of death or even of annihilation met head on as it is in Lasker-Schüler's poems. Pathos in exile poetry, a defense against complete silence (*Verstummen*), can often stretch poetic credibility quite far. Here it reaches, however, a new dimension, for the poems do not languish or wane; they are sharp and radiating.

The language of Lasker-Schüler is more fragile and evocative than that of most poetry written in exile.   Emmy Ball-Hennings called it the "Harfensprache des Herzens" ("harp of the heart"), language possessing all of the qualities that metaphor implies: delicacy, tenderness, and resonance.[26]   In a memoir from 1952, Gottfried Benn wrote of her: "Her themes were variously Jewish, her imagination oriental, but her language was German, a rich, opulent, fragile German"; and Benn went on to call her "the Jewish and the German in a single lyric incarnation!"[27]

Karl Wolfskehl, exiled in 1933, acknowledged himself to be a poet whose traditions came principally from Judaism-- but this confession came for the first time in exile.   That Wolfskehl's soul was not only Jewish, but Mediterranean and German as well, was a fact he never ceased to reiterate.   He built his aesthetic effort upon this triangulation of cultural loyalties.   A historian by avocation, Wolfskehl showed in his poetry a particular sensitivity to the concept of "the broken tradition" of exile, as Vordtriede formulated it.[28]   No other exile poet sought a link with tradition through a view of history as specifically as did Wolfskehl.   In 1938 he emigrated further than any other--to New Zealand.   From there he did not write of himself as an émigré of his own free will, but instead called himself rather bitterly "ein exul immeritus," invoking the figure of Job. His secretary later wrote: "From this moment on [1938] his life stood under the sign of this archetype of human fate. Hesitant and full of faith, the poet submitted to the metamorphosis from Dionysus to Job."[29] So "Job" was born and matured in exile; he had no place in the desolation of Europe; "Renewal comes only from afar," wrote Wolfskehl.[30]

Sang aus dem Exil [Song from Exile],[31] Wolfskehl's poetic contribution to German letters in exile, was of epic proportions. A panorama of Western history and culture, it was the lengthiest single work to be conceived and written by an exiled poet. The work is divided into three parts: "Praeludium," "Mittelmeer" ["Mediterranean"], "Verbannung" ["Banishment"]. The "Praeludium" invokes prophets, old and new, and signs of mystery foretelling German (Western) doom --including the breakdown of language ("Des Menschen Wort vergeht"), a problem close to Wolfskehl's aesthetic soul. The second part, "Mittelmeer," is a scenario of the Mediterranean cultural heritage, past and present. Part three, "Verbannung," explores the fate of the exile. The tense of the work is alternately past and present--the former required by the historical perspective, the latter being consonant with the mythical purpose. Armed with both, Wolfskehl ranged intuitively over the historical past; among the passages of despair, he celebrates, nonetheless, his advancing age.

> Winzer Leid, dich grüss ich, meiner Trauben
> Überschwere Beeren seien dein.
> Herbste! Lang schon gilben meine Lauben:
> Späte Lese bringt den vollsten Wein.
>
> ("Tränen sind") [32]

It should be noted that Wolfskehl went blind in exile and that the visual aspects of his poems are richly ornamental and emblematic.

Of all three sections, "Mittelmeer" is the longest and most expansive. Like the historical novel loved by emigration for its interpenetration of historical periods, "Mittelmeer" is filled with references to the histories of Rome and the Middle Ages, comparing ancient and modern aesthetic glory. Highly sentimental as well as symbolic in his poetic nature, Wolfskehl displays here his supreme affection for this world in the manner of the classicist he became in exile. "Mittelmeer" is the primordial sea of not only all Western beauty, art, and history, but of Wolfskehl's exiled vision.

In one portion of Sang aus dem Exil Wolfskehl gives vent to his considerable personal bitterness over exile, thus disrupting an otherwise controlled piece. His outrage, which he as a German man of letters felt deeply, is authentic, and his vision of exile finds expression beyond what metaphor could present. The outburst is directed specifically at Hitler, although Wolfskehl does not name him:

> Exul! Mich Keltrer, Kellerer des Weins,
> Des Weins, der Wort heisst, Geist, Tau des Gedeihns,

Mich den bestallten Hüter unsres Schreins,
Mich wies ein Wicht in Acht und Aberacht.
Griff mir ans Herz und trieb mich in die Nacht.
                                    ("Ultimus Vatum")[33]

This passage is true exile indignation in a poem that otherwise narrates Western man's trek from prehistoric, through
historic time, to island exile.

Throughout *Sang aus dem Exil*, Wolfskehl opted for the
series of shorter poems rather than a continuous poem, which
might have been feasible at least in "Mittelmeer." Thus
Wolfskehl refers to his work as a cycle, for the poems reflect each other and evolve. A major characteristic of exile
poetry was that it was often too long for what it had to
say; it apparently took more verbal energy than ever to
keep a poem afloat. Wolfskehl packed into an extremely long
series of poems rich images, sweeping themes, and varied
structures, making this work one of the most interesting
to come out of exile.

In 1946, in Los Angeles, California, there appeared
Gedichte aus den Jahren 1908-1945 [*Poems 1908-1945*], an
anthology of poems by Franz Werfel, chosen by him for this
edition shortly before his death.[34] "In the final months of
his life, he made a selection of the poems he thought the
most beautiful," wrote Alma Mahler-Werfel.[35] The book included poems from the years of his exile, 1938-45. Werfel's
poetic themes in exile seemed to grow principally out of the
experience of his own physical deterioration in his last
years: illness, sensations of the body, and death. The
titles of the poems are revealing: "Ballade von der Krankheit" ["Ballad on Sickness"], "Der Kranke" ["The Sick Man"],
"Körpergefühl" ["Body Sensation"], "Ein Genesender spricht"
["A Convalescent Speaks"], "Göttlicher Sinn der Krankheit"
["Divine Meaning of Sickness"], "Totentanz" ["Dance of
Death"], and "Eine Stunde nach dem Totentanz" ["An Hour
After the Dance of Death"]. The fulcrum of this poetry is
both metaphysical and spiritual in its matter: metaphysical
in its abstract exploration of human essence, and spiritual
in its mediation between body and soul. Again and again
Werfel's poetic material circles the mind-body duality of man.
In a short poem "Mensch und All" ["Man and Cosmos"], from
the section entitled "Kunde vom irdischen Leben" ["Tidings
of Earthly Life"], Werfel postulates an integrated universe,
expressed in the poetic-scientific metaphor so dear to earlier
centuries:

Ich ass und trank in jeder Speise
Die Sonne selbst, die ihren Strahl
Umwandelt auf geheime Weise
Zu Wein und Brot beim Erdenmahl.

In meiner Brust die Atemwelle
Lief durch den ganzen Lebensstrom.
In meines Leibes letzter Zelle
Fehlt von Gestirnen kein Atom.

Wie müsst ich sein, der Alldurchkreiste,
Der Schöpfung heimatlich vertraut...
Du aber schufst mich, Gott, im Geiste
So fremd, so urfremd, dass mir graut.36

The need for the body to make the universe whole, the knowledge that the mind cannot perceive, much less envision, without it, this aggressive pursuit of the organization of external
reality, while not unusual in exile poetry, is rare from the
perspective of physical self-doubt and suggests a particular
sense of frailty, heightened no doubt for Werfel by illness.
Greatly removed from his cultural ecosystem, the exile is left
to contemplate, as Werfel does here, his decaying body and
fettered spirit.

Werfel's focus on illness, a condition described alternately as wholly inimical to life ("Ballade von der Krankheit") and as a trial by fire ("Lehr uns zu merken, Gott"
["Teach Us to See, O God"]) is without counterpart in exile
poetry.   Illness is hardly a neutral topic of exile poetry
and, with both physical and psychological decline a continuous threat, the pathology of the exile poet is greatly complicated by illness as a theme.   Lasker-Schüler preferred death
as a poetic topic and thus neutralized questions of process;
death was instead a transcendent arena where imagination
and language were freed.   Werfel has chosen the opposite:
an obsession with spiritual and corporeal change, which he
interprets in a totally negative way.

Formally, Werfel's poetry is much like that of other
exiles: tight stanza forms and a great deal of rhyme.   Because Werfel's subject matter is so theatrically expressed,
one senses this structure to be like armor, quite rigid.   In
a small exercise in defense of his use of rhyme, so curiously
"unmodern," Werfel wrote a sonnet, "Der Reim," which would
bear comparison with Brecht's famous essay, "Über reimlose
Lyrik mit unregelmässigen Rhythmen" ["On Unrhymed Lyrics
with Irregular Rhythms"],37 on the opposing side.   Here is
a peculiarly philological view:

Allein nicht jede Sprache hat geheiligt
Den reinen Reim. Wo nur sich deckt die Endung,
Droht leeres Spiel. Der Geist bleibt unbeteiligt.

Dieselben Silben lassen leicht sich leimen.
Doch Stämm' und Wurzeln spotten solcher Blendung.
In Deutschen müssen sich die Sachen reimen.38

"Die Sachen" undoubtedly bears a double meaning.

Werfel did not really write much poetry in exile.   His
prose is of course more widely known.   However, one of the
most dramatic images to come from poetry of these times, certainly ranking with Brecht's *Aprikosenbäumchen* ("little
apricot tree") and Lasker-Schüler's *blaues Klavier*, is found
in the final lines of "Eine Stunde nach dem Totentanz":   a
chilling and complex image of death summing up Werfel's
poetic interests:

Und während mein Leben sich regsamer bläht und geniesst,
Fühl ich ihn lehnen im hörigen Nebenzimmer,
Wo er unsichtbar raschelnd das Abendblatt liest.[39]

There were many who thought and some who knew that
in exile, poetry had fallen on particularly hard times. Bertolt Brecht was the lyric poet who could write a simple poem
to say just that. "Schlechte Zeit für Lyrik" ["Bad Times for
Lyrics"] reveals a finely honed edge of sensibility on the
subjects of art, writing, aesthetics, exile, and the imagination reflecting upon itself:

Ich weiss doch: nur der Glückliche
Ist beliebt. Seine Stimme
Hört man gern. Sein Gesicht ist schön.

Der verkrüppelte Baum im Hof
Zeigt auf den schlechten Boden, aber
Die Vorübergehenden schimpfen ihn einen Krüppel
Doch mit Recht.

Die grünen Boote und die lustigen Segel des Sundes
Sehe ich nicht. Von allem
Sehe ich nur der Fischer rissiges Garnnetz.
Warum rede ich nur davon
Dass die vierzigjährige Häuslerin gekrümmt geht?
Die Brüste der Mädchen
Sind warm wie ehedem.

In meinem Lied ein Reim
Käme mir fast vor wie Übermut.

In mir streiten sich
Die Begeisterung über den blühenden Apfelbaum
Und das Entsetzen über die Reden des Anstreichers.
Aber nur das zweite
Drängt mich zum Schreibtisch.[40]

It is apparent that exile self-consciousness reached a new
high in the poetry of Bertolt Brecht. The *Svendborger Gedichte* [*Svendborg Poems*] are his most successful poems in and
about exile. There is a level of personal and artistic
acceptance of exile that allows for a certain watchfulness
over his own work, an absorption in immediacies without the
forcing of meaning. Brecht's spare style and language were
well suited to the expression of alienation. He did not cast
about in his poems, as others in exile did, for new ideas,
new words--they were already a part of his craft. In
Brecht, intellectual alienation allied itself with physical dis-
placement, and the result is poetry that is laconic, lucid,
and penetrating:

Heute, Ostersonntag früh
Ging plötzlicher Schneesturm über die Insel.
Zwischen den grünenden Hecken lag Schnee. Mein
        junger Sohn

Holte mich zu einem Aprikosenbäumchen an der
           Hausmauer
Von einem Vers weg, in dem ich auf diejenigen
           mit dem Finger deutete
Die einen Krieg vorbereiteten, der
Den Kontinent, diese Insel, mein Volk, meine Familie
           und mich
Vertilgen mag. Schweigend
Legten wir einen Sack
Über den frierenden Baum.

("Frühling 1938")[41]

The poem makes a powerful and moving statement about art and the world. The tension is delicate as the author tells us he is leaving a poem for the world-in-a-poem.

Brecht wrote particularly of the detestable "oily smoothness of the five-beat iamb" and the "commonness of its clatter," and so set himself apart from the majority of lyric poets in exile who clung tenaciously to traditional features of poetry.[42] Brecht saw this timidity as a false attempt to neutralize disharmony and artificially close off the poem from outside interference. Interestingly, rhymes and stanzas know no politics, for some of the leftist poets with politics or ideologies in common with Brecht nonetheless produced some of the greatest rhythmic and rhyming "clatter"; Brecht knew where the edge of formlessness lay.

Much has been written on Brecht's poetry and the context of exile in which it was born. What is unique-- and self-evident--in Brecht's lyric is the powerful, dramatic realism uniting exile, modernism, and a political ideology. This congenial union of circumstance and poetic proclivity was not met elsewhere in the poetics of exile.

The hope of all literary exiles, from whatever poetic or political sector, was that the voice of literature would be heard. It is therefore not surprising to find an abundance of satire and parody. Both forms are civilized and reflect a given cultural and political landscape. They are usually associated with periods of cultural security rather than cultural disintegration, not only because their success is dependent upon a broad, well-disposed public, but because they themselves serve as a corrective counterweight to cultural excesses. The social character of satire and parody fulfilled two personal and public needs of the exile: the yearning to be heard and the longing for community and continuation. To this extent they are symptomatic of the exile condition. The poet is inclined to these forms to defend himself against the charge that (1) he is himself not truly German, and (2) that he has voluntarily excluded himself from German culture and tradition through emigration.

One of the most obvious styles available to a bellicose exile was caricature. The theater critic Alfred Kerr and the political poet Walter Mehring made extensive journalistic use of the animal cartoon to satirize the Nazis. Kerr's poem "Das braune Lamm" ["The Brown Lamb"] follows the Führer's transformation:

> Gestern noch ein böses Böckchen,
>   Heut ein Lämmchen mit dem Glöckchen;
> . . . .
>
> Aus der Stirn guckt, sonderbar,
>   Ein Hyänen-Augenpaar.[43]

Walter Mehring in "Die Sage vom grossen Krebs" ["The Saga of the Giant Crab"] chronicles Germany and Hitler in the tale of a legendary crab propelled eternally in reverse, a crab that must not be allowed to leave his ancient hiding place lest the clocks and history take a great leap backward.[44] Satirical verse in the works of these two writers, and in writings by a host of others who appropriated the lyric form for various barbed purposes, seems to go beyond traditional notions of this genre in at least two ways: (1) exile satire was written for an international public, whereas satire was usually considered "internal"--that is, for local consumption, a shared cultural joke; (2) by and large, exile satire lacked the level of exaggeration upon which satire usually rests. The exaggerations portrayed were barely commensurate with the incredible cartoons the Nazis seemed to embody to their literary detractors. Where exile satire could enjoy itself was perhaps in its language. Mehring plundered the Nazi tower of babel for the vocabulary of "Arier-Zoo" ["Aryan Zoo"]:

> Wotans-Saurier, Odinsdrachen
>   von der Fresse bis zum Steiss
> Wart ihr hirnlos – war nur Rachen.
> Euer Nachwuchs ist zum Lachen –
>   Pazifistisches Geschmeiss.
>   Züchtet Übermenschen–Affen
>   Führer-Mammots, kolossal
>   Wie sie GOTT im Zorn erschaffen
>   Aus dem Opernarsenal
> Bis der Bärenhäuter-Floh
>   Lindwurmlaus und Auerwanzen
>   Hausen in dem grossen ganzen
>   Rassereinen Arier-Zoo.[45]

Parody, called a "principle of the moderns" by Walter Jens, was perhaps the ultimate exile form, in prose or poetry.[46] Of parody in exile writing, Werner Vordtriede writes: "It is no idle, peripheral phenomenon. It belongs to the mainstream, is a weapon against those who would corrupt all tradition at home . . . ."[47] The importance of parody to the émigré lay in its reactivation of the link that the émigré felt between himself and German tradition. It was an indictment of the "tradition-spoilers" inside Germany, and it required a deftness and sense of ambiguity. "Ich hatte einst ein schönes Vaterland – / So sang schon der Flüchtling Heine," writes Mascha Kaléko in the poem "Emigranten-Monolog," and elsewhere in the same poem she says, "O, Röslein auf der Heide, / Dich brach die Kraftdurchfreude."[48] The use of the famous *Röslein* was obviously not a belittling of Herder or Goethe, nor was Kaléko equating the line with Hitler's slogan of "Kraft durch Freude" ("strength through joy").   Instead, she was mounting an attack upon the abuse of Goethe and the *Heidenröslein*.   The juxtaposition emerges as the center of the greatest of all exile dilemmas: what is truly German?   Mehring echoes the German folksong with "Amsel, Drossel, Fink und Star / . . . / von dem Belt bis an die Saar . . ." in his pursuit of Germanness.[49]   Brecht, too, wrote fierce parody in his *Hitler-Choräle*:   "Nun danket alle Gott / Der uns den Hitler sandte . . . ."[50]

Unlike satire, parody struck at the taproot of the exile's aesthetic self-consciousness, whereas satire was more of a discharge of moral and physical disgust.   Lyricists actually wrote little parody, despite the cultural redefinement so integral to Hitler's plans for the Reich.   Parody offered a forum where the giants of German culture might assemble, or be assembled, for debate.   It seems no coincidence that the three examples given here evoke stellar figures of German history: Luther, Goethe, and Heine, all of whom were considered archetypes of German pride and *misère*.   Perhaps what was lacking for parody among lyricists was not poetic gift or interest, but the requisite ideological keenness so visible in Brecht.

*   *   *

GRENZE

Geschrieben am 2. Juni 1947 beim Überschreiten
der französisch-deutschen Grenze

Als wir über die Grenze kamen,
da sah es drüben genauso aus,
ein Feld war ein Feld und ein Haus war ein Haus,
die Dinge hatten kaum veränderte Namen,
ein Mensch war ein Mensch und ein Tier ein Tier,
die Menschen hatten zwei Arme und die Esel vier Füsse,
die Kleefelder hatten auf beiden Seiten die gleiche Süsse,
auf beiden Seiten blühten Akazien mit gleichem Schwung
und Kampf war Kampf und Arbeit Arbeit und Liebe war
                                    Liebe; und jung
vor seiner Zukunft war auf beiden Seiten
                          das Menschengeschlecht,
die Erde war auf beiden Seiten den ihr befreundeten
                                    Menschen recht,
auf beiden Seiten gab es für die befreundeten
                                    Menschen Erde genug,
Erde und Menschen der beiden Seiten hatten die gleiche
                          Grösse.[51]

Rudolf Leonhard's poem, perhaps the best of his exile, reflects what a returning poet, or any writer, must have felt. The syntactic simplicity is akin to that of Günther Eich in his epoch-making poem "Inventur" ["Inventory"].   Leonhard is tallying, as does Eich, what is left after the catastrophe, not projected or abstracted, but real.   The poem ends near where it begins, though with the feeling, as in "Inventur,"

that the ground, however small, has been covered for now
and some important discoveries made.   "Grenze" stands as
the final gesture of poetry in exile, a poem of cautious,
groping physical confrontation.

The existential situations and decisions facing the exile
poets at war's end were at least as traumatic as the decisions they had faced in the years 1933-38.   Many poets had
died in banishment: Max Hermann-Neisse, Paul Zech, Else
Lasker-Schüler.   Some had turned their backs on Germany
forever: Karl Wolfskehl, Nelly Sachs, Mascha Kaléko, Erich
Fried.   That portion of divided Europe now known as the
"West" witnessed the return of very few poets: Walter Mehring
did settle in Switzerland and Theodore Kramer and Franz
Theodor Csokor, among others, returned to Austria.   Whether
or not they returned, the exiles were defeated in many cases
by the knowledge that their poems were unknown and un-
appreciated in their homelands.   Some were completely disoriented in the postwar literary scene.   Austrian poet Berthold Viertel drew the balance of his own work, a statement
that modestly, but critically, points up feelings shared by
others: "My work had begun in the shifting sand of crumbling relationships.   It remained tentative and subject to
recall.   No undertaking of any size was successful.   There
was no continuity, not even a valid beginning of some tradition that might get through the winter of those seven lean
years."[52]   Yet Walter Berendsohn described the fate of the
lyric in exile thus: "Poetry evolved surprisingly strongly
and well.   The events of the time stirred men and made them
unspeakably lonely in strange lands; while the familiar
world went out of joint, they fled to the haven of the German poem."[53]   Opinion was obviously divided among exile
participants and those sympathetic to exile, but as a new
tradition took shape, the critical review became more negative.   In a collection of critical essays by Hans Mayer and
Stephan Hermlin, the situation of lyric poetry in exile
appears in an altogether different light, albeit a political
and not wholly true one: "We shall have to acknowledge
once and for all that the antiaesthetic posture of the fascist
epoch meant the end (or near-end) of lyric poetry in Germany. Never as in those years was it so clear that the lyric
genre, probably to a greater degree than other art forms,
not only suffers more from historical and geographical limitations, but even dies from it.   The interdependencies are
unpredictable."[54]   Though Hermlin and Mayer are referring
as much to poetry within the Third Reich as without, and
though they ignore the achievement of Gottfried Benn or Oskar
Loerke, the latter half of this statement would ring true for
most émigrés.   Yet the truth about exile poetry must lie in
the middle: lyric poetry neither was of epoch-determining
quality nor was it the end of German poetry.   Exile did seem
to be a caesura, however; it lingered in older traditions, the
threads of which were not picked up by postwar poets.
After the *Nullpunkt* ("ground zero") of 1945, poetry was to
some degree the rejection of the lyrical philosophies of the

thirties: either that poetry had political and social truth or that it had aesthetic truth.

German poetry in exile is to a great extent minor poetry, what J. Isaacs calls the "poetry of direction" as opposed to the "poetry of achievement."[55] Written for drawers, shelves, or suitcases, composed in restaurants, customs stations, or hotel rooms, it is poetry seeking direction. At worst, it consists of false starts, faltering continuation of various traditions, skirmishes with pedantry and didacticism, timid emulations of other poets (Mayakovsky, Rilke, George), pedestrian rhyming, mundane diction, and subject matter that tends to the sentimental. At best, there are sturdy sonnets, much adaptation from other literatures (including such languages as Chinese and Czech), and small, spectacular individual poems. There was also a breath of internationalism in the air, both in exile and in Germany after the war. The work of Eluard, Mayakovsky, W. B. Yeats, and T. S. Eliot is discovered for German letters by Hermlin, Fried, Wolfskehl, and other poets in exile.

History ruthlessly picks out only the winners among exiled poets: Bertolt Brecht and Nelly Sachs are two. Not even new editions have managed to resurrect the efforts of a hundred others. The service performed by exile lyric had more to do with preservation than experimentation--there could be no avant-garde in exile. "Poetry of achievement" surfaces from less troubled waters and is a consolidation of minor poetic achievement and individual genius. Emigration left little time for the cultivation of genius. Nor was a new contemporary sensibility given voice, for Nazi Germany was a puzzlement to contemporaneity--how was a banished poet to cope with such an anachronism? The valiant and prolific years of 1933-39 gave way to despondency about the war. Fewer and fewer volumes appeared toward the war's end. There was a slight upsurge in publications of poetry in 1945-47 as manuscripts emerged from hiding places and publishers of German poetry became available once more, but these poems were rather curiosity pieces, relics among the ruins. The only vision of exile had been a utopian one ill-suited to the postwar years. Most poems went into anthologies, private collections, and occasional reprints.

Perhaps the true matter of exile does lie exposed in the "lesser," the minor poetry, poetry that makes major poetry possible--in this case by default, for the historical novel in exile seemed to flourish to the same degree that poetry seemed to languish. There are a few exceptions of course: Werfel, Sachs, Lasker-Schüler, Goll, Brecht--these seem to be among the best of exile. One or two may prove eventually to be great. Such are the considerations and results of a deliberate investigation of the German lyric in exile.

Notes

[1]Letter to Lina Loos, 26 June 1934, in Franz Theodor Csokor, *Zeuge einer Zeit: Briefe aus dem Exil 1933-1950*

(Munich: Albert Langen–Georg Müller, 1964), p. 71.

[2]Thomas Mann to Eduard Korrodi, 3 Feb. 1938, in Thomas Mann, *Briefe: 1889–1936,* ed. Erika Mann (Frankfurt/M: S. Fischer, 1961), pp. 411–12.

[3]The Aurora Press was founded by poet–publicist Wieland Herzfelde together with Bertolt Brecht, Franz Carl Weiskopf, Heinrich Mann, and Oskar Maria Graf. The press was a reincarnation of Herzfelde's old Malik Verlag, which had been forced out of Prague in 1939.

[4]Walter Berendsohn, *Die humanistische Front: Einführung in die deutsche Emigranten-Literatur (II. Teil)* (Worms: Georg Heintz, 1976), p. 118.

[5]Karl Wolfskehl, *Zehn Jahre Exil: Briefe aus Neuseeland 1938–1950* (Heidelberg: Lambert Schneider, 1959). The following letters register his concern about translation: to Ralph Farrell, 10 Jan. 1939 (pp. 41–44); to D. F., 26 Dec. 1942 (pp. 134–35); to F. O., 30 Nov. 1943 (pp. 167–68); and to Ernst Morwitz, 4 Oct. 1945 (pp. 227–28).

[6]Ernst Weiss in F. C. Weiskopf, *Gesammelte Werke* (Berlin: Dietz, 1960), VIII, 490.

[7]Mascha Kaléko, *Verse für Zeitgenossen* (Hamburg: Rowohlt, 1958), p. 46: "Whenever one of us speaks 'ze lengvich' / He's walking as if on eggs. / Our sentence structure wobbles, or grammar limps, / And when we happen to say a 't-h' correctly, / We feel like celebrating."

[8]Lion Feuchtwanger in F. C. Weiskopf, *Gesammelte Werke,* VIII, 490.

[9]Theodor Kramer, *Verbannt aus Österreich: Neue Gedichte* (London: Austrian P.E.N., 1943), pp. 7, 16, 20, 33.

[10]Jesse Thoor, *Das Werk: Sonette, Lieder, Erzählungen,* ed. Michael Hamburger (Frankfurt/M: Europäische Verlagsanstalt, 1965), pp. 26–27.

[11]Hugo von Hofmannsthal in Weiskopf, VIII, 493.

[12]Carl Zuckmayer, "Kleine Sprüche aus der Sprachverbannung," *Neue Rundschau,* Sonderausgabe zu Thomas Manns 70. Geburtstag, 6. Juni 1946, p. 193: "The foreign tongue is an acid / Cauterizing what has overgrown, / And though the color slowly pales, / The form is purged and slendered."

[13]*Menschheitsdämmerung: Symphonie jüngster Dichtung,* ed. Kurt Pinthus (Berlin: Ernst Rowohlt, 1920), p. 300.

[14]Paul Zech, *Neue Welt: Verse der Emigration* (Buenos Aires: Quadriga, 1939), p. 67: "With the swaying of woolly backs / The horizons revolve for miles. / At intervals, trees hobble as if on crutches. / Lost through an eternity of herds."

[15]Zech, p. 66: "Nor has this valley ever seen a train, / But only crimson–dark water orchids / Heaped in shallow silver vessels. / Multitudes of predators and herons, / The black ibis and the ochre swan, / On willow stumps the peacock often sings / To the screech of ara and toucan."

[16]Werner Vordtriede, "Vorläufige Gedanken zu einer Typologie der Exilliteratur," *Akzente,* 15, No. 6 (Dec. 1968), 574.

[17]Nelly Sachs, *In den Wohnungen des Todes* (Berlin: Aufbau-Verlag, 1947); *Sternverdunkelung: Gedichte* (Vienna: Bermann-Fischer, 1949).

[18]Hans Magnus Enzensberger, "Introduction," in Nelly Sachs, *O the Chimneys: Selected Poems, Including the Verse Play, Eli*, trans. Michael Hamburger, Christopher Holme, Ruth and Matthew Mead, and Michael Roloff (New York: Farrar, Straus and Giroux, 1967), p. x. Bilingual edition.

[19]*O the Chimneys*, pp. 42–43: "We the unborn / The yearning has begun to plague us / The shores of blood broaden to receive us . . . ."

[20]Sachs, *In den Wohnungen des Todes*, p. 52: "Sand in my tattered shoe / That was you . . . you . . . you . . . / Sand I paint, once flesh – / Or goldhair – or blackhair – / Or the kisses and your caressing hand / Sand I paint, sand – sand – sand."

[21]Ibid., p. 51: "Windmills chiming the hour / Like clocks: until all footsteps are erased."

[22]Sachs, *O the Chimneys*, pp. 2–3: "O the chimneys / On the ingeniously devised habitations of death / When Israel's body drifted in smoke / Through the air–– / Was welcomed by a star, a chimney sweep, / A star that turned black / Or was it a ray of sun? / O the chimneys! / Freedomway for Jeremiah and Job's dust–– / Who devised you and laid stone upon stone / The road for refugees of smoke? / O the habitations of death, / Invitingly appointed / For the host who used to be a guest–– / O you fingers / Laying the threshold / Like a knife between life and death–– / O you fingers / And Israel's body through the air in smoke!"

[23]Else Lasker-Schüler, *Mein blaues Klavier: Neue Gedichte* (Jerusalem, 1943); reprinted in *Gesammelte Werke in drei Bänden*, ed. Friedhelm Kemp, 2nd ed. (Munich: Kösel, 1961).

[24]Lasker-Schüler, *Gesammelte Werke*, I, 337: "I have at home a piano that's blue / Though I don't know a single note. / It stands in the dark of the cellar door, / Ever since the world turned savage. / There are four star hands to play upon it / The moonwoman sang in her boat – / Now the rats dance in the clatter. / The keyboard has shattered.... / I mourn the blue corpse. / O sweet angels open to me / – I ate of bitter bread – / The door of heaven while I still live / Though it be against the law."

[25]Ibid., I, 360: "I dream so far from this earth / As though I had died / And would nevermore be flesh and blood."

[26]Emmy Ball Hennings, "Ein Nachruf," in Else Lasker-Schüler, *Dichtungen und Dokumente*, ed. Ernst Ginsberg (Munich: Kösel, 1951), p. 548.

[27]Gottfried Benn, "Rede auf Else Lasker-Schüler," in *Gesammelte Werke in vier Bänden*, ed. Dieter Wellershoff (Wiesbaden: Limes, 1959), I, 538.

[28]Vordtriede, "Vorläufige Gedanken," p. 574.

[29]Margot Ruben in Wolfskehl, *Zehn Jahre Exil: Briefe aus Neuseeland*, p. 18.

[30]Wolfskehl, *Zehn Jahre Exil*, p. 16.

[31]Karl Wolfskehl, *Sang aus dem Exil* (Heidelberg: Lambert Schneider, n.d.).

[32]Wolfskehl, *Sang aus dem Exil*, p. lxii: "Vintager's

sorrow, I hail you, the grapes / Of my clusters be thine. / Harvests! My leaves have long been turning / Late gathering brings the richest wine."

33 Ibid., p. xlv: "Exile! Me - presser, keeper of the wine, / The wine called the word, the mind, the dew of / Me, the appointed guardian of our shrine, / I was declared an outlaw by a wretch / Who seized my heart and drove me into night."

34 Franz Werfel, *Gedichte aus den Jahren 1908-1945* (Los Angeles: Pazifische Presse, 1946).

35 Alma Mahler Werfel in *Gedichte*, p. 7.

36 Werfel, *Gedichte*, p. 151: "I ate and drank in every food / The sun itself, whose rays, / Transformed in a mysterious way, / Became my meal of bread and wine. / In my breast the flow of breath / Coursed through the whole of life's stream / In the farthest cell of my body was / Found every atom of the constellations. / How must I be, through whom all things flow, / Creation my intimate home... / You have created me, Lord, in mind / So strange, so very strange, that I shrink in terror."

37 Bertolt Brecht, *Gesammelte Werke in 20 Bänden*, Werkausgabe edition suhrkamp (Frankfurt/M: Suhrkamp, 1967), XIX, 395-404.

38 Werfel, *Gedichte*, p. 164: "Yet not all tongues have sanctified / Pure rhyme. Where only endings sound together / Lurk empty games. The spirit holds aloof. / Two syllables alike are quickly glued. / But stems and roots will mock such dazzle. / In German it's the things themselves must rhyme."

39 Ibid., p. 161: "And while my life quickens and heals / I feel, in the next room, through thin walls / How he, unseen, reads the rustling evening paper."

40 Brecht, *Gesammelte Werken in 20 Bänden*, IX, 743-44. English version in: Bertolt Brecht, *Poems*, ed. John Willett and Ralph Manheim with the cooperation of Erich Fried (London: Eyre Methuen, 1976), pp. 330-31: "Bad Time for Poetry": "Yes, I know: only the happy man / Is liked. His voice / Is good to hear. His face is handsome. / The crippled tree in the yard / Shows that the soil is poor, yet / The passersby abuse it for being crippled / And rightly so. / The green boats and the dancing sails on the Sound / Go unseen. Of it all / I see only the torn nets of the fishermen. / Why do I only record / That a village woman aged forty walks with a stoop? / The girls' breasts / Are as warm as ever. / In my poetry / A rhyme / Would seem to me almost insolent. / Inside me contend / Delight at the apple tree in blossom / And horror at the house-painter's speeches. / But only the second / Drives me to my desk."

41 Brecht, *Gesammelte Werke*, p. 815. English version in *Poems*, p. 303: "Spring 1938": "To-day, Easter Sunday morning / A sudden snowstorm swept over the island. / Between the greening hedges lay snow. My young son / Drew me to a little apricot tree by the house wall / Away from a verse in which I pointed the finger at those / Who were preparing a war which / Could well wipe out the continent, this island, my people, my family / And myself. In

silence / We put a sack / Over the freezing tree."

42Brecht, "Über reimlose Lyrik mit unregelmässigen Rhythmen," passim.

43Alfred Kerr, *Melodien: Gedichte* (Paris: Editions Nouvelles Internationales/Internationale Verlags-Anstalt, 1938), p. 16: "Yesterday a naughty little buck / Today a lambkin with a bell / . . . / Peering from his brow, how odd - / Two hyena eyes."

44Walter Mehring, *No Road Back*, trans. S. A. De Witt, illus. George Grosz, English and German text (New York: Samuel Curl, 1944), pp. 102-107.

45Walter Mehring, *und euch zum Trotz: Chansons Balladen und Legenden; mit neun Zeichnungen und einem farbigen Umschlag vom Verfasser* (Paris: Europäischer Merkur, 1934), pp. 89-90: "Wotan-saurians, Odin-dragons / From your big mouth to your ass / You were brainless - only skull. / Your successors are a joke - / Pacifistic scum. / Procreating superracial monkeys / Führer-mammoths, colossal / As God might create them in a fit / From an opera arsenal / Till the sluggard-flea / Dragonlouse and forest-bug / Make a home in the whole, big / Race-pure Aryan Zoo."

46Walter Jens, *Deutsche Literatur der Gegenwart*, 4th ed. (Munich: R. Piper, 1962), p. 14.

47Vordtriede, "Vorläufige Gedanken," p. 571.

48Kaléko, *Verse für Zeitgenossen*, p. 48: "I once had a beautiful homeland / So used to sing Refugee Heine," parodies the opening line of Heinrich Heine's nineteenth-century exile lament. The Goethe original "Roselein, roselein, roselein red, roselein on the heather," a short lyric on the picking of a rose, becomes here a flower broken not by human hands but by political cant.

49Mehring, *und euch zum Trotz*, p. 90. The first line of the quotation (from "Arier-Zoo") is taken from a traditional German folk song about the coming of spring, and the second line parodies a line from the German national anthem.

50Brecht, *Gesammelte Werke*, IX, 442: "Now thank we all our Lord / Who sent us Mr. Hitler."

51Rudolf Leonhard, *Deutsche Gedichte* (Berlin: Dietz, 1947), p. 68: "Border: Written on 2 June 1947 upon crossing the French-German border. / As we crossed the border / Things looked the same on the other side / A field was a field and a house was a house / Things had much the same name / People were people, animals animals / People had two arms, the donkey four feet. / Clover fields on both sides smelled of the same sweetness, / The acacia trees on either side blossomed with equal vigor, / And the struggle was struggle, work work and love was love; and young / Facing the future, on either side, was the human race. / The earth on either side was well disposed toward those who befriended her. / On either side there was, for those who befriended her, earth enough, / Earth and people, on either side, were of equal measure."

52Berthold Viertel, *Dichtungen und Dokumente: Gedichte, Prosa, Autobiographische Fragmente*, ed. Ernst Ginsberg (Munich: Kösel, 1956), p. 322.

53Walter A. Berendsohn, "Emigrantenliteratur 1933-47,"
in   Merker/Stammler, *Reallexikon der deutschen Literaturgeschichte* (Berlin: Walter de Gruyter, 1968), p. 342.
54Stephan   Hermlin   and   Hans   Mayer, *Ansichten über
einige Bücher und Schriftsteller* (Berlin: Volk   und   Welt,
1950), p. 197.
55J.   Isaacs,   *The Background of Modern Poetry* (New
York: Dutton, 1952), p. 92.

The Novel in Exile: Types and Patterns
Joseph P. Strelka

The salient fact about the German novel during the Third Reich is its cultivation on foreign soil; virtually all works of any consequence in the genre were produced by writers who left after 1933. This exile of creative genius has an indisputable significance in the sociology of the period's art, but did it also profoundly influence the shape of the novel itself? Unless one examines the complexity of the phenomenon, it would be as easy to claim too much as too little.

From the traditional, realistic novel of the late nineteenth century through the expressionistic experimentation of the first two decades of the twentieth and the postexpressionist, post-Joycean developments between 1922 and 1931, the German-language novel, like the novel in the rest of Europe, manifested a dynamic vitality. Except in regard to a few isolated instances, exile itself did not contribute to further alteration or innovation in the form's fundamental aspects. The basis for the new novel, one should keep in mind, had already been laid by Robert Musil, Hermann Broch, Alfred Döblin, and Hans Henny Jahnn before they went into exile. Moreover, the novelists-in-exile represented almost all hues in the literary spectrum, from the traditionalism of Joseph Roth and Thomas Mann to the modernism of Döblin and Broch, and although the literary approaches of these diverse writers in some cases did change after their expatriation, the change was by no means uniformly in one direction. The novels of Thomas Mann, for example, underwent a transition from traditional to new modes during his exile (a development most conspicuously evident in *Doctor Faustus*, which, undoubtedly for this very reason, he called his "most unrestrained" work), but Döblin's novels, in turning from the unconventional *Berlin Alexanderplatz* [*Alexanderplatz, Berlin*] to the intermediate *Babylonische Wanderung* [*Babylonian Migration*] and the quite traditional *Pardon wird nicht gegeben* [*Men without Mercy*], evince a movement in the opposite direction.

24

But if exile generated no consistent technical advances in the novel's form, it did affect the general character of its content. In the main, this shift was expressed in two distinct ways. The first, illustrated by Mann's forsaking the contemporary ambiance of *Buddenbrooks* and *Der Zauberberg* for the historical setting of *Lotte in Weimar* and the *Joseph* tetralogy, and by Broch's similar desertion of the present of the *Schlafwandler* [*Sleepwalkers*] trilogy for the distant past of *Tod des Vergil* [*Death of Virgil*], involves the employment of the historical past as an oblique comment on the current state of the novelist's world.[1] The second, which is really an alternative manifestation of the same impulse that stimulated the first, simply transfers the accent from the physically real world of specified particulars to the symbolic and general rendering of that world. The case of *Der Mann ohne Eigenschaften* [*The Man without Qualities*] testifies to this latter phenomenon. The initial volume (that is, the first and second parts of Book One in the present edition) assumed, in Musil's own words, that the "subjective depiction of the times that led to the catastrophe must shape the *true matter of the story and always be able to fall back upon it*" (my italics).[2] Two years after the publication of this volume, when Musil, effectively "in exile" in his native Austria after having returned from his chosen home city of Berlin, issued the first thirty-eight chapters of Book Two in 1933, he no longer depended upon the solidity of the external world. The last lines of "Die Umkehrung," the first volume's final chapter, had described the protagonist's isolation--"a condition found not only within but around him, thus uniting both"--as growing "more dense, more vast. It strode through the walls, it extended into the city; without actually expanding, it reached into the world. 'What world?' he thought. 'There isn't any.'"[3] The second volume shows how prophetic these words were to be, for, in it, the external world has practically evanesced and been replaced by the indeterminate contours of subjective experience.

At first glance, both types of indirect depiction of the novelists' world might be seen as merely an instinctive protection against the risk of a tendentiousness that comes of lack of perspective; actually, the phenomenon is much more complex. In some instances, different reactions to diverse political situations produced quite similar results: what Thomas Mann attained from a vantage point relatively free of personal contingencies, for example, was for Musil an outgrowth of exhausting despair. Furthermore, to posit a constant causal connection between exile and the avoidance of a realistically redacted present would be wrong sometimes, as in Joseph Roth's shift from the objective, naturalistic treatment of setting and action in his earliest work to the indirect, timelessly symbolic configuration of *Hiob* [*Job*] (a breakthrough achieved in 1930, well before his exile began), the motivating factors obviously have nothing to do with the circumstances of totalitarianism and exile. The interaction of a myriad elements in a social, aesthetic, historical, and personal context is potentially involved, and to assay the

precise influence of the exile experience in any single instance is a problem of literary criticism incapable of solution within the limited scope of this essay--if, indeed, it is
capable of definitive solution at all. Even so, some observations concerning the effect of exile on the German novel are
pertinent to an overview of this period and may prove helpful toward a better understanding of the phenomenon.

If, as I suggested earlier, the relationship between
the novelist's exile and the content of his fiction can be
more clearly established than the relationship between exile
and form, this is obviously because it was practically impossible for a writer who had witnessed the oppressiveness of a
totalitarian regime and then undergone the intense emotional
process of rejecting its ideology and cutting himself loose
from the fabric of his national identity to wholly escape
having his imagination respond to that agony in his
works. Form tends to be a function of intellect; content of
experience. Yet the nature of the response varied from one
writer to another, and to rest content with a dichotomy that
merely separates novels that directly depict the present from
those that indirectly deal with the central problems of that
present by injecting them into other historical and geographical contexts would be to accept a distinction so superficial
that it is almost without meaning. To do justice to at least
the most important aspects of this literary phenomenon, this
dichotomy should be deepened and essentially differentiated.
Accordingly, I should like to propose a four-part typology
of the novel-in-exile that, though drastically simplified,
accommodates the major varieties: (1) direct rendering of the
contemporary world; (2) indirect rendering of the contemporary world; (3) direct reference to the contemporary world
encased within a portrayal of the past; and (4) indirect
reference to the contemporary world through the portrayal of
the past.

Some examples of each type may serve to clarify the
practical distinctions.

The first type shows the simplest literary reaction to
the events that spurred the authors to emigrate. Oskar Maria
Graf's *Der Abgrund* [*The Abyss*], Plievier's *Stalingrad*,
Seghers's *Das siebte Kreuz* [*The Seventh Cross*], Alfred
Neumann's *Es waren ihrer sechs* [*Six of Them*], Friedrich
Torberg's *Hier bin ich mein Vater* [*Here I Am, My Father*],
and Ernst Lothar's *Der Engel mit der Posaune* [*The Angel
with the Trumpet*] deal directly with the National Socialist
era by depicting specific, concrete events. Regardless of
any symbolic or general significance these events may otherwise imply, the novelists' object is to capture the contemporary experience they describe.

The second type--of which Thomas Mann's *Doctor Faustus* and Broch's *Der Versucher* [*The Tempter*] are superb
demonstrations--illuminates the overpowering experience of
totalitarianism indirectly by focusing on its effect on the
inner sphere of personality and values rather than on the
external record of events. Mann's Faustus is not cast as a
Gestapo agent, a resistance fighter, a general, or any other

exemplar of the contemporary political activism; he is simply
a musician with genius.   Yet Mann's portrait of his protagonist affords a deeper understanding of the times than any
number of depictions of actual National Socialist figures.
From the very outset, when the novel's fictitious narrator,
Serenus Zeitblom, discusses musical genius, the profound
implications of the central theme are already apparent:

> And yet it cannot be denied (and never has been) that
> the daemonic and irrational have a disquieting share
> in this radiant sphere.   We shudder as we realize that
> a connection subsists between it and the nether world,
> and that the reassuring *epitheta* that I sought to
> apply: "sane, noble, harmonious, humane," do not for
> that reason quite fit, even when--I force myself, how-
> ever painfully, to make this distinction--even when
> they are applied to a pure and genuine, God-given, or
> shall I say God-inflicted genius, and not to an ac-
> quired kind, the sinful and morbid corruption of natu-
> ral gifts, the issue of a horrible bargain ....[4]

Broch operates in a fashion similar to Mann's.   Mario Ratti,
the "tempter" of the title, is not a denizen of the Reich Chan-
cellory in Berlin--he does not even wear a brown shirt.   Even
so, Broch's indirect, generalized presentation of life in the
Third Reich, by delving into the psychological, mass psychological, and mythic implications of events in a miniature-
model Tyrolean Alpine village, furnishes an insight into the
period that is not only keener but also more human and
poetic than a pseudojournalistic account of the movers and
shakers in the capitals might have accomplished.

Among the better examples of the third type are Lion
Feuchtwanger's *Der falsche Nero* [*The Pretender*] (in which
Hitler, Goebbels, Goering, and the Reichstag fire are placed
in front of a Roman backdrop) and Hermann Kesten's *Ferdinand und Isabella* (in which the fury of Spanish nationalism, the expulsion of the Jews and Moors, and the institution of the Inquisition obviously refer to the character and
actions of Nazi Germany).   Although one might facilely assume
that this type dictates greater objectivity and a more far-
reaching poetic meaning through its dressing of present
events in historical or regional costume, the opposite is
true.   The very conceit of paralleling the past and the present requires directness, for the device depends upon constant
recognition of the familiar present, and any exploration of
the subtleties of the ostensible historical subject threatens to
confuse that allegorical correspondence.   Furthermore, though
this type avoids the aesthetic risks of lapsing into reportage
or yielding to political cliché that attach to the first type of
exile novel, it is vulnerable to another danger.   Playing on
the direct correspondences to contemporary events can result
in such abbreviation, failure to differentiate, and oversimpli-
fication that not only are both past and present distorted,
but also the artistry that is supposed to be served by the
device will suffer.   To be sure, not all novels written in
this mode succumb to the danger--the works of Feuchtwanger

and Kesten cited above, I hasten to note, are prominent exceptions--but the debilitating trait occurs so often that it can almost be said to be a mark of the breed.

In part because it inherently avoids these pitfalls that come from a constricting directness, the fourth type has produced a higher order of art. Broch's *Tod des Vergil* and Jahnn's *Fluss ohne Ufer* [*River without Banks*] trilogy illustrate the superiority: despite the casual reader's difficulty in perceiving the relevance of the transformation that occurs in Virgil's aesthetic views on the *Aeneid* or of Jahnn's strangely woven fabric of murder, friendship, and harmonious sublimation in musical forms to the nature of National Socialism, these novels--like others of this type--vouchsafe solutions to the contemporary historical dilemma more profound and more conclusive than can be found among the other types. There are several reasons for the paradox that this fiction, though situated at the farthest remove from the facticity of National Socialism, should contain the most basic and searching commentary upon the phenomenon. First, it is free of specious, superficial, or transparent "engagements" that could sink the novel's niveau to the level of the National Socialist clichés it would attack. Second, it exploits the advantage of achieving empathy with the reader through correlations with his inner self rather than through allusions to shared knowledge of external events. Third, it displaces totalitarianism--which made the infinite finite to the point of applying it to pragmatic ends--with the universality that reveals the infinite within the finite.

The last reason, which is the most important of the three, itself leads to a further paradox: novels of this type, which are among the formally more innovative works in this century's fiction, are also among the most traditional in terms of their humanistic, philosophical orientation. (One notes, for example, Broch's Vergil, whose recognition that his perception of life is inadequate in its limitation drives him toward a complementary perception of death, and Jahnn's illumination of the inaccessible, overflowing *Fluss ohne Ufer* of all mortal living flesh on such a grand scale that it overwhelms the possibility of falsehood or reduction.) What Broch succinctly termed the infinite in the finite ("das Unendliche im Endlichen") is the aim Jahnn described when he identified the task of modern art as a quest for unique external forms to express abiding principles: "Progress and evolution in the purposes of art do not exist [and] never did exist," he stated. Art "has its origins in the human tendency toward a state of inner revelation where, as Keppler phrases it, [the artist] imitates his creator. That is, through play and meditation, he achieves new syntheses and glimpses the reflected brilliance of eternal being."[5]

My attempt to outline a possibly typology of the exile novel is of course subject to the problematical difficulties that any taxonomy of intellectual endeavor incurs. First of all, there are mediate forms that resist certain classification. Friedrich Torberg's novel about a Jewish informer for the Gestapo begins as a suspenseful, direct portrayal of the

THE NOVEL IN EXILE 29

contemporary scene.   Further on, however, particularly in
the conversation between the protagonist and his former Jewish religious teacher and in the narrative framework of the
latter half of the novel, it forsakes the convention of the
first type and assumes the characteristics of the second.   In
the case of Musil's *Der Mann ohne Eigenschaften*, it is a
matter of interpretation whether the 1913 setting is sufficiently contemporary to warrant classifying it as a type two
novel, or whether, since the pre-World War I experience is
so remote from the conditions that produced the phenomenon
of exile, it really belongs under type four.   (My own view
is that the latter classification is more appropriate.)

Also, although my typology is based on an analysis
of the novel's contents, it should be pointed out that these
types do manifest certain formal affinities.   In general,
types one and three adhere to the traditional novel form,
whereas types two and four reflect the postexpressionist,
post-Joycean structure of the novel.   If I have not pursued
this topic, it is because to do so would enlarge the discussion beyond the scope mandated by my original point of
departure.

Finally, this typology does not address itself to answer-
ing the myriad questions about the dynamics of exile as a
force in shaping the aesthetic consciousness.   It may raise
some issues and allude to others, but it leaves the major
questions unexplored.   What was the common effect of exile
on novelists?   How did it influence their patterns of response?   How did it affect their productivity?   In what manner did it sway their attitudes toward literature?   Although
these questions are provocative and invite speculation, the
evidence is incomplete and often contradictory.   Exile was a
stimulus that produced a variety of responses, depending on
the idiosyncrasies of the individual author's character and
personal history.   Jahnn found that art offered the only
possibility of achieving genuine harmony; Joseph Roth, who
called his fictional hero Tarabas only "a guest on the
earth," eschewed the purely mundane; Werfel, in *Stern der
Ungeborenen* [*Star of the Unborn*], was attracted to a utopian ideal.   Yet the appearance of a common denominator
in these instances of aversion to the affairs of the world
is misleading.   Musil, for example, found a personal solution
in the lucid mysticism of "the other state of being," but to
interpret his exile experience in terms of a traditional dichotomy of worldliness/other-worldliness would be to be seduced
into a misunderstanding of monumental proportions.   Ödön
von Horváth, to cite a different example, indicted apathy
as the root of the problem in his two-volume novel *Zeit-
alter der Fische* [*Age of the Fish*] and the proposed consideration of "life on this earth" as the solution.   Still
another response was humor--as Hermann Kesten's *Die
fremden Götter* [*The Foreign Gods*] attests.   In a word,
the reactions were so diverse, so multifarious, that it is
impossible to develop a common denominator.   Similarly inde-
terminable is the broad effect of exile on productivity.
Johannes Urzidil almost certainly would never have become a

prolific author were it not for the release of energy caused by his emigration. Stefan Zweig, on the other hand, experienced such a sapping of his creativity that *Balzac*, his projected grand novel of exile, was severely stunted.

Only in the exiles' attitude toward literature was there something approaching uniformity. In "Erdbeben in Chile" ["The Earthquake in Chile"], Heinrich von Kleist had described the effect of a natural disaster on society in terms that apply equally well to the effect of political catastrophe on a literary generation: "Instead of empty chatter for which the world of tea tables used to furnish the subject matter, examples of prodigious deeds were now related. . . ."[6] With the eye of a great artist penetrating to the ambivalence of human response, Kleist wrote: "Indeed, since there was not a soul on that day to whom something heart-stirring had not happened or who had not himself done some generous deed, the anguish in everybody's breast was mixed with so much sweet delight that it was impossible to decide, as she thought, whether the sum of general happiness had not increased on one side by as much as it had declined on the other" (ibid.). In the aftermath of the social breakdown brought about by totalitarianism, the survivors experienced an inner gain that, as a rule, balanced the external deprivation they endured. Among writers, this heightened sense of value took the form of a veneration of literature as art. Whether it manifested itself as an intensified individual ethical consciousness, social commitment, or true piety, the tendency was toward an increased explicitness and concentration on human affairs as the foremost task of art. Art as formalistic play, art for art's sake, or even art for the sake of abstract theory became unthinkable in the face of the events that had driven them to seek havens beyond the borders of their native land.

Despite variations in the styles employed and in the intensity with which this experience was conveyed, the general reaction was basically one: if some expressed themselves in shrouded or sublimated formulations, there was nevertheless a direct commitment to the issues raised by the upheaval; if, in some cases, the gravity and enormity of the events made even serious writing seem unjustifiable self-indulgence, there was also a profound recognition that humanity lay at the core of poetic concern. The overwhelming nature of the catastrophe had a particularly tragic impact on the great writers who, despite their scientific and social interests, had been essentially poets in their innermost being: Robert Musil went through moments when his lay theology loomed more important than the "house of cards" that was his great novel; and Hermann Broch endured periods when, confronting the debacle, he could no longer counter doubts that assailed him about the worth of his writing--only an inner necessity drove him to persist in his literary work at a time when his study of mass psychology seemed more pressing, useful, and significant.

In my view--and, I would hope, in the view of scholars in the future--the importance of the German exile novel lies not only in the literary excellence it produced in uncommon numbers but also in the humanistic earnestness evinced by the critical and historic moral stance of its practitioners. It was an exile novelist who first discerned with utmost clarity the basis of this awesome significance. Broch maintained that science can no longer aspire to the presentation of a unifying vision; only art has the potential to do so. Furthermore, Broch demonstrated in both theory and practice the unique capacity of the novel to fulfill this need for universality. In regard to the task of depicting the totalitarianism of the National Socialist period, the novel, with its comprehensive scope, offered resources no other genre would match. What other form could encompass the manifold aspects of this subject and convey its inner forces in such a way as to scale the metaphysical and magical heights of imagination while also plumbing the depths of its physical roil? The novel alone affords the means of engaging the reader at multiple levels simultaneously, of presenting the full range of human experiences "from the physical and emotional to the moral and metaphysical."[7] In the uniqueness of this all-inclusive vision seen through the lens of man in the modern totalitarian state lies not only the literary achievement of the outstanding German exile novels but also their social and practical relevance to our time. Sadly, since 1933 the menace of totalitarianism has shown no signs of abating. To read these expressions of exile from a world "vexed to nightmare" is to encounter ourselves.

Translated by Frank Gado

Notes

[1] A number of prominent examples could be cited, including Döblin's changeover from *Berlin Alexanderplatz* to *Babylonische Wanderung* and *Amazonas* trilogy, Heinrich Mann's from *Die grosse Sache* [*The Big Deal*] to his great opus *Henri Quatre*, and Bruno Frank's from *Politische Novelle* [*Political Novelle*] to his *Cervantes* [*A Man Called Cervantes*].

[2] Wilfried Berghahn, *Robert Musil in Selbstzeugnissen und Bilddokumenten*, Rowohlts Monographien, 81 (Reinbek bei Hamburg: Rowohlt, 1963), p. 94.

[3] Robert Musil, *Der Mann ohne Eigenschaften* (Hamburg: Rowohlt, 1952), p. 679.

[4] Thomas Mann, *Doctor Faustus*, trans. H. T. Lowe-Porter (New York: Alfred A. Knopf, 1948), p. 4.

[5] Hans Henny Jahnn, *Über den Anlass und andere Essays* (Frankfurt/M: Europäische Verlagsanstalt, 1964), p. 94.

[6] Heinrich von Kleist, *The Marquise of O-- and Other Stories*, trans. and with an Introduction by Martin Greenberg. Preface by Thomas Mann (New York: Criterion Books, 1960), p. 260.

[7] Hermann Broch, "How THE GUILTLESS Came into Being," in *The Guiltless*, trans. Ralph Manheim (Boston: Little, Brown, 1974), p. 288.

Short Fiction in Exile: Exposure and Reclamation of a Tradition

James Rolleston

Writing in 1929, Alfred von Grolman describes the modern literary obsession with individual loneliness and metaphysics as fundamentally alien to the Mediterranean clarity of the *Novelle*, and concludes (despite abundant ongoing evidence to the contrary): "It is a fact, not a value judgment, that for a century no German has been able to write a *Novelle*--in spite of, or perhaps because of, Heyse --and it is a fact that must be acknowledged."[1] Forty-two years later, Theodore Ziolkowski discusses the function of the sonnet for opponents of the Nazi government: "From any perspective, the world of the Third Reich is unmasked as a cultural and human chaos; only form can reestablish order."[2] Taken separately, these statements raise the full spectrum of questions about problems of form in modern literature. Granted that caution is in order regarding authors' own designations of their short fiction:[3] nevertheless, of what use is a formal definition like Grolman's, so strict that it can exist only in a hypothetical literary museum, along with other fragile and rarefied artifacts? At the other extreme Ziolkowski seems to be saying something either very startling or very ordinary: either the sonneteers of whom he speaks employed a new miracle ingredient called "form" to make instant sense out of their world, or writers then, as at all times, confronted reality armed only with their language and the accumulated literary resources of the past.

Taken together, however, the two comments suggest a sea-change in critical approaches to aesthetic matters, brought about by the overwhelming facts of totalitarian government and the resultant universal disruption. In 1929 one could talk of "modern man" as such, a creature given to fragmentation and nihilism, standing at the end of traditions visibly crumbling under the pressures of his brooding and destructive gaze. In one sense the rise of fascism simply confirmed this state of affairs, removing the freedoms that had been so little valued. But the dialectic of devastation gave new life to discussions that had become arid and restored the perspective of engagement to formal questions that had seemed buried under the weight of an ironic determinism. Literary forms could no longer be taken for granted or modified within a continuum; rather, they had to be chosen consciously, reborn as it were, for the government that had obliterated the old world excluded nothing from its assault, not even something so self-evidently "existent" as a literary past. Ziolkowski's title, "Form als Protest," is thus very apt, provided it is not understood in too narrowly political a sense: to the exiles, form was not so much a weapon as a valid starting-point, a locus for the self in a world without alternative roots. As Werner Vordtriede has said: "All great exile writing represents an attempt to save the tradition that has been broken."[4] The break in tradition is an indisputable fact corresponding precisely to all the other catastrophic facts of an exile's life. Traditional forms are thus at issue, indeed inextricably involved in the texture of exile writing. In the exile context the distinction between "traditional" and "progressive" shrinks in importance, in the aesthetic as well as the political sphere, as the two terms come close to being synonymous in the struggle to wrest the German language from its oppressor.

All this is peculiarly relevant to the *Novelle*, with its roots in an explicitly "social" situation linking story, storyteller, and audience. Fritz Lockemann has traced the changing relationships between story and frame from Boccaccio to the nineteenth century, showing how the principle of "order" was identified first with the shape of the fiction itself, then with the society in which it is told, and finally with the artist's a priori insights. Lockemann shows that the frame is no mere artifice but inherent in the very conception of the *Novelle*, and that it is no paradox to call an unframed *Novelle* an "extreme form of the framed *Novelle*" ("Grenzform der Rahmennovelle").[5] This is a fruitful point from which to approach the exile writers, whose relationship with the *Novelle* was, very precisely, one of paradox. Although a degree of self-exiling, of critical distance, was inherent in the relationship between the earliest writers of *Novellen* and their society, that relationship remained one of creative tension; the exiled German writers, however, were totally cut off from a society for which they rapidly ceased to have any understanding or any feeling that could nourish a traditional critical connection. As the gulf of time and geography widened, their anti-Nazi sentiments became either too abstract or too colored with the experience of exile to be artistically usable in relation to contemporary Germany. At the same time, of course, they could never become sufficiently "inside" the societies in which they actually lived even to begin the movement toward valid critical distance. Thus the prerequisites for writing a *Novelle* were absent in their entirety: the principle of order was certainly not to be found in their experiences, but neither could it be situated in any imaginable social or artistic frame. Hence to choose the *Novelle* form was an act of extreme paradox; out of the very absence of any kind

of fertilizing soil the form was, as it were, to be summoned
into existence in order to generate, through its own fictive
momentum, the social perspectives that the author was struggling to articulate.   Here another aspect of the exile's
extreme situation, well summarized by Vordtriede, came to
his aid: "Every expression of exile is absolutely authentic.
The testimony of an untalented man and that of a genius are
genuine in equal measure."[6]   The flattening, reductive quality of the exile experience gives a sharper profile to the
dimension of choice: choice of form and choice of experience,
which must have seemed so arbitrary to the individual
author, blended immediately with the movement of history to
produce, in some cases, an "authentic" piece of literature
such as the same writer might never have managed under
less urgent and extreme circumstances.   One is impressed
by the way differences between "major" and "minor" writers
seem less noticeable in the exile context: Thomas Mann wrote
one of his weakest stories, "Das Gesetz," 1943 ["The Law"],
in exile, and it is hard to find much to enjoy in Carl Zuckmayer's unctuous "Der Seelenbräu," 1945 ["Soul Bridegroom"].[7]
      Mention of these stories, neither of which is called a
Novelle, necessitates a closer examination of the problem
of genre.   In this century a dichotomy has developed, in
theory and to some extent in practice, between the *Novelle*
and the story (I shall use this term as a translation of
Erzählung, although I am aware that in German writings
on the question subcategories are involved):

> The first type is the *Novelle*: it is limited in plot,
> centrally focused, sharply drawn, succinctly aimed,
> takes an unexpected narrative turn, reveals a web of
> structural supports, its tempo is urgent, and it is
> rigorously closed in upon itself; the second type is the
> *story*: it is contrastingly decentralized in narrative
> shape, lingers on situations, unfolds gradually, is
> loosely woven, discrete, dwells more on problems than
> clear epic solutions, is relaxed, a continuum of a
> single notion, and it proceeds at a calm retardant
> pace . . . .[8]

Such dualisms, although generally not applicable in every
detail, are useful starting points, especially in such a context as the exile writers' relationship to the *Novelle*.
For while these writers looked to the *Novelle* as an emblem of the tradition that had been broken and a symbol of
the social dialogue for which they yearned, the sheer fragmented quality of their actual experience demanded expression
in the looser, less binding framework of the short story.
And although I believe the *Novelle* remained the prototype, the conscious goal of most of the exile writers, the
story should not be understood merely as its negative pole.
Although the results are too "impure" to satisfy a theoretician, the works can be grouped according to their underlying
thrust: either they tend toward the *Novelle*, toward the
multiplication of frames and the distillation of reality—or
they tend toward the story, breaking through their own

fictional frames and striving to reenter reality through an accumulation of detail and a generalizing of the narrative voice.   In the *Novelle* the persona of the central character is isolated and enigmatic, and the deeper motives are inaccessible to the narrator; in the story the figure of the hero is blurred, his "personality" tends to merge with its physical context.   He is constantly observing and reflecting on himself, whereas the thoughts of his counterpart in the *Novelle* are often ritualistic and stylized.   Three themes are commonly found in both types of exile fiction: death, time, and art.   For the hero of the *Novelle* death is the ultimate step in a reductive process that begins with the story itself, a suicide in fact or by implication; in the story, on the other hand, death is a moment of extreme intensification, a final experience that generates memories and expands the self toward mythic status.   The story makes fertile use of time-dimensions, juxtaposing history and fiction, past and present to suggest an "overcoming" of time, a regaining of both reality and meaning; in the *Novelle*, by contrast, time is the victor, foreshortening life into a more or less "fateful" framework from which it is powerless to escape.   Works of art, finally, are frequent motifs, expressive of the quest for tradition at the heart of the exile experience: in the *Novelle* the work of art is a kind of residue, a stranded enigma; in the story it is a summation, almost an allegorization of events.

Klaus Mann's remarkable story about the last day in the life of King Ludwig of Bavaria, "Vergittertes Fenster," 1937 ["Barred Window"], illustrates both the basic themes of exile fiction and the specific tendencies toward the *Novelle* as prototype.   Although much exile writing focuses on the period before 1914 as a starting point, this work is explicitly "historical"--and yet we experience history here as the absolute reverse of an escape route.   The opening pages, so important for the self-enclosing structure of a *Novelle*, show the central character in an extreme situation: Ludwig, the last monarch able to indulge the fantasies of absolutism, is effectively deposed as insane and locked in a small room with a barred window surrounded by the magnificence of his own castle, Berg; outside, the Bavarian rain pours down ceaselessly.   With all the antinomies of life--fantasy and monotony, power and impotence, past and present--concentrated into Ludwig's basic situation, Mann allows a crucial question for the exile situation, the question of madness, to unfold before the reader without restrictive value judgments. It is the specific quality of the *Novelle* form that enables him to do this.   There is no explicit frame: the reader is plunged in medias res.   But at the outset he is not "inside" the king, but aligned rather with the servants' viewpoint; the king's words are unrevealing, and, because the word *Blick* ("look," "view," "appearance") predominates, the reader is invited to focus on his face.   Interestingly, this atmosphere continues when the king is left alone: he knows he is being watched.   The reader is allowed into his thoughts only *because* of his sense of being on stage: "I want to seem dignified. . . . No more moaning. . . . Everything depends on putting my thoughts in order" (p. 25). Ludwig's thoughts are thus placed in a frame from the outset so that the reader accepts their stylized quality and is never clear when the border between "public" and "private" is crossed, or even if there is one.   The king's thoughts focus on Richard Wagner and at once two new dimensions are established.   On the one hand Wagner himself, now three years dead, was an "open" character, about whom, unlike Ludwig, a *Novelle* could not have been written: "[Wagner] made his peace with this dreadful modern world that is my destruction" (p. 30).   On the other hand the yearning for death at the core of Wagner's music dramas begins to take hold of the king's mind, both nourished by and warring with the monotony of the rain and the lake outside his window.

Klaus Mann maintains the impetus of his story through a constant generation of new frames.   The frame of history itself is lightly etched in through the counting of the hours and meals; the reader's "knowledge" of Ludwig's coming death is unobtrusively enlisted.   Gradually, too, the theme of art supplements that of time until it comes to predominate. As Ludwig is permitted to walk round his palace, he contemplates his own past embodied in the portraits of him.   And then the king's fictionalizing mind, as if impelled by the twin confines of the barred room and the *Novelle* itself, begins to transform the wretched events of the present: "Ludwig--in thought, facing the bars of the window--views the finale of his own tragedy, like the fifth act of a Schillerian drama" (p. 53).   From Schiller to Wagner and suicide by drowning is a short step.   But Mann does not stop there: the entire drama of Ludwig's final hours becomes itself a kind of frame for the final image of the mourning Empress Elizabeth, a "statue of pain" (p. 95).   The word *Bild* (meaning both "picture" and "image") is almost as common at the end as *Blick* was at the beginning, transforming the narrative into a multiple metaphor of exile, the margin between history and fiction, between feeling and its appearance, between the act of creation and life itself.   As the narrator withdraws explicitly, as he had begun implicitly, into the position of a servant, the "only witness of the grand picture, which the empress now represents beside the bed of her dead friend," he maintains the tension between his own analytical and mythicizing tendencies, asking the rhetorical question whether she was not "blind, like the goddess of fate" (p. 95).

One can argue that all this is self-conscious to a fault, and perhaps it is, although summary discussion necessarily exaggerates the technical aspects.   Certainly Klaus Mann has used a great many props from history and maintained a "conservative" linguistic profile.   But in doing so he has illuminated, from a consciously oblique angle, both the dynamics of German self-destructiveness and a paradigm of the despair and potential madness inherent in any exile situation.   The detachment, the indirection of the *Novelle* form is the key to his achievement.

A prime illustration of what I have termed the tendency toward the short story is provided by what is perhaps, next to *Doctor Faustus*, the most ambitious work generated by the pressures of exile, Hermann Broch's *Die Schuldlosen*, 1950 [*The Guiltless*]. This is a major book, to which no kind of justice can be done here, and my discussion will be restricted to the question of genre, intriguing in itself. In his absorbing postscript Broch says he has collected a group of *Novellen* and linked them together; but the result is quite the opposite of a revival of the *Novelle* cycle. The rather precise subtitle of the work is "Ein Roman in elf Erzählungen" ["A Novel in Eleven Stories"], which points to both the misleading use of the word *Novelle* in the postscript and the real conception of the book: Broch is striving to emulate Joyce's *Ulysses*, to build an overwhelming answer to reality itself through the integration of fragmented genres and perspectives, to achieve and surpass the goals of mimesis through the reimposition of artifice. Despite the elaborate deployment of "lyrical" interludes, entitled "Stimmen" ["Voices"], between the stories, there are essentially no frames here, merely conduits from fiction into reality. None of the characters is clearly focused; indeed clarity is not sought by Broch, whose aim is always to dissolve the boundaries of the individual consciousness while maintaining an aura of existential anguish: "And the self in the bowed head looked down on the trunk which split into legs . . . his self, though embedded in the darkness of the environing night world, was alone" (p. 61). The thrust toward inclusiveness and continuity blurs the outline of all conflicts; indeed the death of a major figure, Melitta, becomes an occasion for the hero's further self-exploration, woven into the texture of his inchoate ego.[9] As the theme of time is played and replayed, it becomes apparent that the book's goal is nothing less than a symbolic reenactment of the entire period 1913–33. The problematic nature of the enterprise becomes evident when the fictional constraints are finally broken open and Hitler himself is invoked directly. For the drive toward reality is simultaneous, perhaps even synonymous, with the drive toward metaphysical abstraction. The challenge to Hitler is phrased thus: "A concrete declaration of war against the Beast's apocalyptic here and now, that is the new watchword of responsibility . . ." (p. 264). The sentence continues for no fewer than fifteen lines. Broch is probably correct, at least inadvertently, in his presentation of a German intellectual's response to the rise of Hitler; but without a functioning system of frames, there is no way for the reader to gain perspective on the speaker's rhetoric. The speech is made by the principal character, A., and at its conclusion we are simply told: "A. had concluded his confession." It is precisely the immediacy of the political challenge that makes the "open" tendencies of the story risky for the exile posture. Can literature enter the political arena directly without revealing all too vividly its inherent weaknesses as a house of words? In his postscript Broch is quite clear that literature has never converted anybody, but

he sees it as an embodiment of a "totality of being." The
consequence is that his book, while striving for an impossible
mastery, becomes instead a symptom of the age it sets out to
symbolize.

Literary groupings, like politics, make strange bed-
fellows; when the two are intertwined, the results can be
stranger still. Tending, like Broch's work, toward the openness of the short story, but endeavoring to embrace their
own relativity in the political context, are a group of stories
written from a left-wing perspective: Gustav Regler's "Der
Tod in der Michaelskirche," 1934 ["Death in St. Michael's
Church"], Günther Anders's "Der Hungermarsch," 1935 ["The
Hunger March"], Eduard Claudius's "Das Opfer," 1938 ["The
Victim"], and Friedrich Wolf's "Lucie und der Angler von
Paris," 1946 ["Lucie and the Paris Fisherman"]. All except
the Claudius (the least interesting) declare themselves to be
Novellen, but by all traditional criteria, on which my own
are merely a variation, this is a misnomer. Lutz Mackensen
suggests the reason, all too bluntly: "A tendentious novella
would be a contradiction in terms. The poet (one cannot
reiterate it often enough) is above all else a creator, not a
harbinger, a pedagogue, or a partisan spokesman."[10] This
is something that perhaps *can* be repeated too often; that a
political *Novelle* is a contradiction in terms is no longer as
self-evident a truth as it used to be. The exile situation,
however, with a dispersed audience and events daily shattering all previous expectations, was an unfavorable starting
point for such an attempt. These writers seem to have
picked on a particular quality of the *Novelle*—the concentrated, extreme situation—as the justification for labeling
their work as such; but it is the concentration of the explod-
ing bullet, reducing all narrative perspective to rubble. The
most innovative of the group is Anders's story, which concerns an attempt by a worker-priest named Om, in Mexico in
July 1924, to mobilize a motley collection of rural workers in
protest against their conditions. Anders has endeavored to
generate the appropriate novellistic "detachment" by removing
tension (we know from an encyclopedia entry concerning Om
in the first paragraph that the hunger march fails); by
incorporating "Brechtian" techniques such as instructional
chapter titles and even a summarizing "song" near the end;
and by the dryness in his style: "Let us be precise: a char-
latan of truth. This won't make Om any better. Just more
available to posterity" (p. 297). But the center of the work
is all too clearly the lengthy debate Om stages with the captured mayor of Barano on issues of the class struggle before
they both are shot and the march disperses. The terms of
the debate do not so much stylize as effectively replace the
nominal participants: and without a strongly profiled "private" dimension at its core, however obliquely portrayed, the
structure of the *Novelle* simply wilts in the Mexican sun,
like the political moment it is attempting to revive.

One certainly cannot complain of a lack of "inner life"
in Regler's story. An activist is mortally wounded trying to
escape from prison and staggers into a nearby church, where

the combination of physical pain, music, childhood memories, and political consciousness (he is roused to a final anger by the tardy and "moderate" anti-Nazism of the sermon) enlarges the moment of his death into a kind of archetype of the committed existence.   The trouble is, of course, that with the passing of the specific occasion the reader ceases to respond to such highly colored prose.   I am not arguing that *all* political statements from the period are necessarily dated (one thinks of the moving conclusion of Chaplin's film *The Great Dictator*); indeed the problem of how to make such statements is a central concern of all exile writers, who were in effect condemned to politics.   But for a political insight to survive the moment it must be carefully validated, embedded in the life of a character whom the reader can know and believe in: the problem is not solved in these "committed" stories.

A more "standard" kind of exile fiction that tends to the pole of story rather than *Novelle* is to be found in the many stories of Lion Feuchtwanger and Franz Werfel.   "Robust" is perhaps the best adjective for these works, none of which claim to be *Novellen*.   Narrative frames are found often enough, especially with Werfel, but they are always conversational rather than formalistic, throwing as many ropes as possible across the gulf between fiction and the substance of history.   These writers seem to believe that by constant involvement with their times, by applying their established literary skills to every scrap or image of genuine experience that comes their way, they will maintain their readers' awareness of the true dimensions of the age they are living through.   This very functional attitude toward the short story (one must remember that both men reserved their "major" utterances for novels) yields a great deal to enjoy and generates striking images of the oddities and surface conundrums of the period.   Two Werfel stories, "Par l'amour," 1938 ["By Way of Love"] and "Weissenstein, der Weltverbesserer," 1939 ["Weissenstein, the World-Reformer"], illustrate the author's ability to encompass seeming extremes of experience within the same unruffled framework.   "Par l'amour" is a very concrete fantasy in which Bertrand, the hero, notices a girl on a commuter train reading a pulp novel and imagines an entire future with her before the train pulls into the Gare Saint Lazare.   The point of the story is the indirection (not until late in the story does Bertrand even see the girl's face): all the details of the story, the world of the pulp novel, the commuter journey and the routine it represents, even the shadows cast by human figures, all serve as mutually reinforcing frames in which the imagined future becomes irresistibly real, incorporating the present moment as a wholly "natural" reference point: "She is reading passionately just as she did the first time they met on the train to St. Lazare" (p. 54).   "Weissenstein, der Weltverbesserer," on the other hand, concerns a deformed Dostoyevskian character who haunts cafés in the year 1911 and whom his friends are always having to get out of trouble.   The author is very frankly among these friends and tells us that the story's interest lies entirely in a chance meeting he has had with Weissenstein in 1914, when the oppressed little man is rapidly becoming metamorphosed into an exultant dictator. There is little point, in such an "open" story, in distinguishing between author and fictive persona; thus Werfel himself says of his creation: "I consider him a secondary role, a supporting actor in God's great tragicomedy. I would not summon him from the underworld, had life itself not lent a poignancy to his story that was more blunt, more daring than any author could have devised" (p. 65). The ethos of the short story could hardly be more concisely expressed: the reader's awareness of Hitler's rise is designed to lift the last veil between fiction and reality.

Ultimately, however, such openness defeats itself. The conversational tone, the accumulation of detail could not do justice to the radical isolation of exile. To probe the compatibility of the experience with a "closed" form such as the *Novelle*, we return to the two most ambitious examples of the genre in these years: Stefan Zweig's "Schachnovelle," 1941 ["The Royal Game"] and Leonhard Frank's "Deutsche Novelle," 1944 ["German Novelle"]. Zweig's well-known story concerns a sea voyage from New York to Buenos Aires on which the narrator finds that a fellow-traveler is the world chess champion, a phlegmatic former prodigy named Czentovic whose entire existence seems absorbed by the chess board. In the course of a challenge match a brilliant player appears, a Dr. B., who is extremely nervous but has a profound understanding of chess. In a long central section he tells the narrator about the horrors of solitary confinement by the Gestapo during which his sanity is saved by a book of chess games. However, the abstraction and division of the self involved in this concentrated study produces a nervous breakdown and persistent instability after his release. In the culminating match with Czentovic, Dr. B. wins the first game but cannot endure the champion's delaying tactics in the second and loses his grip on reality for one disastrous moment. The space needed to give even the bare outlines of the story suggests an important fact about "Schachnovelle": the author is consciously "choosing," directing his story toward the *Novelle* as prototype while retaining fruitful links with the unstylized actuality of the short story. The story reads very easily and the elaborate system of frames—the voyage, the chessboard, the story of Dr. B's past—is deployed like a kind of unseen presence, avoiding all direct hints of the story's symbolism. The profoundly ambivalent significance of chess (a recurring motif in stories of the time, it has an important role in Curt Goetz's "Tatjana") is spelled out only in Dr. B's narration. Chess both saves him and almost destroys him; in its domination of his mind it hints at the tyranny of modern technology, which is "neutral" only if the social fabric is strong enough to contain it. This dimension is reinforced by the figure of Czentovic, who is far from "demonic," but whose value-free impersonality conceals a crude lust for power. In its other aspect, of course, chess embodies the possibility of the

Novelle itself, the formal perfection toward which civilization has striven and which brings its present state into sharp focus. The reductive impulse of the *Novelle*, which I termed central to its value for exile literature, is most delicately handled here: Dr. B. stumbles away—he will not play chess again, and other speculation about him is irrelevant. Through chess we have come to know him, and into the impossibility of chess he withdraws from sight.

Frank's story is far more elaborate and stylized. In the year 1904 the young Michael Vierkant is working in a village where a young noblewoman named Josepha lives. He worships her, but she is psychologically trapped by her "demonic" servant who plans her mental destruction stage by stage. She is very pure, but cannot control her lust to yield to him; after she finally does so, she escapes further humiliation by shooting him and then herself. Michael, whose story intertwines with hers, is the first to find the bodies, takes Josepha's confession and makes it appear as though the servant did the shooting. Forty years later Michael's picture of the scene, with the title "I Would Have Loved Her," is hanging in a New York gallery, a pictorial residue of a drama understood only by Michael. One's response to this work is entirely different from one's response to "Schachnovelle"; far from having links to the short story, Frank's opus could be called an intensified and expanded *Novelle*, a demonstration of *Novelle* techniques on the largest possible scale. Whether it works is another question: the circular quality of the closed rhythm, while entirely consonant with the theme, becomes exhausting and provokes the irreverent wish that Josepha's servant would accelerate his game plan somewhat. The texture is modulated by extensive accounts of Michael's own more concrete (but unfortunately not very interesting) experiences, and by occasional punctuations of the atmosphere of 1904 with brief thoughts about Germany's subsequent history. The title makes plain that Josepha's fate is supposed to parallel that of Germany, and this becomes explicit when the later Michael ponders "the unanswerable question why, for a German, life is no more than the chance to search for death" (p. 99). Frank was communicating with Thomas Mann in California at the time of writing and he evidently hoped to do for the *Novelle* what *Doctor Faustus* was doing for the novel. That he could not succeed should be clear by now from what has been said about the self-contained, reductive nature of the *Novelle* in contrast to the inclusive, expansive tendency of the story, the novel writ small. Nevertheless, a modern critic like Jost Hermand finds the psychology of Germany-as-victim objectionable in itself: "The identical conservative myth of German character is found in the 'Deutsche Novelle' of Leonhard Frank, which in its concentration on the demonic and instinctual reveals a dubious affinity to the ideology of the then rulers of the Reich."[11] This seems harsh. That Frank was no historian is no argument against an attempt at symbolic reenactment of history already past. Moreover, it is of the essence of the exiles' situation that they could not

42   JAMES ROLLESTON

know the reality and were compelled to deploy their imagination and the resources of memory. Hermand's argument seems
much more applicable to the questionable ground occupied
by Hermann Broch in his resolute entry into history and the
implication that his work holds a spiritual key. Frank's
aspirations are much more modest in practice; the historical
dimension as such is minimal (no extensive meditations à la
Doctor Faustus), and a more cogent argument against the
"Deutsche Novelle" is the intrinsic one that the motivation
of the principal characters is inadequate and the narrative
perspective uncertain--Michael's consciousness functions only
as a counterpoint, not as a fully developed frame for the
central action.   Josepha and her servant are thus enigmatic
without being enigmatic enough.

Among the many stories striving to blend the chaos of
the exile experience with the strict modality of the *Novelle*,
I conclude with a brief discussion of three that emphasize
differing qualities of the prototype in an illuminating way:
A. M. Frey's "Ein Mädchen mordet," 1934 ["A Girl Murders"],[12] Alfred Neumeyer's "Laurel Valley," 1939, and Oskar
Jellinek's "Der Freigesprochene," 1945 ["The Man Who Was
Acquitted"].   Frey's story, somewhat conventional in manner
and employing Schnitzler's stream-of-consciousness technique,
presents a girl who has botched an attempted murder of a
woman blackmailing her; she reads of her failure in the
newspaper, visits her lover, a married doctor, who gives
her the drugs and the nurse's uniform to finish the job; she
succeeds, reads of her success in the newspaper, is drawn
to the dead woman's family, finds her lover distant, and
gradually loses the thread of what she has done, finally
drowning herself.   The striking thing about the story is the
way an intense and concentrated situation, a climactic moment
in the heroine's life, is juxtaposed with a persistent and
growing atmosphere of anonymity.   From the moment when
Thekla is confronted with the distorted image of her act in
the newspaper she is borne along like a somnambulist, not
in any doubt about what she has to do, but not able to
regain meaning either.   It is as if she, not the victim, were
dead.   (Hans Weigel wrote an extended fantasy, "Das himmlische Leben" ["Life in Paradise"], about the exile experience of moving in an empty afterlife.)   The persistently
melodramatic quality of the language heightens the sense of
nonexistence at the center of Thekla's consciousness, until
her actual suicide becomes merely the final step in the continuing reduction.   A touch peculiarly characteristic of the
Novelle is the doctor's discovery in his papers, months
later, of a scrap bearing the words, "If I die, it is for
you."   The only residue of Thekla's literally and metaphori-
cally disintegrated existence is this not very authentic sentence.

The movement of Neumeyer's *Novelle* is entirely in the
opposite direction.   When two American students set off into
the Oregon hinterland in search of some Basque shepherds,
they come upon a genuine Greek temple in the middle of the
wilderness, apparently built by a group of Alexander's

officers who had briefly colonized this edge of the New World
after sailing from India.   This is an obvious wish-dream of
the exiled European; the reader is as dumbfounded as the
two students by the naive audacity of the conception.   But
gravely the implications are explored: this living synthesis
of nature and art calls into question all intervening history
and will have a transforming effect on the present when the
world hears of it.   Or will it?   Can its perfection be anything but reduced, made relative, lost?   The students con-
verse with the Basque shepherd who uses the temple as a
good place for his sheep and the simplicity of his phrase,
"a valley of good proportions," makes them decide to leave
it untouched.   It will live in the modern consciousness as
long as they are alive to bear its secret.   Suddenly, at the
story's end, the focus switches: what we have been reading
was told to the narrator in 1918 at a World War I campfire;
it is now 1938.   (Exile writers, most notably Broch of
course, constantly explore the enigmatic symmetries of time.)
The suddenness with which these frames are imposed may
seem clumsy until one reflects that it merely echoes the suddenness of the temple's appearance.   As Frey probes the
contours of monotony and anonymity, Neumeyer delineates the
sudden eruptions of the inexplicable into reality and out of
it again: the exile knows both extremes.   The last sentence
of the *Novelle*, about the faded photograph of what looks
like a Greek temple that the narrator is holding, dissolves
the story's pagan clarity into an enigma: "On the back, in
his large imperious script were the words 'Laurel Valley'
and I can see through the letters as through an open door."
That words come to resemble doors that do not admit or open
only into mirages and dreams is a vivid expression of the
exiled consciousness.
     The sheer availability of literary combinations and
traditions was one of the burdens of freedom in exile.   The
need to choose was ever present: Oskar Jellinek wrote *Novellen* throughout his career, yet in his last one, "Der Freigesprochene," about a barely articulate miner and his community, the reader hears overtones from almost every realm of
the *Novelle* tradition.   The official "choice" Jellinek has
made is the hysterical-naturalistic modality of Büchner's
Woyzeck and Hauptmann's Thiel; but the romantic-mystical
emblem of the mine is also echoed in a simple phrase such
as "the depths he had come to love" (p. 307).   Literature of
the past has become enmeshed in the very texture of the
miner's world and Jellinek's task is to maintain the authenticity of his choices while simultaneously depicting the disintegration of his own synthesis: only thus can both the "real"
and the symbolic quality of the miner's fate be sustained.
That a decisive element of self-conscious intellectuality was
involved was clear to Jellinek, who wrote in 1928, in words
that must have later been vividly underlined by the impover-
ishment and discontinuity of exile: "Today's generation,
skeptical, struggling, seeking, yearns for ideas and concepts
instead of form and vision.   This generation is not opposed
to having ideas made visible, but finds only the idea itself

of any consequence. Moreover, a certain general ability of verbal expression has become commonplace, so that writers, as it were, are talking to audiences of writers, while the idiom of the past echoes across millennia into this modern world like an archetypal religious hymn."[13] In exile, art itself is perpetually in danger of becoming an "idea," and none more so than the *Novelle*, with its traditional expectations of striking subjects, surprising twists of plot, concrete symbols, and the like. Jellinek has countered this danger by writing an analytic *Novelle* (he thought of himself as basically a dramatist), with all the key events in the past. Matthias Benda has murdered his wife's lover after finding them in flagrante delicto, has pleaded insanity and been acquitted; however, although he has no aspirations beyond reintegration into the community (and the community is wholly in favor), his conscience will not let him rest. His world is out of joint, and step by step Benda focuses on different sources of his malaise: he should never have taken a man's life; he should have killed his wife, not her lover; toward the end he finds out that his best friend had already been her lover. Finally he calculates that his own son may well be the progeny of his best friend instead of himself, and this realization leads at last to his own violent death. All this takes place against the twin backgrounds of the mining routine (including a climactic disaster in which Benda, acting instinctively, saves his best friend) and Benda's anxious pursuit of others' opinion of him, for example that of the jurors who voted to convict. Clearly this man is incapable of absorbing the complexities into which he is plunged, and Jellinek shows us, with a minimum of melodrama, the inexorable growth of the web of past events around Benda and the progressive extinction of a mind without internal resources. Especially novellistic is the thematicizing of time; as the natural cycle points ironically toward spring and renewal, Benda performs the last of many mathematical calculations concerning his past--the date of the union between his wife and his best friend plus nine months. The subtle incompatibility of human and natural time conditions the work's rhythm, its conciliatory lulls, its convulsive lurches forward into self-annihilation.

To summarize the formal problem by means of a topos already mentioned in connection with "Laurel Valley": a repressed character in *Die Schuldlosen*, Hildegard, is perpetually wandering about outside the door of the lodger's room, whereas Josepha, heroine of "Deutsche Novelle," is to be found in bed most of the time, waiting for the tempter to come through her door. The short story gathers the details of experience while summoning all its energies to pass through the door into life itself; the *Novelle* probes the logic of its enclosed space with the compelling awareness that what is outside the door is poised to crush its logic into meaninglessness. In both cases the sensation of the door's existence, the enigmatic opening into wholeness or the void, is what locks the self-limiting shape of short fiction into the concreteness of the exile experience. The claustrophobia of the hotel room and the vastness of the American continent both fuel the same vision of an uprooted human being in a continuum of infinite meanings, of literary traditions and historical processes, all of them suggestive, none of them binding. To this existence on a perpetual threshold, the precision without preconditions inherent in short fiction offered some relief, some hope of validity.

Notes

[1] Adolf von Grolman, "Die strenge Novellenform und die Problematik ihrer Zertrümmerung," in *Novelle*, ed. Josef Kunz, Wege der Forschung, 55 (Darmstadt: Wissenschaftliche Buchgesellschaft, 1968), p. 165. All English translations, except for that of Broch's *Die Schuldlosen*, are by me.

[2] Theodore Ziolkowski, "Form als Protest: Das Sonett in der Literatur des Exils und der Inneren Emigration," in *Exil und innere Emigration: Third Wisconsin Workshop*, ed. Reinhold Grimm and Jost Hermand, Wissenschaftliche Paperbacks, Literaturwissenschaft, 17 (Frankfurt/M: Athenäum, 1971), p. 165.

[3] Three of the canonical *Novellen* in Benno von Wiese's survey were not called such by their progenitors. Brentano's "Geschichte vom braven Kasperl und dem schönen Annerl," Chamisso's "Peter Schlemihls wundersame Geschichte" and Hofmannsthal's "Reitergeschichte" are all *Geschichten* ["stories"]. The point is made by Joachim Müller, "Novelle und Erzählung," in *Novelle*, p. 468.

[4] Werner Vordtriede, "Vorläufige Gedanken zu einer Typologie der Exilliteratur," *Akzente*, 15, No. 6 (Dec. 1968), 574.

[5] Fritz Lockemann, "Die Bedeutung des Rahmens in der deutschen Novellendichtung," in *Novelle*, p. 338.

[6] Vordtriede, "Vorläufige Gedanken," p. 558.

[7] All bibliographical information concerning the texts under discussion is given in the checklist following the Notes. The word "Seelenbräu" is a pun on "Seelenbräutigam."

[8] Müller, "Novelle und Erzählung," pp. 472–73.

[9] Wolfgang Düsing sees the fact that the hero is "not so much a self-sufficient individual as representative of an epoch shattered by crises" as an integrative element in Broch's quest for a new genre. "Der Novellenroman," in *Jahrbuch der deutschen Schillergesellschaft*, 20 (1976), 542.

[10] Lutz Mackensen, "Die Novelle," in *Novelle*, p. 400.

[11] Jost Hermand, "Schreiben in der Fremde," in *Exil und innere Emigration*, p. 27.

[12] This *Novelle* was awarded first prize by the exile journal *Die Sammlung* in a competition for *Novellen* in September 1934. The citation reads: "This story was unanimously awarded the first prize in *Die Sammlung*'s competition. The judges were Heinrich Mann, Bruno Frank, and the editorial staff of the magazine." No criteria are given for the award and the fact that the second prize was given to

Gustav Regler's "Der Tod in der Michaelskirche," discussed above, suggests that no great significance should be read into it. The competition was not the only one, however; in 1943 the New York weekly, *Der Aufbau*, had a "Competition for the Best German Novelle" written in exile; the winner was one Josef Brügel. Clearly the *Novelle* as a form was of conscious importance to the exile writers.

13Oskar Jellinek, "An den Dichter kommender Zeiten" ["To the Poet of Future Times"], in Jellinek, *Gedichte und kleine Erzählungen*, ed. Richard Thieberger (Vienna: Paul Zsolnay, 1952), pp. 341-42.

A Checklist of Short Fiction

A checklist of short fiction considered in the course of the article follows. For reasons of space, a few of the texts could not be discussed.

Anders, Günther.   "Der Hungermarsch." *Die Sammlung*, 2, No. 6 (Feb. 1935), 294-314.

Broch, Hermann. *Die Schuldlosen*. Zurich: Rhein-Verlag, 1950.   English version: *The Guiltless*, trans. Ralph Manheim. Boston: Little, Brown, 1974.

Claudius, Eduard. "Das Opfer," in *Salz der Erde*. Halle: Mitteldeutscher Verlag, 1969.

Feuchtwanger, Lion. "Die Lügentante" and "Venedig (Texas)," in *Odysseus und die Schweine und zwölf andere Erzählungen*. Berlin: Aufbau-Verlag, 1950.

Frank, Leonhard. *Deutsche Novelle*.   Munich: Nymphenburger Verlagshandlung, 1954.

Frey, A. M.   "Ein Mädchen mordet." *Die Sammlung*, Nos. 1 and 2 (Sept., Oct. 1934), 16-29, 87-100.

Goetz, Curt. *Tatjana: Eine Legende*. Hamburg: Rowohlt, 1949.

Jellinek, Oskar. "Der Freigesprochene," in *Gesammelte Novellen*.   Ed. Franz Karl Ginzkey.   Vienna: Paul Zsolnay, 1950.

Lackner, Stephan. *Das Lied des Pechvogels*. Constance: Südverlag, 1950.

Mann, Klaus. *Vergittertes Fenster: Novelle um den Tod des Königs Ludwig II. von Bayern*.   Frankfurt/M: S. Fischer, 1960.

Mann, Thomas. "Das Gesetz," in *Die Erzählungen*. Frankfurt/M: S. Fischer, 1966.

Neumeyer, Alfred.   "Laurel Valley" and "Im Namen der Vernunft," in *Treue und andere Novellen*. Heidelberg: Schneider, 1948.

Oberländer, Friedrich.   "Menschensohn und Wechslerssohn," *Die Sammlung*, 2, No. 8 (April 1935), 403-16.

Polgar, Alfred.   "Veilchen," in *Standpunkte*.   Hamburg: Rowohlt, 1953.

Regler, Gustav. "Der Tod in der Michaelskirche." *Die Sammlung*, 2, No. 3 (Nov. 1934), 124-43.

Sochaczewer, Hans. "Die Botschaft der Ermüdeten." *Die
    Sammlung*, 2, No. 4 (Dec. 1934), 182–200.
Speyer, Wilhelm. *Señorita Maria Teresa: Eine spanisch –
    kalifornische Erzählung*. Zurich: Werner Classen, 1951.
Urzidil, Johannes. *Der Trauermantel: Eine Erzählung aus
    Stifters Jugend*. New York: Friedrich Krause, 1945.
Walter, Fritz. "Gold und Schwarz." *Die Sammlung*, 2, No. 5
    (Jan. 1935), 241–51.
Weigel, Hans. *Das himmlische Leben: Novella quasi una
    fantasia*. Vienna: Alfred Ibach, 1946.
Werfel, Franz. "Par l'amour," "Weissenstein, der Weltver-
    besserer," and "Die wahre Geschichte vom wiederher-
    gestellten Kreuz," in *Erzählungen aus zwei Welten, III*.
    Ed. Adolf Klarmann. Frankfurt/M: S. Fischer, 1954.
Wolf, Friedrich. *Lucie und der Angler von Paris: Novel-
    len*. Berlin: Aufbau-Verlag, 1946.
Zuckmayer, Carl. "Der Seelenbräu," in *Die Erzählungen*.
    Frankfurt/M: S. Fischer, 1952.
Zweig, Stefan. "Schachnovelle," in *Stefan Zweig: Eine Aus-
    lese*. Ed. J. Hellmut Freund. Vienna: Carl Ueberreuter,
    1968. English version: "The Royal Game," trans. B. W.
    Huebsch, in *The Royal Game*. New York: Viking, 1944.

German Drama in Exile: A Survey

Ernst Schürer

The recent scholarly interest in German exile literature
has focused not so much on the literature itself as on the
reasons for the forced emigration, the difficulties and hardships faced by exiled writers abroad, the working conditions,
and the official and popular attitude toward the exiles in
the different host countries. Only a few literary genres,
such as the novel and the sonnet, have come under closer
scrutiny, whereas scant attention has been paid to the drama.
During the 1969 Stockholm Symposium on "German Literature
by Exiles from the Third Reich," Helmut Müssener underlined
the importance and the problems of basic research and asked
for a booklist according to genres:

> It would indicate which genres were preferred; it would
> induce those concerned with literary criticism to ask
> the question: Why does the list look like this? Did
> authors write fewer plays because there were no stages
> that could produce them? Did they write lyrical poetry
> because this literary form is best suited for the expres-
> sion of personal feelings? Did one write novels because
> one was unemployed and had time to waste?[1]

Different literary forms of expression were indeed differently affected by the conditions of exile. Exiled writers were
hard pressed, because they had to find publishers for their
works and try to reach German audiences, or else have their
books translated. Most easily translated were historical and
other novels, as well as autobiographical and personal
accounts of persecution and Nazi terror. Such books appealed
also to the natives of the exiles' host countries, and with
these, famous novelists such as Lion Feuchtwanger, Thomas
Mann, Emil Ludwig, Franz Werfel, and Erich Maria Remarque
were able to further their renown and make a living in the
English-speaking world. For lyrical poetry no such market
existed: it is difficult to sell even under normal conditions,
and few publishers in exile were willing and irresponsible
enough to risk publishing poems for a very limited audience.
Nevertheless, lyrical poetry flourished, as it seems many

48

writers used this form to express their homesickness and their experiences in exile even though hardly a chance existed for publication. But the difficulties of these writers paled in comparison with those of the dramatists, whom F. C. Weiskopf has justly called the "problem children of the literary emigration."[2] Even if a playwright was able to have his work published--and plays were printed by publishing houses like Querido and exile journals like *Das Wort*--he also needed a stage for their performance. Until 1938 he could still turn to some theaters in Austria, Switzerland, and parts of Czechoslovakia, although the Nazis through their embassies and representatives exerted strong pressure on the theaters and governments in these countries to exclude the works of emigrants and accept only noncontroversial plays. Often they were successful, but after the occupation of Austria and Czechoslovakia, Switzerland alone remained as a haven, with the Zurich Schauspielhaus as the most famous of theaters that still accepted and performed the works of exiled playwrights.[3] In countries where German was not the native language, the dramatist encountered added difficulties, because the German theatrical tradition was alien to a public accustomed to its own theatrical traditions and stage conventions and not willing to accept unfamiliar aesthetic and formal ideas; people were also not inclined to listen to political topics that did not concern them. Moreover, these countries did not, as a rule, have subsidized or repertory theaters, and the commercial ones were more than reluctant to launch a production that would spell financial disaster if it failed. Because most German dramatists were not known internationally, they had to be introduced to audiences and their plays had to be made palatable; therefore we find many adaptations.[4] But very few were successful or yielded any royalties to their authors. This situation has been pointed out by literary critics and dramatists alike. Matthias Wegner states: "The literary genres--lyrical poetry, the novel, drama--were after all not preferred in the same proportions as in 'normal times.' The drama could hardly develop in exile, because German-speaking theaters that made performances possible were lacking. . . . The portrayal of life in exile remained a prerogative of lyric poetry and especially of the novel."[5] Robert E. Cazden describes the plight of the dramatist in exile in the United States in even stronger terms: "In contrast to the novelist, the émigré dramatist found almost no market for his wares whether written in German or English. The German drama had always been neglected on the New York stage and lack of opportunity for performance naturally precluded much chance of publication."[6] These statements by critics are corroborated by the complaints of the dramatists themselves. Bertolt Brecht remarked repeatedly that he needed a theater to observe the actual staging of his plays, because only then could he observe his theories in action and correct his mistakes: "It is impossible to complete a play without having a stage. The proof of the pudding . . . Only the stage decides about possible variants. Since *Johanna* [*Saint Joan of the Stockyards*] everything I have written has not been tested, except *Die Mutter* [*The Mother*] and *Rundköpfe* [*The Round-heads and the Peakheads*]."[7]   To Walter Benjamin he explained: "They not only have taken away my house, my fish-pond and my car, they also have robbed me of my stage and my audience. From my point of view I cannot admit that Shakespeare was basically a greater writer. Because he also could not have written for the stockroom."[8] "Plays remain unpublished in our drawers. Novels find an audience,"[9] Kaiser confided to his friend Julius Marx in 1941. A litany of similar statements by exiled dramatists could easily be compiled. It must be added that few articles on the drama by critics or playwrights appeared in journals published in exile, and in articles on exile literature in general dramatists and their plays were not mentioned at all or only in passing.

It is amazing that in spite of all these difficulties, a large number of plays were written and even performed.[10] In the Academy of Arts in East Berlin an Archive for German Theater and Film in Exile has been established, where the works of the exiles and materials about their productions are collected. During the Second International Symposium on German Exile after 1933, Curt Trepte presented a paper based on materials in the archive. Considering the fact that very little has been said about the drama, it comes as a surprise to read that no fewer than 420 dramatists lived in exile in forty-one countries. According to the information of the archives, they wrote 724 plays, 108 radio plays, and 398 film scripts.[11] Although few of these plays were ever performed, their existence alone proves that most playwrights did not despair but hoped for the day when they again would have access to the German theater.

It is rather ironic that exiled dramatists were confronted by the greatest personal challenge of all exiled writers and were experiencing the greatest financial difficulties, because in Germany in general they had been better known and were more successful economically than most novelists and poets. However, their fame also placed them in greater danger. To explain this phenomenon, a few words about the German theater before and during the Weimar Republic are in order. Since before the turn of the century, Berlin with its many stages had been not only the capital of Germany, but even more so that of the theatrical world. During the twenties it was the mecca to which all aspiring playwrights traveled hoping for a breakthrough, and even the critics came there from all over Germany to see what was new and avant-garde. Outside Berlin there were theaters in all larger cities and even in many smaller towns, financially subsidized and supported by the communities. If an author was successful in Berlin, his play would usually be taken over by the theaters in Weimar, Dresden, Leipzig, Munich, and other cities, and the financial rewards of a resounding success like Brecht's *Dreigroschenoper* [*Three Penny Opera*] were substantial. Besides Bertolt Brecht, other famous playwrights such as Ernst Toller, Georg Kaiser, Friedrich Wolf, Walter Hasenclever, and Carl Zuckmayer began their rise to fame in

Berlin. Most of these writers were committed liberal progres-
sives, socialists, and pacifists, and because of their ideological and political convictions declared opponents of nation-
alists and in particular of the National Socialists. There
were very few Communists or Nazis among the playwrights,
although both the political left and right considered the theater important in their struggle for power, a tool for dissemi-
nating their ideology and propaganda. When Hitler became
chancellor in 1933, most playwrights realized that they would
become favorite targets for the Nazis and that they were in
grave danger. Brecht, Toller, and Wolf were among the
first to flee. Their plays were banned on all German stages.
Others, such as Kaiser, stayed in Germany for a certain time,
but remained silent, whereas still others, such as Zuckmayer,
found a temporary refuge in Austria. The ruling Nazi party
now placed a total claim on art, viewing it as a means of
controlling and influencing the population, and German theaters were put under the supervision of the Minister of Public
Enlightenment and Propaganda, Joseph Goebbels, whereas
Hermann Göring, as prime minister of Prussia, controlled the
state theaters in Berlin. This control became law in May
1934 when the new law governing the theaters (*Reichsthea-
tergesetz*) was passed. A few dramatists, among them Arnolt
Bronnen and Hanns Johst, stayed in Germany and served the
cause of the Nazis. The party asked for political and historical plays characterized by national spirit, plays that
would extol the strength and heroism of the German soldier
while paying homage to the *Führer*. But in spite of such
hectic activity the Nazis did not create a new trend in the
theater; the production statistics of the German theaters
before and after 1933 prove that the successes of the Nazi
dramatists were minimal, and that classical and nonpolitical
plays were preferred.[12]
     The exiled dramatists at first fled into neighboring
countries that had stages where their plays could be performed; German was spoken in some of them and in others
there were German minorities. Following Hitler's triumph and
the occupation of Austria and Czechoslovakia, they were
forced to resume their wanderings. Brecht's flight in the
years 1933-41 from Czechoslovakia to Austria, Switzerland,
France, Denmark, Sweden, and Finland, and finally to California by way of Russia, with trips to Moscow, Paris, and
New York in between, graphically illustrates the hardships
most authors had to endure. It is indeed amazing that they
kept producing at all. However, under the pressures of this
life some lost courage and turned to other genres. Fritz von
Unruh had already left Germany for Italy in 1932; he at
first continued working on new plays, but then, convinced
that as a dramatist he would be condemned to silence, turned
to the novel. The same applies to Georg Kaiser, who from
1938 on began writing novels and lyric poetry. Ödön von
Horváth turned to the novel after 1936 to expose fascism, and
Franz Theodor Csokor wrote a novel about his experiences in
the German-Polish war of 1939. But these and the majority
of the dramatists also continued writing plays in the hope

that they would be performed at some time in the near or distant future. It is to these plays that we now turn our attention.

We must first address ourselves to the question whether exile drama can be considered a subgenre in the dramatic field or whether it should be considered simply as a special literary phenomenon. Can it be defined as a specific type of drama during a specific period of German literary and political history? When we speak of the drama of expressionism and the drama of the subsequent "new objectivity," we group together plays with more or less specific thematic and formal characteristics written during certain chronologically defined periods in modern history. However, when referring to the exile drama, we point, at least superficially, first of all to a fact extraneous to the drama itself, namely that it was written by a playwright living in exile. This certainly cannot be the determining criterion for defining exile drama, because the criteria for definition should be vested in the plays themselves. Not all plays written in exile can be defined as exile dramas, just as not all plays written even during the heyday of naturalism and expressionism can be classified as being naturalistic or expressionistic, because many authors continued to write neoclassical or romantic pieces. As far as length of time is concerned, the exile of most authors lasted as long, twelve to fifteen years, as the periods of *Sturm und Drang* ("storm and stress"), naturalism, expressionism, or new objectivity. There is, however, a basic difference: the previous literary periods had their origin and were caused by the opposition of writers to existing artistic, social, and political conditions and usually developed over a long period of time before culminating in a so-called literary movement. The thematic and especially the formal characteristics of the specific literature developed and matured slowly, especially in the case of the pioneers. Naturally there were also camp followers who then exploited the situation and imitated the prevailing literary canon. In the case of exile literature there was no such period of incubation, because exile was in most cases a condition imposed on writers suddenly and without warning by an outside political power. Most exiled writers were opposed to the prevailing social conditions and the reigning political philosophy and party and had often already expressed this opposition in their previous writings, but they were not rebelling against any prevailing literary trend or in the process of developing a new one. Or, if they had been members of the literary avant-garde and had been experimenting with modern forms, this had nothing to do with their exile. On the contrary, these authors were forced by the exigencies of exile and by political and economic considerations to turn away from experimentation, to reject modern forms and use traditional, usually realistic styles and structures to make their plays acceptable to as many stages as possible and their message understandable to the whole audience instead of just to a few insiders. Concerning his play *Die Rundköpfe und die Spitzköpfe* [*The Roundheads and the Peakheads*], Brecht

wrote to Karl Korsch in an ironic manner about some friends
who had advised him of the necessity of choosing either a
reactionary content or a reactionary form: "but both together
are too much of a good thing."13 Playwrights also had to
take into account that their plays usually had to be performed by small companies and would be produced on small
budgets and in small theaters, not on the large stages of
Berlin. They no longer had at their disposal a complicated
technical apparatus such as Piscator had used in his productions, nor could they operate on big budgets. This often
meant a return to the traditional form of the well-made play,
the revue, or even the sketch.

Since the exile dramatists held different philosophical,
political, and social views, preferred certain topics, proclaimed different literary ideals, and had different talents,
the over 700 plays written by them differ vastly in style and
structure. Nevertheless, we find a common characteristic in
the majority of them, namely a return to realistic and naturalistic forms. This holds true especially for the works written during the first years of exile. Authors like Walter Hasenclever and Friedrich Wolf had already joined this trend
toward a new objectivity and a new realism, as the literary
period during the twenties was called, before the beginning
of their exile, and their writing in exile is stylistically
only a continuation of their earlier production, whereas other
writers like Brecht and Kaiser reverted to these forms for
practical purposes. Plays of this type could be more easily
translated, and they were also more acceptable to audiences
in foreign countries, for instance here in the United States,
where plays of this type still dominated the stages. This
does not mean, however, that writers did not continue to
experiment. Especially during the war, without any hopes of
having their plays performed, but already thinking of a
return to Germany, they again occupied themselves with aesthetic and formal problems. Brecht again comes to mind: in
the first years of exile he was quite willing to make concessions as far as style and structure were concerned in
order to have his plays performed, but later he wrote his
theoretical treatise, the *Kleines Organon für das Theater*
[*Short Organon for the Theater*] and his best plays, among
them *Mutter Courage* [*Mother Courage and Her Children*],
Leben des Galilei [*Galileo*], and *Der gute Mensch von
Sezuan* [*The Good Woman of Sezuan*]. While working on the
last play, Brecht remarked: "I can develop the epic techniques and finally get back to a high standard. For your
drawer you don't need to make concessions."14 Brecht continued work that he had begun long before 1933, although
the question might be asked whether he would have written
these plays if it had not been for the leisure the conditions
of exile forced upon him. He would much rather have worked
as a director and popularizer, as he did after his return to
Germany. But are these plays, even though written in exile,
truly representative of exile drama? They are listed everywhere as examples of Brecht's new epic theater--as contrasted to the old dramatic theater that he rejected--and the

fact that they were written in exile is usually not even mentioned.

     This leads to the conclusion that structurally and sty-
listically drama in exile cannot be looked upon as a separate
unit in the development of German literature since 1890, because it tends to be realistic and is patterned after the
drama of naturalism and the documentary play (*Zeitstück*)
of the twenties. But drama in exile is in a more literal and
true sense documentary theater (*Zeittheater*), a drama mainly
determined by its topics.   In his "Preliminary Thoughts Concerning a Typology of Literature in Exile," Werner Vordtriede
states that the "exiled poets themselves are the first exile
typologists."[15] It is not form, he thinks, but the authenticity
of the content, a predilection for specific topics, and a specific vocabulary that define literature in exile.

     In his article on the methodology of German antifascist
drama,[16] Bernhard Reich hardly discusses the formal methods
of the playwrights; instead he brings examples of the three
main topics discussed in the plays--race, class, and the
struggle against the Nazis inside Germany--and explains how
the authors deal with these topics. The plays listed according
to these categories are indeed important documents of exile
drama; they have in common their political motivation.   This
political nature of the drama is the single most important
characteristic of exile drama. In exile even the apolitical
writer had to become political, because it was for political
reasons that he had been forced to leave his country.   The
political motive might exist only in the minds of his enemies,
as for them the racial issue was also political, but this
forced the victim of this policy to reflect upon it. An author
like Georg Kaiser considered pacifism a purely humanitarian
topic, but for the Nazis it was eminently political and reason
enough to persecute the author of such plays and prohibit
his works.   Indeed, there existed a "Zwang zur Politik," a
"coercion to politics," as Thomas Mann called it.   Walter
Benjamin, himself in exile, expressed the political nature of
drama in exile in his discussion of Brecht's *Furcht und
Elend des dritten Reiches* [*The Private Life of the Master
Race*]: "The theater of emigration can only make a political
drama its concern. Most of the plays that ten or fifteen
years ago brought together a political audience in Germany
have been overtaken by events. The theater of emigration
must begin all over again; not only its stage, but also its
drama has to be rebuilt."[17] Benjamin is referring to the
plays of the expressionists and to the documentary plays of
Weisenborn, Bruckner, Lampel, and Wolf that attacked the
ills of the Weimar Republic but ignored the danger of fascism. That Benjamin now considers the fight against Hitler
and the analysis of fascism as the foremost task of the drama
is obvious. But in his essay on German exile literature since
1933, subtitled "A Dialogue between Politics and Art,"[18]
Alfred Döblin stresses the fact that the playwrights, although
united through their experiences as emigrants and their fight
against a common enemy, are not to become advocates of a
specific political party or program but rather committed

writers, in whose works the social and political side of human life is always taken into account. The playwrights are not encouraged to write tendentious dramas (*Tendenzdramen*), although there are enough of them, but rather plays that will raise the level of political consciousness of the audience, that is, political drama in the best sense of the word.

Eschewing formal innovations and experiments, dramatists turned their attention to the call of the day. Their plays can be divided into three broad categories according to topic: by far the largest and most diverse category is that of the antifascist plays; it dominates the field to such an extent that it is generally regarded as exile drama par excellence. The second group consists of plays about life in exile and the problems and troubles that beset the emigrant; in a certain sense this kind of play deserves the name of exile drama more than the first one. The third group—and there exists some doubt whether plays in this group should be counted as exile drama—comprises all plays that do not belong to the above outlined two categories; these plays were written for entertainment, for production on exile stages to keep the German theater alive and attract audiences who were not interested in antifascist or problem dramas. Although the plays are thematically not directly concerned with exile, personal references and "hidden themes"[19] relate them to the drama in exile. The traces of the psychological impact of the exile experience in the works make them interesting and revealing in a comparison with the literature produced within the borders of the Third Reich.[20] In general, it can be said that the playwright came closest to fulfilling in his works the mission of the German writer in exile as outlined by Klaus Mann:

> On the one hand he had to warn the world of the Third Reich and enlighten it about the character of the regime, while at the same time keeping in contact with the "other, better Germany," the illegal, secretly resisting one, and supplying the resistance movement at home with literary materials; on the other hand he had to keep alive abroad and continue to develop through his own creative contribution the great tradition of the German spirit and the German language, a tradition now without a home in the land of its origin.[21]

The antifascist plays are protest dramas (*Kampfdramen*). Their basic aim is to inform the world about the political program of the fascists and the realities of Nazi rule in Germany. They call for resistance against the tactics used by the new rulers to suppress personal and political liberties and urge the audience to join the fight for freedom of thought and individual human rights against mass hysteria and chauvinistic nationalism. They were also a valiant attempt to counter the pernicious and blatant propaganda of the Nazis. Jewish playwrights hoped that the excesses caused by the fascist racial ideology and the fate of the Jewish people in Germany would open the eyes of the people who looked upon Hitler as a bulwark against communism. To the

Western democracies it had to be made clear that just as Hitler did not adhere to democratic rules in national politics, he would use every available method to gain his international goals; the aggressive tendencies that the Nazis had displayed in crushing political opposition at home would be applied more ruthlessly in international affairs in spite of Hitler's constant protestations of peace--his lust for power and gains would only be increased by the vacillating and conciliatory stance of the countries he was dealing with.

For the socialist writers, the fight against Hitler was furthermore a fight for a better world order against the evils of capitalism, and Communist dramatists were very much interested in establishing a united popular front against the fascists. Liberal writers wanted to examine in such plays as Hermann Broch's *Die Entsühnung*, 1934 [*The Atonement*], the economic, social, and political reasons for the fall of the progressive and democratic Weimar Republic and for the rapid acceptance of totalitarian ideologies by large parts of the population. Since the beginning of World War I, history had moved at such a fast pace that the contours of historical events and decisions had become blurred. It seemed necessary to analyze these events in detail, point out past mistakes, and try to arrive at conclusions and results for use in future political situations.

The preferred types among the antifascist plays were *Zeitstücke* (literally, "plays about the times"), parable plays, revues, and one-act plays or short sketches. The choice of a specific type of play was usually dictated by the personal preferences and the artistic and political objectives of a playwright, often already displayed in his earlier production; his choice had structural and stylistic consequences. The *Zeitstück* is a type of documentary play that had become popular in the twenties; it serves to examine contemporary social and political problems such as drug addiction, divorce, capital punishment, abuses in youth homes and schools, secret armaments, and conditions in the military by selecting a specific, individual case and presenting it in such a way as to throw the problem under examination into sharp focus. Very often the plot was based on an actual occurrence, a well-known crime or a trial, that had made headlines in the newspapers. Court procedures and debates are favorite devices of the documentary play, with the accused--whose crimes have been caused by social circumstances--arraigned against the bureaucracy and class justice of the state. The interrelationship between his private life and the political happenings are emphasized and therefore recognized by the audience: the fate of an individual attains universal significance.

Some of the most famous authors of documentary plays were active in exile; they included Friedrich Wolf, Ferdinand Bruckner, Ernst Toller, and Peter Martin Lampel, although not all continued cultivating the genre. Wolf, a medical doctor and since 1928 member of the German Communist party and of the Union of German Proletarian and Revolutionary Writers, had been successful with *Cyankali*, 1928 (a play that dealt with the question of unwanted pregnancy, abortion, and the infamous paragraph 218 of the Civil Code, which defines and sets the punishment for abortion. In his next play, *Die Matrosen von Cattaro*, 1930 [*The Sailors of Cattaro*], Wolf depicted the unsuccessful revolt in the Austrian navy in 1918, whereas his antifascist comedy *Die Jungen von Mons*, 1932 [*The Fellows of Mons*] was based on documentary materials from England. His play about the Chinese revolution, *Tai Yang erwacht*, 1931 [*Tai Yang Awakens*], was produced by Erwin Piscator, who envisioned it as an epic and didactic demonstration; however, his attempt met with little success. When in the year before the Nazi takeover the regular theaters refused to accept Wolf's plays because of the political and financial risks involved, they were performed by so-called actors' collectives that were politically oriented.

In 1933 Wolf had to flee to Paris, where in the same year he published *Professor Mamlock*, the first, most effective, and most often produced play directed against the racial theories of the Nazis. Like other documentary plays, it is based on an actual event: in Mannheim a Jewish doctor had committed suicide after having been evicted from his hospital. The authenticity of the play is further strengthened by the fact that Wolf named Mamlock's antagonist Dr. Hellpach--Wilhelm Hellpach was a noted scientist and professor who had become an apologist for the racial theories of the Nazis. In the play these theories are shown to be scientifically untenable as well as barbarous in their application. The phrases of the Nazi commissar are contradicted by his own behavior. Mamlock is a liberal democrat with strong moral and ethical convictions who believes in the law and tries to keep profession and politics separate.[22] He is opposed to the leftist parties and vainly protests against the lawless actions of the Nazis. Except for a few young Communists--always the heroes in Wolf's plays--all colleagues and friends of Mamlock abjectly bow to and acquiesce in the wishes of the commissar in the hope that they will be able to keep their jobs and coexist with the Nazis.

In his play, Wolf tries to explain how the Nazis were successful in consolidating their power by the use of terror and intimidation; the opposition parties--except for the Communists--refused to fight, trusting the laws of the Weimar Republic without realizing that these could no longer protect them. Before his suicide, Mamlock recognizes his mistake and tells his friends: "Your cowardice will supply the enemy with new weapons. *There is no greater crime than not wanting to fight where one has to take a stand!*"[23] This is the message of a play that was successful because it did not merely paint in black and white, but presented differentiated characters on both sides in a convincing plot. The characters--from the young idealistic Nazi, taken in by the rhetorics of heroism, truth, comradeship, and loyalty, to the nationalistic Jew--are a representative spectrum of German society in 1933. The audience could also easily identify and sympathize with Mamlock, much more so than with the central character in Ferdinand Bruckner's *Die Rassen*, 1933 [*The Races*].

The hero of this play is Karlanner, an aimless and searching student at a German university. In spite of initial resistance he is duped into becoming a member of the new community proclaimed by the Nazis. But the brutal behavior and the crimes of his comrades finally open his eyes; he warns his friend, allowing her to escape abroad, while he stays behind after killing the Nazi leader. Bruckner had already explored the psychological condition of young people in *Krankheit der Jugend*, 1926 [*The Malady of Youth*], and he continues this task in *Die Rassen*: the audience learns much about Karlanner's private problems, but little about the political situation. Bruckner decries the fact that German youth failed in the task of making democracy strong, but his play does not possess the same persuasive force as Wolf's *Professor Mamlock*. Nor does Bruckner finish his drama with the optimistic ending so typical of the plays of Wolf and other progressive antifascist writers. Bernhard Reich countered criticism against these positive conclusions so contrary to the realities of the political situation in Germany after 1933 by denying that they are schematic: they are rather prophetic and impart to the audience the necessary confidence for the struggle toward a better future. "The revolutionary artist cannot leave the world of his play without giving a most sincere testimony to the invincibility of the forces of revolution. Every painting of his age he wants to sign with this truth. That is his good right," Reich asserted.[24]

The racial question was also treated by Paul Zech in *Nur ein Judenweib*, 1935 [*Only a Jewess*], and Stephan Lackner in *Der Mensch ist kein Haustier*, 1937 [*A Human Being Is Not a Pet*]. At that time even comedies were written about it, *Rassokraten*, 1934 [*Raceocrats*], by Peter Kast, and *Gandha*, 1945, by Fritz von Unruh.[25] Bertolt Brecht based his satirical parable *Die Rundköpfe und die Spitzköpfe*, 1934 [*The Roundheads and the Peakheads*] on Shakespeare's *Measure for Measure* and Heinrich Kleist's story *Michael Kohlhaas*. In the land of Jahoo the workers learn to their dismay that the regent and the wealthy landowners are using the racial theories of the demagogic Iberin only for their political ends; in the final analysis, a capitalistic peakhead is still better than a proletarian roundhead. Brecht underestimated the fanaticism of the fascist leaders and their followers when he thought that Hitler was merely a puppet in the hands of the German industrialists and that his racial theories were only a ploy to win the workers over to his side. He was able, however, to portray certain facets of the Nazi movement such as Hitler's skillful use of rhetoric, his appeal to the petty bourgeoisie and to the farmers, and the terror of Hitler's SA and SS troops.

The consolidation of Nazi rule in Germany and the international recognition accorded to Hitler, fascist intervention in Spain, and the growing military strength and aggressiveness of the fascist states led to a shift in topics away from the racial problem to the dramatic presentation of conditions in Germany and the struggle of the resistance movement in the homeland and in occupied countries after the beginning of the war. These plays were in many cases the result of wishful thinking, a desperate attempt to counteract the triumphs of fascism. The passive resistance advocated in the early plays now gives way to a summons to armed opposition against this threat to the whole human race. However, some plays are based on known cases of opposition. Ernst Toller, an often disappointed pacifist and untiring fighter against fascism, modeled his *Pastor Hall* (1939) on the case of Pastor Niemöller; an active opponent of the Nazis, he preached against the evils of the regime in his church in Dahlem and was thereupon imprisoned in a concentration camp until the end of the war. Carl Zuckmayer's *Des Teufels General*, 1946 [*The Devil's General*] is partially based on the life and death of Ernst Udet. These and other plays, among them Theodor Fanta's *Die Kinder des unbekannten Soldaten*, 1935 [*The Children of the Unknown Soldier*], Johannes Wüsten's *Bessie Bosch*, 1936, Gustav Wangenheim's *Margarethe Biswanger*, 1938, Ferdinand Bruckner's *Denn seine Zeit ist kurz*, 1943 [*For His Time Is Short*], Friedrich Wolf's *Patrioten*, 1943 [*Patriots*], Rudolf Leonhard's *Geiseln*, 1945 [*Hostages*], and Günter Weisenborn's *Die Illegalen*, 1945 [*The Illegal Ones*] were attempts to picture on the one hand the political oppression, on the other hand the lonely but determined struggle of the resistance fighters against moral scruples, opportunists, and collaborators and against a watchful and dangerous enemy who employed every means to crush all opposition. Johannes R. Becher's *Winterschlacht*, 1942 [*Winter Battle*], Hermann Greid's *Die andere Seite*, 1944 [*The Other Side*], Wolf's *Dr. Lilli Wanner*, 1944, and Zuckmayer's *Des Teufels General*, 1946, show the growing disillusionment among the German soldiers and officers, their gradual recognition of the criminal nature of the war they are fighting, and the resulting change in their attitudes and actions.

The historical development of fascism in Austria and Spain also provided playwrights with materials. Wolf used the bloody suppression of the Viennese socialist workers by Dollfuss in February 1934 as the topic for his drama *Floridsdorf* (1935); he places the blame for the failure of the revolt on the vacillating and inactive Social Democrats. Bertolt Brecht's *Die Gewehre der Frau Carrar*, 1937 [*Señora Carrar's Rifles*] bears the message that at times it is necessary to fight--and in 1937 that meant at the side of the Republican forces in Spain. Señora Carrar is a pacifist who forbids her sons to march to the aid of the Republic until the oldest is killed by fascists. Then she awakens to the challenge and recognizes that to preserve freedom one must be willing to pay a price, even if it is the supreme one. Because of its actuality, this play was performed repeatedly; it was also well suited for performances on small stages. Georg Kaiser's *Der Soldat Tanaka* [*Private Tanaka*], produced in 1940 by the Zurich Schauspielhaus, is an attack on militarism in general, although the play is set in Japan. In another of his works, *Die Spieldose*, 1942 [*The Music box*], the happiness of a peasant family in Brittany is destroyed by the war. Kaiser was very much aware of the militarism of the Nazis; he realized that it was systematically fostered under the dictatorship, and he therefore wanted to warn the world.[26]

Although the plays mentioned focus on similar topics, structurally and stylistically they are very different. Brecht readily admitted that he had used what he considered an anachronistic naturalistic style to heighten the popular appeal of his play; Wolf's dramas combine a tight structure with a realistic dialogue, whereas Becher's drama is diffuse with unconvincing, long lyrical monologues in blank verse that betray the author's expressionistic heritage and the influence of Shakespeare's drama. His figures are also shallow and unconvincing types. Bruckner's psychoanalytical approach leaves its traces in the style of his plays, whereas Zuckmayer's drama shows a combination of naturalistic, expressionistic, lyrical, and Schillerian elements. Weisenborn employs modern epic elements to keep the audience detached and allow it to judge for itself, but he defeats his own purpose by inserting sentimental love scenes. The plays of Communist writers are usually ideologically oriented, with set types instead of individual characters and the inevitable optimistic ending dictated by socialist realism. On the other hand, many of these plays are tightly constructed and well suited for the émigré stage.

Several dramatists chose the parable play to present a more objective view of the reasons for the rise of fascism, to make this background more comprehensible to audiences abroad, and to use satire to its fullest extent. Brecht's *Die Rundköpfe und die Spitzköpfe* (1934) has been mentioned already; in *Der aufhaltsame Aufstieg des Arturo Ui*, 1941 [*The Resistable Rise of Arturo Ui*], the author uses the gangster milieu of Chicago to make Hitler's rise and his criminal actions more readily understandable to an American audience. In Ernst Toller's satirical comedy *Nie wieder Friede*, 1936 [*No More Peace*], Napoleon, residing in heaven, wagers that the convinced pacifists in Dunkelstein, an Andorra-like small country, can be turned into fierce warriors in the twinkling of an eye--and he is right. In his "modern fairy tale in three scenes," *Der Rattenfänger bei den Schildbürgern*, 1938 [*The Pied Piper Among the Gothamites*], Albin Stübs warns the Sudeten Germans not to follow the example of Gross-Schilda by letting themselves be lured to their doom by the ratcatcher Kasimir.

Historical plays had already become very popular around 1930; they were used by playwrights of different political persuasions to present modern social or political problems in historical costume. Napoleon and Frederick the Great were portrayed as leaders who saved and transformed nations, whereas historical revolutions and the peasant revolt were topics that pointed to the need for revolutionary change. The exiles continued this trend; for them recourse to history was at times dictated by censorship in the host countries. Nonetheless, in most cases it was easy for the

audience to draw the necessary analogies and parallels.   In
Ferdinand Bruckner's comedy *Napoleon der Erste* , 1936 [*Napoleon the First*], certain characteristics and decisions of the
hero point to Hitler, who was indeed often compared to the
French emperor and called the Napoleon of the twentieth century.   The main character in Georg Kaiser's *Napoleon in
New Orleans* (1941) is an impostor who defrauds a fanatical
admirer of the emperor of his wealth.   Kaiser equates the
false Napoleon and his companions with Hitler and his criminal cohorts.   A self-characterization of the protagonist is
clearly a total condemnation of Hitler, his methods of terror,
and his lust for power.   In his comedy *Konflikt in Assy-
rien* , 1938 [*Conflict in Assyria*], Walter Hasenclever drama-
tizes the biblical story of Queen Esther and King Ahasverus.
With the help of Mordecai, Esther is able to foil the plan of
Haman, the King's advisor, to have all Jews in the kingdom
killed and their property confiscated.   Haman expresses his
hatred for the Jews in speeches that abound with the anti-
Semitic phrases of Hitler.   The satire of the play is directed
against the racial ideology of the Nazis.   In Fritz von
Unruh's *Charlotte Corday* (1933) the heroine's murder of
Marat is justified as necessary in the struggle against political tyranny.
     As a subgroup of the historical plays, dramas based
on famous literary and historical models should be pointed
out.   Brecht's use of a Shakespearean play has already
been mentioned.   Brecht and Feuchtwanger also collaborated
on *Die Gesichte der Simone Machard*, 1943 [*The Visions of
Simone Machard*], a modern adaptation of the Joan of Arc
theme with realistic and visionary elements.   Simone feels
that she is a reincarnation of Joan and that she must save
France.   Brecht also lets the hero of Jaroslav Hašek's novel
continue his passive resistance against the military and the
state in his *Schweyk im Zweiten Weltkrieg*, 1944 [*Schweyk
in the Second World War*].   Friedrich Wolf's *Beaumarchais*
(1940) sounds the call to revolution, but the author of
Figaro refuses to join in the fighting and expresses his
trust in the power of the word before he leaves Paris to go
into exile.
     The revue has been one of the most widely used forms
for the effective dissemination of political propaganda.   With
its satirical thrust, it had been used extensively during the
Weimar Republic to show the face of the times, and in exile
it became even more important because it could be presented
by small ensembles on makeshift stages without great expense.
Brecht's *Furcht und Elend des dritten Reiches* (1938) presented life in Germany in twenty-four realistic scenes based
on eyewitness accounts and newspaper reports.   The common
tenor of all scenes is the all-pervading atmosphere of fear,
distrust, and terror that leads to disintegration of family
life, loss of human dignity, and perversion of justice and
even of scientific inquiry.   For performances and for specific audiences, certain scenes could be selected because they
are basically self-contained and of different literary quality.
During an evening of theatrical entertainment, one-act plays

by different authors were often performed, such as Wolfgang
Langhoff's *Im Bunker* [*Solitary Confinement*], dealing with
his experiences in a concentration camp, Arthur Koestler's
Sammeltransport [*Mass Deportation*], Anna Seghers's *Ver-
höre* [*Cross-Examinations*], and Gustav von Wangenheim's
Helden im Keller [*Heroes of the Underground*].

Although the flight from Germany and life in exile presented many difficulties to playwrights, it is not found very
often as a topic.   For most writers the political task was
more pressing; personal problems could also be better described in novels and autobiographies.   One of the most
famous exceptions is Franz Werfel's *Jakobowsky und der
Oberst* [*Jacobowsky and the Colonel*]; for the plot of his
"comedy of a tragedy," Werfel used his own experiences as a
refugee escaping from the advancing German armies in France,
as well as those of a fellow refugee with whom he later
shared the royalties from the performances of the play.   In
the comedy a haughty, reactionary anti-Semitic Polish colonel
and a liberal German Jewish businessman team up to escape
from their common enemy.   On their flight, only a few steps
ahead of the Nazis, they come to understand and appreciate
each other.   Werfel succeeds in showing the difficulties of
the refugees and portrays their desperate physical and spiritual situation.   That he was able to do this in a comedy
is even more admirable.   Ödön von Horváth's *Hin und her*,
1934 [*Back and Forth*] shows the exile as a victim of the
bureaucracy and the laws of the states.   Evicted by one and
not admitted by the other, he becomes a displaced person,
a nonentity, condemned to living on a bridge crossing the
border.   In *Figaro lässt sich scheiden* , 1936 [*Figaro Gets
a Divorce*], he deals with the financial and psychological
problems of the emigrants, and the adjustments in their lifestyle they must make because of their altered personal situations.[27]

Exile drama is *littérature engagée*.   Should therefore
the normal aesthetic norms and criteria be applied when
evaluating plays, or should judgment be suspended in this
case?   For the exiled dramatist the political demands of the
hour were most pressing, and he had to decide in favor of
the realistic and politically effective approach, even if this
meant neglecting or disregarding literary quality--to him
aesthetic norms and modern forms were of secondary importance.   The necessities of the political struggle dictated
the thematic and formal considerations we encounter again
and again in the dramas of exile.   As Wolf had expressed
it, art was a weapon in the struggle for the progress of
society, and to explain and change the world was the primary aim of these authors--but one should not forget that
the mirroring of reality and service in the progress of mankind are facets of all worthwhile literature.   Therefore, the
aesthetic criteria need not be lowered or suspended when
judging exile literature, yet certain matters, such as the
reasons for the shunning of modern forms and the turning
away from experiments, should be taken into consideration.
There are good and bad plays, as in any other period.

Because they focused on certain topics, many plays seemed dated after the defeat of Germany and the end of the war, often unjustifiably so. When German stages would not perform their plays because of this, playwrights returning from exile were very disappointed. However, there were also other reasons for the rejection of these plays: the German population did not want to be reminded of its shortcomings, callousness, and political mistakes. It felt that it had been punished enough by the war and that life itself had taught it the lessons it needed to learn. Morever, the murder of millions of Jews, Poles, Russians, and Germans in concentration camps, the horrors and the suffering during the war, the ruthless extermination of all political opposition, and the brainwashing of a whole population had so far surpassed everything portrayed in the plays that the evils of Nazism described in them paled in comparison with reality. Such feelings of guilt among the German people and their inability to identify with the exiles meant that dramas about life in exile also found no audience. A purely literary reason why these plays were not performed should also be mentioned: during the twelve years of dictatorship, theaters had been closed to modern foreign drama, and now the plays of O'Neill and Williams, Sartre and Camus, Eliot and Fry, Anouilh and Ionesco were eagerly welcomed by German audiences and their production was encouraged by the occupation forces, while the dramas of the exiles gathered dust in archives. In the Western zone foreign plays and German classics dominated the stages for over a decade and only in the sixties did the documentary dramas of Rolf Hochhuth, Heiner Kipphardt, Peter Weiss, Tankred Dorst, and others begin to reexamine the phenomenon of fascism, war, and concentration camps. There is no doubt that the exile writers exerted a powerful influence on the younger playwrights—Peter Weiss had been exiled himself. One notable exception to this general neglect was Carl Zuckmayer's *Des Teufels General*. Zuckmayer's play was enthusiastically welcomed by the German public, staged more than 2,000 times, and made into a movie. In this drama Zuckmayer succeeded exceedingly well in portraying the atmosphere in Nazi Germany. German audiences could easily identify with Harras, the hero of the play, and sense themselves as victims of fate, of a superhuman power, without having to pay the ultimate price like Harras or to come to a realization of their own guilt in the rise of fascism.[28]

In the Soviet-occupied part of Germany, exiled dramatists played a much more active role in reconstruction. Several of the exiled playwrights returned to East Berlin, where they were welcomed with open arms. Brecht founded the Berlin Ensemble in 1949, Becher became Minister of Culture, Wolf was appointed ambassador, and their plays were performed by the state-controlled theaters. And whereas the theaters in the Western zone of the country were intent on presenting avant-garde, experimental, and absurd plays, the realism of the exile production fitted the call for social realism in the theaters of the Eastern zone. Many young playwrights continued writing in this tradition, and their plays became stagnant variations on a theme.   Only Brecht persisted in experimenting with his theories concerning a dialectical and didactic theater, in which he tried to balance aesthetic and political functions.   Brecht's drama, not completely shaped, yet very much influenced, by his exile, has in turn provided much stimulation to young dramatists in the German Democratic Republic.

However, the influence that exile drama exerted is not a true indicator of its importance, nor does the fact that many plays were never produced and that others are no longer performed detract from its significance.   In a time when a totalitarian regime dictated what was to be German literature, exile drama upheld the true humanistic tradition and represented the other Germany.   Whereas the drama of the Third Reich was thematically reactionary and formally anachronistic, exile drama attempted to stay relevant.   Although many of its characteristics were dictated by its fight against fascism, it tried to preserve a high literary quality and later even attempted to find new forms of expression. Its cultural value is not so much vested in its literary qualities, however; it will rather live on as a document of protest against the terror of the Nazi regime at a time when it was still courted even by foreign governments.   Drama in exile is living proof that not all Germans fell under the spell of Nazism and that the conscience of the nation was still awake. The dramatists recognized the barbarism and militarism of fascism, they were able to differentiate between chauvinistic nationalism and true patriotism, and they never tired of raising their voices in protest as they gave to an unbelieving and reluctant world signals of a danger that it recognized only when it was nearly too late.

Notes

[1] Helmut Müssener, "Die deutschsprachige Emigration nach 1933: Aufgaben und Probleme ihrer Erforschung," *Moderna Språk: Language Monographs* , No. 10 (1970), p. 11.   Except where indicated, all translations into English are my own. Since the completion of this essay the following studies about drama in exile have been published: Gudrun Klatt, *Arbeiterklasse und Theater: Agitprop-Tradition--Theater im Exil --Sozialistisches Theater* (Berlin: Akademie Verlag, 1975); *Deutsches Exildrama und Exiltheater: Akten des Exilliteratur-Symposiums der University of South Carolina 1976* , ed. Wolfgang Elfe, James Hardin, and Günther Holst, Jahrbuch für Internationale Germanistik, Reihe A: Kongressberichte, 3 (Berne: Peter Lang, 1977); Peter Diezel, *Exiltheater in der Sowjetunion 1932-1937: Deutsches Theater im Exil* (Berlin: Henschel, 1978).

[2] F. C. Weiskopf, *Unter fremden Himmeln: Ein Abriss der deutschen Literatur im Exil 1933-1947* (Berlin: Dietz, 1948), p. 27.

3 Cf. Hans Mayer, "Theater in der Emigration," in *Verbannung: Aufzeichnungen deutscher Schriftsteller im Exil*, ed. Egon Schwarz and Matthias Wegner (Hamburg: Christian Wegner, 1964), pp. 288-94.

4 E.g., S. N. Behrman's adaptation of Franz Werfel's original play *Jacobowsky and the Colonel* (New York: Random House, 1944); Ernst Toller's *No More Peace*, which was translated by Edward Crankshaw, with the lyrics adapted by W. H. Auden (London: John Lane The Bodley Head, 1937); Ernst Toller's *Pastor Hall*, trans. Stephen Spender and Hugh Hunt; *Blind Man's Buff*, by Ernst Toller and Denis Johnston (New York: Random House, 1939).

5 Matthias Wegner, *Exil und Literatur: Deutsche Schriftsteller im Ausland 1933-1945*, 2nd ed. (Frankfurt/ M: Athenäum, 1968), p. 174.

6 Robert E. Cazden, *German Exile Literature in America 1933-1950* (Chicago: American Library Association, 1970), p. 144.

7 Bertolt Brecht, *Arbeitsjournal, I: 1938 bis 1943*, ed. Werner Hecht (Frankfurt/M: Suhrkamp, 1973), p. 122 (30 June 1940). Brecht here actually uses part of the English proverb "The proof of the pudding is in the eating" to express his conviction that the success of a play is determined on the stage.

8 Walter Benjamin, *Versuche über Brecht*, ed. Rolf Tiedemann, edition suhrkamp, 172 (Frankfurt/M: Suhrkamp, 1967), p. 135.

9 Cited by Walther Huder in the "Nachwort" to Georg Kaiser, *Stücke, Erzählungen, Aufsätze, Gedichte*, ed. Walther Huder (Cologne: Kiepenheuer & Witsch, 1966), p. 786.

10 The productions of the exile theater in various countries and the extreme difficulties under which the directions and groups labored have been described in detail by Hans-Christof Wächter in his study *Theater im Exil: Sozialgeschichte des deutschen Exiltheaters, 1933-1945, mit einem Beitrag von Louis Naef*, "Theater der deutschen Schweiz" (Munich: Carl Hanser, 1973). Wächter concentrates exclusively on plays written and produced in exile. He modestly asserts that it is not his aim to give a "literary analysis and evaluation of these plays" (p. 13), but with its extensive bibliography and the list of plays written in exile, his book is invaluable for the study of the drama in exile. In November 1973, the director of the Academy of Arts in West Berlin, Dr. Walther Huder, presented an exhibit under the same title (Exhibit and Symposium "Theater im Exil, 1933-1945," Akademie der Künste, Berlin, Nov. 1973). In connection with this exhibit, writers, directors, and critics met at a colloquium and discussed their experiences in exile and the relevance of this experience for our times. Following the exhibit, Dr. Huder directed for three semesters a research seminar on "Theater in Exile 1933-1945" at the Free University of Berlin that resulted in a publication by Hermann Haarmann, Lothar Schirmer, and Dagmar Walach, *Das 'Engels' Projekt: Ein antifaschistisches Theater deutscher Emigranten in der UdSSR (1936-1941)*, Deutsches Exil

1933–1945, 7 (Worms: Georg Heintz, 1975), and unpublished research reports by F. Werner, "Erwin Piscator im Exil: Zur Praxis antifaschistischen Theaters," B. Hopf and G. Kulas, "Das Züricher Schauspielhaus: Eine deutschsprachige, antifaschistische Bühne," and M. Brand and B.-U. Endriss, "Fritz Kortner: Seine Entwicklung zum linksbürgerlichen Künstler."

[11] Curt Trepte, "Deutsches Theater im Exil der Welt," in *Protokoll des II. internationalen Symposiums zur Erforschung des deutschsprachigen Exils nach 1933 in Kopenhagen 1972*, ed. Helmut Müssener and Gisela Sandqvist (Stockholm: Deutsches Institut der Univ. Stockholm, 1972), pp. 520–56. Cf. also Curt Trepte, "Archiv Deutsches Theater und Filmschaffen im Exil," *Mitteilungen der deutschen Akademie der Künste zu Berlin*, 5, No. 1 (Jan./Feb. 1967). At that time the holdings of the archive were much less complete. Cf. p. 12: "Over 300 . . . German-speaking dramatists, librettists, and authors of works for the film, cabaret, and radio; app. 450 dramatic works written during the emigration; app. 800 productions in the German language or that of the country of asylum; names and, in part, professional résumés of app. 2,400 exiled artists."

[12] Cf. Uwe-Karsten Ketelsen, *Heroisches Theater: Untersuchungen zur Dramentheorie des Dritten Reiches* (Bonn: H. Bouvier, 1968).

[13] Klaus Völker, ed., *Brecht-Chronik: Daten zu Leben und Werk*, Reihe Hanser, 74 (Munich: Carl Hanser, 1971), p. 67.

[14] Bertolt Brecht, *Arbeitsjournal*, p. 45 (15 March 1939). Cf. also Ulrich Weisstein, "Bertolt Brecht: Die Lehren des Exils," in Manfred Durzak, ed., *Die deutsche Exilliteratur 1933–1945* (Stuttgart: Reclam, 1973), pp. 373–97.

[15] Werner Vordtriede, "Vorläufige Gedanken zu einer Typologie der Exilliteratur," *Akzente*, 15, No. 6 (Dec. 1968), 556.

[16] Bernhard Reich, "Zur Methodik der deutschen antifaschistischen Dramatik," *Das Wort*, 2, No. 1 (Jan. 1937), 63–72.

[17] *Die neue Weltbühne*, 34, No. 26 (1938), 825. Quoted from Walter Benjamin, *Versuche über Brecht*, p. 44.

[18] Alfred Döblin, "Die deutsche Literatur im Ausland seit 1933: Ein Dialog zwischen Politik und Kunst," *Aufsätze zur Literatur* (Olten: Walter, 1963), pp. 187–210.

[19] Guy Stern, "The Plight of the Exile: A Hidden Theme in Brecht's *Galileo Galilei*," in *Brecht Heute--Brecht Today: Jahrbuch der Internationalen Brecht-Gesellschaft*, 1 (Frankfurt/M: Athenäum, 1971), 110–16. See also the revised version published in this volume.

[20] Wegner, *Exil und Literatur*, p. 225.

[21] Cited according to Trepte, "Deutsches Theater im Exil der Welt," p. 521.

[22] Gotthold Mamlock was a "deutschnationaler Jude" ("nationalist German Jew") and an influential member of the editorial office of the *Berliner Tageblatt*. Cf. Hans Albert Walter, *Deutsche Exilliteratur, 1933–50*, I: *Bedrohung und*

Verfolgung bis 1933 , Sammlung Luchterhand, 76 (Darmstadt: Luchterhand, 1972), p. 80.

[23] Friedrich Wolf, *Professor Mamlock: Ein Schauspiel* (Leipzig: Reclam, 1958), pp. 60–61.

[24] *Das Wort*, 2, No. 1 (Jan. 1937), 68.

[25] Cf. Petra Goder, "Moralist der Appelle: Zur Exilproblematik im Werk Fritz von Unruhs," in Durzak, *Die deutsche Exilliteratur 1933-45*, pp. 499–508.

[26] Cf. Ernst Schürer, "Verinnerlichung, Protest und Resignation: Georg Kaisers Exil," in Durzak, pp. 263–81.

[27] Walther Huder, "Ödön von Horváth: Existenz und Produktion im Exil," in Durzak, pp. 232–44.

[28] Cf. Volker Wehdeking, "Mythologisches Ungewitter: Carl Zuckmayers problematisches Exildrama *Des Teufels General*," in Durzak, pp. 509–19.

Journalism in Exile: An Introduction

Hanno Hardt

I

Prior to the Nazi takeover Germany's press reflected the political diversity and the cultural and artistic interests that characterized life during the Weimar Republic. Among those who worked as journalists in Berlin or Frankfurt, or who contributed regularly to leading newspapers like the *Vossische Zeitung, Berliner Tageblatt,* and *Frankfurter Zeitung* or political magazines like *Die Welt am Montag, Das Tage-Buch,* or *Die Weltbühne,* were men and women who represented the highest professional standards and the best intellectual tradition of German journalism.

The mass media, and particularly the press, became one of the first targets of the Nazi regime in its attempts to silence the opposition and to secure all channels of mass communication for its own propaganda purposes. Journalists experienced the seriousness of the political situation and the consequences for freedom of expression and a free press almost at once. As early as 1933 the position of the German press drastically changed with three major developments: the establishment of the *Reichsministerium für Volksaufklärung und Propaganda* (Ministry for Public Enlightenment and Propaganda), the passage of the *Reichskulturkammergesetz* (Chamber of Arts and Culture Act), and the ratification of the *Schriftleitergesetz* (Editorial Act). The results not only were strict government controls over the flow of information; they also affected the organization of the press as a free enterprise and the working conditions for professional journalists.

After the passage of the *Schriftleitergesetz*, liquidation of press property proceeded at a rapid pace; publishers who did not follow the regulations of the *Reichskulturkammergesetz* lost not only their positions, but also their property. Journalists who did not meet the requirements of the *Schriftleitergesetz* were forced to leave the profession; this law specified that editorial positions could be held only by German citizens and not by individuals who had been deprived of their citizenship, or who were Jews or had been married to Jews.   It was a law that closely resembled the 1920 Nazi party program with its regulations for the press.   The impact of the *Schriftleitergesetz* was reflected in an increasing number of announcements about resignations, changes of profession, or retirements carried in the *Deutsche Presse*, a leading professional journal.   From its pages emerges the first chapter in the history of German exile journalists.   Many careers of promising young journalists and experienced professionals ended in the columns of the *Deutsche Presse* with an announcement of their resignations followed by a comment like "Sec. 5,3," in reference to a section of the *Schriftleitergesetz* that declared that editors "must be of Aryan descent and must not be married to a person of non-Aryan descent."[1]   Immediately after the passage and enforcement of the law, the exodus of journalists began, first from the editorial offices of their respective papers and then from Germany.

An example of how deeply this law affected the operation of the press is provided by the *Frankfurter Zeitung*, one of Germany's most respected newspapers at that time. Of thirty-one staff members who were dismissed either immediately after 1933 or some time later, a majority emigrated and about one-third of them reached the United States.   Among them were Arthur Bogen, Otto Hirschfeld, Hans Kohn, Max Nürnberg, Wilhelm Constaedt, Siegfried Kracauer, Kurt Lachmann, Soma Morgenstern, Wilhelm Rey, Frederick H. Rosenstiel, and Heinrich Simon.[2]

In addition, the Nazi regime proceeded with its policy of discrediting journalists who had fled the country to engage in professional activities in Prague, Amsterdam, or Paris, where groups of German intellectuals gathered to continue their fight against Hitler with the aid of a number of German-language publications.   The most active members of the "exile" press corps were stripped of their German citizenship and their names were published in the *Völkischer Beobachter*, the leading Nazi newspaper.   For instance, among the individuals who were listed in the issue of 13 June 1935 under the headline that announced: "36 Traitors Tossed Out," were ten journalists and publicists whose professional affiliations were also given in the following manner: Hermann Budzislawski (editor, *Nachtexpress*, *Tribüne*), Peter Bussemeyer (*Frankfurter Zeitung*), Max Gruschwitz (editor, Breslau scandal sheet), Kurt Häntzschel (editor, *Neues Wiener Journal*), Werner Hirsch (editor, *Rote Fahne*), Hans Joel (editor), Friedrich Kummer (editor in chief, Deutscher Metallarbeiterverband), Franz Pfemfert (editor, *Die Aktion*), Viktor Schiff (editor, *Vorwärts*), and Paul Westheim (journalist). A few months later, the *Völkischer Beobachter* of 4 March 1936 added several journalists to the above roster.   The individual journalists and their designations were: Kurt Doberer (engineer, journalist), Hans Finsterbusch (SPD editor, *Volkszeitung*, Dresden), Erich Goldbaum (artist, journalist), Erich Hamburger (contributor, *Berliner Tageblatt*), Fritz Lachmann (Ullstein editor), Herbert Stahl (editor),

Heinz Pol (*Welt am Abend*), Carl Paeschke (editor, SPD Silesia), Bernhard Menne (*Die Tribüne*, *Rote Fahne*).

The Nazi regime also compiled blacklists of journalists and writers and published secret guides to the subversive press and literature abroad. For instance, a 1936 listing of active anti-German journalists and writers contains over 200 names, starting with Alexander Abusch, editor in chief of *Gegen-Angriff* and ending with Arnold and Stefan Zweig, "both Jewish writers, authors of anti-German propaganda articles and pamphlets."[3] The 1937 *Leitheft* [*Guidebook*] provides historical materials, listings of major organizations, and publications of emigrants and contains the names of key figures among German emigrants. The publications are identified in terms of their political, racial, or religious contents, that is, Jewish (*Pariser Tageszeitung*, *Neue Weltbühne*, *Das Neue Tage-Buch*, *Die Wahrheit*, *Das Wort*); Communist (*Deutsche Volkszeitung*, *Volks-Illustrierte*, *Rundschau*); other Marxist groups (*Neuer Vorwärts*, *Neue Front*); Catholic (*Der Neue Weg*, *Der Deutsche in Polen*, *Der Christliche Stände-Staat*); and the Strasser group (*Deutsche Revolution*).[4]

There was, then, in various parts of Europe a resistance movement well known to the Nazi regime that actively engaged in the publication of newspapers and magazines that addressed themselves to the political situation in Germany. Among the staff members were journalists from many parts of Germany as well as writers and political refugees. By and large, the years immediately preceding the invasion of Austria and Czechoslovakia and the beginning of World War II proved to be the most active ones in the lives of many exiled journalists. Under the threat of Nazi rule over a large part of Western and Eastern Europe, many journalists and publicists continued their flight across the Atlantic. This essay will deal with this second phase of the German emigration, the retreat from Europe and the arrival in the United States. Although the specific history of exile journalists and their institutions in the United States remains to be written, this is an attempt to describe general social, political, and economic conditions of the time as they affected the situation of German journalists as professionals in exile.

II

The journalist, like the writer who arrived in the United States, faced the problem of crossing a language barrier to pursue his professional career on the staff of native media organizations. A failure to master the English language resulted in employment that required less than perfect understanding of the language or employment by organizations that accepted German language articles. The latter market consisted of the German-language press abroad (mostly in Switzerland), or of the so-called foreign language press in the United States.

According to a study of the Americanization of emigrants at that time by Donald Peterson Kent, only twenty-three of forty-seven journalists included in the sample "were able to continue in the field of journalism in the United States. Of those currently earning their livelihood by writing, two were writing for German language publications, one was writing in German for overseas broadcasts, and three were able to write in German and be translated into English. The remaining fifteen were writing in English."[5] Kent suggests that journalists were among a group of people who were less likely than other emigrants to become citizens because they felt that their transfer to a new culture was more difficult. Kent is also of the opinion that poor command of the language was accompanied by indecision about remaining in the United States. He points out, in addition, that there were many political refugees among the journalists.[6] Thus an argument can be made that these journalists were forced to make additional decisions that affected their professional careers beyond what could be considered a temporary delay of their activities. They had a choice of joining the American mass media, the German-language press in the United States, the exile press, or of changing their professional objectives; some were virtually forced by circumstances into retirement.

The German journalist who entered the United States in the thirties encountered a press that was headed for advertising growth and economic success and a broadcasting system that was also created in the image of the free enterprise system, the 1934 Communication Act and the establishment of the Federal Communications Commission notwithstanding. As William Allen White so aptly described it, journalism was "once a noble calling; now it is an 8 per cent investment and an industry."[7] Also, American newspapermen and women had just succeeded in organizing against economic threats and exploitation by their publishers; they had founded the American Newspaper Guild under the leadership of Heywood Broun and affiliated with the labor movement. In addition, the press was under some fire from the public, which criticized its sensationalism. There were many who advocated that free speech be prohibited, especially on subjects like socialism, communism, and Nazism.[8]

Also, the émigré journalist learned that the American press, unlike its counterparts in Germany, emphasized objective reporting and a particular style of writing that stressed factual accounts and reserved interpretation and personal reactions largely for the editorial pages. This kind of journalism stressed names in the news and played up local events, activities that were often considered trivial by German standards of professional journalism. It was practiced mostly in small-town dailies and country weeklies, but larger newspapers in metropolitan areas also reflected a kind of provincialism that was unknown to most journalists from abroad. Human interest stories and sensationalism prevailed, whereas the discussion of foreign news, the interpretation of economic issues, or the in-depth coverage of cultural affairs were missing as regular features in most American newspapers.

The émigré journalist also soon discovered that his American counterpart did not exist; that is to say, the American journalist of that time typically was a craftsman who had learned his trade on the job more often than in a school of journalism.   He was not an educated man in the sense of having had a prior professional career in a different field or of holding a university degree; instead, he relied on his ability to write and edit copy.   Words were his business, not ideas or ideologies.   He saw his own strength in his ability to use language for purposes of communicating facts and events to large numbers of individuals, and he believed in the tradition of American journalism as an important independent force in the democratic process.   At the same time, he was underpaid, easily replaced, and often unable to improve his own position because of his lack of education or option to change his professional career.   Thus even after the German journalist had overcome the language problem, American journalism remained another world of professional activities.

III

It is not surprising, therefore, that a majority of German journalists who joined the American press as free lancers or staff members worked for magazines or newspapers of national and international status, whose editorial policies reflected political or intellectual concerns not normally shared by the rest of the American press.   A listing of over 130 German journalists and their professional associations compiled by this author includes, among others, *Commonweal* (Richard Arvay), *New York Herald Tribune* (Julius Bab, Heinz Pol), *Washington Post* (Fritz Cahen), *New York Times* (Leopold Schwarzschild), *American Mercury* (B. F. Dolbin), *Esquire* (George Froeschel, Franz Höllering), *Newsweek* (Joachim Joesten), *Time* (Heinz Liepmann), *Christian Science Monitor* (Hans Natonek), and the *New Republic* (Franz Schoenberner).

Among the more successful German journalists in the United States was Curt Riess, who arrived in 1934 and managed to work for French publications as a foreign correspondent as well as for such magazines as *Esquire* (1938–45), *Saturday Evening Post* (1940–44), and *Colliers* (1940–43). As a war correspondent he was later attached to General Eisenhower's headquarters in Europe.   Others were Kurt Korff and Kurt Szafranski; the former was associated with the Hearst organization, both had participated in the conceptual development of *Life* magazine, which became a highly successful picture magazine in North America and the focal point of American photojournalism under the influence of a number of émigré photographers.   Szafranski also became cofounder of the Black Star Picture Agency in New York City, whose president was Ernest Mayer (owner of Mauritius photo agency) when it became one of the most important picture agencies in the United States.   Alfred Kantorowicz began as a contributor to the broadcasting field and succeeded in becoming an executive for the Columbia Broadcasting System; and Hans B. Meyer advanced to the position of chief of the German section of the Voice of America.

Alternative professional careers were suggested by the presence of a large number of German-language publications. The history of the German-language press in the United States reflects the important social and political role of the German immigrant throughout the centuries, from the founding of the country through World War II. German-language dailies in the United States reported a weekly circulation of nearly 2 million copies in 1938, which declined to about 800,000 by 1945. The largest daily newspaper was the New York *Staats-Zeitung und Herold*, whose weekly circulation ranged from 351,066 copies in 1939 to 211,926 in 1945. Other large daily newspapers that provided information in the German language throughout the war, cited here with their circulations at the beginning and end of World War II, include the Philadelphia *Gazette-Democrat* (251,000 to 183,400), Omaha *Tribüne* (157,590 to about 84,000), Chicago *Abend-post* (147,303 to 63,972), Cincinnati *Freie Presse* (103,551 daily to 18,599 weekly), Cleveland *Wächter und Anzeiger* (92,760 to 90,618), Milwaukee *Deutsche Zeitung* (84,000 to 78,799), and Rochester *Abendpost* (80,112 to 78,799). The Detroit *Abendpost* (prewar daily circulation 202,048) and the Baltimore *Correspondent* (prewar daily circulation 151,873) dropped to publication schedules of three times and twice a week respectively with less than comparable circulation statistics.[9] In addition, there were a number of weekly newspapers, among them the Winona *America-Herold und Lincoln Freie Presse* (72,716 to about 55,000).[10]

These newspapers and a host of other smaller German-language publications constituted the potential field of employment for émigré journalists. However, these media had already undergone a process of Americanization in terms of their news style and treatment of events; they also represented a press that had suffered politically and economically after World War I, when anti-German sentiments were strong. As a result, the German-language press had retreated from political involvement and avoided controversial issues. It became an ineffective and perhaps even irrelevant medium in terms of social and political functions associated with the press in general. Wittke has observed: "By 1940, papers like the Cincinnati *Freie Presse*, the *Wächter und Anzeiger* of Cleveland, and the *Tägliche Tribüne* of Omaha contained almost no editorial comment."[11]

Given the peculiar position of the German press in the United States and its attempt to avoid controversy, it may not come as a surprise that only a few émigré journalists sought or found employment with one of the established German-language publications, because many of these emigrants were politically committed and represented a potential threat to the neutral position sought by the German press, a position that, by the way, did not even allow for an aggressive anti-Hitler stance. As Roucek suggested, the majority of the German-language press sidetracked "the issue of the war, a difficult feat in any language, but particularly so in German."[12]

An American assessment of the involvement of the German press was provided by *Fortune* magazine. In a review of the foreign language press, *Fortune* listed a number of pro-Nazi papers, among them the *Portland Nachrichten* (Oregon), the *Taylor Herold* and *Waco Post* (Texas), the *Milwaukee Deutsche Zeitung*, and the *Deutscher Weckruf und Beobachter* (New York City), the organ of the Nazi movement in the United States. The same survey listed the *Florida Echo*, the *Schenectady Herold-Journal* (New York), the *Gross Daytoner Zeitung* (Ohio) and the *Neue Volks-Zeitung* (New York) as anti-Nazi newspapers. The article concluded with the statement that "the greater part of the German-language newspapers try to be cautious and diplomatic. Their editors for the most part, are definitely partial to Germany, but avoid open Nazi propaganda."[13]

On the other hand, one of the largest employers of émigré journalists and an exception in the history of journalism was the *New Yorker Staats-Zeitung und Herold* (Hellmut Brann, Robert Groetzsch, Erika Guetermann, Rolf Nürnberg, and Hilde Marx, among others). It remained the largest German-language newspaper throughout this period. Because it was located in New York City, it was also most accessible to those journalists who arrived in New York and remained there.

Perhaps it can be said in conclusion that the attitude of the German-language press toward the employment of émigré journalists and the recognition of their work remained indifferent unless a newspaper was taken over by an emigrant. For instance, Cazden reports that after Willy Pollack took over "editorial control of the National Weeklies, the largest chain of German-language papers in the United States," advertising space for the promotion of German writers and the review of their work became available, indicating a change of policy.[14]

Unfortunately, events like the takeover of established German-language publications by émigré journalists were rare. Instead, the lack of a vigorous, "native" German press in the United States was balanced by the introduction of a new type of press that represented the world of the German émigré journalists as they understood their professional roles and their calling at this time in their careers. This short-lived but highly successful press of socialist, Communist, and Jewish interests among German emigrant groups became another alternative for émigré journalists; in particular, it attracted the politically active and committed journalists who had looked in vain for the kind of advocatory journalism with which they had been associated in Germany and during their years in European exile.

The German press in exile, so to speak, was successful in terms of its ability to organize a large number of talented journalists into editorial staffs or groups of regular contributors to serve not only the community of German-speaking emigrants but also their American supporters as interpreters of the social and political conditions in Germany and the United States. These newspapers made available "German" ideas and ideologies and provided at least one basis for a discussion of the future of Germany and the future of the German immigrant in the United States. Finally, this press gave purpose and direction to the lives of a group of professional journalists and writers whose involvement in German culture and politics virtually prevented their absorption into the new cultural and political environment as well as into the professional world of American journalism.

The *Neue Volks-Zeitung* (1932-49) was dedicated to the interests of the working people and served as an organ of the Social Democratic party in exile. It was started under the direction of Siegfried Jungnitsch, who was followed by Gerhart H. Seger in 1936. At that time the paper came under the dominance of a number of émigré journalists, among them Karl Jakob Hirsch, Rudolf Katz, Friedrich Stampfer, and Hilde Walter. Others were Julius Epstein, Wilhelm Sollmann, Max Barth, Robert Groetzsch, and Alexander Stein. The paper, whose circulation dropped from 21,850 in 1934 to 17,632 in 1949, was supported by "numerous German-American socialist and trade union groups, many of whom used the paper as a kind of organizational news bulletin."[15] Nevertheless, Seger intended to appeal to a wider audience than the German emigrant community; he suggested that his newspaper was more than just another paper established to help fight Hitler, and his attempt to "Americanize" advertisements and makeup of the newspaper supports his claim.[16] At the same time efforts were made to distinguish the *Neue Volks-Zeitung* from the bulk of the German-language press in the United States, which was thought to fall below the standards of acceptable journalism. Arthur Schwerdtfeger comments that when compared to German weeklies in the United States most of the former Prussian provincial press looked like metropolitan newspapers.[17] It is obvious, however, that concessions had to be made to the newspaper readers, with the result that American professional know-how and ideas about the presentation of facts and information were utilized in the communication of the specific ideological or intellectual goals of émigré journalism.

A more typical example of this merger of American format and German content was the founding of the *Deutsches Volksecho* (1937-39), which represented the interests of the Communist movement. It was the continuation of the *Arbeiter*, an earlier paper that had been the voice of the German Bureau of the Communist party in the United States. The *Deutsches Volksecho* appeared as a tabloid and featured a variety of services designed to attract all age groups and women as well as men. Consequently, the paper had regular pages for women and for young adults; there was sports coverage for the male reader and a proletarian comic strip. In addition, articles in English appeared in the newspaper, a factor that may have contributed to the alleged appeal of the *Deutsches Volksecho*, which at one time was supposed to have reached a circulation of over 35,000 copies. The Americanization of the newspaper was the work of Stefan Heym, the editor, and Alfons Goldschmidt, who became the publisher of the *Deutsches Volksecho* in 1938. It seemed, however, that this type of journalism, which tried to combine the packaging of information of the commercial press with the ideological content of a Communist newspaper, did not succeed. Consequently, Heym tried to interest the *Neue Volks-Zeitung* in a merger when he was unable to attract enough readers for his newspaper from American sympathizers and the German-language community, but specifically from among the subscribers of the *Neue Volks-Zeitung*. After two years the *Deutsches Volksecho* was discontinued. In the same year another Communist weekly, the *Volksfront* (1934-39) in Chicago, which had been edited by Erich von Schroetter and Hermann Jacobs, alias Martin Hall, also disappeared from the German-language market without replacement by a similar publication.

One of the most successful newspapers of this time, however, was *Aufbau* (founded in 1934), which became an international institution and the leading German-language newspaper during the height of the immigration to the United States. A creation of the German Jewish Club in New York, *Aufbau-Reconstruction* served as a platform for the Jewish community in the United States and became the lifeline for thousands of emigrants. The paper introduced the emigrant to his new home and appealed to the loyalty of the emigrants to the United States; it also upheld the Jewish traditions and promoted the undeniable German heritage of most of its readers. Under its editor Manfred George, who held the position since 1939, the newspaper acquired a distinguished staff of émigré journalists; it is almost safe to say that a majority of the German writers and journalists at one time or another contributed to the pages of *Aufbau* during the period following George's appointment. Among his closest journalistic collaborators were Siegfried Aufhäusser, Josef Maier, Therese Pol, and Ruth Karpf; Richard Dyck and Kurt Hellmer were assistant editors; Vera Craener was women's page editor and Arthur Holde, music critic. Others included Max Behrens, sports editor; B. F. Dolbin, Robert Groetzsch, Erika Guetermann, Ivan George Heilbut, Hilde Marx, Carl Misch, Rolf Nürnberg, Max Osborn, Kurt Pinthus, Heinz Pol, Ludwig Wronkow, and Michael Wurmbrand. Hans E. Schleger became advertising director in 1938 and Wronkow was named circulation manager in 1939.

Under the direction of George the newspaper increased its circulation from about 13,000 copies in 1940 to over 30,000 in 1944; this growth was accompanied by a rise in the advertising volume, which made *Aufbau* a successful newspaper in a competitive New York market. In 1941 *Aufbau* merged with *Neue Welt*, the organ of the Jewish Club of Los Angeles, and offered a West Coast supplement.

Cazden's assessment of *Aufbau* is quite correct when he observes: "The general literary excellence of the paper, the many first printings of prose and poetry by authors such as Thomas Mann, Werfel, Zweig, and Brecht, the numerous book reviews, discussions of all aspects of German, Jewish, and American culture--all contribute to make the *Aufbau* an indispensable source for any literary or cultural history of the emigration."[18] This kind of broad coverage also made *Aufbau* a viable alternative to its German-language competitors, the *Neue Volks-Zeitung* and the *Staats-Zeitung und Herold*.

It should be stressed, however, that *Aufbau* under the leadership of George maintained an editorial position that made the newspaper a modern-day successor to immigrant newspapers of the last century; that is to say, George saw one of his major contributions in paving the way for the acculturation of the Jewish-German immigrant. *Aufbau* by and large did not get involved in controversies between various political factions among German emigrants; it did not take editorial stands on questions of Social Democratic or Communist domination of debates ranging from the popular front movement to the political future of post-Nazi Germany. Instead, George believed in loyalty to the concerns of the United States, particularly in the war effort against Nazi Germany. He basically continued an editorial policy that was stated in the first issue of *Aufbau*: "If we succeed in reaching our goals, this paper will become the newspaper of thousands of German Jews in the service of the Jewish race and our new homeland."[19] There is no doubt that *Aufbau* contributed more to the reunification of families, for instance, and to the welfare of German-Jewish immigrants, than any other newspaper.

Another German-language publication that became a forum for émigré journalists was *Solidarität* (1906-54), the official organ of the Workmen's Sick and Death Benefit Fund of the United States of America. Otto Sattler, the editor of the monthly magazine,[20] provided a number of German journalists with an opportunity to write for the publication.

Although *Aufbau* employed a considerable number of émigré journalists, there were still others whose arrival in the United States marked the end of their journalistic career. Given the wide variety of professional expertise and specialized knowledge in various fields and the advantage of academic training among German journalists, self-employment or employment as college professors or as researchers in the academic field was not uncommon.

Among the individuals whose careers moved in these directions were Hellmut Brann, who taught at Columbia University and Rutgers University before he became editor of the *New York Staats-Zeitung und Herold*, and Alfred Einstein, who served as professor of music at Smith College. Paul Frölich conducted historical research, and Hans Habe was a writer and author before he joined the U. S. Army and helped design the postwar press in West Germany. Egon Jameson worked in the State Department during the Roosevelt, Truman, and Eisenhower administrations. Siegfried Kracauer published studies on film and the Nazi movement, among them *Propaganda and the Nazi War Film* (1942) and *From*

Caligari to Hitler: A Psychological History of the German Film (1947). Carl Landauer joined the University of California at Berkeley in 1936. Ernst Erich Noth, editor of *Books Abroad*, was also a member of the University of Oklahoma faculty. Felix Pinner published his *Wirtschaftsanalyse* ("economic analysis") in New York. Kurt Pinthus joined the Columbia University faculty as an expert on theater. Richard Plant was professor of German at New York City College. Guenter Reimann published on financial and economic matters. Willy O. Somin worked for the U. S. Office of War Information. Gustav Stolper was joined by his former colleague in Germany, Georg Katona, as copublisher of *Information*, a news service for business organizations. Katona later moved to the University of Michigan.

Others utilized their talents and special interests in different fields of endeavor. Eric Godal took a stab at establishing a satirical journal; *TNT* made a short appearance in 1942. Gert von Gontard became an assistant to Max Reinhardt in Hollywood and founded the Players from Abroad company in New York. Siegmund Salzmann joined Disney production in Hollywood and created *Bambi*, one of the most successful Disney cartoons. Will Schaber worked for the British Information Services. Siegfried Thalheimer worked as an art dealer in New York, and Hans Wallenberg founded a printing company before he joined the military service in 1942.

On the other hand, one of Germany's most respected journalists, Georg Bernhard, editor of the *Vossische Zeitung*, member of the Reichstag, and founder of the *Pariser Tageszeitung*, lived a quiet life in New York until his death in 1944. His colleague, Julius Elbau, the last editor of the *Vossische Zeitung*, also retired from active involvement in the German-language press until after the war. Both represent a group of individuals who, often by choice, avoided the confrontation with the professional environment of the exile press.

The story of the German émigré journalist and writer has not yet been told; there are many individuals whose careers were interrupted and destroyed by the Nazi takeover. Others became highly successful and respected members of their professions in the United States and abroad. Their individual histories together with the history of German journalism as a profession in American exile may reveal the contribution of German journalists not only to American culture, but also to the development of the mass media.

Notes

[1]H. Schmidt-Leonhardt and P. Gast, eds., *Das Schriftleitergesetz vom 4. Oktober 1933 nebst den einschlägigen Bestimmungen* (Berlin: Carl Heymans Verlag, 1938), p. 54. Translation mine.

2Reported in *Gegenwart-Sonderheft: Ein Jahrhundert Frankfurter Zeitung, 1856-1956*, "Die Redaktion der F.Z./ Bericht über ein Vierteljahrhundert," pp. 56-57.

3"Reich Propaganda Ministry Blacklists of Authors and Journalists," Headquarters United States Forces; European Theater, Information Control Division, Intelligence Section. Ref. No.: DE 496/DIS 202.

4*Leitheft: Emigrantenpresse und Schrifttum*, issued by the Reichsführer-SS, Der Chef des Sicherheitshauptamtes, March 1937. Reprinted in Herbert E. Tutas, *N.S. Propaganda und deutsches Exil, 1933-39* (Meisenheim/Glan: Anton Hain KG, 1973), pp. 135-88.

5Donald Peterson Kent, *The Refugee Intellectual: The Americanization of the Immigrants of 1933-1941* (New York: Columbia University Press, 1953), pp. 28-34.

6Kent, pp. 28-34.

7As quoted in George Seldes, *Facts and Fascism* (New York: In Fact, Inc., 1943), p. 244.

8The survey in *Fortune* (Feb. 1940) was part of an effort to discover the public attitude toward the American press. Part of these results were reprinted in Robert W. Jones, *Journalism in the United States* (New York: E. P. Dutton & Co., 1947), pp. 566-67.

9Circulation figures and estimates have been compiled from listings in the 1938 and 1945 issues of the *Ayer Directory of Publication* (Philadelphia: Ayer Press). The directory is published annually.

10*Ayer Directory.*

11Carl Wittke, *The German-Language Press in America* (Lexington: University of Kentucky Press, 1957), p. 283.

12Joseph S. Roucek, "The Foreign Language Press in World War II," *Sociology and Social Research*, 27 (July/Aug. 1943), pp. 462-71.

13Ludwig Oberndorf, "The Foreign Language Press," *Fortune*, 22, No. 5 (Nov. 1940), 90-104.

14Robert E. Cazden, *German Exile Literature in America, 1933-1950: A History of the Free German Press and Book Trade* (Chicago: American Library Association, 1970), pp. 118-19.

15Cazden, pp. 118-19.

16Joachim Radkau, *Die deutsche Emigration in den U.S.A.: Ihr Einfluss auf die amerikanische Europapolitik 1933-1945*, Studien zur modernen Geschichte, 2 (Düsseldorf: Bertelsmann Universitätsverlag, 1971), p. 146.

17Radkau, p. 147.

18Cazden, p. 63.

19Quoted from a short history of *Aufbau* by Alfred Prager, "Kurzgeschichte des *Aufbau*," *Aufbau* (New York), 21, No. 13 (1 April 1955), 23.

20Personal information in a letter from Will Schaber to John Spalek.

Selected Bibliography

The following books and articles provide some basic information about the literature of émigré journalists and their publications. Additional sources can be found in more general works about exile literature, theater, and film.

Arndt, Karl J. R. and May E. Olson, eds. *The German Language Press of the Americas, 1732-1968*. Munich: Dokumentation, 1965; an enlarged edition was published in 1976.

Cazden, Robert E. *German Exile Literature in America 1933-59: A History of the Free German Press and Book Trade*. Chicago: American Library Association, 1970.

Franck, Wolf. *Führer durch die deutsche Emigration*. Paris: Editions du Phénix, 1935.

Friedrich Ebert Stiftung, ed. *Die deutsche politische Emigration, 1933-1945: Katalog zur Ausstellung*. Bonn-Bad Godesberg: Forschungs-Institut der Friedrich-Ebert-Stiftung, 1972.

Habe, Hans. *Im Jahre Null: Ein Beitrag zur Geschichte der deutschen Presse*. Munich: Kurt Desch, 1966.

Halfmann, Horst. *Zeitschriften und Zeitungen des Exils, 1933-1945*. Leipzig: Deutsche Bücherei, 1969.

Hardt, Hanno, Elke Hilscher, and Winfried B. Lerg, eds. *Presse im Exil: Beiträge zur Kommunikationsgeschichte des Exils, 1933-45*. Munich: K. G. Saur, 1979.

Hase, Martin von. "Verzeichnis verbotener Schriften in der ersten Hälfte des zwanzigsten Jahrhunderts." *Börsenblatt für den deutschen Buchhandel*, No. 13 (12 Feb. 1952), p. 54, and "Eine Nachlese" in No. 44 (30 May 1952), p. 218.

Heide, Walther. *Handbuch der deutschsprachigen Zeitungen im Ausland*. Essen: Essener Verlagsanstalt, 1940.

Hurwitz, Harold. *Die Stunde Null der deutschen Presse: Die amerikanische Pressepolitik in Deutschland 1945-1949*. Cologne: Wissenschaft und Politik, 1972.

Kuehl, Michael. "Die exilierte deutsche demokratische Linke in USA," *Zeitschrift für Politik*, 31, No. 4 (1957), 273-89.

Langkau-Alex, Ursula. "Deutsche Emigrationspresse. (Auch eine Geschichte des 'Ausschusses zur Vorbereitung einer deutschen Volksfront' in Paris.)" *International Review of Social History*, 15, part 2 (1970), 167.

Maas, Liselotte, ed. *Handbuch der deutschen Exilpresse 1933-1945*. 2 vols. Munich: Carl Hanser, 1976, 1978.

Misch, Carl, ed. *Gesamtverzeichnis der Ausbürgerungslisten 1933-38*. Paris: Verlag der Pariser Tageszeitung, 1939.

Oberndorf, Ludwig. "The German Press in the United States." *The American-German Review*, No. 6 (Dec. 1939), p. 14.

Paetel, Karl O. "Deutsche Publizistik in der Emigration." *Der Tagesspiegel* (Berlin, Germany), 18 Oct. 1946.

_____. "Die Presse des deutschen Exils, 1933-45." *Publizistik*, 4, No. 4 (July/Aug. 1959), 241-52.

Paetel, Karl O.   "Die Zeitschriften des deutschen Exils." *New Yorker Staats-Zeitung und Herold*, 3 Nov. 1946.

Radkau, Joachim. *Die deutsche Emigration in den USA: Ihr Einfluss auf die amerikanische Europapolitik 1933-1945*. Studien zur modernen Geschichte, 2. Düsseldorf: Bertelsmann Universitätsverlag, 1971.

Schaber, Will, ed. *Aufbau Reconstruction: Dokumente einer Kultur im Exil*. New York: The Overlook Press; Cologne: Kiepenheuer & Witsch, 1972.

Sternfeld, Wilhelm.   "Die 'Emigrantenpresse.'" *Deutsche Rundschau*, 79, No. 4 (1950), 250-59.

_____.   "Press in Exile: German Anti-Nazi Periodicals 1933-1945." *Wiener Library Bulletin*, 3, No. 3/6 (1949), 31; and No. 1 (1950).

Exile and Existentialism

Henri R. Paucker

Even before 1933 Erich Kästner had written sarcastically about a German "Unity Party," meaning the totalitarian National Socialists and their Nazi party:

> Als die Extreme zusammenstiessen,
> begriff Max Müller, wie nötig er sei.
> Und er gründete die Partei
> aller Menschen, die Müller hiessen.
>
> Müller liebte alle Klassen.
> Politische Meinungen hatte er keine.
> Wichtig war ihm nur das Eine:
> Sämtliche Müllers zusammenzufassen . . .

"Müller" met with great success because of one measure in particular:

> Diese Müllermehrheit wies
> alle aus, die anders hiessen . . .
>
> ("Die deutsche Einheitspartei")[1]

The authors exiled from Germany are precisely those "non-Müllers." They come from the most diverse social backgrounds and voice the most diverse political, philosophical, and aesthetic opinions. The absurd and arbitrary policy of Nazi "cultural control" created exile literature; thus the essence of exile writing is elusive, and the basis of its existence is itself absurd and arbitrary. Taken together, this literature reveals a variety of phenomena that are difficult to bring under a single rubric. For example, do Thomas Mann and Bertolt Brecht have anything else in common beside their shared California exile?

Not only is there no single, comprehensible identity among these countless writers. For the critic, this multiformity presents an additional complication: the individual style of some writers was often totally undisturbed by exile, allowing them simply to continue a previously established, personal literary tradition. Using a critique of style, for example, is it actually possible to distinguish a "before"

and "after" text by Thomas Mann?   Again, the only criterion
that remains is the arbitrary, extraliterary phenomenon of
exile itself.   Yet the idea that "exile literature" is nothing
more than the writings of Kästner's "non-Müllers" is equally
untenable, for it connotes blind acceptance of the Nazi program's criteria for cultural control.   Kästner clearly and
neatly indicated the absurdity of such distinctions, making
it tempting simply to brew up an existential, after-the-fact
raison d'être for exile literature, and to look for any principle that fits.

A comparative approach seems most appropriate.   The
literature of France in those same years, that is, "existentialist" literature and the literature closely associated with
this movement, is so permeated with the concepts "exile" and
"alien" that a comparison literally invites itself.

This present attempt will be a more or less three-
pronged approach: exile as a literary motif; the characterization of the exile hero; and the factors that led to his
isolation.   In all three areas, there is clearly perceptible
agreement: exile literature appears to be the literature of
those who were exposed to the identity crisis in an over-
whelmingly personal way.   To undertake an analysis of this
crisis, as the French existentialists themselves did, is certainly appropriate in this study.

In view of the wealth of material under consideration,
it goes without saying that in our context it can only be a
question of "directional indicators."   Only individual examples will be used for illustration, and much that is relevant
will be omitted.

I. Exile as a Literary Motif

The "given" from which all else proceeds is exile itself.
It is apparent from the outset how frequently the phenomenon
of isolation, of exclusion, occurs in the literature of the
thirties and forties.   Oddly enough, this is equally true for
literature that does not explicitly have exile as a theme,
and it is true even for work conceived or written before
1933.

In Hermann Broch's trilogy *Die Schlafwandler* [*The
Sleepwalkers*],[2] the protagonist of each volume attempts
to overcome his solitude and become socially integrated.   When
the "romanticist" Pasenow does not succeed in this by donning
a uniform, the "garb of a foreign value system" (p. 572),
it is not in the least surprising.   But the "realist" Hugenau,
who appears to get on rather well in his world, is also
isolated in the end from his fellow citizens by a "chasm,"
by a "dead region of silence" (p. 679).   At the conclusion
of *Die Kapuzinergruft* [*The Crypt of the Capuchins*],
Joseph Roth's Baron von Trotta stays behind, alone in his
café, while the shutters outside are closed.   Even his mother,
who was more able to cope with life than Trotta, had only
apparently been able to maintain contact with the external

world: without admitting it to anyone, she had gone deaf.
Ulrich, Robert Musil's *Mann ohne Eigenschaften* [*The Man
without Qualities*], is not only unable to adapt but withdraws to an island with his twin sister.

Such motifs are not new: "outsiders" had long been
Kafka's protagonists.   K's search for judges and authorities
in *Der Prozess* [*The   Trial*] and *Das Schloss* [*The Castle*],
the waiting of the man from the country in "Before the Law,"
the country doctor in the story of the same name, alone in
the winter night---all these reflect isolation that, although
in another way, characterizes most of Thomas Mann's characters from *Tonio Kröger* to *Der Zauberberg.*   Others were
fugitives, like Pont in Arnold Zweig's *Pont und Anna.*   In
the southerly calm of Lake Como, Pont yields to grief over
his lost loved one, and not until the final sentences of the
narrative does he understand the duty he must perform in
Germany.   Klaus Mann's heroine in the novel *Flucht in den
Norden*   [*Journey into Freedom*] is also a fugitive.   As the
author explains in his diary *Der Wendepunkt* [*The Turning Point*], the heroine ignores her guilty conscience and
gives in to a love affair rather than participate in the
struggle against fascism in Paris.[3]

Thus in literature before, during, and after 1933 there
appear certain themes and motifs that are shared with, but
not independent of, the special exile literary situation.   It
is not only the protagonist of exile who lives in the alienation, the isolation of a figurative, if not literal, exile.
From this perspective exile literature demonstrates only one
aspect of a larger, more generalized development.

The possibility that merely chance coincidences are at
play here is dispelled by a glance at the literary situation
in neighboring France.   The significance that the motif of
isolation had acquired there emerges clear and unmistakable.
In the work of Camus terms such as "exile" and "alien"
become key ideas and emerge in several titles: *L'Etranger*
[*The Stranger*], *L'Etat de siège* [*State of Siege*], *L'Exil
et le royaume* [*Exile and the Kingdom*].   Almost every
hero in Sartre's drama acts upon this primal experience.   In
Les Mouches [*The Flies*], Orestes perceives that he is a
"stranger" in his own native city.[4]   Hugo, in *Les Mains
sales* [*Dirty Hands*], attempts through political assassination to purchase membership in the party whose members continue to scorn him as "bourgeois."[5]   St. Exupéry's characters
are aviators, for whom separation, elevation above everyone
and everything, remains an insatiable need.   And "frater-
nité," attainable only in the extreme threat of war, appears
for a number of characters in André Malraux's novel *L'Espoir* [*Days of Hope*] to be the most important, if not the
only, motive for participation in the Spanish Civil War.[6]

II. The Characterization of the Exiled Hero

More important than these parallels is the fact that
the protagonists are sketched in a similar psychological

manner--their isolation is not a matter of chance. Many of these characters complain that they are "weightless." Like St. Exupéry's aviators, they "hover," foreign and indifferent above indifference itself, in the passivity of the homeless, belonging to no group. In the chapter concerning the "utopia of the precise life" in *Der Mann ohne Eigenschaften* Musil points out the difficulty incumbent upon those who, like Ulrich, want to remold, recast themselves rather than give way to "fixed laws": "No one knows how such a person should spend his day, since surely one cannot hover continually in the act of creation."[7] Sartre's Orestes also experiences this "hovering" over things in *Les Mouches*. He constantly complains about not being more attached to the earth and yearns for the weight of one who belongs.[8] In the final act, having purchased acceptance through the murder of his mother and stepfather, he is delighted by the "weight" he has at last acquired.[9]

The youthful grace and lightness that is characteristic of all these figures is the result of this absence of weight: they are elegant and versatile within high society (like many protagonists of Roth's, like Musil's Ulrich, like the characters of Thomas Mann), intellectual and witty (Sartre's Hugo and his wife Jessica), feather-light riders (Anouilh's Thomas Becket and Frisch's Don Juan).[10] Not accidentally, a whole series of exile writers took stands that correspond to this analytic scheme. These were writers who adopted the Nazi epithet "Journalist" as a personal mark of distinction. One of their most important representatives, Klaus Mann, hovers continually above and among various groups to which, in spite of all attempts, he cannot unconditionally attach himself. In *Der Wendepunkt* he calls this hovering in empty space the typical fate of an "intellectual between two World Wars."[11]

This buoyancy is represented over and over again as an affliction. From the vantage point of the isolation theme, such a treatment is understandable and a further trait common to all these characters. There is, correspondingly, the one possibility they all recognize as a solution to their problem: commitment. The weight of an act of commitment would mean belonging, the attainment of their highest goal. But it is precisely this act of integration in which they do not succeed. They remain egocentrically captive to the consciousness of their own weightlessness. They do not break through the glass armor of subjectivity; the objective remains unattainable. For the intellectual Hugo everything remains "sport," "a role," "inauthenticity."[12] Thomas Becket is incapable of "loving"; even the loss of the loved one or his material possessions is "easy" for him.[13] Klaus Mann, whose entire work can be considered an analysis and description of this one crisis, sees himself as a latecomer, a successor, a "son"[14] of the bourgeois-romantic tradition. He now participates, with horror and fascination, in the demise of this very tradition. The committed act proves to be doubly impossible for these characters: because they do not have the "stuff" for political-social commitment, and because--had fascism not made it impossible--they would have preferred to escape into their personal erotic-philosophical interests rather than take a political stand. This was the course chosen by Klaus Mann's heroine.[15] Because of the inevitability of catastrophe, however, the "futility" of all action is predicated from the outset, particularly for writers. "Futility" is the keynote of literary endeavor: Klaus Mann,[16] Hermann Broch,[17] Stefan Zweig, and Günther Anders[18] speak of it continually. Like Camus' Sisyphus, these characters vainly roll their boulder uphill, knowing from the start it will only roll down again.[19]

Given such extensive parallels, it is no wonder that psychology generally agrees on its own view and understanding of the literary hero of these years. A study from the Jungian school[20] recognizes and examines in the existential hero of France a type of *puer aeternus*, a perpetual adolescent. The flight from clear commitment (or simply the inability to make a commitment), youthful charm as a consequence of weightlessness and hovering, are explained as a delayed or not yet completed puberty. Not only is the narrator in *Le Petit Prince* boyish, separated from the world of adults, but he considers himself to be totally misunderstood by the "grandes personnes" and finally ceases wanting to belong to them at all.[21] In Sartre's *Les Mains sales*, Hugo says of himself: "At times I would give my right arm to become a man this instant; other times it seems to me I wouldn't want to outlive my youth."[22] Indeed, he is continually addressed as "petit" by his beloved enemy Hoederer. In *Der Mann ohne Eigenschaften*, Ulrich's refusal--or inability--to become a man with qualities may also be brought into this context: it is the hesitation of the juvenile to become "grown up," to push forward from the freedom of all available possibilities to a single irreversible reality, to produce "biography." Not coincidentally, Max Frisch, who unceasingly questions individual identity throughout his work, wrote a drama entitled *Biografie* [*Biography*], in which an "adult" disavows the empirical limitations of biography and struggles back to that point from which everything could have been different.[23] That the problem of the *puer aeternus* did not disappear from literature at the end of the Second World War is attested to not only by Frisch, but also by Alfred Andersch, whose motif of flight belongs equally well in this context--as does his distinction between freedom and empirical limitations of choice in *Die Kirschen der Freiheit* [*Cherries of Freedom*].[24]

A similar pattern of indecision or indecisiveness can be seen in Kafka's work as well as in his life--for example, in his various attempts to get married.[25] The complexity of relationships between men and women is indeed a further indication of the psychological parallel between the protagonists of German and French literature. Again it is Jung's *puer aeternus* syndrome: the *puer aeternus* carries with him the possibility of Don Juanism or homosexuality. By avoiding marriage as one of the most decisive forms of commitment (Don Juan), or by rendering it impossible (homosexu-

ality), the *puer* remains in the realm of pure weightlessness
--to quote from *Der Mann ohne Eigenschaften*:   he is a
"being as the embodiment of his possibilities, the potential
being."[26]   With incest, Musil's Ulrich adds a further possibility to both of the Jungian ones.   Incest belongs to the
puer aeternus because the love between brother and sister
likewise leads only apparently from one to the other: in
reality Ulrich loves and finds himself in his twin sister.
He remains in the weightless sphere of the individual self,
in "exact Utopia," outside reality.   He disdains reality as
possibility that became reality "by accident."[27]   In the works
of Hermann Broch[28] and Klaus Mann the homoerotic element
is more or less distinct.   It is indicative of the egocentric
isolation of the protagonists.

Interestingly enough, isolation, the inability to conform, was linked to the phenomenon of puberty by other,
nonpsychologically oriented critics as well.   In his diary
Die Schrift an der Wand [*The Handwriting on the Wall*],
Günther Anders, whose earliest works anticipated French
existentialism and whose entire *oeuvre* has remained at
least related to it,[29] refers verbatim to this puberty to which
the exile authors were condemned:

> The expression "old boy" suddenly sounded meaningful
> . . . Because we occupied the *chambres garnies* of a
> temporary existence, because we regarded our weekday
> as a mere intermezzo, because we arranged our life
> as only an antecedent to the day after tomorrow . . .
> we engaged in a totally *invalid life*, in a condition
> that, on the basis of its similarity to the lifestyle of
> adolescents, could be labeled "puberty" . . . The
> choice of puberty was the accursedly great sacrifice
> that we had to make for our determination . . . the
> determination not to integrate ourselves, to continue
> to cry "that cry of rage that we had taken up on our
> very first day. . . ."[30]

III. *The Reasons for Isolation*

Jung's *puer aeternus* may thus be viewed as a contemporary literary model that transcends the mere fact of geographical exile and is capable of providing a coherent structure for the exile experience as reflected in literature.   This
overall coherence, this partly literary-symbolic anticipation
of political exile and the larger meaning attributable to the
theme, is genuinely amazing.   But is this enough to confirm
a relationship and not just a mere similarity?   One cannot
speak of such a relationship until the factors that led these
protagonists into exile reveal their own parallels.   If such
parallels exist, exile literature would present (to the extent
it is shaped by the fact of exile) a parallel to existential
literature in France.   The experience of exile could be considered symptomatic of the existential mode of perception;
and the literature that mirrors this experience could be

tentatively understood within the theoretical categories of French existentialism.

As with every historical event, even such a singular occurrence as the National Socialist years, one looks for causes, development, and consequently prefigurations. The final sentences of Heinrich Heine's *Zur Geschichte der Religion und Philosophie in Deutschland* [*Religion and Philosophy in Germany*] were often interpreted as a foreshadowing.[31] Seen from a contemporary perspective, the signs were much more distinct. Literature aimed at politics around 1930 is full of warnings of impending catastrophe. Kästner's *Fabian* is direct and explicit. It is more surprising that even such generalized representations as *Der Mann ohne Eigenschaften* and *Die Schlafwandler* mesh with the portrayal of the great yearning for a *Führer*--the word occurs more than once and in critical passages in both novels![32] It is significant that in both cases the call for a *Führer* appears as a consequence, as an unavoidable result of a fully elaborated crisis.

This crisis is depicted not only by Musil but also by Broch as a *crisis of the (bourgeois) ratio*, as a doubting of the rational comprehensibility of the bourgeois world and its "values." The *Führer* appears as the one who would take away decision from the individual and make possible the flight from a rationalism that has become impossible, into irrationalism. This failure of rational knowledge, the "opposition between man who seeks to know and the world, which is stubbornly silent," is also found in Camus, in his *Le Mythe de Sisyphe*.[33] Out of this opposition of forces, Camus states, "arises absurdity." Because National Socialism was consciously irrational (one need only think of Gottfried Benn's and Ernst Jünger's rejection of rationality, their preference for "blood" and "race" over the "dissecting" Jewish intellect)[34] and espoused unquestioning submission to a leader, in total consequence of the crisis of reason, one can speak of a related literary situation in Germany and France. If one examines *Der Mann ohne Eigenschaften* on this basis a distinct parallel emerges. Ulrich is introduced in a significant way: the furnishing of his house presents itself to him as an insurmountable task if done alone, because the knowledge of *all* previously created styles prevents him from using *one*.[35] The same problem arises when the leading opponents of intellect, science, and art meet at the house of Ulrich's cousin, Diotima. There, brought together by a very real political circumstance, they seek in vain for the one exalted principle that will be binding on all things. Thus already at the novel's beginning such "immediate and pertinent questions" dissolve "into a vast multiplicity of doubt and possibility--according to those considered most knowledgeable" (p. 105). Such a "vast multiplicity of doubt and possibility" is contrasted with the utopia of the "precise life" (p. 252). Because reality breaks up into a "vast multiplicity," Ulrich relieves *ratio* of the duty to comprehend this reality and subscribes instead to the "utopia of essayism" (p. 256). According to this precept of Ulrich's, nothing is static, perpetual, or certain. The "utopia of essayism" requires instead that one be open in every direction: ". . . as an essay in the course of its paragraphs apprehends one idea from many sides, without ever exhausting it completely--for an idea that is totally described instantly loses its fullness and degenerates into a *concept*, he mused--to be able to view and manipulate the world and one's own life as accurately as possible" (p. 257). The real man, the man who is present in reality, is no longer the central concept of his thinking, rather "man as embodiment of his possibilities, the potential man, the unwritten law of his existence" is central (p. 258). Ulrich is a man without qualities because he continually recreates himself, places possibilities above the casual realities. Slightly reminiscent of the *puer aeternus*, Ulrich says he "hesitates to make something of himself: a personality, a profession, a specific nature of being . . ." (p. 257). Without claiming to represent Musil's concept of "essayism" in detail, it may be affirmed that he proceeds with, or even relies on, a growing impossibility to apprehend reality by rational means.

Other characters in the novel, whose intelligence is less obvious than that of Ulrich, express this clearly. General Stumm, for example, who can think only in military terms but who is more qualified to evaluate the situation than his more brilliant friends, speaks with bluntness of a "civilian mob" (p. 383). Even he finds that "this business is damned complicated." Brutally summarizing the endless fragmentation of the *ratio*, he presents a possible solution to the crisis: "the best thing would be if sometime a real fool would come across these indissolubilities, somebody like Joan of Arc, who could maybe help us!" (p. 1063). His is not the only such suggestion. To Meingast, for whom Ludwig Klages was the model, it is more important that in Geneva "there is a French boxing teacher, than that the analyst Rousseau once worked there" (p. 852). He believes: "the idea of salvation has always been antiintellectual." His advice accordingly is: "The world today needs nothing more than it needs a good, strong madness" (p. 852). Even Arnheim-Rathenau, whose generally admired education places him intellectually far above Stumm and Meingast, talks of the "wish . . . for stability and guidance." This lack, he believes, "is universal in today's world" (p. 1057).

The circumstances in *Die Schlafwandler* are similar. The splintering of the *ratio* corresponds here to the incessant "decay of values." The "value core" of the Middle Ages is lost; fragment values develop inconsistently and in contradiction: in total "metaphysical disregard."[36] This closeness to the terminology of the existentialists cannot be missed: man feels himself "ostracized," "hurled into nothingness, into chaos."[37] "For this reason we yearn for the '*Führer*'-- so that he will furnish us with motivation for an event that without him we can only call insane."[38]

The sensation of being "ostracized" or "hurled into nothingness" is closely related to the crisis of reason. The "strangeness" from which the characters of Camus and Sartre emerge has no other explanation. "Even thinking leads no further," Camus wrote in *Le Mythe de Sisyphe*. Man is "a stranger to himself and to this world"; he is "equipped with no other aid than reason, which negates itself." Absurdity, the epistemological symbol for what in literature is this "strangeness," is defined by Camus as "the opposition between the man who asks and the world, which remains stubbornly silent."[39]

In light of the above, exile literature is more than the work of authors, to quote Kästner, with "other names." Of course the National Socialist label "Jew" connotes as always an arbitrariness devoid of class or political distinctions. But it has one inescapable consequence: no matter how deep the crisis of reason, the experience of absurdity, may have been among individual authors, the leap into "madness" and "intoxication," the willingness to be "led," was impossible for them as exiles. Even those among them whose work exhibited quasi-fascist traits could not fall prey to the "error" of a Benn. Exile authors could not escape the crisis of Sartre and Camus. The escape into fascism did not offer itself to them--obviously not to those who were banished, and by the same definition, not to those who had always fought against it as an ideology.

Günther Anders, in the passage concerning the "puberty" of exile authors, says that they were forced "to make time."[40] Exile literature is the literature of those who, voluntarily or involuntarily, were exposed to the point of departure of the French existentialists in the most direct and brutal manner. Exile is the basic existential situation of man par excellence, and the literature of exile mirrors the history of ideas, frostbound for twelve years on this mountain peak of crisis.

IV.   Exile Literature from an Existentialist Viewpoint

The crisis in which the exile authors find themselves thus corresponds to the starting point in the thought of the French existentialists: the point of departure of Camus in *Le Mythe de Sisyphe*, or of Sartre's Roquentin in *La Nausée*, who "experiences" the existence of a tree root, an experience for which there is no category of thought.[41]

For the exiled author as for the French existentialist, a theoretical solution to this crisis is clear: voluntary submission, action, commitment. But in both cases nearly insurmountable obstacles stand in the way. It is precisely the existential hero, the "intellectual" Hugo in *Les Mains sales*, who as the *puer aeternus* cannot accept commitment. To him everything remains a "part to be played," a temporary performance, and his intellect lays bare its arbitrary and disobliging nature. A philosophical corollary is the knowledge that an objective, rationally apprehended goal of *engagement*, of commitment, a basic "value system" in

Broch's sense, cannot be found.   Sartre's formula "existence precedes essence"[42] is the problem in a nutshell.   The essence of man, what he is and what he ought to be as expressed through the categorical imperative, cannot be apprehended because it does not exist.   Every commitment is arbitrary, absurd, and "in vain."   As with Musil's Ulrich, it is a question of continual recreation of the self, whereby the number of possibilities threatens to overwhelm the one existing, accidental reality.

An exile author faces the same problem.   The need for commitment in the struggle against the spread of fascism is beyond question.   But he perceives just as clearly difficulties that he can scarcely hope to overcome.   He conceives his own essence above all as bearing the stamp of the bourgeois-romantic, that is, subjective tradition based on the individual.   His concern is therefore not political writing, although he knows it to be necessary.   To him, the difficulty appears even more immense when viewed from the perspective of an "outsider."   The onset of catastrophe became increasingly evident following the National Socialist seizure of power; it could not be halted even by political means. Where then should any concrete hope have existed for outlawed, scattered refugees and their most powerless of all weapons, literature?   The effort they undertake "in spite of everything," that is to say "absurdly," is finally "in vain." Even attempts to unite all exile authors into a single united political front failed.   But they did not fail by mere accident.   The bourgeois intellectual is in his heart a sceptic by nature.   He cannot pledge hiimself unconditionally to a single party.   The commitment that he continually fulfills, as did Klaus Mann, remains provisional.   It remains tentative, like that of his great predecessor in exile to whom he likes to refer: Heinrich Heine.   Heine had certainly committed himself, yet never gave up his reservations.   One need only be reminded of his complex relationship to every doctrinaire aspect of communism or socialism.

A dual movement is revealed as the fundamental structure of French existentialism: a dissolution of ties to the world as a result of the crisis of the rational faculty, and the plunge back into the world in the form of commitment. Between the two lies the focal point of exile literature, and the locations of individual authors may be plotted in relation to this point.   From here it is possible to take up a classification of the seemingly divergent individual writers within the exile group.

The difficulty discussed earlier of finding a common denominator, other than California exile, for Thomas Mann and Bertolt Brecht would, from this vantage point, work out as follows.   The prefascist attitude of Thomas Mann at the time of the *Betrachtungen eines Unpolitischen* [*Reflections of an Unpolitical Man*], with its acknowledgment of the irrational-romantic, proved more and more untenable in the light of political events.   Mann turns away from romanticism and finds a new model in the Enlightenment.   In this reorientation brought on by fascism he is aligned with

Brecht.   Both make, although with different means and a different object in view, an appeal to reason.   Brecht's alienation effect, combating empathy, and Mann's "recasting of myth" into the rational area of intellectual irony (as he wants his *Joseph* tetralogy to be understood)[43] coincide at this point and express the same attitude toward National Socialist irrationalism.

Consequently, what was called the focal point of exile literature above is clearly the center of the reorientation that Thomas Mann undergoes between 1933 and 1945.   Although he initially rejected, then avoided, all political involvement, Mann finally shifted and, after Eduard Korrodi's polemical essay in the *Neue Zürcher Zeitung*,[44] came to terms with active participation in political events.   This step then began to evince itself, although only indirectly, in his exile writing.

Authors like Klaus Mann, Hermann Broch, and Alfred Döblin illustrate this focal point of crisis with utter clarity. The difficulty of definitive commitment presented itself to them over and over again for the reasons shown.   As for Klaus Mann, insight into the necessity of commitment, his repeated attempts to free himself from the bourgeois romantic tradition, and the continued evidence of his experience that this was not possible, are his basic theme.

By contrast, Bertolt Brecht, Anna Seghers, Arnold Zweig, and others represent that group of authors who are spokesmen for commitment.   That there were also those among them who "needed" exile, in the sense of a deeply personal, unavoidable confrontation with crisis, is verified by the works of Arnold Zweig, which are a paradigm for this question.   The basic movement and evolution in its entirety is mirrored in his development: from romantic, aestheticizing subjectivism, to crisis (intensified by the experience of fascism), and finally unequivocal political commitment.

Translated by Adrienne Ash

Notes

[1]"When the extremes clashed against one another / Max Mueller saw clearly his role. / He founded the Party of Muellers / the name 'Mueller' was everyone's goal. / Mueller was fond of all classes. / He had no political sight. / Only one thing was important: / That all the Muellers unite. / . . . This plurality of the Muellers / Expelled those with other names. . . ."   Erich Kästner, *Gesammelte Schriften, I: Gedichte* (Cologne: Kiepenheuer & Witsch, 1959), pp. 265-67.   Unless indicated otherwise, all English translations are by the translator of the article.

[2]Hermann Broch, *Die Schlafwandler: Eine Romantrilogie* (Zurich: Rhein-Verlag, 1931-32).

[3]Klaus Mann, *Der Wendepunkt: Ein Lebensbericht*, Fischer Bücherei, 560-61 (Frankfurt/M: S. Fischer, 1963), pp. 298-99.   (Originally published in 1949.)

[4]Jean-Paul Sartre, "Les Mouches," *Théâtre I* (Paris: Gallimard, 1947), pp. 13–24 (Act I, scene 1).

[5]Jean-Paul Sartre, *Les Mains sales: Pièce en sept tableaux*, Livre de poche, 10 (Paris: Gallimard, 1965), pp. 24–28 (Act I, scene 3).

[6]André Malraux, *L'Espoir: Roman*, Livre de poche, 162–63 (Paris: Gallimard, 1970), pp. 34, 98, 270. (Originally published in 1937.)

[7]Robert Musil, *Der Mann ohne Eigenschaften*, ed. Adolf Frisé (Hamburg: Rowohlt, 1952), p. 254.

[8]Sartre, "Les Mouches," *Théâtre I*, pp. 24–29 passim (Act I, scene 2).

[9]Sartre, "Les Mouches," pp. 119–21 (Act III, scene 7, last).

[10]Jean Anouilh, "Becket ou L'Honneur de Dieu," *Pièces costumées* (Paris: La Table Ronde, 1960), pp. 150, 153, 154; Max Frisch, "Don Juan oder Die Liebe zur Geometrie," *Stücke* (Frankfurt/M: Suhrkamp, 1962), II, 12–13, 19.

[11]Mann, *Der Wendepunkt*, pp. 380–81.

[12]Sartre, *Les Mains sales*, pp. 59–71 passim (Act III, scene 1).

[13]Anouilh, "Becket ou L'Honneur de Dieu," pp. 184, 221–22; English version: *Becket or The Honor of God*, trans. Lucienne Hill (New York: Coward-McCann, 1960), p. 44: "Gwendolyn: . . . My Lord cares for nothing, in the whole world, does he? Becket: No."

[14]Klaus Mann, *Kind dieser Zeit: Eine Autobiographie* (Munich: Nymphenburger Verlagshandlung, 1965), p. 261. (Originally published in 1932.)

[15]See notes 3 and 11.

[16]Mann, *Der Wendepunkt*, p. 326.

[17]See Hermann Broch, *Der Tod des Vergils* (New York: Pantheon Books, 1945).

[18]Günther Anders, "Dichten heute: Aus Tagebüchern," *Die Wandlung*, 4, No. 1 (Jan. 1949), 40, 50; *Philosophische Stenogramme* (Munich: C. H. Beck, 1965), p. 51 and passim.

[19]Albert Camus, *Le Mythe de Sisyphe* (Paris: Gallimard, 1942).

[20]Marie-Louise von Franz, *The Problem of the Puer Aeternus* (New York: Spring Publications, The Analytical Psychology Club of New York, 1970).

[21]Antoine de Saint-Exupéry, *Le Petit Prince* (Paris: Gallimard, 1956), pp. 9–11.

[22]Sartre, *Les Mains sales*, p. 138 (Act IV, scene 3); English version: "Dirty Hands," *No Exit and Three Other Plays* (New York: Vintage Books, 1957), p. 191.

[23]Max Frisch, *Biografie: Ein Spiel* (Frankfurt/M: Suhrkamp, 1967).

[24]Alfred Andersch, *Die Kirschen der Freiheit: Ein Bericht* (Frankfurt/M: Frankfurter Verlagsanstalt, 1952).

[25]Cf. Henri Paucker, "Der Einbruch des Absurden. Zwei Interpretationen der Struktur von Kafkas Denken," *Neophilologus*, 55, No. 2 (April 1971), 175–90.

[26]Musil, *Der Mann ohne Eigenschaften*, p. 258.

[27]Musil, p. 369.

[28]Especially in *Der Tod des Vergil*.

[29]Günther Anders, "Die Weltfremdheit des Menschen," Lecture for the Kant Society in Frankfurt/Main and Hamburg, 1929.   Published in French: "Une Interprétation de l'apostériori" and "Pathologie de la liberté. Essai sur la non–identification," *Recherches Philosophiques* (Paris), 4 (1934/35), 65–80, and 6 (1936/37), 22–54.

[30]Günther Anders, *Die Schrift an der Wand* (Munich: C. H. Beck, 1967), pp. 76–77.

[31]Heinrich Heine, "Zur Geschichte der Religion und Philosophie in Deutschland," *Werke und Briefe* (Berlin: Aufbau Verlag, 1961), V, 308.

[32]See Broch, *Die Schlafwandler*, especially the end of part II: *Esch oder die Anarchie*, and Musil, *Der Mann ohne Eigenschaften*, end of part II.

[33]Camus, *Le Mythe de Sisyphe*, p. 44.

[34]Cf. Ernst Loewy, *Literatur unterm Hakenkreuz*, Fischer Bücherei, 1042 (Frankfurt/M: S. Fischer, 1969), pp. 43–54.

[35]Musil, *Der Mann ohne Eigenschaften*, pp. 19–21.

[36]Broch, *Die Schlafwandler*, pp. 474–77.

[37]Broch, p. 686.

[38]Broch, p. 403. See also pp. 685, 599.

[39]Camus, *Le Mythe de Sisyphe*, pp. 36, 44.

[40]Anders, *Die Schrift an der Wand*, pp. 76–77.

[41]Jean-Paul Sartre, *La Nausée*, Livre de poche, 160 (Paris: Gallimard, 1938), p. 183; English version: *Nausea*, trans. Lloyd Alexander, introd. Hayden Carruth, A New Directions Paperback, 82 (New York: New Directions, 1969), pp. 129–30.

[42]Jean-Paul Sartre, *Existentialism and Human Emotions* (New York: Philosophical Library, 1957), p. 13.

[43]Thomas Mann, "Briefe an Karl Kerényi," *Gesammelte Werke* (Frankfurt/M: S. Fischer, 1960), XI, 630–32, 653.

[44]Eduard Korrodi, "Deutsche Literatur im Emigrantenspiegel," *Neue Zürcher Zeitung*, 26 Jan. 1936.   Cf. also Klaus Schröter, *Thomas Mann in Selbstzeugnissen und Bilddokumenten*, Rowohlts Monografien, 93 (Reinbek bei Hamburg: Rowohlt, 1964), p. 110.

The Reception of the German Writers in Exile by the American Liberal Press 1933–1945: Changes and Trends

Carol Paul-Merritt

The subject of the reception of German exile literature by the American press during the period of National Socialist rule is quite complex, owing in no small measure to two factors, one of external and one of internal origin: (1) the great variety of American publications that dealt to some degree with aspects of exile and Nazism, and (2) the unavoidable subjectivity involved in evaluating the political, social, and literary orientation of the periodicals in question. In the present discussion, therefore, it will be possible to present only a brief overview of the intricate political and cultural situation in the United States during this period and to delineate some basic trends in the reaction of the American press to those writers in exile whose chief literary vehicle was the German language.

It is our contention that the liberal press paid considerably more attention to the exiled writers, their dilemmas, and their activities than did the more conservative periodicals and newspapers between 1933 and 1945. This premise is based on several factors, by no means the least of which was the relative dearth of other than minimal or negative press coverage of exile-related issues by such politically conservative publications as the Hearst newspapers. Although no attempt will be made here to analyze the role of American conservatism at that time, it should be noted for present purposes that the movement was of significance as a potent countercurrent to the more liberal trends that played on the American political-intellectual stage. In fact, a bitter and often vicious battle was waged by the left-wing press in particular against the "forces of reaction"--the "enemies of the people"--as embodied particularly in William Randolph Hearst, the Communist-hunting Dies Committee in Congress, a large part of the American Congress itself, and assorted "tycoons," "warmongers," and munitions manufacturers. Not surprisingly, the most unyielding and sensationalistic accusations and attacks against the right were undertaken by avowedly revolutionary periodicals such as *New Masses*, a Communist journal established in 1926, and *New Theatre*, established in 1934 as a monthly organ of the New Theatre and New Dance League.

An attitude especially relevant to this survey was the tendency of conservatively oriented organizations and individuals to distrust refugees[1] and frequently to associate them with communism. This suspicion of Communists combined with a strong tradition of isolationism in America could hardly work to the advantage of even the highly talented and well-known exiles who sought a haven here. Thus the vociferous rantings of the left-wing extremist press may have been an overreaction against this two-pronged phenomenon; conversely, they may have been simply a reflection of the emotionalism that seemed to permeate publications of this type. The following item, quite typical of the attitude and editorial style of *New Masses*, serves also to illustrate aspects of the antialien mood prevalent in some circles:

> Legislators, driven into paroxisms [*sic*] of fright by the bedtime stories Hearst and his confreres are telling them about the imminence of revolution, are feverishly pouring bills into their respective Houses to crush every phase of the movement of the working class . . . to improve its lot. The attack is, as usual, being made especially on the foreign born[,] and deportation bills of every size . . . and shape are flooding Congress. The most important . . . is the administration bill which grants the right to the government to arrest without a warrant any "alien subject to deportation . . . ." There are . . . others of varying stringency. One would force all "aliens" to take out naturalization papers within twelve months after the passage of the bill. Another is the notorious Dies Bill, defeated last year, that would deport all alien Communists. A third would cut off all immigration for ten years.[2]

Some conservative groups, such as the American Legion, also opposed the entrance of refugees into America, ostensibly for economic reasons. Speaking at the annual midwinter conference of the Kentucky branch of the Legion in 1938, the national commander expressed the following, apparently official viewpoint: "While the Legion sympathizes with these oppressed people . . . it is opposed to admitting immigrants at this time because of our economic situation and the fact that many aliens already here have not been assimilated . . . ."[3]

Unfortunately, the Visa Division of the State Department seemed to concur with the Legion, in action if not specifically in motivation, for the difficulty of gaining entrance to the United States appeared to increase almost proportionately as Hitler and the Axis gained control of ever greater portions of Europe. One of the most insidious of the obstacles placed in the path of refugees was the ruling of 1 July 1941, which provided that no visa would be granted to those leaving German-occupied territory who were forced to leave behind any relatives. Coupled with this ruling was an incredibly bureaucratic measure requiring submission of proof by potential emigrants that they could obtain an exit permit and a transit visa before an American visa would be granted--yet such papers were impossible to get in Europe unless the American visa already existed.[4] An almost immediate reaction to this ruling was well illustrated by the sarcastic conclusion to an editorial published in the *Nation*: "If only the [State] department had thought of this earlier, it could have shut out Thomas Mann and Einstein."[5] Both the *New Republic* and the *Nation* were unswerving in their support of refugees from the Nazi terror and in their demand for an easing of the restrictive immigration laws that seemed to reflect the dominant isolationist sentiment in the United States at this time.[6]

Obviously, attitudes such as those of the American Legion and the Visa Division of the State Department, deeply embedded as they were in the fabric of the national structure, could only be detrimental to individuals seeking freedom from the oppressive measures of totalitarian regimes. What then may be said of the antithetical viewpoint? May a legitimate case be made for favorable reception of the exiled Europeans in the United States? Did something akin to an "exile aura" exist in this country, and if so, what role did press awareness of the events leading to its genesis play in its development?

Although the interrelation between the economic, social, and artistic spheres of activity lies only tangentially within the scope of this survey, answers to the above questions must be considered to some degree within the framework of this interrelation. An evaluation of the reception of the German exiles in America--be they writers, intellectuals, musicians, or scientists--is contingent upon the establishment of certain features of the sociocultural atmosphere of the thirties.

That a relationship exists between traumatic economic upheaval with its attendant social disillusionment and an extreme, sometimes militant reaction was clearly indicated in the America of this period. The frustrated energy generated from such a situation seeks both an object upon which to vent itself and an outlet for its release. For American artists and intellectuals, the Depression and soon thereafter fascism, with their soul- and culture-destroying consequences, provided ideal targets toward which they could direct their anger and desperation. The revolutionary attitude that art should be a weapon for social change quickly became both focal point and outlet.[7]

Implicit in the popular left-wing view that both capitalism and fascism were antagonistic to the development of culture was the connection between revolutionary cultural activity and the battle against fascism. In 1934, for example, *New Theatre* unequivocally affirmed the determination of ". . . revolutionary theatre workers the world over . . . [to] continue the fight against war and fascism, for a social system in which the arts and sciences serve not the Morgans and the Mellons, the Rockefellers and the Rothschilds, the Krupps and the Comité des Forges, but the mass of mankind."[8]

In his excellent introduction to Himelstein's study of the New York theater between 1929 and 1941, John Gassner evaluates the emotional components of this new activism:

> A great fear of . . . evading or having evaded one's social responsibility . . . pervaded the world of the artist and the intellectual. . . . Engagement to a cause became a guilt-enforced virtue that was to lead to some kind of activism such as signing a petition or a protest, marching in a parade, and writing a story, poem or play of so-called social consciousness. Thus *enthusiasm*, an important factor in the practice of the arts, became a ferment in the depressed nineteen-thirties . . . .[9]

And so was born the fervent antifascist "cause orientation" of the decade--a period, incidentally, often labeled the "red decade" in American politics and culture.

This was a decade charged with both positive and negative excitement, for the forces emanating from the disaster of 1929 manifested themselves in greatly varied forms that allowed the disenchanted and the aware to voice their despair, to proclaim their views, and to become socially involved. For instance, many periodicals came into being with considerable fanfare and flourish, and although a number were quite short-lived and often died of financial starvation, others had long and colorful lives. To the first category belonged such journals as *Blast, Scope, Monthly Review, Leftward*, and *Left Front*--their titles are fairly indicative of their tone and orientation. In the second group were publications such as *New Theatre, Partisan Review, Anti-Nazi News, Twice A Year*, and *Direction*--these ranged the spectrum from decidedly left-wing to moderately and intelligently liberal. However, no matter at what point on the liberal political scale these were located, they all shared at least one trait in common: their hatred of fascism, either on the basis of their opposing political orientation (for example, *New Theatre, Partisan Review, Anti-Nazi News*), or on the basis of humanitarian concern (*Twice A Year, Direction*, and Klaus Mann's *Decision*, established in January 1941).

Organizations reflecting the growing sociocultural awareness in America during the decade are too numerous to specify in detail. It is sufficient here to observe that, in general, they were at least tinged by political coloration and on occasion completely permeated by it. The problem of assessment, however, is greatly increased by the fact that a variety of such groups, although labeling themselves "nonsectarian" or "nonpolitical," were in reality quite definitely neither.[10] In an illuminating article Max Eastman, a well-known former Trotskyite who had become a critic and analyst of the Communist movement,[11] detailed three Communist-front organizations chosen from a list of over 100 existing in the United States in the thirties. It was his premise that these groups exploited the developing antifascist climate to further their own ends.[12] One typical group was the American Committee for

Struggle Against War, founded in 1932, which underwent no
fewer than four name changes by 1941, each one reflecting
the current political mood in the United States.[13]

   In the 1930s also arose such organizations as hundreds
of workers' theater groups.   In fact, the theater became
in many ways an early nucleus around which large numbers
of artists and intellectuals rallied in the hope of creating
a substantial new direction for the arts.   As an embodiment
of the reform-inspired dreams of "the newly radicalized
depression intelligentsia, it pulled into its orbit those writ-
ers--and their numbers were legion--who, surprised by the
economic crisis of the early 30's . . . discovered politics."[14]   Naturally, the hard-core Communists were quick to
seize this opportunity to turn to their advantage the mounting dissatisfaction with the existing order; by capitalizing
on both the ills of the Depression and the hopes of the
liberal intellectuals for reform, they "attempted to infiltrate
and control the American stage . . . [in the belief] that
the theatre could help foment their revolution against . . .
capitalism and all of its . . . evils."[15]

   Although a number of middle-class intellectuals felt
that the answers to the contemporary dilemma were to be
found in workers' movements and proletarian agitation, many
of them either gradually modified their ideas or channeled
their energy into other realms of expression.   It must be
acknowledged, however, that their initial involvement was
sufficient to alter the heretofore relatively passive and
neutral position of the arts in America, thus paving the way
for sympathetic action on behalf of the artists and writers
who fled their European homeland in the name of moral
freedom.   No matter what forms were assumed by the manifestation of interest in the concept of art as a viable weapon
in the arsenal of democracy, all of the views and activities
basically reflected a common belief in the "humanizing function" of art, as Malcolm Cowley aptly put it.[16]   And precisely this faith in the humanizing function of art was an
element that attracted many American men and women of
letters to the camp of the cultural émigrés, who by virtue
of their very act of emigration became transfigured, in a
sense, into a collective symbol of the ideals for whose realization the Americans themselves were striving.   Furthermore,
there is little doubt that the heroic appeal of the exile
situation contributed to the interest taken by numerous intellectuals and representatives of the press in the cause of the
German exiles.[17]

   The above factors thus became important stimuli for
the increasingly energetic concern of Americans with exile
activities.   This concern was not only reflected in journalism, but also led to involvement in congresses of the P.E.N.
Club and the League of American Writers, as well as in the
following diverse groups: (1) the German-American League
for Culture, founded in 1935;[18] (2) the American Guild for
German Cultural Freedom, 1936;[19] (3) the German Academy
of Arts and Sciences in Exile, 1936;[20] (4) the Protective
Association of German Writers--originally the Schutzverband

Deutscher Schriftsteller--reestablished in New York in 1938 and subsequently affiliated with the American P.E.N. Club as the German-American Writers' Association;[21] (5) the Emergency Rescue Committee, particularly active after the invasion of France in mid-1940 and credited with saving about 100 Germans from the Gestapo;[22] (6) the Exiled Writers' Committee, another active rescue organization, but of different political hue;[23] and (7) the University in Exile of the New School for Social Research in New York.[24]

An excellent point on the subject of involvement was made by the editors of the lucid periodical *Twice A Year*. They observed that the person who requires freedom to exist, such as the artist, is not justified in simply accepting this vital condition without participating in its maintenance: he "cannot fail to take responsibility for creating and preserving for all [persons] that freedom without which he cannot himself function--and which must exist beyond national boundaries."[25]

One of the most significant areas of exile activity proved to be that of the various writers' congresses and conferences held throughout the world between 1933 and 1943. This is true for several reasons, including the fact that the staging of these meetings created a focus upon which news coverage could be concentrated, thus providing a valuable source of publicity for the activities of writers and intellectuals. The seventeen congresses of those years brought together at different times such diverse exiles as Becher, Brecht, Bredel, Feuchtwanger, Leonhard Frank, Herzfelde, Kantorowicz, Kisch, Ludwig, the Manns--Erika, Heinrich, Klaus, and Thomas--Ludwig Marcuse, Münzenberg, Plievier, Regler, Renn, Seghers, Toller, Uhse, Werfel, Friedrich Wolf, Arnold Zweig, and Stefan Zweig. The reception in the press and by American intellectuals of congresses and writers provided a sort of emotional barometer for the prevailing political mood at any given time.

Four writers' organizations ranging in orientation from basically nonpartisan to militantly activist sponsored these events. In the first division belongs the International P.E.N. Club, the least politically oriented of the four; the other three were the Union of Soviet Authors, the League of American Writers, and the International Association of Writers for the Defense of Culture. A logical assumption, therefore, would be that a fairly predictable correlation existed first, between the attendance of certain exiled German writers at particular congresses and their political leanings, and second, between the coverage by specific publications of certain events and the political bias of the publications in question. Such a correlation was frequently present, especially in regard to the first point. For instance, the political idealism and/or liberal, socialist, or Communist orientation of German writers such as Becher, Bredel, Herzfelde, Plievier, Toller, Graf, Klaus Mann, and Friedrich Wolf undoubtedly was an impetus for their participation in the First All-Union Congress of Soviet Authors held in Moscow in August and September of 1934.

In his history of German exiled writers, *Exil und Literatur*, Matthias Wegner explains their participation as follows: "The uncertainty about the victory of the western democratic nations over Hitler, the desire for political engagement of literature in the struggle against fascism, the might of the Soviet Union--all these factors must have favored an increasing attraction to communism."[26] It is perhaps indicative of the early flush of revolutionary fever in the United States that no less than nine articles, letters, and editorials dealing with this congress appeared in the *New York Times* alone, and that such varied journals as the *New Republic*, the *Living Age*, *New Masses*, and *International Literature*[27] published articles dealing with the event. Unfortunately, however, relatively scant attention was paid by these publications to the many Germans involved.[28]

Possibly the first really significant gathering insofar as the German exiled writers were concerned was the First International Congress for the Defense of Culture, meeting in Paris during the week of 21 June 1935 under the auspices of the Schutzverband Deutscher Schriftsteller,[29] a liberally oriented organization founded in 1908 that had dissolved and been reestablished in Paris in 1933 when the National Socialists came to power; among its new founders were Alfred Kantorowicz, Alfred Kurella, Rudolf Leonhard, Ludwig Marcuse, Gustav Regler, Max Schröder, and Anna Seghers. Of the many German émigré writers participating in the conference, some were already based in Paris (Kisch, Regler, Uhse), and numerous others were residing at least in France (Feuchtwanger, Kantorowicz, Alfred Kerr, Leonhard, Heinrich Mann, Marchwitza, Marcuse, and Seghers). The aim of the meeting was to discuss the contemporary literary and political situation and so contribute to a clarification of the objectives and methods involved in the defense of intellectual freedom. Many members of the Schutzverband belonged also to the Communist party, and the majority, of course, were already in exile.

Despite the impressive display of unity by European writers at this event,[30] American press coverage--particularly of the Germans' role in it--was again relatively meager, both quantitatively and qualitatively: not one reference was listed in the *New York Times Index*; only two appeared in the *New Republic*, one of which was a letter urging attendance by Americans, signed by the American Organizing Committee of the Congress--itself composed of members of the League of American Writers; and one article each was published by the *Living Age*, the *Saturday Review*, the *Partisan Review*, and the English-language edition of *International Literature*. The coverage of the congress by these periodicals tended to concentrate either on the role of the Soviet delegates or on the international tone of the event, with emphasis on the British and French delegations. Of course, liberal or Marxist representatives of these three national groups--for example, Ilya Ehrenburg, Aldous Huxley, E. M. Forster, John Strachey, André Gide, André Malraux, Romain Rolland--were better known in the United States of this time than were most of the German Marxist exiles in attendance, and speeches by Marxists comprised the greater portion of German representation.[31]   In addition, a case might be made for somewhat chauvinistic press coverage, based on the observation that both authors of the articles in the *Living Age* and the *Saturday Review* were members of the seven-man British contingent.[32]

It seems apparent that the liberal American press had not yet beaten a path to the door of the exile cause. A further possible explanation for the meager press coverage might be that, although some 250 writers representing thirty-eight countries attended, the most important official American speakers numbered only two: Waldo Frank, president of the leftist League of American Writers, and Michael Gold, an active Marxist who had been elected to the executive committee of the League at its inception during the First American Writers' Congress several months earlier. Perhaps the strong left-wing coloration of the Paris congress, as well as American preoccupation in 1935 with matters of immediate internal economic and social consequence, were additional factors in the lack of coverage.[33]

In general, the amount of coverage granted by the liberal American press during the first five years of the European struggle not only to the writers' congresses but also to the situation of the German exiled writers was fairly sporadic compared with that extended them as the thirties drew to a close and events in Europe impinged more strongly on the American consciousness: by the end of the decade the fascist threat had approached too close to be ignored. This in turn seemed to inspire closer interest in these congresses and in the writers as symbols of antifascism. In the early and mid-thirties, fascism, although considered a despicable phenomenon, was still too remote and abstract to be perceived emotionally, particularly by the majority of traditionally isolationist Americans.

Of course, certain other events seemed to elicit early flurries of press activity: for example, the infamous book burnings of May 1933;[34] the so-called "retirement," also in May, of well-known writers from the illustrious Prussian Academy of Arts;[35] and the publication on 25 August 1933 of the first of various denationalization lists of prominent Germans.[36]   No doubt the events of May contributed significantly to the greater interest shown by the press in the highly dramatic P.E.N. Club Congress held at Ragusa, Yugoslavia, several months after Hitler had assumed power.[37] It may be said with some certainty that only this congress and the Soviet Writers' Congress of 1934 received more than cursory treatment in the press during the early years of the National Socialist regime.

Not until after the annexation of Austria in March 1938 did the activities of the exiles strongly begin to attract the limelight in the United States. This was due partially to the greater rapidity with which "safety lands" available to the exiles started disappearing at this time: one year after Austria came the seizure of Czechoslovakia, closely followed by the "attachment" or invasion of Poland, France, Denmark, Norway, Holland, and Belgium; by mid-1940 hardly a country in Central Europe was untouched by the Nazi plague. The North American continent thus replaced Europe as an available exile haven. In fact, as early as the beginning of 1938, New York had become the most important center for the exiled German intelligentsia. According to Klaus Mann, "the more critical the situation in Europe became, the more the exiles, the famous as well as the less famous, pressed toward America."[38]

A rather notable secondary development occurred shortly after the annexation of Austria. This was the world-wide revival of interest in the books of exiled German authors. Despite the elimination of Austria as a primary outlet for books published in German, there was reported an almost immediate and increased demand for books of German writers by the ten publishing houses in Holland, Switzerland, and Czechoslovakia that handled, among others, the works of Einstein, Feuchtwanger, Thomas Mann, Remarque, and Stefan Zweig. Writing in reference to the results feared from the Austrian seizure, Heinz Liepmann stated: "But suddenly a curious reaction occurred. The civilized world protested in its own way against a further curtailment of the publication of books by liberal German authors . . . ."[39] Liepmann illustrated his point with the following statistics: between August 1937 and August 1938, sixty-one books were published by these houses, of which 241 translations were made. By contrast, the *Börsenblatt für den deutschen Buchhandel*, the official publishers' organ in Germany, reported that 331 translations of some 2,031 literary works were to be made for outside distribution during the same period.[40] These ratios speak for themselves.

Press interest in two significant writers' congresses held within one month of each other in mid-1939, the World Congress of Writers and the Congress of the League of American Writers, seems to reflect clearly the effect of Hitler's increasingly aggressive foreign policy on American public opinion. For example, the sheer quantity of articles on the World Congress of Writers, held at the New York World's Fair under the auspices of the American Center of the International P.E.N. Club during the second week of May, was unparalleled for any such prior event, including the 1933 P.E.N. Congress. Eight articles in the *New York Times* alone--some of them very lengthy--as well as articles and editorials in the *Publishers' Weekly*, the *Saturday Review*, the *New Republic*, *Twice A Year*, *Time*, and even the *Commonweal*, dealt in considerable detail with the 1939 Congress and the participating German writers. A further distinguishing feature of that event was the strikingly greater degree of political awareness shown by the P.E.N. Club, which until about that time had been known in more liberally oriented literary circles as a fairly uncommitted group that in general had seemed unable to make a decision for strong political involvement in any cause.

It is certainly possible that the handing over of Czechoslovakia to Hitler via the infamous Munich Agreement in September 1938 by Chamberlain of Britain and Daladier of France as well as the increased Nazi persecution of the Jews in November 1938 may have thrust the truth of Hitler's intentions upon the consciousness of greater numbers of Americans, even before these aims became crystallized in the actual seizures of countries not yet under the control of the National Socialists. For although Britain and France did not declare war on Germany until nearly four months after the P.E.N. Congress, the handwriting on the wall was visible for those with the eyes and the will to read it.

Over thirty countries were represented among the writers in attendance at the World Congress of Writers, and not surprisingly, far more German exiles were present than at any P.E.N. conference held since Hitler's assumption of power. For example, the speakers at the first of the four sessions, whose topic was "How Can Culture Survive Exile?," included Ferdinand Bruckner, Annette Kolb, Klaus Mann, Ernst Toller, and Arnold Zweig; and speakers at subsequent sessions and related private functions were Alfred Döblin, Erika Mann, Thomas Mann, Erich Maria Remarque, Franz Werfel, and Carl Zuckmayer.[41] The list of prominent literati from at least twenty-nine other nations reads like an international *Who's Who*: Sholem Asch, Max Ascoli, Raoul Auernheimer, Giuseppe A. Borgese, Pearl Buck, Henry Seidel Canby, André Maurois, Karin Michaelis, Jules Romains, Ignazio Silone, Hendrik Willem van Loon, Lin Yutang. The basic theme of the congress was the very timely one of the position of writers in the world crisis and methods of securing the liberties essential to literary creation, and the topics of the other official sessions reflected this concern. In addition to the question of culture and exile, the following subjects were treated: "The Writer's Responsibility for the Crisis of Today and the World of Tomorrow," "The Ivory Tower or the Soap Box?," and "Writing Contemporary History."[42]

In his welcoming speech to the delegates at the opening session, International P.E.N. Club President Jules Romains struck the tone that was to dominate the conference with his declaration that ". . . those who wield the pen must abandon any neutrality toward the world's affairs and take strides against those who wield the sword in the present world conflict of nations and ideas."[43] He continued on this note throughout his address, pointing out the responsibility of all writers to ". . . call the . . . attention [of each member of the public] to the unprecedented perils which today assail civilization, peace, liberty and the dignity of the human person."[44] Dorothy Thompson, president of the American P.E.N. Center, developed the international theme further and rather more graphically by noting: "Never, in the memory of any one in this hall, have so many of our guild been men without a country. . . . [or] been in prison or in exile. For in much of the world today the word itself has been made captive. It walks in chains. Those who would free it do so at the risk of their own lives." Her observation, "Some who have taken that risk are here among us, and we welcome them,"[45] was a clear acknowledgment of the numerous exiled authors in attendance.

In general, the consensus of the press seemed to be that the P.E.N. Club had at last come of age by maturing into an organ humanely and passionately committed to the ideals of liberty and freedom in an inhumane world of militarism, power plays, and repressive state control. As the *New Republic* declared in a brief editorial summarizing the conference:

> The meeting was under the general guidance of "P.E.N.," which is usually regarded as a mildly right-wing group and which has tried for years to keep out of politics. But in one country after another, politics have caught up with its members, dozens of whom have been sent to concentration camps or forced into exile. The tone of the speeches at the recent congress was such that they would have been called decidedly Leftist only a couple of years ago. Democracy was applauded, fascism denounced and creative workers in the arts were called upon to play their part in rescuing the world from the darkness that threatens it.[46]

The third biennial Congress of the League of American Writers, held in New York during the first weekend of June 1939, also received considerable press coverage, and although the reports were not so much greater quantitatively than they had been for the two previous congresses in 1935 and 1937, they evinced a much broader awareness of the exiled European writers than ever before. For instance, the speeches of various exiles were printed in their entirety,[47] and one of the topics of a major session was "Writers in Exile," a subject that appeared to indicate a basic and perhaps official acceptance of the reality of that situation by American intellectuals. In fact, the first two sentences of the official "Call" to the congress illustrated a decided recognition of the exile condition as an unhappy consequence of the spread of ideological oppression: "In the last two years, writers in other countries have sacrificed their lives and suffered exile and imprisonment. They have proved that the preservation of every form of culture is inseparable from the struggle of the people everywhere against those forces that seek the death of liberty in our time."[48] Press coverage of this conference was found in the following sources: *Direction*, *International Literature* (English edition), the *New Republic*, the *Saturday Review*, *Twice A Year*, the *New York Times*, and the *American Mercury*. Some periodicals, notably the *New Republic* and the *Saturday Review*, carried more than one article or editorial.

As of 1938–39, the American press showed a heightened interest in exile issues and problems. Certain publications devoted entire issues to exiled German and European writers and artists: *Direction* in December 1939, *Twice A Year* in its double issue of 1939–40, the *Saturday Review* in October 1940, and *Decision* in October 1941.[49] Nor was exile merely a short-lived journalistic curiosity, for concurrent happenings such as benefits in the forms of manuscript sales and dinners were not only publicized by the press, but were on occasion actively sponsored by members of the press and various cultural organizations. A partial list of such activities would include auctions of manuscripts and books sponsored by the League of American Writers in February 1939 and January 1940; a dinner sponsored by the Committee of Publishers in October 1940 that raised $15,000 to rescue some twenty writers still in Europe and sought by the Gestapo (responsibility for applying the funds was delegated to the Exiled Writers' Committee of the League of American Writers); and a reception held by the American P.E.N. Club in October 1940 to raise money for stranded Europeans as well as for needy Europeans already in the United States.

A further indication of interest in the exile cause on the part of the press was the increased frequency with which essays and reports dealing specifically with the concept of exile and its related aspects appeared as of 1938-39. Included in this category were articles not only by Americans in the *Literary Digest*, the *Nation*, the *New York Times*, and the *New Republic*, but also by Germans (Ernst Bloch, Wieland Herzfelde, and Ludwig Renn, among others) in such publications as *Anti-Nazi News*, the *Living Age*, the *New Republic*, the *New York Times*, and the *Saturday Review*.

One other factor deserving mention as a barometer of interest is the large variety of reviews appearing in the American press that treated works by German writers. A cursory glance at the *New York Times Index* alone for the years in question provides ample substantiation of this assertion. Periodicals that consistently published reviews of exiles' books would include the *Nation*, the *New Republic*, and the *Saturday Review*; numerous other journals and magazines presented at least occasional discussions of such works.

Between 1933 and 1945 it is possible to distinguish three phases of what we shall label "exile consciousness" by the American press; these may be divided chronologically. As has been indicated, the early period encompassed approximately the first five years of National Socialist rule and was given its most spectacular impetus by the flames of 10 May 1933, which heralded the start of an insane and world-wide fury. The middle phase, impelled by the events of March 1938 and underscored by the increasing exodus from Europe, fell predominantly into the years 1938 to 1940.

The final period of exile consciousness existed from approximately 1941 to 1945 and differed in several vital respects from the two previous phases. No doubt active American participation in the European and Asian conflicts was a factor in the changed orientation. Eventually, when the conquest of Germany seemed inevitable to many, the question of reconstruction prompted numerous analyses of the German "soul" and "national character" in the writings of intellectuals and others who wondered about the future of the country and how the nightmare that was Hitler could be prevented from recurring.[50] The stormy conflict between proponents of quite disparate views of Germany was succinctly summarized in the editorial introduction to an amazing document written by Ernst Toller and published on the fifth anniversary of that playwright's death: "The anniversary of Toller's death finds a controversy raging between those who have faith in the structure of a democratic postwar Germany and others who regard such ideas as dangerous illusions."[51]

For example, in 1943 the liberal *New Republic* had published an editorial criticizing the German people en masse for their lack of effective opposition to Hitler and his minions.[52] This editorial was not an isolated instance. Nor were the effects of the controversy over Germany limited to Germans within the Third Reich, for gradually an almost fundamental distrust of the German "spirit" developed that seemed to color rather indiscriminately the American attitude toward the concept "German." This did not bode well for a constructive view of the future Germany or for American reaction to the German exiles. The human tendency to generalize occasionally swept these men and women, expatriates though they were, into a fold of increasing national hostility. Near the end of 1942, the American P.E.N. Center had held a dinner meeting at which publisher Clifton Fadiman spoke on Germany and included some negative comments on the dangerous aspects of the German "national character." According to Norman Cousins, chief editor of the *Saturday Review* , whose letter of rebuttal and warning was published on the following day, Fadiman, although setting off ". . . the biggest forensic explosion the P.E.N. Club . . . ever felt . . . [and thus bringing] more life to the P.E.N. than it [had seen] in years . . . unwittingly and unintentionally played into the hands of a school of thought that [seemed] to be gaining ground in the last few months [and that represented] a great potential danger."[53]

It is obvious that the greater number of writers banished from the Third Reich underwent long, arduous periods of suffering and difficulty. Although press interest served to some extent to illuminate and to mitigate their plight, it could not entirely alleviate it. For the uniquely individual nature of the writer as an artist and the position thrust upon him by the perceptions arising from a creative imagination are not easily reconciled with organized efforts, no matter how well intentioned. The condition of exile imposed extreme difficulties upon the German writers cast out from the land that had borne and nurtured their creativity. Far more traumatic than the physical hardships they endured was the emotional and psychic deprivation they suffered, caused not only by enforced alienation from a once-loved native land, but also by the tremendous problems encountered when they were driven into countries whose language was an unfamiliar creative vehicle and whose alien cultures established subtle psychological barriers.

In summary, a notable trend in the involvement of the liberal American press on the "exile scene" seems to

have been a decreasingly revolutionary orientation: the interest of such radical publications as *Anti-Nazi News*, *New
Masses*, and *Partisan Review* in the exile cause had by the
late thirties been replaced by that of less extreme and more
"respectable" publications such as *Direction* , the *Living
Age*, the *Nation*, the *New Republic*, the *Publishers'
Weekly*, the *Saturday Review*, and *Twice A Year*. This
trend may have been connected with the more general public
disfavor into which communism fell as the Depression deepened and the fortunes of fascism rose. A decline in an
interested readership large enough to support many left-wing
journals may have been a factor, due in part to the disen-
chantment with the tenets of communism felt by numerous
formerly sympathetic intellectuals, and in part to the desire
of the public for quantitatively and qualitatively more pro-
American orientation in its journalism. Moreover, many of
the exiled Germans who appeared later in the United States
did not hold the extreme political convictions of their earlier
counterparts, thus making their plight more palatable to
Americans on the whole. Whereas left-wing periodicals would
not be particularly interested in these Germans, moderate
publications saw in them an opportunity to enhance their
journalistic status by appealing to the traditional American
sympathy for the underdog and admiration for the heroic
idealist. Generally, it may be observed that from about
1938 on, interest in the German exiled writers and their
activities became the almost exclusive domain of the less
radical segments of the liberal press, reflecting the corresponding political modifications occurring on the American
scene and supplanting the representatives of leftist ideology
of the earlier nineteen-thirties.

Notes

[1]That exiled writers were recognized to be political
refugees was indicated in a resolution adopted by the
Authors' League of America, Inc., and addressed to the
State and Labor Departments of the United States government
as early as May 1933, even prior to the book burnings of
10 May of that year. The relevant statement read as follows: "Resolved, That the council of the Authors' League of
America request the State Department and the Department of
Labor to take whatever steps may be necessary to permit
German authors who so desire to come to America as political refugees." "Aid to Germans Urged: Authors League Wants
Writers Admitted as Refugees Here," *New York Times*, 3 May
1933, sec. 1, p. 11. The League was an organization of
somewhat moderate political leanings, representing about
2,000 American writers. A further reference to cultural
exiles as refugees was made some months later in an ada-
mant appeal published by the *Christian Century*, which
called itself "An Undenominational Journal of Religion":
"Maintain the American Tradition!" (Editorial), *Christian
Century*, 50 (6 Sept. 1933), 1099.

[2]"Editorial Comment," *New Masses*, 14 (19 Feb. 1935), 4.

[3]"Would Bar Refugees: Legion Head Opposes Immigration under Present Conditions," *New York Times*, 5 Dec. 1938, sec. 1, p. 10.

[4]"Persecuting the Refugee" (Editorial), *New Republic*, 105 (18 Aug. 1941), 208.

[5]"The Shape of Things" (Editorial), *Nation*, 153 (5 July 1941), 3.

[6]One of the most informative articles on the subject of support for refugees was published early in 1941 and took note of work being done by various independent organizations to aid Jews, Catholics, and antifascists *per se*. An appended list of thirty-four principal American refugee-aid groups, their addresses, and their functions included the following: American Friends' Service Committee, *Aufbau* (the German-language periodical edited by Manfred George and based in New York, which numbered among its activities an employment agency that placed about 150 refugees a month), Emergency Rescue Committee, Exiled Writers' Committee, International Relief Association, Salvation Army, and Unitarian Service Committee. See Albert Horlings, "Who Aids the Refugee?" *New Republic*, 104 (13 Jan. 1941), 43-46. See also Herbert A. Strauss and Leonard P. Liggio, "Einwanderung und Radikalismus in der politischen Kultur der Vereinigten Staaten von Amerika," in *Deutsche Exilliteratur seit 1933*, Band I: *Kalifornien*, ed. John M. Spalek and Joseph Strelka (Bern: Francke, 1976), pp. 168-94.

[7]As *New Theatre* announced in one of its early editorials: ". . . the slogan, 'Art is a weapon in the class struggle,' has penetrated the broadest strata of worker-artists the world over . . .," *New Theatre*, 1 (Sept. 1934), 3.

[8]Ibid. A similar although less sensationalistic observation was published in the initial issue of the sleek radical journal *Partisan Review*. Presenting their aims, the editors stated: "We propose to concentrate on creative and critical literature, but we shall maintain a definite viewpoint-- that of the revolutionary working class. Through our specific literary medium we shall participate in the struggle of the workers and sincere intellectuals against imperialist war, fascism, national and racial oppression, and for the abolition of the system which breeds these evils." "Editorial Statement," *Partisan Review*, 1 (Feb./March 1934), 2.

[9]John Gassner, "Politics and Theatre" (Foreword), in Morgan Himelstein, *Drama Was a Weapon: The Left-Wing Theatre in New York 1929-1941* (New Brunswick, N.J.: Rutgers University Press, 1963), p. xi.

[10]The following examples may be cited in this regard: the New York-based Non-Sectarian Anti-Nazi League to Champion Human Rights, established in 1934; the Hollywood Anti-Nazi League for the Defense of American Democracy, established in 1936; and the National Committee on Justice for Victims of Nazism. Asserting that the anti-Nazi leagues of America were basically Communist-front groups, Senator Jack Tenney, a militant anti-Communist who headed the Fact-

Finding Committee on Un-American Activities of the California Legislature during the mid-forties, stated that "Anti-Nazi Leagues flourished in the United States[,] and the Anti-Nazi League of Hollywood grew to considerable proportions. The comrades in America and California exploited to the fullest the growing horror in the minds of all Americans of the brutality rampant in Hitler's Third Reich." Jack B. Tenney, *Red Fascism: Boring from Within . . . by the Subversive Forces of Communism: An Exposé and Manual of Communist Strategy* (Los Angeles, Calif.: Federal Printing Co., 1947), p. 75.

[11]He published two rather incisive studies: *Stalin's Russia and the Crisis in Socialism* (New York: W. W. Norton & Co., 1940) and *Marxism: Is It Science?* (New York: W. W. Norton & Co., 1941). An informative article on Eastman was written by Edmund Wilson: "Max Eastman in 1941,' *New Republic*, 104 (10 Feb. 1941), 173-76.

[12]Eastman declared: "Almost every one of [these 100] represents the drawing into the . . . network of hundreds of prominent Americans, and the use of their names and money for causes they actually despise." Max Eastman, "Stalin's American Power," *American Mercury*, 53 (Dec. 1941), 671-80; here: p. 678.

[13]The Committee evolved into the League Against War and Fascism in 1934, when Hitler was seen as a threat; into the American League for Peace and Democracy in 1936, when indignation arose against the Stalin purges; into the American Peace Mobilization in 1939, after the Hitler-Stalin Pact of August; and into the American People's Mobilization in 1941, when the Nazis attacked Russia.

[14]"This Quarter" (Editorial), *Partisan Review*, 6 (Fall 1938), 8.

[15]Himelstein, p. 3.

[16]Malcolm Cowley, "Art Tomorrow," *New Republic*, 79 (23 May 1934), 34-36.

[17]See Martin Gumpert, "Exiled Writers and America," *Publishers' Weekly*, 140 (4 Oct. 1941), 1376-79. This article was a condensation of the chapter "Writer and Exile" from Gumpert's book *First Papers*, trans. Heinz and Ruth Norden (New York: Duell, Sloane and Pearce, 1941). See also Erika and Klaus Mann, who in their book, *Escape to Life*, clarified their aim as having been: "To demonstrate and describe in a graphic manner not individual persons banished . . . but rather an entire complex culture--the true German culture that has at all times been a creative part of world culture--now the victim of Nazi fanaticism." Erika and Klaus Mann, *Escape to Life* (Boston: Houghton Mifflin Co.; Cambridge, Mass.: The Riverside Press, 1939), p. viii.

[18]The League was a progressive organization with national headquarters in Chicago, more than twenty local chapters, and ". . . over 120,000 members through its affiliated clubs, organizations, singing societies, *Turners* and youth groups." Hans Meyer, "New Blood for American Democracy," *Direction*, 2 (Dec. 1939), 28. Headed by the historian and union leader Otto Sattler, it was probably the

largest and certainly one of the most active and militant of the anti-Nazi groups, distributing literature, issuing statements, and organizing and participating in public demonstrations. See Walter Mueller, "Report on the German-American League for Culture," *Direction*, 2 (Dec. 1939), 29.

[19]According to its founder and guiding light, Prince Hubertus zu Löwenstein, the Guild was dedicated to ". . . keeping the German language alive in exile [by means of] Scholarships, printing guarantees, subsidies and any other means of intellectual or material promotion." Löwenstein, *Towards the Further Shore* (London: Victor Gollancz, Ltd., 1968), p. 176. It also arranged lecture tours, sent representatives to congresses, and in general ". . . strengthen[ed] the contact between the German exiles and the world public" (Erika and Klaus Mann, *Escape to Life*, p. 316). American leaders in the Guild included Governor Wilbur F. Cross of Connecticut, Senator Robert F. Wagner, Dr. Alvin Johnson of the New School for Social Research, Dr. Robert M. Hutchins of the University of Chicago, Dr. Frank Kingdon, and Henry Seidel Canby of the *Saturday Review*. Well-known exiled members included Thomas Mann, Lion Feuchtwanger, Alfred Neumann, Fritz von Unruh, Franz Werfel, and Otto Klemperer. See "This Week," *New Republic*, 91 (26 May 1937), 58. See Löwenstein, pp. 179-80, for a more comprehensive list of German members, including Hermann Broch, Alfred Döblin, Sigmund Freud, Erwin Piscator, and Paul Tillich. Manfred George, editor of *Aufbau*, also discussed the Guild in his article, "German-Americans vs. Nazi Propaganda," *Direction*, 2 (July/Aug. 1939), 6-7. In addition, specific details regarding the activities of the Guild are to be found in at least ten articles in the *New York Times* between 1937 and 1940.

[20]Löwenstein states that he had established the Academy concurrently with the Guild and ". . . had the [Academy] entrusted with the functions of what was called the 'European Senate' of the Guild" (*Towards the Further Shore*, p. 177). The president of the Division of Arts and Letters was Thomas Mann, and Sigmund Freud headed the Sciences Division. In the words of Dr. Volkmar von Zühlsdorf, assistant secretary of the Guild, the Academy provided ". . . some temporary community, a visible centre of gravity [for the] . . . emigrated authors, artists and scholars . . . ." (ibid.). In reality, then, the Academy was not truly autonomous, but was rather the European branch of the Guild, and most of the American and European members and sponsors were associated with both groups, working in conjunction with one another on such projects as writers' contests and the publication of books by German exiled writers. See Löwenstein, pp. 177-78; also "This Week," *New Republic*, 88 (26 Aug. 1936), 60.

[21]As the Nazis increased their European conquests, the Schutzverband established branches in Prague, Brussels, Copenhagen, and England, and in 1938 moved to the United States as the Schutzverband Deutsch-Amerikanischer Schriftsteller; its first president was Oskar Maria Graf, and its vice-president was Ferdinand Bruckner. Thomas Mann was

honorary president.   The Association represented about 150
writers and was very active in New York City; it cooperated
with colleges and cultural organizations as well as with
the German-American League for Culture in arranging varied
events and programs in the fields of literature, art, music,
and science.   Another area of concentration was the provi-
sion of aid to German, Austrian, and Czech nationals interned in France; the Association had "established a connection with French authorities in order to work for [their
release] . . . ."   See "Cultural Front" (Column), *Direction*,
2 (Dec. 1939), 30.   A third area was the instruction of German and German history in American high schools and colleges, for which a special school committee was created.   See
Manfred George, "German-Americans vs. Nazi Propaganda,"
p. 6.

[22] The Emergency Rescue Committee was headed by Dr.
Frank Kingdon, former president of Newark University, and
included the following Americans on its executive board:
Dorothy Thompson, Dr. Robert M. Hutchins, and radio commentators Elmer Davis and Raymond Gram Swing.   According
to *Newsweek*, the E.R.C. worked "in cooperation with the
State Department."   See "Saving Writers from Hitler," *Newsweek*, 16 (28 Oct. 1940), 53.   Its chief aim was to faci-
litate the rescue of antifascist Germans and nationals of
Nazi-occupied countries--in particular well-known individuals.
The magazine noted that in addition to having "saved more
than a hundred persons from the Nazis [to date, the group
had] information on the whereabouts of some 500 more and
promise[d] to keep on with the salvage work as long as
possible" (p. 54).   See also Wolfgang D. Elfe, "Das Emergency Rescue Committee," in *Deutsche Exilliteratur seit
1933*, Band I: *Kalifornien*, ed. John M. Spalek and Joseph
Strelka (Bern: Francke, 1976), 214-19.

[23] The Exiled Writers' Committee was another well-
publicized group devoted to the rescue of stranded exiles in
unfriendly territory.   It differed from the E.R.C. in its
organizational and political affiliations, that is, with the
leftist League of American Writers, through whose efforts it
had been founded.   The American liberal writer Dashiell
Hammett was chairman of the Committee and in June 1941 was
also elected president of the League itself.   According to
one source, the Committee ". . . [had] been instrumental
in bringing more than sixty anti-Nazi authors to this continent."   S. J. K., "The Roving Eye" (Column), *Wilson
Library Bulletin*, 16 (June 1942), 847.   However, some
twenty-five of this group were still financially dependent
on the Committee, among them Egon Erwin Kisch, Ludwig
Renn, Anna Seghers, and Paul Westheim (ibid.).   That the
League of American Writers should establish a rescue organization for its European colleagues is not surprising, because
its ideological orientation was so strongly opposed to that
of fascism, particularly as embodied in Hitler's brand of
totalitarianism.   As left-wing author Albert Maltz asserted
in his keynote speech regarding the position taken by the
League's fourth congress on the issue of war and peace,

"The defense of culture, yesterday a matter of Europe, is today the burning problem of American life." Maltz, "4th Annual Congress," *Direction*, 4 (Summer 1941), 2-3. For an interesting discussion of the antipathy between the E.R.C. and the Exiled Writers' Committee, as well as of the machinations employed by each to garner publicity for its work while subtly blackening the reputation of its counterpart, see "Exiles" (Books), *Time*, 36, No. 20 (11 Nov. 1940), 80.

[24]The New School itself was a liberally oriented institute founded in 1919 and dedicated to the study of sociological and political problems. Instrumental in aiding hundreds of exiled antifascist writers, intellectuals, and artists, it not only provided a forum for their theories and ideas via lectures and speeches, but made available as well teaching positions for some at its University in Exile--its Graduate Faculty of Political and Social Science--which was composed of exiles such as Arnold Brecht, Emil Lederer, Jacob Marschak, Kurt Rietzler, Hans Staudinger, Leo Strauss, and Max Wertheimer. Other well-known exiles who worked at the New School were Erich von Kahler, who was professor of history and the philosophy of history in 1941-42, Carl Zuckmayer, who taught in Erwin Piscator's Dramatic Workshop in 1940, and Hermann Broch, who conducted studies in mass psychology there between 1942 and 1944. For a fairly comprehensive discussion of the New School and the University in Exile, see Joachim Radkau, *Die deutsche Emigration in den U.S.A.: Ihr Einfluss auf die amerikanische Europapolitik 1933-1945*, Studien zur modernen Geschichte, 2 (Düsseldorf: Bertelsmann Universitätsverlag, 1971). See also Charles Scott Lachman, "The University in Exile," B.A. Honors Thesis Amherst College, 1973.

[25]Editors' Statement, *Twice A Year*, 10-11 (Spring/Summer 1943, Fall/Winter 1943), 13.

[26]Translated from: Matthias Wegner, *Exil und Literatur: Deutsche Schriftsteller im Ausland 1933-1945* (Frankfurt/M: Athenäum, 1967), p. 135.

[27]*International Literature* was the English language edition of the Communist journal *Internationale Literatur*, the chief organ of the International Association of Revolutionary Writers. It was also published in Russian, French, and Chinese. Left-wing writer Johannes R. Becher, who had been denationalized in March 1934, was the editor in chief of the German edition for ten years, 1935-45. After the dissolution of the I.A.R.W. in 1935, however, the contributors to the German edition included non-Communists. The individual national editions of this journal differed strongly from one another.

[28]The only periodical that devoted more than cursory attention to the Germans participating in the Moscow Congress was *Neue Deutsche Blätter: Monatsschrift für Literatur und Kritik*. This Communist-oriented exile journal appeared in Prague from September 1933 to August 1935 under the editorship of Wieland Herzfelde. In its first anniversary issue of September 1934, pp. 713-53, were printed numerous speeches presented in Moscow; this proved to be the best

total coverage that I was able to find of the event. Another exile periodical granting some space to the activities there was *Die Sammlung*, 2 (Oct. 1934), whose publication life was identical to that of *NDB* and whose editors and sponsors included Klaus Mann, André Gide, Aldous Huxley, and Heinrich Mann. Of the American press, the *New York Times* provided the most comprehensive information on general events, although it did not print speeches in any detail.

29 For a good if understandably biased review of the background and activities of the Schutzverband, see Alfred Kantorowicz's article, "Fünf Jahre Schutzverband Deutscher Schriftsteller im Exil," *Das Wort*, 3 (Dec. 1938), 60–76.

30 Several additional factors contributed to the unity of the Schutzverband Deutscher Schriftsteller. The first was the establishment in Paris of the Deutsche Freiheitsbibliothek on 10 May 1934, the first anniversary of the book burnings, its purpose being to collect and make publicly available through an International Antifascist Archive all those books burned, forbidden, and otherwise defamed by the Third Reich. Headed by a steering committee composed of prominent French, British, and German personalities including André Gide, Romain Rolland, H. G. Wells, Lion Feuchtwanger, and Heinrich Mann, it drew such international support that, according to Kantorowicz, even the Nazi press was forced to react, thus informing all antifascist sympathizers in Germany ". . . that we were living and working effectively" (Kantorowicz, "Fünf Jahre Schutzverband," p. 65). From now on the SDS and the Bibliothek cooperated closely on all questions and actions concerning the ". . . militant . . . intellectual . . . emigration" (ibid.). A second unifying factor was the participation by many SDS members in the Moscow Writers' Congress of 1934, which further strengthened the ideological unity of the organization.

31 In his fairly objective article on the congress, Malcolm Cowley--who also contributed on occasion to *New Masses* and who had been one of the signers of the "Call for an American Writers' Congress" issued some months earlier-- did mention that the German delegation was "entirely composed of exiles." Although not specifying any points made by the Germans in their addresses, he did include the exile delegation among those three that he considered "especially brilliant," the other two being the French and the Soviet groups. Cowley, "The Writers' International," *New Republic*, 88 (31 July 1935), 339.

32 E. M. Forster, "Writers in Paris," *Living Age*, 349 (Sept. 1935), 63–65. This article had been published originally in the *New Statesman and Nation*, an independent leftist weekly in London. The other reporter-delegate was Amabel Williams-Ellis, who wrote "A Parliament of Writers," *Saturday Review*, 12 (3 Aug. 1935), 17.

33 By way of contrast, the much greater interest displayed by the *New York Times*, for example, in the similarly revolutionary Moscow congress might be explained as a journalistic venture into the labyrinth of a uniquely significant historical phenomenon. The importance of the Soviet con-

ference lay not only in its being the first held in the USSR since the Revolution, but also in its value as the first manifestation of unity by the recently established Union of Soviet Authors--the previous organization, the Association of Proletarian Writers (R.A.P.P.), which had been much more dogmatic and party-oriented in its official attitude, had expired over two years earlier. See the report of Robert Gessner, one of the United States delegates: "The Funeral of the R.A.P.P.," *New Republic*, 82 (24 April 1935), 307-08.

34 The *New York Times* obviously considered this event important enough to warrant headline exposure on its front page. See "Nazis Pile Books for Bonfires Today; 25,000 Volumes Gathered by Berlin Students--Other Cities to Follow Suit; A New Code for Schools; Dr. Frick Tells the Ministers of Education Present System Is Unfit for Reich," *New York Times*, 10 May 1933, sec. 1, pp. 1, 11. Several related articles were printed in that newspaper on the same day: Frederick T. Birchall, "Propagandist Art Is Nazis' Demand; Goebbels Tells German Stage Leaders Artist Must March at Head Politically; No Art for Art's Sake; Minister Also Thinks the Jews Will Be Eliminated from the Field 'Without Legislation,'" *New York Times*, 10 May 1933, sec. 1, p. 10; also "Helen Keller Warns Germany's Students; Says Burning of Books Cannot Kill Ideas," *New York Times*, 10 May 1933, sec. 1, p. 10. See also "Join Fight on Hitlerism; United Synagogue and Women's League Support Protest," *New York Times*, 10 May 1933, sec. 1, p. 10.

35 See "Prussian Arts Academy Loses Most of Its Noted Members" [Special cable to the *New York Times*], 7 May 1933, sec. 1, p. 13. This was perhaps the earliest step in the Nazification of culture in the Third Reich. Included in this "retirement" were the following illustrious Germans: Alfred Döblin, Ludwig Fulda, Georg Kaiser, Bernhard Kellermann, Thomas Mann, René Schickele, Jakob Wassermann, Franz Werfel, and Fritz von Unruh--Heinrich Mann and Käthe Kollwitz had been forced out as early as 15 February. As the *New York Times* succinctly phrased it, the change was brought about ". . . as a result of the nationally minded reorganization of the literary section of the . . . Academy. . . . [A]lmost the only writers of international reputation left of the old membership are Gerhart Hauptmann and Ricarda Huch. Bernhard Rust, the Prussian Education Minister, promises that reorganization of the composers and graphic arts will come next" (ibid.).

36 One of the number of repressive official measures instituted against potential enemies of the state after the establishment of the Third Reich was a law of 14 July that decreed the National Socialist German Workers' Party to be the only political party in Germany. Enemies of Germany as defined under this law were subject to denationalization and imprisonment and were considered to have no legal status within the state. See Frederick T. Birchill, "Nazis Seize Goods of 33 Foes in Exile; Annul Citizenship; Hitler Decree Proscribes His Most Prominent Enemies for Outspoken Criticism; Scheidemann Is Included; Bernhard, Feuchtwanger

and Heinrich Mann Are Also among Those Affected; List of First of Series; All Whom the Regime Regards as Inimical to Its Interests Are Slated for Ban," *New York Times* , 26 Aug. 1933, sec. 1, pp. 1, 3.

[37] This international congress, held on 25–27 May 1933, in Ragusa (Dubrovnik), was highly charged with emotion for several reasons: (1) the reactions evoked by the standardization and limitation to Nazi requirements of the P.E.N. branch within Germany; (2) the conflict between delegates stimulated by the recent eviction from the German group of such eminent German authors as Lion Feuchtwanger, Emil Ludwig, Thomas Mann, and Erich Maria Remarque. Ernst Toller very audibly attended the congress as a representative of the exiled Germans, and in a sympathetic obituary published shortly after Toller's suicide, *Saturday Review* editor Henry Seidel Canby referred to this conference as having been the "first encounter between the new forces of repression in the . . . Reich and the outside world of artists and intellectuals." "Ernst Toller" (Editorial), *Saturday Review*, 20 (3 June 1939), 8.

[38] Translated from: Klaus Mann, *Der Wendepunkt: Ein Lebensbericht* (Frankfurt/M: S. Fischer, 1952), p. 403. Ten years earlier Mann had published an English-language version of the book: *The Turning Point: Thirty-Five Years in This Century* (New York: L. B. Fischer, 1942). These two books, despite their similar titles, are in reality two different books written for readers of two distinct language cultures. See Mann's explanation of this point in the Afterword of the German work, p. 544.

[39] Heinz Liepmann, "Books by Emigré German Writers: Demand for Exiles' Works Increased at Time of Anschluss," *New York Times Book Review* , 2 Oct. 1938, sec. 6, p. 8.

[40] Ibid.

[41] "World Congress of Writers," *New York Times Book Review* , 30 April 1939, sec. 7, p. 16.

[42] "Writers' Congress at Fair," *Publishers' Weekly*, 135 (29 April 1939), 1607.

[43] "Writers of World Asked to Condemn the 'Mystics of Violence'; Romains Demands End of Neutrality; Tells Writers It Is Time for the Pen to Fight the Sword in World Crisis; 500 at Congress in Fair; Dorothy Thompson and Pearl Buck Address the Delegates from Thirty Countries," *New York Times* , 9 May 1939, sec. 1, p. 18. The *Publishers' Weekly* printed an editorial in praise of Romains's position, concluding with the opinion that the "publisher and the bookseller today can no more withdraw to an ivory tower than the author." Frederic G. Melcher, "'The Time Has Come to Take Sides,'" *Publishers' Weekly*, 135 (13 May 1939), 1749.

[44] "Writers of World Asked to Condemn the 'Mystics of Violence' . . . ," *New York Times*, 9 May 1939, sec. 1, p. 18.

[45] Ibid.

[46] "No More Ivory Tower" ("This Week"), *New Republic*, 99 (24 May 1939), 59.

47 See the "German, Italian and Exile Sections" in the Special Double Number of *Twice A Year*, 3/4 (Fall/Winter 1939, Spring/Summer 1940), 135-49. These pages encompass the speeches given at the General Delegates' Session of the Third American Writers' Congress by Ernst Bloch, G. A. Borgese, Klaus Mann, Thomas Mann, and Bodo Uhse. As the editors state in their "Introductory Note" to this special issue, these speeches, as well as materials by Kahler, Fried, Toller, Chiaromonte, and Roditi were included as samples of attitudes held by ". . . contemporaries who have been not only oppressed by, but have stood out against fascism, oppression and decadence in Europe" (Removable Insert-- no page number).

48 "Call to the Third American Writers' Congress," *Direction* (Special Congress Issue), 2 (May/June 1939), 1. The Call was signed by over seventy American writers, including Van Wyck Brooks, Erskine Caldwell, Malcolm Cowley, Lillian Hellman, Albert Maltz, Dorothy Parker, S. J. Perelman, Edwin Seaver, Irwin Shaw, Upton Sinclair, Irving Stone, Louis Untermeyer, Carl Van Doren, and William Carlos Williams. It is also of interest that several articles by exiled writers and articles concerning aspects of exile activity appeared in this issue: "House for Exiled Writers" by F. Menaker, a "Message from Heinrich Mann," "German American Writers' Association" by Erika Mann and Ferdinand Bruckner, and "The Living Spirit" by Ernst Bloch (pp. 24-29).

49 *Decision* was an exception to the group in that this particular issue was not devoted in toto to German literary exiles. Rather, its editors included in the regular number a "German Anthology" that offered creative and analytical work by Bertolt Brecht, Alexander Moritz Frey, Stefan George, Hermann Kesten, Gustav Regler, and Peter Viereck. In addition, two politically oriented essays were published: "Germany's Role in World Politics" by E.R.C. member Frank Kingdon, and "The German European" by Heinrich Mann.

50 This is illustrated in *The Readers' Guide* for July 1943 to April 1945, to cite one source. Of the approximately thirty-one articles listed under the heading "Germans," about fourteen, or nearly half, dealt with some aspect of the German "spirit" or "condition." Some representative examples are the following: F. W. Foerster, "After the defeat of Nazism, what? German people essentially identical with Hitler and responsible for Hitler"; J. P. Warburg, "Can the Germans cure themselves?"; R. Moley, "Don't call them vandals; it isn't fair to the Vandals"; E. Ranshofen-Wertheimer, "Germans and the German problem"; O. Oppenheimer, "The soul of postwar Germany"; "Are Germans incurable?"; and "Root of German evil." These articles appeared in such moderate and right-of-center periodicals as the *Christian Century*, *Commonweal*, *Newsweek*, and the *New York Times Magazine*.

51 Editorial introduction to Ernst Toller, "Are We Responsible for Our Time? Prophetic Commentaries from the Unpublished Papers of a Literary Giant," *Saturday Review*, 27 (20 May 1944), 5-8. Here: p. 5.

[52]"The Germans and the Nazis" (Editorial), *New Republic*, 108 (4 Jan. 1943), 4.

[53]Norman Cousins, "Open Letter to Clifton Fadiman" (Editorial), *Saturday Review*, 25 (7 Nov. 1942), 10. Cousins felt that this school of thought represented ". . . the idea that all Germans are alike, that there is something in the physiological makeup of the German people that prevents them from living as civilized human beings. . . . According to the same idea, militarism and barbarism are boiling in the blood of every German, and have been boiling there for two thousand years." He pointed out the dangerous parallels between this type of thinking and the racist arguments used by the National Socialists to justify their actions, noting further that "[r]egarding any people as an entity is dangerous" (ibid.).

The Exile's Choice: Brecht and the Soviet Union[1]

John B. Fuegi

> "Actually I have no friends there. And those in Moscow do not have any either--like the dead."
>
> Brecht, July 1938[2]

> "The intellectual isolation here is unbelievable; compared to Hollywood, Svendborg was a world center."
>
> Brecht, September 1941[3]

The question of why Brecht chose to spend a considerable portion of his exile period in capitalist Hollywood rather than in socialist Moscow takes us to the center of some of the most complex personal, political, aesthetic, and historical problems not only of Bertolt Brecht but also of *at least* one generation of artists in this century whose lives and works have been ground between the claims of massive and conflicting political and aesthetic ideologies. A tentative answer to the question of Brecht's choice should point us back beyond this single figure to a reexamination of the close relationship of the German and Russian aesthetic avant-garde in the first thirty-five years of the twentieth century.

In order to understand the complexity of Brecht's choice, and the choice of those many artists who shared a similar political and aesthetic point of view, it is necessary for us to cast our minds back to the period when the avant-garde in the arts flourished in such profusion. It is helpful to attempt to return for a while beyond the searing experience of the worst excesses of Stalin's "personality cult," the sterile and crashingly dull products of the "socialist realists," to that dazzling sunburst of aesthetic endeavor from Moscow that illuminated the West. We must now attempt to remember those whose very memory Stalin ordered destroyed. We need to remember most particularly Blok, Mayakovsky, Kherzentzev, Eisenstein (now remembered mainly for his film work), Evreinov, Tairov, Vakhtangov, Simonov, Okhlopkov, Tretiakov, Meyerhold, and the aesthetic theorist Shklovski.

119

This roll call of authors of some of the most brilliant Soviet aesthetic experiments of the early twentieth century is a roll call also of those people most brutally assaulted as "formalists" by Zhdanov, charged by Stalin in 1934 to cast all Russian art in the socialist realist mold.   Of crucial importance to the central preoccupation of this paper is the fact that this list is also a roll call of those people in the Soviet Union who were closest to Brecht in a political, aesthetic, and personal sense.   I shall try to show here how close these ties actually were and to trace briefly the historical rise and fall of the kind of aesthetic experimentation in Russia that anticipated and that was so sympathetic to the German exile.   As we shall see, it is only in such a context that Brecht's choice of Hollywood over Moscow becomes really understandable.

In the first two or three years of the new century an erstwhile student of Stanislavski who became *the* focal point of what would later be called "formalist" experimentation in theater, V. E. Meyerhold, had already evolved a full-fledged antiillusionary or nonnaturalist theater.[4]   With considerable satisfaction Meyerhold quotes in 1902 the thesis of his friend, the poet Valery Bryusov: "It is time for the theater to stop imitating reality" (*Meyerhold*, p. 39).   Working from this premise Meyerhold sought also to prevent his audience from forgetting they were in a theater.   In the words of Leonid Andreyev, another poet caught up with Meyerhold in developing "the theatrical theater":[5]   "In the stylized theater the spectator should not forget for a moment that an actor is *performing* before him, and the actor should never forget that he is performing before an audience, with a stage beneath his feet and a set around him."[6]   In a note from 1907, Meyerhold himself states as his first principle of diction: "The words must be coldly 'coined' free from all tremolo and the familiar break in the voice.   There must be a total absence of tension and lugubrious intonation" (*Meyerhold*, p. 54).   He adds in another note of the same year: "If an actor of the old school wished to move his audience deeply, he would cry out, weep, groan and beat his breast with his fists.   Let the new actor express the highest point of theater just as the grief and joy of Mary were expressed: with an outward repose, almost *cóldly*, without shouting or lamentation.   He can achieve profundity without recourse to exaggerated tremolo" (*Meyerhold*, p. 55).   Of considerable interest here is the fact that not only does Meyerhold come up with a full-blown theory of cool acting (at a time when Brecht was but nine years old), he sees that such acting can have a profound emotional effect on an audience: "Wherever it was necessary to convey the extreme of passion, resort was made to a device of the grotesque: in order to reinforce the impact of dramatically intense scenes, the passages of intervening narrative were delivered in an unusually cool style, almost devoid of feeling and emphasis.   The actors' moves either preceded or followed their lines.   All movements were treated like dance steps [a Japanese device], regardless of whether they were meant to express any emotion or not" (*Meyerhold*, p. 65). A year later movement itself became a device for eliciting emotion. Anticipating Brecht's use of gestures, Meyerhold notes: "The essence of human relationships is determined by gestures, poses, glances and silences. Words alone cannot say anything. Hence there must be a *pattern of movement* on the stage to transform the spectator into a vigilant observer" (*Meyerhold*, p. 56).

None of this, I would hasten to add, struck Meyerhold and his colleagues as being particularly new. Again and again he substantiates his theories with references to earlier aesthetic practice[7]--he regards his work more as restorative than innovative. Although he does not himself generate at this time a Russian equivalent for the German *Verfremdung* ["alienation," "estrangement"], we know from his close relationship with Shklovski that he is perfectly aware of the device as an ancient and honorable aesthetic category. In a note of 1911 he quotes E. T. A. Hoffmann writing on Jacques Callot's drawings: "Even in his drawings from life (processions, battles) there is something in the appearance of the lifelike figures which makes them at once *familiar yet strange* [Meyerhold's italics]" (*Meyerhold*, p. 141). It is extremely likely that Brecht's own term *Verfremdung* is a direct translation of Shklovski's *priem ostranneniia*, which John Willett renders as a "device for making things strange." It is significant that Brecht first uses the term *Verfremdung* after his 1935 trip to Moscow.[8]

From all this it is clear that a full decade before the Russian Revolution and before Brecht had even entered his teens, a number of technical devices we in the West tend to associate with Brecht and the epic theater were in use in Russia. All that was lacking in Meyerhold's prerevolutionary theory and practice (and this was only a partial lack) was the direct application of his theater theory to political causes. With this addition following hard on the heels of the Revolution, Meyerhold's dramatic theory and practice in both its aesthetics *and* its politics anticipates that of Brecht in all essential particulars. In contrast to Evreinov and Tairov, who shared many of Meyerhold's aesthetic ideas, Meyerhold himself immediately and unreservedly placed his aesthetics at the disposal of the Revolution. As Anna I. Miller observed in 1931 of Meyerhold: "He is a born revolutionist, not an evolutionist: he would smash the old mould to release a new truth. He is heart and soul with the new government: why haggle over the relation of propaganda to art when there are millions of workmen, soldiers and peasants illiterate or half-educated, seizing each bit of encouragement which the theater can offer them in their advance toward the communistic ideal?"[9] Meyerhold's stance and even his dress become resolutely proletarian; he becomes the director of the governmental theater organ of the revolutionary Soviets. Gorchakov notes in *The Theater in Soviet Russia*:

He [Meyerhold] wanted to link the theater arts
with the age of the proletarian dictatorship, and so he
struck out sharply and mercilessly against the acting
"priesthood."   A stage is not a temple, he asserted.
Its brick walls and "machines for acting" do not distinguish it in any way from a factory.   An actor on
the stage is a member of the actors' guild and wears
the same proletarian "street clothes" as any worker.
His work contains no bourgeois obscurantism of any
sort.   It is based on materialist science and is subor-
dinated to methodology principles known to every Soviet
worker.10

So devoted was Meyerhold to the Soviet cause and to
revolutionary art that he had no difficulty following a 1927
party directive:

Promote those productions that reflect the characteristic features for the era of socialist construction
through which we are living and that are permeated
with the spirit of the proletarian class struggle. . . .
Struggle against the intensified attempts by agents of
the new bourgeoisie to win over the stage . . . to a
repertory that is middle-class, salonish, boulevardish,
and ideologically hostile . . . .   Try to continue the
ousting of the most harmful survivals from the art that
originated in the feudal period of landed proprietors,
and the period of bourgeois decadence.11

Working closely with Mayakovsky and Sergei Tretiakov,
Meyerhold continued to produce huge political spectacles.
Just a year later, however, with the end of the relative
artistic freedom associated with the New Economic Policy
(NEP, introduced in 1928), Meyerhold and all his associates
came under ever more pressure for alleged formalism in their
artistic experimentation.   By the time of Brecht's first visit
to Russia in 1932 Mayakovsky had already committed suicide,
Stalinist supporters were entrenched in positions of power
in the cultural world, and Meyerhold and Tretiakov
(Brecht's closest personal friend in the Soviet Union) were
already under some open fire.   Tretiakov's *I Want a Child*
(subsequently adapted by Brecht), a play that Meyerhold
tried repeatedly to stage, was denounced by the highest
authorities as "a slur on the Soviet family."   Meyerhold did
not help matters by deliberately staging those works of his
close friend Mayakovsky that transparently lampooned Stalin
and the Soviet bureaucracy.   Tretiakov, the author of "a
slur on the Soviet family," who also had a keen interest in
Japanese and Chinese affairs, was viewed with suspicion in
a Russia becoming ever more isolationist.   But much of this
was not visible on the surface.   What the general visitor
still saw on the stages of the Soviet Union, even as late as
1936 and 1937, were magnificently innovational productions
by Meyerhold and people trained by Meyerhold as he continued to compete successfully with those stages dominated
by Stanislavski and his close associates.12   On his 1932 and
1935 visits to Moscow, Brecht arrived in time to hear the

swan song of Soviet experiment in the arts.   But as those
who knew what was going on behind the scenes in Moscow
would tell Brecht, only socialist realism (and this most narrowly defined) would hereafter be tolerated in the arts.
    At the 1934 conference, Zhdanov made public Stalin's
official policy statement on the arts.   Perhaps as disturbing
to Brecht as Zhdanov's speech was the general tone of adula-
tion for Stalin at the 1934 Congress.   Boris Souvarine notes
in his *Stalin, A Critical Survey of Bolshevism*: "During
the Congress a continuous hosanna went up from dawn to
dusk on the 'steel colossus,' the 'great engineer,' the
'great pilot,' the 'great master,' the 'great architect,' the
'great disciple of the great master,' the 'greatest of the
theorists,' the 'finest of the Leninists,' and finally the
'greatest of the great . . . .'"[13]   Brecht's own loathing for
all "greatness" and for pomp and circumstance is sufficiently
well substantiated for us to predict his response, not only
to this treatment of Stalin but also to Stalin's smiling acceptance of such torrents of monstrous, inflated flattery.   It is
of some interest to note Brecht's own response to Souvarine's
book.   In California in 1943 he noted in his diary: "Just
read Souvarine's depressing book about Stalin" (*Arbeits –
journal*, 19 July 1943).   Right after the conference, Tretiakov
wrote to Brecht in guarded terms about the implications of
the turn of events.   They must, he writes, get together personally, as such matters are difficult to handle in letters.
"There are," he continues, "a number of new developments
that must be discussed and studied.   And I would like to
do this especially with you."   The arts, as Tretiakov at the
very center of things and with his sensitive antennae so
well knew, stood "at a turning point" (BBA 447/134-40).   The
battle lines would now be more severely drawn and it would
become, in a literal sense, a question of life and death as
to where one stood as an artist in relation to this socialist
realist line.   Artists such as Tretiakov, Meyerhold, Okhlopkov, Eisenstein, Pasternak, and the German émigré Bernhard
Reich knew that everything depended on where this line was
to be drawn and how Stalin's directive was to be interpreted.   The experimenters in the arts would now attempt
to gain a hearing for a point of view that held that being
proexperimentation in the arts could not and should not be
interpreted (as their enemies would vehemently maintain) as
an attack on the Soviet Union, on Stalin, and the development of socialism.   Under socialism, they would maintain,
there could be and indeed must be toleration for a wide
range of artistic expression.   But to maintain this in the
Soviet Union in 1935 was to oppose Stalin directly.   And
Stalin, for millions at home and abroad, had become by this
time the very incarnation of the Soviet Union.[14]   Complicat-
ing matters further was the need to establish a united political and artistic front against Hitler.   The experimenters
wished neither to weaken the antifascist position by internal bickering nor to subscribe to a supposedly antifascist
set of artistic dicta that were, as they knew all too well,
virtually identical in form with the aesthetic dicta of the
Third Reich.

In practical political terms, in Moscow in the thirties, the battle that swirled around the term "socialist realism" was to be decided not so much by artists as by those critics who seized and held positions of power within the Communist party hierarchy or on the editorial boards of the most important review bodies and literary journals.[15]   The deaths in those years of 98 of the 139 members of the Central Committee were paralleled by the pressure put upon anyone in the artistic world who dared to deviate from the Zhdanov-Stalin line.[16]   It is of considerable significance to note that almost all of Brecht's Soviet friends would find themselves in the "deviationist" camp.

Esenin, a Berlin acquaintance from the early twenties, had committed suicide in 1925, as Mayakovsky was to do in 1930.   Lunacharski, former freewheeling commissar for education and another old Berlin acquaintance, died in 1933. Bucharin, who spoke vigorously against Zhdanov's 1934 pronouncement, was liquidated in 1938.   Brecht's greatest political admirer in the Soviet Union, the former Communist premier of Hungary, Bela Kun, was killed in 1937.[17]   Gorki also was dead, possibly murdered by the secret police.   Tretiakov, whose loyalty to Stalin considerably outstripped that of Brecht and who had seemed the very model of the loyal Soviet artist,[18] by all accounts Brecht's closest Soviet friend, was arrested in 1937, tried peremptorily on a trumped-up charge, and then executed.   His wife, Olga Victorevna, simply for being the wife of a "traitor," was to spend nineteen years in various concentration camps.   Meyerhold, after one last bold speech against the validity of the socialist realist line, was arrested in 1939 and shot early the next year.[19]   Meyerhold's wife was murdered in their Moscow apartment by unidentified thugs.   Eisenstein, having dealt with Stalin's paranoid reception of *Ivan the Terrible* and the hostility evoked by the outright destruction of *Bezhin Meadow*,[20] was forced into silence.   Pasternak, whom Brecht would ask in 1955 to translate his Stalin Prize acceptance speech,[21] turned from original work to translation.   Mandelstam was dead and his wife on the run from the secret police.[22]   Tairov, who had done the first production of a Brecht play in the Soviet Union, lost his Kamerny Theater by official decree in 1934.   Of particular importance to Brecht was Nikolai Okhlopkov's loss of control of the Realistic Theater in 1938.   This student of Eisenstein and Meyerhold had long wanted to do (and had in fact agreed to do) Brecht's highly symbolic *Die heilige Johanna der Schlachthöfe* [*St. Joan of the Stockyards*] (Reich, p. 371).

The physical and artistic destruction of Brecht's Russian friends was paralleled in the same years by the treatment of many of his German acquaintances who had left Nazi Germany for the Soviet Union.   Bernhard Reich and his wife Anna Lazis, both friends from Brecht's Munich days, were coming under increasing pressure to conform.   The actress Carola Neher, a close friend, was on trial on a vague charge of high treason, while Brecht, from his Danish exile, sought to intervene on her behalf.   Alexander Granach, another actor friend, left hurriedly for Hollywood after a brief spell of imprisonment and interrogation in the Soviet Union. Even Erwin Piscator, who had been made most welcome when he first arrived in the Soviet Union in 1931, left on the eve of the purge trials. For years he had been able to obtain work only with the utmost difficulty, and before his precipitous departure he read the riot act on Soviet aesthetics to no less a person than the then first secretary of the Central Committee, Kaganowitsch.[23]   As much of this as world conditions permitted would be transmitted to Brecht. From Zurich in January 1937 a letter reached Brecht from Brentano (BBA 481/4-5) that another of their friends was rumored to be in difficulties. A Russian source was spreading the word in Prague and Vienna that Ernst Ottwalt was a Nazi spy and was in jail on this charge. Slatan Dudow wrote from Paris complaining about the Hay-Lukács clique in Moscow and what they were doing to ruin Marxist aesthetics.

As this partial listing indicates, "the operation of the thirties," correctly characterized by Bernhard Reich in 1970 as one that "grossly injured Leninistic principles" (Reich, p. 352), destroyed virtually everyone in the Soviet Union with whom Brecht had any political aesthetic rapport. It should not surprise us, therefore, that the Marxist Brecht replied in the negative to his friend Walter Benjamin's comment on Moscow: "But you have friends there." Or that he would add ominously: "And those in Moscow do not have any either--like the dead."[24]

We now know from Brecht's unpublished correspondence, diary entries, and essays published after his return from exile in 1948 that the dark tide that engulfed so many of his most loyal Marxist friends and artistic collaborators was one that he tried to stem in every way open to him. In constant fear of being swept up by the Gestapo or Hitler's advancing armies, and with a United States visa by no means assured, Brecht acted circumspectly. His fear for the safety of himself and his family was matched, however, by his fear of giving comfort to his Nazi enemies by publicly disagreeing with his supposed Moscow friends, the group in control of the major international journals, *Das Wort* and *Internationale Literatur*. Within the framework of these two formidable restrictions, Brecht waged war against his Moscow detractors and vigorously supported his ever-dwindling roster of Moscow friends.

When Brecht had agreed in 1936 to join (by mail from Denmark) the editorial staff of the Moscow-based, German-language journal *Das Wort*, he had hoped to work with compatible people such as his fellow editors, Willi Bredel (then fighting in the Spanish Civil War) and Lion Feuchtwanger (in exile in the south of France). Unfortunately, the absentee editorship of the three editors on the journal's masthead meant that the journal was really controlled by Zhdanov-oriented people who were actually on the spot in Moscow. Gradually both *Das Wort* and *Internationale Literatur* (under the managing editorship of Brecht's friend Johannes R. Becher) became more and more vehement in their attacks on the kind of artistic production to which Brecht was committed. From generalities, circumlocutions, and vague comments on "certain" persons departing in "certain" ways from the established aesthetic-political line, the one-sided public debate passed to naming names and to open attacks on specific works. Under normal circumstances adverse criticism of the person of an author or the tone of his works, no matter how vituperative that criticism may become, is not a matter of life and death. In Moscow in the thirties, particularly the late thirties, conditions were, to say the least, not normal. Stalin's passion for conformity and obedience in all areas of Russian life increased as intelligence reports came in on Nazi invasion plans. For Georg Lukács (as the major apologist for socialist realism) then to link Sergei Tretiakov and Bertolt Brecht by name with the bourgeois decadents[25] was tantamount to condemning them to a prison sentence or even to death.

Although Brecht maintained a steadfast public silence in the face of published attacks and at least one violently abusive personal letter from Julius Hay,[26] he fought vigorously behind the scenes for the lives and aesthetic principles of his friends. A letter written to a certain "Lieber Doktor"[27] in Moscow in 1937 vigorously defends Carola Neher, warns against Julius Hay, and says flatly that the supposedly "Marxist" aesthetics of Hay and others like him are highly questionable. Another letter to "liebe maria" asks about the fate of Mikhail Kolzov and says explicitly that he knows Kolzov has worked without rest for the Soviet Union. He complains also about *Das Wort* and says it is now empty of content. In a friendly and frank letter to Bredel (BBA 1856/04), Brecht complains openly about Lukács and says that this whole debate is destructive of party unity and should be suppressed. The opinion of Lukács, he says emphatically, is not "die marxistische." Another letter, to Becher, says essentially the same thing (BBA 1386/07). In a letter to Brentano in Switzerland (BBA 481/06), Brecht apologizes for the way Brentano's work has been reviewed in *Das Wort* and dissociates himself from this kind of reviewing. Even more explicitly, in a diary entry of July 1938, Brecht says flatly of the dean of the socialist realist critics, Lukács: "How this man moves into all the positions vacated by the proletariat! This talk about realism, which they happily managed to corrupt like the Nazis did socialism" (BBA 283). Or as Brecht was to note in his diary in December 1947, as he weighed the prospect of settling in East Berlin and having to deal once again with his old enemy: "I am reading Lukács' edition of the Goethe-Schiller correspondence. He analyzes how the German classical authors come to terms with the French Revolution. Once again, not having one of our own, I shudder to think that we will now have the Russian Revolution with which to 'come to terms'" (BBA 283/05). Or, commenting directly on those Russian socialist realist models that Lukács wished everyone to emulate:

Genuine investigations are either not attempted or they assume the character of a trial. The atmosphere is shockingly unproductive, malicious, personal, authoritarian, and servile all at the same time. This is clearly not an atmosphere in which a vital, provocative, exuberant literature could flourish. In fact, not only is there no significant novel, but such kitsch novels as those of Alexey Tolstoy are even considered good. And there is not *one* drama, not *one* dramatic figure, comic or tragic; not *one* linguistic achievement, not *one* philosophical quality in any play and all this in a theater of very high potential.[28]

These sentiments, expressed privately by Brecht before the death of Stalin--some of them guardedly in print from 1954 on--indicate clearly why Brecht was not prepared either in the thirties or in 1947 to voluntarily cram his writing into Georg Lukács' and Zhdanov's pseudo-Marxist mold. Further, as we have seen, even had Brecht been willing to attempt to do this, it is reasonably clear that he was far too closely identified with Piscator, Eisenstein, Mayakovsky, Tretiakov, and Meyerhold for his very life to be safe in the USSR in the late thirties and early forties. As Brecht's close associate in his last years, Käthe Rülicke-Weiler, has pointed out: "Asked by visitors which Soviet artists had influenced his work, Brecht named Eisenstein, Mayakovsky, and Meyerhold; one must add the name of Tretiakov, whose great agitprop plays Brecht came to know from the productions of Meyerhold, whom he knew as a friend and considered his teacher."[29] Or, as she adds a little later, secure in the knowledge that all these men had been posthumously cleared of any wrongdoing against the Soviet state and were in fact again being studied there, Brecht as a poet was perhaps closest of all to Mayakovsky, the author of the satirical plays *The Bath* and *The Bedbug*.

When we see how close Brecht was to the major but now largely forgotten victims of the formalist witch hunt, when we know how open he was in his antagonism (at least in his conversation and correspondence) to Lukács, Hay, Erpenbeck, Kurella, and other "enemies of production" and *Apparat-schiks*, we can see perhaps how wide of the mark Marianne Kesting is when she says of Brecht's decision not to settle in Moscow in 1941: "It is possible that Brecht found employment possibilities wanting also in Moscow."[30] Likewise, Martin Esslin seems to have forgotten for a moment the sheer physical danger Brecht was in in Moscow in 1941 when he writes: "It is a sign of Brecht's uncanny shrewdness in such matters that he, an ardent and convinced supporter of the party and eager to participate in its propaganda activities, should have resisted the temptation of settling in the Soviet Union."[31]

What Brecht as a Marxist revisionist knew and where his shrewdness did come into play was in the enunciation of the principle that the first duty of the bearer of truth is to stay alive. Then, possibly, so he seems to have thought, the time would come when change might be possible, and Marxism might be given a human face.   In Sweden, at the end of September 1939, Brecht noted bitterly in his notebook: "The talk one hears everywhere about the bolshevik party having reformed itself from the bottom up, is most certainly incorrect.   More likely is the misfortune that it has not changed at all . . ." (BBA 276/9).

On 5 October 1940 he entered in his diary the laconic note: "Today chose America . . ." (BBA 277/53).   The choice was one of expedience only and was made for him by the Hay-Lukács clique in Moscow and by positive efforts of several individuals in the United States to gain an entry visa for him.   So Brecht was forced to hurry across the full breadth of the land that, despite its faults, he continued to love and to sail for Hollywood to join "the sellers of lies."   In Hollywood he would write to his close friend, the Marxist theoretician Karl Korsch: "The intellectual isolation here is unbelievable; compared to Hollywood, Svendborg was a world center."[32]

Of the place where he could not choose to go in 1941 and of the socialist experiment, he wrote in an undated fragment: "One cannot say: freedom rules in the proletarian State, Russia.   But one can say: liberation rules there."[33] The dream remained for the Marxist exile, although the realities of 1941 forced upon him an ideologically distasteful choice.   Neither those charged with the rewriting of Soviet history nor those who would have us believe that the United States was some kind of democratic Holy Grail[34] for Bertolt Brecht can draw much comfort from the exile's choice.

Notes

[1]This paper explores, on the basis of some new and otherwise unpublished evidence, territory that was first opened by John Willett in *The Theatre of Bertolt Brecht: A Study from Eight Aspects* (London: Methuen, 1959), and that was then examined in somewhat greater detail by Marjorie Hoover in her fine essay, "V. E. Meyerhold: A Russian Predecessor of Avant-Garde Theater," *Comparative Literature*, 17, No. 3 (Summer 1965), 234-50.   I am indebted to the Bertolt-Brecht-Archiv in Berlin (cited hereafter in the text as BBA), the Houghton Library at Harvard, and Brecht's heirs for letting me use unpublished notebooks, diaries, and letters of Brecht.   Additional material on Brecht's relationship to Soviet aesthetics is drawn from Klaus Völker's excellent article, "Brecht und Lukács: Analyse einer Meinungsverschiedenheit," *Suhrkamp Kursbuch 7* (Frankfurt: Suhrkamp, 1966), pp. 80-101.

[2]Quoted by Walter Benjamin, *Versuche über Brecht* (Frankfurt: Suhrkamp, 1966), p. 133.   Unless otherwise indicated, translations in this article are mine.

[3]The remark is made in an unpublished letter in the Karl Korsch papers at Harvard's Houghton Library.

[4]Many of Meyerhold's basic writings are now available in English in *Meyerhold on Theatre* , translated and edited with critical commentary by Edward Braun (New York: Hill and Wang, 1969). Subsequent references to this volume are given as *Meyerhold* in parentheses in the text. In Russian there is a more complete collection: V. E. Meyerkhol'd, *Stat'i, Pis'ma, Rechy, Besedy* (Moscow: "Iskusstvo," 1968), 2 vols. For a general survey of what came to be known technically as formalism, see Victor Erlich, *Russian Formalism: History, Doctrine* (The Hague: Mouton, 1955). Space does not permit an exposition of the highly technical reasons that compelled Meyerhold to separate himself from the "formalists." See Hoover, "V. E. Meyerhold."

[5]The phrase "the theatrical theater" stems from Tairov, who may have received the idea from either of Georg Fuchs's books: *Die Schaubühne der Zukunft* (Berlin: Schuster & Loeffler, n.d.) and *Die Revolution des Theaters: Ergebnisse aus dem Münchener Künstler-Theater* (Munich: Georg Müller, 1909).

[6]*Meyerhold* , p. 63. The original letter was written about 1907.

[7]Georg Fuchs was perhaps the single most important influence on Meyerhold. See n. 5 above. Meyerhold quotes Fuchs again and again and always with approval.

[8]See Bernhard Reich's memoirs, *Im Wettlauf mit der Zeit: Erinnerungen aus fünf Jahrzehnten deutscher Theatergeschichte* (Berlin: Henschelverlag, 1970), pp. 371-72; cited hereafter as Reich in parentheses in the text.

[9]Anna Irene Miller, *The Independent Theatre in Europe: 1887 to the Present* (New York: R. Long & R. R. Smith, 1931), p. 374.

[10]Nikolai A. Gorchakov, *The Theater in Soviet Russia*, trans. Edgar Lehrman (New York: Columbia University Press, 1957), p. 203.

[11]Gorchakov, p. 265. The quotation originally appeared in *Puti razvitia teatra* , pp. 503-04, in 1927. Curiously enough, Stanislavski, who became the model to be emulated in Soviet theater, would still have been viewed in 1927 as a remnant of the feudal period.

[12]Excellent accounts of the relationship of the two main forces in Russian theater of the twenties and thirties are available in English. See particularly Norris Houghton, *Moscow Rehearsals* (New York: Harcourt, Brace and Co., 1936), and Harold Clurman, *The Fervent Years* (New York: Hill and Davy, 1957), pp. 150 ff.

[13]Boris Souvarine, *Stalin, A Critical Survey of Bolshevism* , trans. C. L. R. James (New York: Alliance Book Corp., Longmans, Green and Co., 1939), p. 580.

[14]See n. 12 above. Brecht observed to Benjamin in 1938 that "writers over there simply have a difficult time." As Brecht said to Benjamin: "It is already construed as intentional, if the name Stalin does not occur in a poem" (Benjamin, *Versuche über Brecht* , p. 129). See also Benjamin's recollection: "Brecht speaks of his inborn hate for the clergy, inherited from his grandmother. He makes it apparent that

those who have adopted and used the theoretical precepts of Marx will always constitute a priestridden clique" (*Ver- suche* , p. 128).

[15]Brecht was extremely conscious of this distinction. He confided bitterly to Benjamin: "They are enemies of pro- duction. Production is suspect to them. One cannot trust it. It is unpredictable, one never knows what may come of it. And they themselves do not wish to produce. They only want to play the white collar foreman and to have control over the others. Each of their critiques contains a threat" (*Versuche*, p. 132). The specific persons referred to here (as the context of this remark makes clear) are Lukács, Kurella, and Gabor. We might also add Erpenbeck, Hay, and Wolf.

[16]One example of such literary decimation may serve for many. In 1936 *Internationale Literatur* carried eleven names on its masthead. By 1938 only the hardy peren- nial, Johannes R. Becher, is still listed.

[17]One does not know how many attempts on his life he had survived prior to this. See Reich, pp. 342-43.

[18]The sociologist friend of Brecht, Fritz Sternberg, reports in *Der Dichter und die Ratio: Erinnerungen an Bertolt Brecht* (Göttingen: Sachse & Pohl, 1963):

> The discussion was about the Soviet Union, which had just begun the forced collectivization of agriculture under Stalin. It was sharply criticized. Tretiakov, who had taken part in the discussion in the beginning, became progressively more reticent. Suddenly, however, he turned to Brecht and exploded: "Where have you led me? There are enemies of the party here, enemies of the Soviet Union!" Brecht replied. "What do you mean? We were criticizing Stalin's collectivization, which seems to me quite justifiable." And when Tretiakov then began to quote some speech of Stalin's, Brecht interrupted him and explained: Sternberg is correct; Marxists are not interested in what statesmen say about their political stance, but rather with what they do. (pp. 23-24)

It is of considerable significance to note that in at least one account written by a highly sympathetic Western journalist, the Tretiakov family is treated as the ideal family unit in the new Soviet state. For specific details I am particularly indebted to a close friend of the Tretiakov family, Professor Herbert Marshall, Director of the Center for Soviet and East- European Studies in the Performing Arts at Southern Illinois University. Professor Marshall spent the years 1930-37 in the Soviet Union and was closely associated with Meyerhold, Tretiakov, and Eisenstein. Inasmuch as he also knew Hanns Eisler and Brecht personally, he is a valuable source of information on the relationship of many of the German émigrés to Soviet experimenters in the arts.

[19]As part of the de-Stalinization process, much of Meyerhold's work has been reissued in the Soviet Union. Of particular importance is *Vstrechi s Meierkhol'dom* (Moscow:

Vserossiĭskoe teatral'noe obshchestvo, 1967), where the editors state flatly: "V. E. Meyerhold was arrested in 1939 on the basis of false information and killed on 2 February 1940, a victim of illegal repression" (p. 13). The victim has now been given an important place in the six-volume official history of the Soviet dramatic theater: *Istoria sovetskogo dramaticheskogo teatra v shesti tomakh* (Moscow: Izdatel'stvo "Nauka," 1966–1971). Interestingly enough, however, a great deal of Tretiakov's work is still suppressed in the USSR.

20 Professor Marshall, now working on an official English edition of Eisenstein's writings and drawings, has told me how fanatically every last print of *Bezhin Meadow* was sought out and destroyed in the Soviet Union.

21 Brecht's choice of Pasternak was a highly significant political-aesthetic act in 1955. The choice made a great impression on Pasternak, who said that he had thought up to that point that Brecht was a Stalinist hack.

22 See Nadezhda Mandelstam's chilling account of the treatment she and her husband received for failure on the part of Iosip Mandelstam to join the general chorus of inflated praise for Stalin and for Stalin's aesthetic policies: Nadezhda Mandelstam, *Hope Against Hope: A Memoir* (New York: Atheneum, 1970).

23 See Reich, pp. 347–48, for a detailed account of Piscator's stormy meeting with Kaganowitsch and for Reich's flat statement about the purges that Piscator just missed: "In August began the well-known affair of the thirties, which severely injured the principles of Leninism. Piscator never returned" (p. 352).

24 Benjamin, *Versuche*, p. 133.

25 On the cover of the Brecht-Archiv copy of *Internationale Literatur: Deutsche Blätter*, 8, No. 7 (1938), there is an identifying note in Brecht's hand: "Lukács Dekadenzen." In Brecht's Danish notebook, 27 July 1938, we find: "There are concepts that are difficult to combat simply because they exude such ennui. For example *Decadence*" (BBA 275/2). The specific subject of much of Brecht's ire was the polemical and threatening tone of much of Lukács' writing, particularly the essay "Marx und das Problem des ideologischen Verfalls," *Internationale Literatur*, 7 (1938).

26 BBA 1386/13. Brecht's reply (BBA 1386/15) in the face of Hay's fanatical vituperation is a model of diplomacy and firmness.

27 The "Doktor" is Lion Feuchtwanger (BBA 478/76).

28 Quoted by Völker, with no source or date given, "Brecht und Lukács," pp. 86–87. Materials actually derive from Brecht's *Arbeitsjournal*, p. 636. Date of entry, 16 Oct. 1943; place, Hollywood. Brecht's most important essay on the topic of socialist realism, even though still a very guarded one: "Weite und Vielfalt der realistischen Schreibweise" ["Breadth and Variety of Realistic Modes of Writing"], was first published in 1954, in *Versuche*, No. 13.

[29]Käthe Rülicke-Weiler, *Die Dramaturgie Brechts* (Berlin: Henschelverlag, 1966), p. 110.   This list of influences acknowledged by Brecht himself differs markedly from the list given in his printed works.   The verbal list directly confirms the importance to Brecht of precisely those loyal Soviet artists who were silenced, committed suicide, or were executed for daring to propose that formal aesthetic experimentation must have a place in a socially and aesthetically viable socialist society.   The particular value of Rülicke-Weiler's book is that not only did she know Brecht personally, she also has a first-hand knowledge of the Russian language and Russian theater and film.   She knows, therefore, precisely what she is doing in linking Brecht's name (as he did himself) with a list of confirmed deviationists from the creed of socialist realism.   It is difficult to overstress the lack of reliability of Brecht's heretofore *published* comments on his "formalist" friends' achievements and the contempt that Brecht repeatedly expressed for socialist realist nonachievements in the arts.   What lies behind all this surely is Brecht's hesitancy in openly attacking (1) the Soviet Union, (2) policies of the USSR, and (3) the personal architect of those policies, Joseph Stalin.   Unpublished materials in the so-called *Stalin-Mappe* of the Bertolt-Brecht-Archiv will, when published, shed new light on Brecht's view of Stalin and of Stalin's policies.   See also n. 33 below.

[30]Marianne   Kesting,   *Bertolt   Brecht*   (Reinbek   bei Hamburg: Rowohlt, 1959), p. 106.

[31]Martin Esslin, *Brecht: The Man and His Work* (Garden City, N.Y.: Doubleday, 1961), p. 160.

[32]See n. 3 above.

[33]BBA 73/03, portfolio entitled "Politische Aufsätze und Fragmente," or Bertolt Brecht, *Gesammelte Werke in 20 Bänden*, Werkausgabe edition suhrkamp (Frankfurt/M: Suhrkamp, 1967), XX, 103.   Here particularly the text in the *Gesammelte Werke* gives a radical misapprehension of Brecht's position.   The unpublished BBA text from which the *GW* fragment is derived goes on to say: "die frage, ob man die diktaturen befürchten muss, hängt ab von der frage, ob man . . ." ["The question of whether one must fear dictatorships depends upon the question of whether one . . . ," BBA 95/08].   This unpublished openended fragment is, of course, much less emphatic in its endorsement of the USSR than the published fragment suggests.

[34]Materials soon to be published will show how strong an interest the FBI had in Brecht and how close Brecht came to being arrested when he left America hurriedly after his appearance before the House Unamerican Activities Committee.

The Plight of the Exile: A Hidden Theme in Brecht's *Galileo Galilei*

Guy Stern

Most studies of Brecht's *Galileo Galilei*, some at length, others in passing, have pointed out the frequent references to Brecht's own life and times in a drama based at first glance solely on the biography of a seventeenth-century scientist. Schumacher, for example, characterizes the drama as "related to [Brecht's] times in a complex way"; Weideli observes: "The autobiographical elements in it seem to be numerous."[1] Yet neither Brecht scholars nor Brecht himself, in his numerous and sometimes contradictory explanations of his drama,[2] have commented upon a subsidiary theme in it, the plight of Germany's exiles, which at the time of the drama's genesis (1938–39) was both topical and autobiographical.

Evidence for Brecht's abiding and profound concern for the refugees from Hitler Germany emerges, of course, from other works of that period, for example, from his *Furcht und Elend des dritten Reiches* [*Private Life of the Master Race*] and from such poems as "Auf einen Emigranten" ["On an Emigrant"], "Klage des Emigranten" ["Emigrant's Lament"], "Über die Bezeichnung Emigranten" ["Concerning the Label Emigrant"], "Gedanken über die Dauer des Exils" ["Thoughts on the Duration of Exile"], and "Landschaft des Exils" ["Landscape of Exile"].[3] Also the dialogue *Flüchtlingsgespräche*, 1940–41 [*Dialogues of the Refugees*],[4] Brecht's most extensive pronouncement on the plight of the refugees, was written only shortly after the first version of *Galileo*. Significantly, one of the participants of this dialogue is a physicist, an inspiration probably derived from his work on *Galileo*. It appears, therefore, that Brecht's own experience as an exile affected a drama based on a historical person, who was neither an exile nor a fugitive himself. Brecht, in short, accommodated a theme, the introduction of which was difficult and which occasionally seems forced.

Four aspects of the exile experience permeate the drama: the flight, economic straits, loss of identity, and intellectual suppression of the refugees. Flight, the necessity of "chang-

ing one's country more often than one's shoes,"[5] had become
a way of life to Brecht; even his departure from the United
States resembled one.   It is therefore understandable that
Brecht has his hero prepare for flight as prudently as did
Brecht at various stages of his exile.   In past interpretations of the play, this prudence on the part of Brecht's
protagonist is often overlooked.   Misled by Galileo's dis-
claimer, "I cannot see myself as a refugee. My comfort means
too much to me,"[6] critics have explained Galilei's seeming
inertia as resulting from his myopic view of danger, love
of comfort, and even as a mirror of Brecht's own passivity
in staying in East Berlin despite the restraints on him.
Zimmermann observes: "He [Galileo] refuses to acknowledge
the immediate danger to his life and rejects an opportunity
to escape, whereby [the drama] . . . does not actually make
it clear whether he fails to recognize the real danger or
whether he only wishes to shun the discomforts and annoyances involved in flight . . . ."[7]   And Lucke adds: "Just
as Galileo refuses to flee to Venice (scene 2), so Brecht himself, despite intellectual oppression and forced compromises,
remains in East Berlin after all."[8]   But Galilei, as a close
reading of the text reveals, is dissembling during his conversations with Vanni, the ironmonger.   Unbeknownst even
to his daughter, Virginia, to whom he feigns the same type
of blind optimism, he has prepared for flight: "We are not
going home from here, but to Volpi, the glass cutter. We
have made arrangements that a wagon, full of empty wine-
barrels, always stand ready in the adjoining courtyard of
the inn, to take me out of the city" (III, 1321).[9]   Earlier
in the play (III, 1290) Cardinal Barberini observes that
Galilei wears no masks.   Both he and Brecht's critics under-
estimate Galilei's ability to dissemble.

The theme of flight and emigration is struck again at
the end of the drama.   Andrea, Galilei's student, is preparing to emigrate to Holland (to Strassburg in the first version
of the drama).   A border guard challenges him:

> THE GUARD: Why are you leaving Italy?
> ANDREA: I am a scholar.
> THE GUARD to the Scribe: Enter under "Reason for
>   leaving country": Scholar. (III, 1343)

In addition, Brecht uses a device of the epic theater
to link past and present.   A transparency displayed at the
beginning of the scene injects the author into the play:

> The great book o'er the border went
> And, good folk, that was the end.
> But we hope you'll keep in mind
> You and I were left behind.
> May you now guard science's light
> Keep it up and use it right
> Lest it be a flame to fall
> One day to consume us all.[10]

Hence in one terse dialogue and a brief rhyme Brecht
accuses his age and country--more so than seventeenth-

century Italy—of forcing intellectuals into exile. Being a scholar had become a reason sui generis for emigrating.[11]

Brecht's flight from Germany brought him freedom coupled with deprivation; this was typical of the fate of the refugee. Brecht in fact felt strongly that the exile countries unconscionably made deprivation the price of freedom. In his *Flüchtlingsgespräche* (XIV, 1456) Kalle, the metal worker, is "hospitably received" in Denmark, but callously exploited as a garbage collector; later on in the work we hear of a physician, a renowned specialist in asthmatic ailments, who works in a clinic "where he was allowed to work as an orderly without pay" (XIV, 1467). Brecht's protest against economic exploitation in exchange for freedom carries over into *Galileo*:

> THE CURATOR: Do not forget that while the Republic may not pay as much as certain princes, it does guarantee freedom of scientific investigation.
> GALILEO: Your protection of intellectual freedom is quite a lucrative business, isn't it? By pointing out that the Inquisition rules and burns in other places, you acquire excellent teachers cheaply. You compensate yourselves for the protection from the Inquisition by paying the worst salaries. (III, 1241 f.)[12]

It is unlikely that the historical Galilei ever made such a pronouncement. But if we substitute "National Socialism" for "Inquisition" in the passage above, Brecht's Galilei would be voicing the precise thoughts of the author and of Brecht's fellow exiles, who like him were paid considerably less than they deserved.[13]

Brecht, in the same passage and throughout the drama, shows that even this vaunted freedom is not unalloyed—and that it is particularly precarious for foreigners. To make his point, Brecht has his protagonist recall the fate of Giordano Bruno, who was delivered up to the Inquisition by the Republic of Florence, the supposed protector of freedom. In trying to exculpate his government, the curator cites the historic "party line," that Bruno was extradited not for his heresies, but because he was a foreigner:[14]

> THE CURATOR: Not because he spread the teachings of Mr. Copernicus [was he extradited to Rome] . . . but because he was not a Venetian and had no employment. (III, 1241)

This argument is unconvincing from the start. It is furthermore demolished completely by subsequent speeches and also fails in its purpose to assuage the fears of Galileo. Hence its function within the play is difficult to fathom. But it makes perfect sense as a topical reference. In the *Flüchtlingsgespräche* deportation hangs heavily over the exiles: they speak with rather desperate humor of the time "when we are to be unceremoniously deported" (XIV, 1386). Also, in another scene, the two colloquists must subject themselves to the fearsome task of seeking renewal of their Finnish residence permits (XIV, 1425). Deportation to Germany meant imprisonment and death for the exiled intellectuals as surely as extradition to Rome did, in its time, for Giordano Bruno.

Brecht, in the drama's final scene, took pains to point out the parallelism between the seventeenth and the twentieth centuries regarding thought control and flight from it. In a passage added, significantly, *after* the completion of the first draft, Galileo says: "Watch out when you travel through Germany, with the truth under your cloak" (III, 1341).[15] This warning appears rather gratuitous, if intended for someone smuggling Galileo's *Discorsi* out of Italy; during the Thirty Years' War ownership of the manuscript would have been dangerous in some parts of Germany and not hazardous at all in others. Also this warning is inconsistent with the assertion by a reliable source--the pope himself--that Galileo, far from having to fear Catholic Germany, has powerful friends at the court of Vienna (III, 1324). But the warning became an effective dramatic device to show the analogy between the Inquisition and the Nazis, and the necessary flight from the one as well as the other.

Finally, Brecht's use of dates referring to historical events in the seventeenth century, which are not absolutely essential to the drama of Galileo, tends to emphasize the parallelism. Dates such as 1633 and 1637 evoke the memory of events precisely 300 years later. They also evoke parallelism between the life of Brecht as an exile and that of Galileo as an intellectual exile--choosing the seventeenth-century equivalent of "inner emigration." Occasionally Brecht attributed his persecution by the Nazis in part to the Marxist tenor of his didactic plays: "Then [Mr. Brecht] . . . asked you too often where the riches of the rich come from / And right off you abruptly chased him out of the country" (verse added to the "Salomonlied").

The year 1932 falls into this specific period of Brecht's creativity with the completion of such works as *Die Mutter* [*The Mother*] and *Kuhle Wampe*. Brecht appears to imply that one of the factors that led to the silencing or intellectual exile of Galileo was the application of his teachings to the socioeconomic and political arena. In fact, scene 10 in *Galileo Galilei* is a didactic play in a nutshell proceeding from the observation of a neutral scientific fact, the earth revolving around the sun, to a utopia of the class struggle in which the master is a satellite of his servants. Brecht as the embattled and endangered writer of didactic plays joins hands across several centuries with Galileo Galilei, who inspired didactic satire, the Shrovetide Plays. Warnings of the consequences of such boldness appeared both in Brecht's life and in his fictionalized account of Galileo's. The barring of the second performance of *Die Mutter* [*The Mother*] in 1932, the political censorship of his film *Kuhle Wampe*, and the boycott of his plays made "the circles around Brecht sense, correctly, political motives behind the dubious intervention of the authorities,"[16] whereas in the play the words of the ballad singer, a figure that frequently acted as Brecht's spokesman, warn that a dangerous dog must be muzzled: "If you remove the muzzle from a rabid dog, he'll bite" (III, 1315).

The next year, or so Brecht seems to argue, both he and Galileo pay the price for carrying abstract insights to their logical conclusion. The forces that compel Brecht's involuntary emigration, "When I Was Driven into Exile" (VIII, 416), drove Galileo into his intellectual exile. With one spatial reference that consciously or subconsciously reinforces the temporal one, Brecht drives home the parallel. In '33 both Brecht and Galileo started a prolonged residence (see stage directions III, 1330) in a *Landhaus* ("country house"). To list the dates in this abbreviated and more striking form is a legitimate device because Brecht himself had recourse to this manner of emphasizing the point in one of the versions of the play. Recently a scholar has suggested that Brecht elevates his exile experience to a poetic level, which transports the trauma of the exile to the realm of the legend.[17] As far as the relationship of these two exiles--actual or intellectual--is concerned, Galileo becomes Brecht's "legendary" alter ego.

The story of hidden themes in *Galileo Galilei* has a sequel. When Brecht readied his drama for a production in the United States, he collaborated on the translation with Charles Laughton. Laughton, who had no personal reason to share Brecht's continuous preoccupation with exile and flight, eliminated the passages quoted above, including the one relating to truth being threatened in Germany. Brecht reluctantly consented to these deletions, his reluctance not totally removed by his realization that Laughton was often cutting away excrescences rather than vital parts of the play:

> The more incisive changes in the structure of entire scenes or even of the work itself were made solely to facilitate the forward movement of the action . . . L. [Laughton] treated the "printed text" with a revealing, sometimes brutal indifference that the playwright [*Stückeschreiber*] was seldom able to share. What we created was a script; the performance was everything. It was impossible to persuade him to translate portions that the dramatist was prepared to omit in the production, but that he, however, wanted to rescue for the "book." The most important thing was the stage performance, for which the text was only the means, the vehicle: the text was used up in the production; it was consumed like powder in fireworks.[18]

When Brecht prepared the final version of the play, this time with the help of Elisabeth Hauptmann, Benno Besson, and Ruth Berlau, three collaborators far less "brutal" than Charles Laughton, he retained and restored each one of the references to exile and flight. He must have felt that these passages, though unessential for the "forward movement of the action," were vital to the personal and universal statement he wished to make. Of course, had Brecht commented upon the restoration of this theme, he might have had recourse to a proverb, one of his favorite modes of expression. In seeking a reason for his hero's need to communicate his scientific findings, Brecht hypothesizes that "out of the abundance of the heart the mouth speaks." The same proverb may explain the introduction of a theme into the play that is scarcely detectable at first glance, but nevertheless basic to the drama.

On the other hand, the process of inclusion and restoration may have been far less conscious. In the one instance in which Brecht explains the restoration of one of the passages under discussion, he seems to be less than candid. As Käthe Rülicke recalls:

> Brecht also deleted the comment about the Republic as "those parts of the world that lie in complete darkness, where the gloom had even increased." Germany no longer lived in the dark night of fascism, and it was hoped that a new era had actually dawned. To be sure, Brecht left the sentence: "Watch out when you travel through Germany, with the truth under your cloak," untouched and he quipped during a rehearsal: "It is dangerous to show up in Germany with the truth under your coat; this has been a fact since the peasant wars. One must be very careful when uttering the truth."[19]

This remark, as the tone of the description implies, was meant to be more jocular than self-analytical.

The discovery of this particular hidden theme in Brecht's *Galileo* may, beyond its pertinence for Brecht scholarship, help solve a problem of classification in modern German literature. One of the earlier books on exile literature suggests that we will arrive at a valid typology of the genre only if we discover traces of the exile experience in works thematically divorced from it.[20] In *Galileo* we have a striking example of such a transplanted exile landscape.

As far as Brecht scholarship is concerned, the theme of exile and exiles adds yet another enriching complexity to the "complex topicality" of this polychromatic work.

Notes

[1] Ernst Schumacher, *Drama und Geschichte : Bertolt Brechts* Leben des Galilei *und andere Stücke* (Berlin: Henschel, 1965), p. 70, and Walter Weideli, *The Art of Bertolt Brecht* (New York: New York University Press, 1963), p. 109. Also see Gerhard Szczesny, *The Case against Bertolt Brecht*, trans. Alexander Gode (New York: F. Ungar, 1969). Because most of the sources for this paper are not available in English translations, the English versions in the text are my own.

[2] See Werner Hecht, ed., *Materialien zu Brechts* Leben des Galilei (Frankfurt/M: Suhrkamp, 1963).

3 For an excellent analysis of these poems as "exile literature" see Werner Vordtriede, "Vorläufige Gedanken zu einer Typologie der Exilliteratur," *Akzente*, 15, No. 6 (Dec. 1968), 556-75, especially pp. 556 f. and 560.

4 "Flüchtlingsgespräche," in Bertolt Brecht, *Gesammelte Werke in 20 Bänden*, Werkausgabe edition suhrkamp (Frankfurt/M: Suhrkamp, 1967), XIV, 1381-1515. All references in the text are to this edition, indicated by volume and page numbers.

5 See *Gesammelte Werke*, IX, 525.

6 Bertolt Brecht, *Gesammelte Werke*, III, 1318. Unless otherwise noted, all references to *Galilei* are to the third version as it appears in *Gesammelte Werke*, III, 1229-1345.

7 Werner Zimmermann, *Brechts* Leben des Galilei: *Interpretation und didaktische Analyse*, Beihefte zum *Wirkenden Wort*, No. 12 (Düsseldorf: Schwann, 1965), p. 20.

8 Hans Lucke, "Schulpraktischer Kommentar zu Brechts Leben des *Galilei*," *Der Deutschunterricht*, 20 (June 1968), 81.

9 The reference to Galileo's contemplated and thwarted flight appears in the third (USA) version. See Brecht, *Life of Galileo*, in Ralph Manheim and John Willett, eds., *Collected Plays* (New York: Pantheon Books, 1970), V, 77. The absence of this motif from the first (Danish) version is attested to by Werner Mittenzwei, who examined the *Ur-Galileo* in the Brecht Archive. See his *Bertolt Brecht: Von der* Massnahme *zu* Leben des Galilei (Berlin: Aufbau, 1962), p. 263.

10 In Manheim and Willett, V, 96 (*Gesammelte Werke*, III, 1342).

11 Lucke, p. 82, calls attention to the autobiographical elements in this scene: "The emigration of Andreas reminds one of Brecht's emigration . . . ."

12 Schumacher, p. 240, attests to the fact that the scene with the curator was already part of the first version.

13 Brecht's precarious financial position during the genesis of *Galileo* can be gleaned from the (previously unpublished) letters of Margarete Steffin, quoted in Schumacher, p. 381, n. 8.

14 The expedient substitution of a pretended or at least secondary reason for Bruno's deportation instead of the real one conforms to historical facts. See William Boulting, *Giordano Bruno* (London: K. Paul Trench, Trubner & Co., 1916), p. 291.

15 For an account of this addendum and its subsequent retraction in the US version, see Schumacher, pp. 116 and 155. On p. 37 he also reprints the slightly variant wording of the first version.

16 Kurt Fassmann, *Brecht: Eine Bibliographie* (Munich: Kindler, 1963), p. 62.

17 Peter Paul Schwarz, "Legende und Wirklichkeit des Exils," *Wirkendes Wort*, 19 (1969), 267-76. I am also indebted to John Fuegi for calling my attention to some of the parallels between important dates in Brecht's life and those specifically cited in *Galileo Galilei*.

[18]*Materialien*, pp. 42 f.

[19]Käthe   Rülicke,   "Bemerkungen   zur   Schlussszene" in *Materialien*, p. 96.

[20]Matthias   Wegner,   *Exil   und   Literatur: Deutsche Schriftsteller   im   Ausland   1933-1945* (Frankfurt/M: Athenäum, 1967), p. 227.

Hermann Broch in America: His Later Social and Political Thought

Michael Winkler

Of all the authors who found asylum from Nazi persecution in the United States, Hermann Broch is the only novelist to achieve world stature for the books that he wrote and for those that he could not complete as an exile. And it is the essential characteristic of his most intensely productive years as a poet and thinker that he wrested his creative accomplishment from the potentially shattering experience of the émigré's isolation. He had to conquer that spiritual loneliness that comes with the loss of faith in the justifiability of one's work. All through the years after his precipitous flight from Vienna, Broch lived with the terrible possibility that he might become a specter or caricature of the homeless European intellectual: dedicated to social and political theories in a country that has little patience with contemplative speculation; reluctant to accept the habits and values of a society whose language he could never learn to use with grace, precision, or dignified pathos; forced by his refugee existence to perfect an esoteric style that is altogether alien to the native literary tradition and, consequently, unable to establish any contact with a desperately needed new readership.

Thus it is only natural that the circumstances of his life in exile produced in Broch a persistent tension that was sustained by two principal antagonistic forces. On the one hand, there was his almost frenetic desire to contribute to a better understanding of the world through the artistic representation of a most intense process of self-examination and through an ethically motivated mission of political enlightenment. This he offered in return for the gift of physical survival. On the other hand, there was the recurrent apprehension that his work was destined to be hopelessly futile or inadequate in the face of the destructive course of political events. This inner conflict more than any other single factor reflects the particular nature of Broch's intellectual situation in America, and he sought to resolve it in a manner unique among refugee novelists in this century. For in addition, and often enough in preference, to his artistic and aesthetic concerns as a writer of fiction he attempted to formulate a comprehensive system of thought that would prove with the precision of philosophical deduction and with the stringency of mathematical cognition that a humane social order and an ethical politics were possible and practically attainable even in his own time. This type of work he considered the intellectual's principal obligation in an era in which Western civilization appeared doomed to destroy itself with that inevitable logic that is the mark of its disjointed and fragmented sense of values. And even after the defeat of Hitler, mankind seemed to him threatened with continued degradation. For his contemporaries appeared incapable of overcoming their progressively more "panicked" spiritual disorientation in any way other than submitting to the false security and protection of what he perceived to be rival systems of totalitarian oppression. Against this prospect of complete dehumanization through either capitalistic or communistic enslavement, he sought to develop the philosophical foundation for a new society. It was his aim to advance a practical theory of participatory mass democracy in the postwar world that would be as "scientifically" conclusive as the doctrine of historical materialism. In its recognition of the individual human being's absolute right to freedom and dignity, his system of "totalitarian" or "total" democracy, moreover, would prove itself to be of greater plausibility and spiritual persuasiveness than its ideological opponent. He considered it a speculative achievement most urgently in need of practical realization.

It is a social theory that reflects a lifelong habit of eclectic philosophical speculation and political observation. Nevertheless, it was most decisively influenced by Broch's experiences, preoccupations, and perspectives as an intellectual in exile. Thus a description of its most salient aspects will be given its proper context only if we recapitulate briefly the course of his life and the extent of his work in America.

Broch had seriously considered the possibility of emigration as early as the spring of 1935, but did not actually leave Austria until July 1938. The decisive experience was his incarceration in the district jail at Bad Aussee in Styria, where he was detained in "protective custody" from 13 March to 31 March on suspicion of leftist political leanings and intellectual negativism. His passport was confiscated, and he had to report to the police authorities in Vienna immediately upon his release. His English visa, which Willa and Edwin Muir, the translators of his trilogy *The Sleepwalkers* (1931–32), were able to obtain for him in the meantime, had inadvertently been forwarded to Paris, where Broch had originally planned to go. When it was finally returned he took the first opportunity to fly to London. With nothing in his possession but one suitcase, he stayed there for a few days with the novelist and translator Sidney Schiff (1869–1944), the friend of James Joyce and Marcel Proust, before he proceeded to the university town of St. Andrew's in Scotland. The Muirs had invited him to stay with them. To cover the bare minimum of his living expenses, the English P.E.N. Club had secured for him a stipend of £7 per month for twelve weeks so that he could continue his work on the *Virgil* manuscript.   On 2 October, two days after the signing of the Munich Pact, Broch left England on board the *Statendam* and half a month later arrived in New York City, where he rented a small room in a boarding house on Upper Amsterdam Avenue across from Columbia University.   Because he had no reliable means of support and was practically unknown in America, he continued at first most determinedly to expand the *Virgil* material and hoped as well to complete the so-called *Mountain Novel*[1] for publication.   But despite the advantages of New York City's Public Library, Broch's work did not progress satisfactorily, especially after he fell ill during the winter months.   He was therefore very relieved when Henry S. Canby, the editor of the *Saturday Review of Literature* , invited him to spend a few months at his country home in Killingworth, Connecticut.

Shortly after his arrival in America, Broch had received some help from the American Guild for German Cultural Freedom, which became a regular monthly stipend of $50 in March 1939.   At the end of July he was sent a check for $75 for the publication of a chapter from his novel in Thomas Mann's journal *Mass und Wert* .[2]   Early in June he accepted an invitation to spend three months at the artists' colony Yaddo near Saratoga Springs, New York, to continue work on the *Virgil* novel.   This afforded him the first opportunity to write in relative tranquility.   But his request for an extension was denied, and Broch was glad to accept an offer from Albert Einstein to spend a month's time from 15 August in his house in Princeton while he was on vacation with his family.   Thereafter Broch rented a room at 11 Alexander Place near the university, where he was soon to meet Erich Kahler, who was teaching at Princeton as a guest professor from Cornell University and in whose house at 1 Evelyn Place he was a guest for most of the next ten years.   His very modest material needs were barely met by an honorary gift from the American Academy for Arts and Letters and by a stipend from the John Simon Guggenheim Memorial Foundation, which had informed him at the end of March 1940 that it would support his work on the *Virgil* novel with a fellowship that was eventually extended until December 1941.   In February 1942, when his situation was desperate, Broch was sent a supplementary check for $150.   His theories on mass hysteria, initially supported by a small grant from the Oberlaender Trust of the Carl Schurz Memorial Foundation, began to occupy him full-time and over the years grew to some 300 pages.   They were meant to form the nucleus of a three-volume study on mass psychology, the publication of which, Broch had hoped, would secure him a position at Princeton's Institute for Advanced Study or at the New School for Social Research, whose founder Alvin Johnson had strongly encouraged his work.   But in January 1942 the outlook for his future appeared catastrophic because the Rockefeller Foundation had not responded at all to a positive appraisal of

Broch's projected work and of his qualifications that Einstein, Kahler, Thomas Mann, and Johnson among others had
signed.   Another description of his studies was submitted
in the form of a thirty-three-page outline3 through Professor
Hadley Cantril of Princeton University's Office of Public Opinion Research, and this time his proposal was accepted for
funding.   Broch was notified at the end of April that he
would be paid a salary of $2,000 for one year, starting
1 May, to study mass psychological phenomena in history
as Cantril's assistant.   On 13 June 1943 his stipend was
officially extended at the same rate of compensation for a
period of twenty months until 31 December 1944.
      But his artistic integrity compelled Broch to spend
much of this time, and especially almost all of 1944, on the
expansion, revision, and stylistic perfection of *Der Tod des
Vergil* [*The Death of Virgil*], which had gone through
eight versions. Its appearance was finally scheduled for the
spring of 19454 as a simultaneous publication of both the
American translation by Jean Starr Untermeyer, which was
printed in December 1944, and the German original, which
in fact did not appear until the late summer of 1945.5   This
epic poem in four parts deals with the emotional, intellectual, and spiritual experiences of the dying Roman poet who,
during the last twenty-four hours of his life, reexamines his
entire existence as an artist, as a citizen of the empire,
and as a companion of the mighty.   Despite his recognition
that he had spent his most precious years in the vain pursuit of the idol of beauty and thus without regard for his
human obligation to help his fellow man, he decides not to
destroy the manuscript of the *Aeneid*, but to give it to
Augustus as a humble act of friendship and to grant his
slaves their freedom.   Thus prepared through his contrition
to experience the mysteries of the unknown dimension beyond
death, he returns his immortal soul to its divine origin, and
his spiritual essence is remerged in a process of mystical
union with a primal totality that is beyond comprehension.
      The immediate impact of this novel, for which an exten-
sive subscription campaign had been launched, upon the
literary world of New York can at best be called minimal.6
It was distributed in a very small edition without the custo-
mary forms of advertising, and it was received with a mix-
ture of awe, reserve, and critical misunderstanding.   The
income from its sale could not, at any rate, support Broch
for even a very short time.   Therefore, he decided to accept
some essayistic work of a literary nature on commission.7
This he considered a not unpleasant diversion, but it did
contribute in the long run to his increasingly desperate
awareness that he needed to publish another major work
soon, but that he might not find the time to finish a single
one of his major projects.
      After 1945, his declining energies and his very limited
resources were further drained by a seemingly unending flood
of letters from abroad, all of which he answered personally
and often at great length, and by the self-denying obligation to send food parcels to friends in Europe.   Also a

series of painful and complicated physical ailments were
added to these burdens. First, he spent nearly the entire
month of April 1947 in a Princeton hospital with a broken
forearm. An accident in the house of Mrs. Untermeyer the
following year forced him to return to a clinic, where his
recovery from the complication of a fractured hip and a her-
nia operation extended from 17 June 1948 to 6 April 1949.
And even though her insurance paid all of his medical expenses, the persistence of dental problems proved to be a painful and costly affliction. When Broch's continued bad health
necessitated his vacating the upstairs room in Kahler's
house, he returned briefly to New York City and took a room
for a time in the very modest Hotel Wales on Madison Avenue
at 92nd Street. From 2 May to the end of July 1949 he
stayed in New Haven at Yale University's Saybrook College
as a Poet in Residence. This honorary position, which he
held mostly during the summer vacation, did not develop into
a more substantial association with the university, and,
after the beginning of a new semester, Broch found a room
in the Duncan Hotel at 1151 Chapel Street. At the end of
the year he moved to a room in a student boarding house
at 78 Lake Place. At Yale he enjoyed the friendship and
company of Thomas and Sidonie Cassirer, of Curt and Emma
von Faber du Faur, of the historian Hajo Holborn and his
wife Anne-Marie, and of Hermann Weigand, who in 1949 had
succeeded in having him appointed an Honorary Lecturer in
the German Department, a position with no material benefits
other than a small monthly compensation that Yale paid from
a private "anonymous" donation and occasional free meals.
    One of Broch's last sources of financial support was
a stipend from the Bollingen Foundation for which he had
applied with the help of Hannah Arendt, who was a reader
and consultant for the foundation's publisher, Kurt Wolff's
Pantheon Books. Broch received the sum of $1,200 for what
appeared at first a rather inconsequential duty. He was
to contribute the introduction to an edition of collected prose
writings by Hugo von Hofmannsthal.[8] This essay, which he
had promised to finish by October 1947, turned into a major,
although fragmentary, analysis of Vienna during that prewar
period that his first novel had analyzed with primary attention to the distinctly German cultural environment. His monograph, *Hofmannsthal und seine Zeit* [*Hofmannsthal and
His Times*],[9] examines the sociology of décor and of bad
taste in fin-de-siècle Vienna. It shows Broch's interpretation of the social phenomena and human experiences underlying linguistic structures to be a forerunner, along with
Walter Benjamin's work, of critical structuralism.
    At the same time Broch was beginning to formulate the
outlines of his political theory, and he returned concurrently
to one of his earliest concerns: a mathematical and linguistic
theory of cognition. But even though he used the enforced
leisure of his hospital stay to expand the Hofmannsthal essay
from the requested sixty pages to three chapters of nearly
four times the originally intended length, the monograph was
never completed.[10] Therefore Broch had to accept an advance

from a prospective American publisher, Alfred Knopf, whose reader Robert Pick knew that a nearly publishable manuscript existed of the *Mountain Novel*. Knopf made it a condition for printing any of Broch's philosophical work that the novel should be finished first. Broch agreed to complete the book by 1 July 1950 and received an advance of $1,800 in June 1949. However, he did not start rewriting it for a second time until the beginning of 1951. A very probable reason for this is the fact that he had been engaged since the middle of 1949 in another major project that also had started rather inconspicuously. His friend Herbert Burgmüller, who was the literary advisor of the Munich publisher Weismann, had easily obtained Broch's permission to collect his old stories in a single volume. But upon reading the galley proofs, Broch found his early work to be so utterly inadequate that he expanded it to more than twice the original length by adding new narrative material and placing it into lyrical frames. The result of this transformation is the "Novel in Eleven Stories," *Die Schuldlosen* , 1950 [*The Guiltless*].11 This book was hardly finished in February 1950, after fifteen months of concentrated work, when Broch had to devote much time and energy to the corrections of the French translation of *Der Tod des Vergil* [*La Mort de Vergile*, 1952].12

The fear of being unable to complete any of his theoretical work and the precarious financial circumstances of the last two years of his life were so acute again that Broch often worked up to eighteen hours a day. He hoped for a major literary prize and for a kind of recognition that would allow him to face old age with dignity. But even though he received some minor honors, Broch did not find a source of income that would have prevented his physical collapse from overwork. On the morning of 30 May 1951 he was found dead in his room of a heart attack. It was only then that the extent of his financial obligations became apparent. His Viennese library, which had just been brought to this country, had to be sold immediately, and for several years the entire income from his books had to be used to pay off his debts.13

Broch had died in virtual obscurity. To be sure, a small group of admirers in Germany who sought to prepare his eventual return and his first publisher, Daniel Brody, used their admittedly limited influence in his behalf. But they succeeded in little more than fostering certain rumors that spoke of his productive association with prestigious universities and the generous support for his studies from famous foundations. And in America not even flattering legends surrounded his name.14 Beyond the immediate circle of a few close friends, most of whom were fellow émigrés, his work was almost totally unknown both to a lay audience and to the professional colleague. A major reason for this, no doubt, is the fact that, between 1938 and his death, Broch had published practically none of his theoretical work.15 But even if he had, it is doubtful that he would have gained much of a following, for his philosophical concerns, his method of inquiry, and his style do not lend themselves to easy comprehension or to critical and popular acceptance.   And they had always been contrary to or at least different from the practices of his academic peers. This was especially true for his concern with political theory, to which so many refugee intellectuals were drawn from moral compulsion even when it was not part of their original interests and professional training, and for the discipline of American sociology, which was revolutionized with the arrival of German émigré scholars in New York.   That is to say, Broch was working in an area in which the native proficiency in "field studies" had produced, in conjunction with the political experiences and with the theoretical models developed by European thinkers, some of the best results of intellectual cooperation or of mutual influence.   And he was working, practically speaking, outside of a normal academic or intellectual environment that could have provided its own kind of stimulation, correctives, or at least a partial division of labor.   In these circumstances, Broch was attempting nothing less than to advance the system of a comprehensive social theory that would include all major aspects of human cognition, and he sought to accomplish this through no other intellectual effort than his own.   To the specialist it must appear that he approached this overwhelming task with the innocence of an insistent dilettante or with the confidence of the gifted amateur.

The last project of a distinctly political nature in which Broch had been engaged before he left Austria was his "Aufforderung an einen nicht existenten Völkerbund" ["Appeal to a Nonexistent League of Nations"].[16]   In 1937–38 he had begun to correspond with a number of prominent Europeans to whom he had sent the text of this resolution along with a commentary and a letter of invitation to the prospective signers, hoping that this document would become a collective and representative political appeal that could be publicized widely.   It contains a number of principles and specific proposals to this "highest European forum for peace" for the preservation and protection "of the individual human being's integrity and of the continuity of culture and of its values."   For obvious reasons Broch could not pursue this plan in Europe after his arrest, but shortly following his arrival in the United States he returned to it, hoping that his appeal would be published.   Even though his hopes were disappointed, he did not give up practicing that form of political activity that, to a refugee intellectual and noncitizen, must have appeared the most directly productive.   He cooperated with a group of American and émigré scholars in drafting a document entitled *The City of Man: A Declaration of World Democracy*, which was issued by seventeen cosponsors in November 1940.[17]   It consists of a Declaration and Proposal to which is appended an explanatory note on the origin and plans of the American "Committee on Europe" from its inception in October 1938 to the formulation of its proposals after conferences in Atlantic City, New Jersey, and Sharon, Connecticut.[18]   This document advocates a "universal and total democracy [as] the principle of liberty and life which the dignity of man opposes to the principle of slavery and spiritual death represented by totalitarian autocracy" (pp. 27–28). It seeks to advance "the concept of a vital democracy [that] must be dissociated from the notion of a disintegrated liberalism" (p. 31) and that is conceived as "nothing more and nothing less than humanism in theocracy and rational theocracy in universal humanism" (p. 33). Its economic basis is envisioned as "pluralistic and flexible" (p. 56), with the factory, "in whose self-contained despotism Fascism found an early blueprint of world-wide regimentation," serving no longer as "the Bastille of the proletariat" but turning into a place where the "youth of nations" learn the "skill of production in patience rather than the craft of destruction in terror" (p. 57). A Bill of Duties supplementing the pledge in the Bill of Rights that no private property shall be taken for public use without just compensation would make it economic policy "that no private property can be tolerated outside the framework of just social use" (p. 58). This New Testament of Americanism, which "must identify itself with World Humanism," infused the best aspects from the tradition of American pragmatic idealism with a European component of moral fervor and a utopian spirit that were unshaken by the harsh experience of the early war years in justifying "America's leadership" (p. 65) in the fight against totalitarianism. Her world-trusteeship is considered a privilege for which the "objective circumstances of history" (p. 64) have chosen her and that should be the beginning of a new world order, that of the Brotherhood of the City of Man.

Broch continued this kind of promotional work with a fragmentary "Memorandum an die 'American Guild,'" in which he describes briefly the historical and political background of German émigrés in the United States, recapitulates some of his ideas on the benefits of international institutions, and defines the future obligations of the Guild in the context of his theory of "totalitarian humanism."[19] He had also worked out, as early as April and May 1939, a twenty-three-page "Vorschlag zur Gründung eines Forschungs-Institutes für politische Psychologie und zum Studium von Massenwahnerscheinungen" ["Proposal to Establish a Research Institute for Political Psychology and for the Study of Phenomena of Mass Aberration"], which he had envisioned as a future addition to the New School for Social Research in New York City.[20] Its principal objective would be to coordinate the empirical investigations and the statistical data of a collective research effort based upon a cognitive model whose structure is sufficiently comprehensive to reflect the full extent of mass psychological problems. As a plausible model to replace the mechanistic systems of the nineteenth century, that is, the economic model of Marxism and the psychoanalytical model of Freud, Broch advanced the outline of an anthropological value system that contains the theoretical foundation for his later work in this field. Only the concrete individual person, and not such mythical entities as

a "mass soul" or a "mass consciousness," is the legitimate
object of investigative and speculative concern; and: the
proper balance between man's rational and irrational acquisition of the unknown quality world, which produces his
beneficial social, cultural, and religious institutions, is
seriously threatened in disoriented modern man, especially
in the population of the big cities, because his metaphysical
fear of dying, of loneliness, and of the unknown is no
longer productively restrained or exploited through a value-
directed process of establishing spiritual and communal
bonds.   His confrontation with an intellectually and emotionally impenetrable reality brings about a loss of consciousness (and a reaction of "panic") or a hypertrophic discharge
of "life" energy (in a reaction of "ecstasy") and it leads
to those social alliances and political allegiances that have
made this an age of psychopathic doctrinarism.   Broch saw
the spreading of fascist totalitarianism, which he believed
would soon conquer all of Europe and might engulf even the
New World, as the consequence of a religious and spiritual
dissociation, of a loss of the fundamental religious verities,
and of the resultant ethical fragmentation.   His intellectual
contribution to the defeat of Nazism, which he called his
part in the "fight against the contagious disease," could
therefore not be merely psychoanalytical but had to include
all disciplines of social inquiry.   Thus it was only natural
that Broch would also formulate ideas on the redistribution
of world power and on the Russian totalitarian state.[21]
        Once more, apparently in October 1945, he tried to
find an institutional outlet for implementing his ideas when
he submitted to the New School a paper on the "Philosophical
Tasks of an 'International Academy'" with two appendices:
"Practical Educational Suggestions" and "Special Research
Tasks."[22]   It would be the main purpose of such an institution to become the intellectual center for an exact "scientific" study of man as the perfectly humane being, to provide the critical methodology for a democratic revolt against
institutional repression, and thus to formulate the cognitive
critique for a general theory of peace and humanitarianism.
Broch also sought support from the Bollingen Foundation for
a manuscript library that would collect the important literary documents of this time, and he drafted a "proposal for
the establishment of a fund for the publication and promotion
of valuable scientific works."[23]   To the United Nations he
submitted, in 1946, a "Proposal for a Law to Protect Human
Dignity,"[24] which was dutifully received and filed in the
organization's archives.   UNESCO, however, where his proposals for the establishment of research institutes eventually
ended up gathering dust, invited him to participate in a
discussion section on international educational problems.   His
accident of May 1948 prevented his attendance, so that his
sixty-page position paper, "Philosophische Grundlagen inter-
nationaler Erziehung" ["Philosophical Foundations of International Education"], was not included in any further delib-
eration.[25]

All of these projects reflect Broch's urgent concern with practical solutions to the problems of the immediate postwar years when the fact of the atomic bomb and the prospect of continued warfare between the two rival economic and political systems made him fear for the very survival of nonauthoritarian institutions. He knew that this was a time of tremendous historical change and he had become more and more disillusioned with the ability and willingness of the democratic system of government as practiced in his adopted country to resist the lure of totalitarian solutions. He wrote to a friend in July 1946 that it was only now, and not during the Hitler years, that he really felt he was in exile.[26] His political theory and his attempts to discover laws that would make the shape of future events predictable were conceived at a time when Broch, as an American citizen, seriously contemplated his return to Europe because he thought the chances for a practical realization of his ideas were better there.

His political theory, of which only the synopsis of a condensed summary was published during his lifetime,[27] is a direct outgrowth of his mass psychology: his definition of an earthly absolute and his theory of human law (*Menschengesetz* as opposed to divine or natural law) as its model of justice. This earthly absolute is explained as the absolute reprehensibleness of human enslavement and as the secular line of demarcation that establishes all consequent rights as duties. Broch saw a modern world that, in the guidance of human affairs, has substituted the partial authority of economic values as an absolute directive for a balanced hierarchy of interdependent verities. It thus faces the inevitable prospect of a totalitarian subjugation of mankind, because the economic value system needs to protect its operative territory against the claims of potential rival systems. The world is abetted therein by a continuous barrage of ideological pressure, which in turn leads to political and other forms of enslavement, so that man cannot but fall into moral apathy and total indifference to his and his fellow man's humanity. Against the "scientifically" predictable realization of total economic gratification through bellicose and revolutionary suppression of all opposition or difference, a process of pacifist evolution must be instituted that, instead of inciting the masses to bring about the ethically abnormal for the sake of a dogma, must succeed in preventing the occurrence of abnormal historical periods, that is, those whose value logic demands the totalitarian abolition of human dignity. A totalitarian humanism alone, understood as a world party with an authority that transcends state sovereignty and eventually to be concentrated in an international court of law and, subsequently, other institutions, can prevent the most destructive consequences of a continued cold war between the capitalist and the Bolshevist economic systems. And only through the implementation of such a utopia, Broch believed, could Western democratic countries regain what they had lost, politically and morally, to Marxist communism, and a just order could be found for the

world. His fear, however, was that America, where he had
experienced firsthand the advantages and shortcomings of
democracy, might not be mature enough[28] to accept the practi-
cality of his vision and thought.

Notes

[1] The earliest conception of this novel may go back to
1932. It was planned as a "religious" novel about people
in a remote mountain village whose allegiance, in the first
version of 1935–36, is torn between confidence in Mother
Gisson, an old woman with the region's traditional peasant
wisdom, and Marius Ratti, an itinerant laborer who promises
a new time. He challenges her authority after she rejects
his plea to accept him as her disciple, and in the end he
brings about the ritualistic killing of her granddaughter.
The fragmentary second version, written in 1936, expands
the underlying pattern of the Demeter–Persephone myth and
of the *magna mater* archetype and was intended as the first
part of a trilogy. The final and shortest version exemplifies
some aspects of Broch's theory concerning the style of old
age and emphasizes more directly the political implications
of plot and characters. Material from each of the three
versions was combined in Felix Stössinger's 1953 edition, *Der
Versucher* [*The Tempter*]. A critical edition in four volumes
of all the pertinent typescripts was prepared by F. Kress
and H. A. Maier. It appeared as *Der Bergroman* [*The Mountain Novel*] in 1969 (Frankfurt/M: Suhrkamp). The only
texts translated into English are two plot summaries with
descriptions of what Broch had intended to accomplish with
this novel. They were written for prospective American publishers. See also Timothy Casey, "Questioning Broch's *Der
Versucher*," *Deutsche Vierteljahrsschrift für Literaturwissenschaft und Geistesgeschichte*, 47, No. 3 (1973), 467–
507.

[2] It was the slightly shortened chapter "Die Angst"
["Anxiety"] that appeared in *Mass und Wert*, 2 (July/Aug.
1939), 748–95. Other published excerpts include the "Intro-
duction to a Peasant Novel" in the anthology *The Heart of
Europe*, edited in 1943 by Klaus Mann and Hermann Kesten
(New York: L. B. Fischer), pp. 588–92, and "Theodor Sabest,
Wirt und Fleischer" ["Theodor Sabest, Innkeeper and Butch-
er"] in *Austro-American Tribune*, 5, No. 4 (Nov. 1946), 3.

[3] It is entitled "A Study on Mass Hysteria: Contributions
to a Psychology of Politics; Preliminary Table of Contents"
and has been published as an appendix to volume VII, 257–
82, *Erkennen und Handeln* [*Perception and Action*]:
Essays II (edited by Hannah Arendt in 1955) of his *Gesammelte Werke* , which appeared in ten volumes between 1952
and 1961 (Zurich: Rhein Verlag). This edition will hence-
forth be referred to as *GW*. It is gradually being supplanted, however, by the annotated paperback edition of
Paul Michael Lützeler, which appears in the series suhrkamp

taschenbücher (Frankfurt/M: Suhrkamp) and will be the most comprehensive Broch edition upon its completion.

[4]The publisher was the émigré Kurt Wolff, whose Pantheon Books, Inc., in New York also brought out a new edition of *The Sleepwalkers: A Trilogy* in 1948.

[5]A British edition was published the following year in London by Routledge & Kegan Paul. A new printing with an introduction by Hannah Arendt appeared in 1965 (New York: Grosset & Dunlap).

[6]A front-page review in the *New York Times Book Review* of 8 July 1945 did not reach its readers because of a strike. In addition, there were altogether fifteen notices and reviews in different types of American papers and journals.

[7]Aside from short reviews and evaluative descriptions of books for American publishers, this includes his essay "Die mythische Erbschaft der Dichtung," which was written in honor of Thomas Mann's seventieth birthday for a special edition of *Neue Rundschau*, 6 June 1945, pp. 68–76. This essay was republished in *GW*, VI, 239–48 and appeared as "The Heritage of Myth in Literature," *Chimera*, 4, No. 3 (Spring 1946), 33–41; "The Style of the Mythical Age," an introduction to an English translation of Rachel Bespaloff's monograph *On the Iliad* (New York: Pantheon, 1947), pp. 9–33 (and *GW*, VI, 249–64); and "Geschichte als moralische Anthropologie: Erich Kahlers *Scienza Nuova*," *Hamburger Akademische Rundschau*, 3 (1948), 406–16, which was translated into English as Broch's contribution to a *Festschrift Kahler*, ed. E. L. Wolff and H. Steiner (New York: Van Fechten Press, 1951), pp. 18–30.

[8]The edition of Hugo von Hofmannsthal, *Selected Prose*, did not appear until 1952 (New York: Pantheon; and London: Routledge & Kegan Paul). Broch's "Introduction" (pp. 9–47) was published first in its German original as "Zu Hugo von Hofmannsthals Prosaschriften," *Neue Rundschau*, 62, No. 2 (1951), 1–30, then in *GW*, VI, 150–81 as chapter III of the monograph, which has not been translated in its entirety.

[9]See also *GW*, VI, 43–181 and its republication with an introduction by Hannah Arendt as volume 94 of Piper Bücherei (Munich: Piper, 1964).

[10]In addition to the material published, the Broch Archive at Yale University Library (=YUL) has six fragmentary drafts. One of them, seventy-two leaves of an original typescript with MS corrections, is entitled "IV. Der Turm von Babel" ["IV. The Tower of Babel"]. A bibliography of YUL material was prepared by Christa Sammons, "Hermann Broch Archive: Yale University Library," *Modern Austrian Literature*, 5, No. 3/4 (1972), 18–69.

[11]*Die Schuldlosen: Roman in elf Erzählungen*, introd. Hermann J. Weigand, *Gesammelte Werke*, V (Zurich: Rhein-Verlag, 1950). English translation: *The Guiltless*, trans. Ralph Manheim (Boston: Little, Brown and Co., 1974). It is a not altogether successful combination of reinterpreted elements from the Don Juan myth with character types from the

Hitler generation whose various forms of moral indifference and political apathy contribute to the rise of Nazism, even though they all are legally "Innocents." This book may have realized at least partially one of Broch's early plans, the so-called "Tierkreis Erzählungen" ["Stories of the Zodiac"], which were an attempt to write a representative story about each sign of the zodiac.

12It was done by Albert Kohn for Gallimard in Paris.

13This library was bought by Joseph Buttinger and became part of his Library of Political Science in New York City. In 1971, Buttinger donated most of it, including the Broch library, to the University of Klagenfurt. See Joseph Buttinger, "Aufbau und Auflösung einer Bibliothek," *Archiv: Mitteilungsblatt des Vereins für Geschichte der Arbeiterbewegung*, 13, No. 1 (Jan.-March 1973), 3-11.

14Broch is still almost totally unknown in America, even to people seriously interested in literature who, unfortunately, cannot consult much valuable introductory writing in English. The only sources with extensive information are Theodore Ziolkowski's essay *Hermann Broch* (1964), which is vol. 3 of the Columbia Essays on Modern Writers; Jean Starr Untermeyer's recollections "Midwife to a Masterpiece," in her *Private Collection* (New York: Knopf, 1965), pp. 218-77; and Ernestine Schlant, *Hermann Broch*, TWAS, No. 485 (Boston: Twayne, 1978).

15He published only four occasional pieces in American journals: a short essay, "Ethical Duty," which appeared in the "Exile Writers Issue" of the *Saturday Review of Literature*, 19 Oct. 1949, p. 8; a very pedestrian piece of satirical prose, "Adolf Hitler's Farewell Address," in the same magazine, 21 Oct. 1944, pp. 5-8; a review of Werner Richter's book *Frankreich von Gambetta bis Clémenceau* in the *Review of Politics*, 10, No. 1 (Jan. 1948), 141-44, of which his friend Waldemar Gurian was the editor; and an appreciation of Elisabeth Langgässer's novel *Das unauslöschliche Siegel* as "The Indelible Seal: A Novel of the Pilgrimage of Faith," *Commentary*, 10 (Aug. 1950), 170-74.

16Its text is published in a volume of selected political essays: Hermann Broch, *Gedanken zur Politik*, ed. Dieter Hildebrandt, Bibliothek Suhrkamp, 245 (Frankfurt/M: Suhrkamp, 1970), pp. 24-36, from page 25 of which the following quotations are taken. All the material pertaining to this project was edited by Paul Michael Lützeler under the title of *Völkerbund-Resolution: Das vollständige politische Pamphlet von 1937 mit Kommentar, Entwurf und Korrespondenz*, Brenner-Studien, 2 (Salzburg: Müller, 1973).

17It was published in New York by Viking Press. Page numbers of my quotations from it are given in parentheses.

18These preparatory meetings took place on 24-26 May and 24-25 August 1940. The secretary of the Committee, Giuseppe Antonio Borgese, author of, among other books on the subject, *Fascism in Action: A Documented Study and Analysis of Fascism in Europe*, prepared at the instance and under the direction of Representative Wright Patman (Washington, D.C.: U.S. Govt. Printing Office, 1947), later headed the Committee of Fifteen, which became the Committee to Frame a World Constitution. Its thirteen conferences between Nov. 1945 and July 1947 and its magazine, *Common Cause* , published monthly thereafter, led to the publication of a *Preliminary Draft of a World Constitution* (Chicago: University of Chicago Press, 1948) as proposed and signed by eleven scholars, among them Erich Kahler, but not Broch. It includes a Declaration of Duties and Rights, a Grant of Powers, and the outline of a constitution for a Federal Republic of the World with commentaries.

[19] His two-page "Report on my activities in rescuing endangered European Writers, June 1940–October 1941" is a practical concomitant and refers to his efforts on behalf of, among others, Paul Schrecker, Gustav Ichheiser, Paul Amann, Werner Richter, Franz Blei, and Franz Werfel. In the summer of 1940, he was engaged in seeking official support from the United States Departments of Justice and of State for his proposal of an "Emigree Loyality [sic] League." YUL has also fragmentary "Vorschläge für den 'Council for Democracy,'" six leaves of proposals for effective propaganda in support of democracy.

[20] A second version of July 1939 exists at YUL in the form of a carbon copy of a twenty–two–page typescript.

[21] YUL has a German typescript "Machtumorganisierung der Welt" ["Worldwide Reorganization of Power"], thirty–six leaves with MS corrections, of which there is also an English translation in three copies, and a fragmentary draft "Der Russische Totalitätsstaat" ["The Russian Totalitarian State"], twenty–six leaves with MS corrections.

[22] A longer German version was tentatively entitled "Gründungsaufruf für eine internationale Universität" ["Proclamation for the Establishment of an International University"], of which YUL has a carbon typescript of sixty leaves with corrections and a fragment of two other versions. The English text is an original typescript of forty–one plus eight leaves with MS corrections by an unidentified reader. It was preceded by another draft of ten leaves entitled "Bemerkungen zum Projekt einer 'International University,' ihrer Notwendigkeit und ihren Möglichkeiten" ["Comments on the Project of an 'International University,' on Its Necessity and Potential"], of 1944, which was introduced by brief confidential observations on the institutional context in which this project might be realized. Most of this material was published in 1969 as vol. 301 of edition suhrkamp under the misleading title: Hermann Broch, *Zur Universitätsreform* , ed. with a commentary by Götz Wienold.

[23] YUL has a two–page original typescript with MS corrections, a carbon typescript, and the original typescript of an earlier version of this proposal.

[24] The German original, "Forderung nach einem Gesetz zum Schutz der Menschenwürde" ["Call for a Law to Protect Human Dignity"], was translated by J. S. Untermeyer and exists as a carbon typescript of nineteen leaves with MS corrections. There are also two other typescripts of thirteen

and seventeen leaves at YUL. The English version has fifteen pages.

[25]In 1950, lack of time prevented his accepting an invitation to participate in the Congress for Cultural Freedom which met in Berlin on 26–30 June. He sent an address, "Die Intellektuellen und der Kampf um die Menschenrechte" ["Intellectuals and the Struggle for Human Rights"], which was published in *Literatur und Kritik*, No. 54/55 (1971), pp. 193–97.

[26]See *GW*, VIII: *Briefe von 1929 bis 1951*, ed. Robert Pick (1957), 257.

[27]*Neue Rundschau*, 61, No. 1 (1950), 1–31. Its title is "Trotzdem: Humane Politik; Verwirklichung einer Utopie" ["Nevertheless: Humane Politics; Realization of a Utopia"]. Vol. VII of *GW* has two chapters of a fragmentary essay "Politik: Ein Kondensat" (pp. 203–55), vol. IX has three fragmentary essays from the material dealing with the theory of history and politics. It also contains, on pp. 235–36, Broch's incomplete "Autobiographie als Arbeitsprogramm" ["Autobiography as a Program for Future Work"], which has not been translated and is the most coherent description of his theoretical work, although not always a chronologically and factually accurate one. Other MSS at YUL from this field of interest are entitled: "Bemerkungen zur Utopie einer International Bill of Rights and of Responsibilities" ["Remarks on the Utopia of an . . ."], forty-five leaves with two shorter English versions and one shorter German version; "Economical Slavery," four leaves; "Pamphlet gegen die Hochschätzung des Menschen" ["Pamphlet Against the High Esteem in Which Man Is Held"], nineteen leaves, fragmentary, and drafts for other versions; "Strategischer Imperialismus," fifty-five leaves and variants; a draft, "Theorie der Geschichtsschreibung und der Geschichtsphilosophie" ["Theory of Historiography and of the Philosophy of History"], 104 pp. manuscript; a draft "Über Marx," ten leaves; a fragmentary draft "Totale Humanität, unbequem aber möglich und notwendig: Über die Grundlagen der gegenwärtigen Weltpolitik" ["Total Humanitarianism, Uncomfortable but Possible and Necessary: Concerning the Foundations of Contemporary World Politics"], eleven leaves; an outline of a planned book "Zur Diktatur der Humanität innerhalb einer totalen Demokratie" ["Toward a Dictatorship of the Human Spirit within a Totalitarian Democracy"]; "Demokratie vs. Faschismus, 1946," seventy-eight leaves.

[28]On this see his letters to Frank Thiess of 24 May 1948 and to Herman Salinger of 29 Sept. 1950 in *GW*, VIII, 290 and 405–06. Broch's political theories have, to my knowledge, elicited no response whatever from American social and political scientists or from fellow exiles if we except the introductory and largely descriptive comments of his friends Hannah Arendt and Erich Kahler. Thinkers like Herbert Marcuse and Ernst Bloch, who have found a wide international following in the past years, even though they also worked in complete isolation while in America, stand at the opposite end of the political spectrum. Despite the fact that their philosophy

seeks to define antidoctrinarian concepts of socialist democracy and centers on the practical potential inherent in utopian thought, there are absolutely no points of contact with
Broch's speculations.

Lion Feuchtwanger: The Hazards of Exile

Lothar Kahn

On a gray morning in November 1932, Lion Feuchtwanger left from a Berlin railroad station for London, the first leg of a lecture trip to the United States. He did not remotely suspect that he was forever taking leave of German soil. For almost alone among the Weimar artists who were anathematized by Hitler or who rejected him, Feuchtwanger was doomed to an exile, begun unwittingly three months before Hitler's appointment as chancellor of Germany, that would last until his death. Yet this cold fact is deceiving. Feuchtwanger would have cherished a return to Germany, at least after 1948, though not as a permanent resident. He was eager to renew old ties, visit the haunts of younger days, observe with typical curiosity the changes that political events do—or do not—bring about in the lives of men. But Feuchtwanger, whose citizenship petition was held in perennially active status without ever being finally acted upon, was unwilling to risk what was shortly to happen to his friend Charlie Chaplin—prohibition of his return to the United States. For despite occasional criticisms, Feuchtwanger had begun to regard America as his home. He was too attached to his California mansion, his quiet lifestyle, his established work patterns, and his American readers to contemplate renewed uprooting and resettlement. Although Feuchtwanger was wholly sincere in separating Nazis from Germans—at no time during his exile did he accept the equation—he probably could not make his peace with German life after so many years of banishment. Also, the failure of West Germans to interest themselves in his work after the initial desire to catch up was a silent disappointment. Politically he questioned the failure of the Bonn regime to rid itself of Nazis in top echelons of government. As for the GDR, in which his work was well received, where Brecht and Arnold Zweig had resettled, and where, two days before his death, Heinrich Mann had been planning to go, Feuchtwanger did not seriously consider it as a permanent residence. One can only speculate about his reasons. Feuchtwanger could not have forgotten the fears he had expressed regarding the

157

Soviet Union ten years earlier, just before embarking on his
Soviet journey. The USSR was a dictatorship, he had stated,
and he knew that as a writer he was driven from within to
give unrestricted expression to his feelings, thoughts, and
experiences, "regardless of individuals, class, party and
ideology. And so, despite my personal feelings, I was mis-
trustful of Moscow."[1]

His suspicions had decidedly weakened with time, but
deep inside they had not been entirely allayed. To be sure,
he viewed the Eastern societies with sympathy--in fact, a
a growing sympathy--but also one that had distance as a
safeguard for his writer's precious freedom. Tüverlin, one of
the main characters of *Success* and a virtual stand-in for
Feuchtwanger, had changed, but not completely. The conflicts between his Marxism and his independence had never
been fully resolved.

But in Feuchtwanger's known sympathy for the Eastern
societies lies one of the trenchant clues to Feuchtwanger's
exile, which, beginning in 1936 and ending with his death,
was in life characterized by his attraction to the "rational
societies"[2] and by the negative responses that this attraction
occasioned in others. Not only did his sympathies endanger
his life in France in the summer of 1940, bringing denunciation from fellow refugees of different political orientation,
but they caused him frequent embarrassment in the United
States and eventually kept him from becoming a full member
of the American community. Yet despite his attraction, as
Jean Améry and others have pointed out,[3] Feuchtwanger never
allowed this sympathy to dominate his work or even to become
clearly apparent. Even when he dealt with topics like
social injustice, domination of one group by another, the
engagement of the artist, or revolution and revolutionary justice, his strong leftist orientation became discernible, but no
more. Although he was capable of an imprudent statement
and perhaps even a foolish assertion, he remained in the
quiet of his study a wise man, a man who retained his intellectual perspective, a distance that enabled him to maintain
a sound level of judgment. The same balance permeates his
work. Wherever he injects into a novel an advocate of communism, he also provides a proponent of democratic freedom;
wherever there is a fascist, there is a communist or a democrat. Feuchtwanger's work, more than his life, is a series
of political-social tensions, of philosophic polarities, of
belief and skepticism. Sympathy, yes; attraction, yes; an
irrevocable commitment, no!

I

It is true that Feuchtwanger in exile suffered fewer
serious hardships, economic upheavals, or general vicissi-
tudes than fellow artists in exile. But because of envy in
some and lack of comprehension in others, there has been
a regrettable tendency to belittle the strong hand, the determination, the capacity for living, the brand of civic courage,

and--though he denied it--physical courage in the shaping of his destiny. Although he deserves full credit for this fortitude in adversity, one cannot deny that Feuchtwanger had one major advantage over his comrades in Sanary or later in Santa Monica. Feuchtwanger had, prior to exile, a vast reading public abroad, one that perhaps equaled or even exceeded the one he had acquired in his own country. This must have been a source of puzzlement before his banishment; after 1933, the presence of an already established readership for his works substantially increased his security in strange lands.

And yet, when Feuchtwanger returned home from his American lecture trip in March 1933, he knew that there would be a period of financial uncertainty. He joined his wife, Marta, then skiing in Austria. As a favorite target of Nazi attack, he was warned that this area close to the German border was physically unsafe. There had been kidnappings, and he might be considered an attractive target. Feuchtwanger thus left for Switzerland, and in the quiet of the Swiss mountains he mulled over the immediate future. It was questionable that he could rearrange his work habits and abandon that rigorous method and discipline of work that he had adopted in the 1920s, and do so without psychic-creative trauma. He was now accustomed to dictating, but how could he afford a secretary? A trusted friend had visited the Feuchtwangers' bank in Munich, but his distant relations were disinclined to risk their own safety by releasing his account. Depressed by the loss of his fortune, his Berlin villa (which was ransacked by Brownshirts), and his beloved library, Feuchtwanger nevertheless resolved to move. Much earlier he had contemplated temporary or even permanent residence on the Italian or French Riviera, and now he could transform hardship into the realization of an old dream. In the spring of 1933 the Feuchtwangers moved to the fishing village of Bandol, close to Toulon, stayed briefly at the Hotel Grand Réserve--where Thomas Mann put in an unexpected visit--and with the arrival of his secretary almost immediately returned to work. For reasons he attributed to human failure, his second *Josephus* volume had not been removed in time from his Grunewald villa, and he did not attempt to rewrite it for well over a year. The shape of European history to come was signaled by the arrival in Sanary, the Feuchtwangers' new residence, of a Sidney Gilliat, a British screen writer. Gilliat came at the request of Prime Minister Ramsay MacDonald, whom Feuchtwanger had met in London. MacDonald was urging the German author to write an anti-Nazi scenario. Because Feuchtwanger had little experience with film technique, Gilliat was prepared to assist him. The result was *The Oppermanns* , but by the time the scenario was completed, the British government had decided upon a course of polite persuasion of Hitler. Feuchtwanger felt free to take matters into his own hands, and rewrote *The Oppermanns* as a novel.

Feuchtwanger's working time was increasingly taken up now with letters from readers inquiring above all about

conditions within the Third Reich. He realized that he would
have to bow to fate and accept the loss of writing time. He
also recognized that, like it or not, he would be drawn
actively from his preferred "contemplation and delineation"
into the antifascist struggle. He himself had been officially
deprived of his German citizenship in the late summer of
1933, having the considerable honor of appearing on the
first list of "former citizens" published 27 August 1933. He
now endorsed virtually every anti-Nazi organization that
sought his name and help. But with active participation,
he also recognized that his host nation was not as solidly
anti-Hitler as it appeared on the surface. There were powerful sources that discerned in the German dictator a possible
savior from social change and the evil of Bolshevism. These
people, outwardly staunch patriots and antifascists, were
not averse only a few years later to proclaiming: "Better
Hitler than Blum." Britain and France, according to Feuchtwanger's informants, would be weak and uncertain allies
in the defeat of fascism. Slowly, gradually, Feuchtwanger
began to see in the Soviet Union the sole, reliable bulwark
of antifascism.

In 1935 he began to receive unofficial invitations to
visit the Soviet Union, whose "humanist" experiment had always intrigued him. But he had also detested the cult of
Stalin and the loss of freedom for "brainworkers," including
independent authors like himself. Despite his reluctance to
visit the USSR, he finally undertook the journey. He was
impressed on the whole, had a lengthy interview with Stalin,
and published his generally favorable report on what he had
seen and heard. In the company of then United States
ambassador Joseph E. Davies he attended the Purge Trials.
Like Davies, Edward Snow, and others, Feuchtwanger--per-
haps naively--believed the defendants guilty of the conspira-
torial charge against them. The visit to Moscow and the
book based on it, *Moscow 1937: My Visit Described for
My Friends* , did not gain Feuchtwanger many friends. In
fact, they evoked angry cries from many quarters, from
Nazis howling in Germany to Social Democrats accusing him
of stupidity or collusion. It is true that after 1937 he
regarded the Soviet Union as more than a mere defense
against Nazism or just an interesting social experiment. He
now believed that experiment deserving of wider interest and
broader support, and he became ever more intolerant of
Western elements who would unreservedly and a priori condemn the Soviet Union.

More than ever before, Feuchtwanger signed antifascist
appeals, messages to the Spanish Loyalists, and "writers'
manifestoes" of one kind or another. With Brecht and Bredel,
though with little active participation, he edited *Das Wort*,
published in Moscow. The conviction had grown meanwhile
that his original assertion upon Hitler's accession to power--
that Hitler meant war--was approaching realization. He was
urged by his secretary and friends to use his American visa,
but for once he was loath to act. Marta Feuchtwanger
uncharacteristically stayed on the sidelines and did not

encourage him.   Later he confessed a probable motive beyond
the obvious ones of having to pack again and leave once
more a cherished abode and a setting he adored.   There was,
he wrote, the writer's natural curiosity to see and observe.[4]
The story of his first brief internment in May 1940 is set
forth in *The Devil in France*, as was his later and more
harrowing confinement, the near-fatal illness at Les Mille,
his futile trip to the Spanish border, his renewed internment
at Nimes, and his escape, dressed as a woman, from the
camp.   Dressed in this manner, he wrote in the concluding
paragraph of this autobiographical work, he was driven off
out of reach of the Devil in France (p. 261).

    This was a half-accurate statement at best.   He left
the camp, to be sure, and the Vichy regime's hostile supervision, but he still had to spend six weeks at the villa of
a morally committed American consul.   There, typically, he
immediately continued work on *Josephus and the Emperor*,
the final volume of his trilogy.   Yet he could not shut out,
even if he wanted to, the sound of Nazi boots.   Danger was
lurking everywhere.   He was dependent on others to plot his
escape from France.   He heard with stoic calm how Varian
Fry's attempt to use an escape vessel was foiled.   Then he
learned of the perilous plan, soon to be implemented, of
spiriting him and Marta across the Pyrenees into unpredictable Spain and finally to spy-infested Lisbon.   In this
adventure he was guided by a Unitarian minister, the Rever-
end Mr. Sharp, who watched over his every step.   Danger
did not cease until Sharp's wife gave her sailing ticket to
Feuchtwanger.   He was never again to set foot on European
soil.

    Feuchtwanger was psychically exhausted aboard the
transatlantic steamer, was uncommonly reticent, and slept
for long hours on deck.   But as soon as he arrived in New
York, he became his old quiet yet forceful self.   Upon settling at the St. Moritz Hotel, he hired a new secretary and
immediately went to work.   He sought dominance over his
affairs, and fought his lingering fatigue with work and by
attending the many affairs in his honor.   He did not permit
himself to be disconcerted when a factually inaccurate attack
appeared in *Time*, assaulting his ties with the Soviet Union.[5]
Yet his continued defense of the Soviet Union in the face of
the Hitler-Stalin pact (which, as a result of private information, he persisted in regarding as a Soviet tactic to gain
time) made his political position difficult and his social
evenings at times uncomfortable.   When after so many years
on the sunny Côte d'Azur he found the New York climate
insufferable, he heeded the invitations of friends to settle
in California.   He arrived there early in 1941.   He tried
hard to assist others who were stranded (like Brecht) to
come to the United States.   In turn, he was helped in finding a new permanent residence, no easy task because he
moved six times in all.   Thereafter, he appeared to become
truly the "peaceful anchorite of Pacific Palisades."[6]   The
remaining eighteen years were characterized by an unrelent-
ing control over his time, a remarkable discipline over him-

self, a rigid daily routine from which he deviated but rarely. He sought vigorously to economize that which, with increasing age, would become ever more precious: time. There were books he still wanted and needed to write, and he was determined that they would be written.

Until Hitler's defeat in 1945, Feuchtwanger engaged in the kind of political activism in which exiles have traditionally engaged against those who have banished them. But Feuchtwanger's activism was limited to a kind that is natural and legitimate in a writer: guiding the thought of those readers who had placed their trust in him. Otherwise exile did not substantially alter Lion Feuchtwanger. Except for a period in Sanary during which, perhaps beset by problems of middle age, he would work less well, Feuchtwanger remained quintessentially a man dedicated to his art and his mission, a man who had turned from his earlier passivity and submissiveness to fate and was now more inclined actively to direct his destiny.

Feuchtwanger's own life supplied the most forceful argument for a thesis he had advanced in his novel *Paris Gazette*, namely that exile made the strong stronger and the weak weaker. It had crushed people he knew: Hasenclever, who had committed suicide at Les Mille, Stefan Zweig, with whom he had corresponded, and Toller. On the other hand, it had strengthened Thomas Mann and Brecht, who seemed irrepressible, and failed to crush Heinrich Mann, who was nearly forgotten in exile. It had damaged Döblin; it had hurt Arnold Zweig. It affected Feuchtwanger's life; it did not alter its basic quality. It did, however, significantly affect and alter the nature of his literary work.

II

His output after 1933 mirrors the outlines of his life. The years in France were filled with books he could not or would not have written in Germany, or without the menacing presence of the Hitler movement. Thus *The Oppermanns*, written in haste between April and October 1933, almost converted him, though only temporarily, into a political publicist. The book was to be a fictional instrument of alerting a cynical and smug outside world to the horrible events in cultured Germany. Despite the haste with which it was written, the novel contained superb characterizations that reflected Feuchtwanger's understanding of both the best and worst in German-Jewish life and of the conditions that made Nazis of ordinary men and also of less ordinary ones. The second *Josephus* novel, *The Jew of Rome*, when Feuchtwanger finally sat down to rewrite it, was different from the lost version in several respects--all of which mirrored the changes that had been wrought in world affairs in the previous one and a half years. *The Pretender* , written in 1935-36, the story of the false Nero, was an anti-Nazi book in historical guise. It made vividly clear the infinite misery to which mediocre and criminal leaders could condemn a people.

Feuchtwanger's travel report on the Soviet Union, *Moscow 1937*, might not have been written at all, for without Hitler conceivably there would have been no trip, certainly none as long, searching, and controversial. The most poignant of Feuchtwanger's novels in exile was his second major *Zeitroman* (topical novel), *Paris Gazette* (1936-39). This undeservedly forgotten work transformed the author's own experiences and observations of the effects of exile on others. He depicted the continued relationship of refugees to the homeland, the hold of a criminal regime on the banished, and the reach of that regime as it seeks beyond its borders for additional power--and finds it. In the novel, despite tribulations, the composer Sepp Trautwein actually grows stronger as he recognizes the duty of the artist to involve himself against injustice. But his wife Anna, to whom he had been greatly attached, can bear no longer the anxieties of a world grown strange and treacherous. The novel continues many of the themes of Feuchtwanger's greatest topical novel, the equally neglected *Success* . The third Josephus novel, *Josephus and the Emperor* , which Feuchtwanger was writing when the Nazi hordes overran France, might have featured a less arbitrary Domitian, and a different conclusion might have been reached concerning Josephus's end. The autobiographical *Devil in France* (1940-41) was possible only because once again Hitler was in close pursuit, this time more awesomely threatening than in 1933. Both the play, *The Visions of Simone Machard* , written in collaboration with Brecht, and the novel *Simone* , written by Feuchtwanger alone, were fictional interpretations of Feuchtwanger's impression that the French bourgeoisie had betrayed the country. Brecht, in fact, suggested the play after reading Feuchtwanger's account of his experiences in France. *Double, Double, Toil and Trouble* (1941), by far Feuchtwanger's weakest novel--he himself regarded it as a failure--purported to delineate the "mythical origins of the Third Reich by depicting the alleged influence of an astrologer on Hitler."[7]   Once again Feuchtwanger came under attack for supposedly underestimating the *Führer*. He had ridiculed Kutzner-Hitler in *Success* (1927-30), in the late twenties; he had mocked him by implication in *The Pretender*; now, he seemed to be presenting him in the light of the occult, hardly a proper presentation for a man who had almost conquered the whole of Europe. But, as Feuchtwanger countered, he was fully conscious of the evil the Hitlers were capable of perpetrating and had already committed; he simply refused to regard their "accomplishments" as more than the mediocre acts of men who simply had the advantage of ignoring all inhibitions and conscience.

His initial exile in France and his later one in the United States combined with his interest in the Soviet Revolution made him return, around 1943, to a subject he had long held under consideration: the relationship between the French and American Revolutions. The result was *Proud Destiny* (1944-46). Reading in preparation for this novel, Feuchtwanger had immersed himself in American history and

come upon the fascinating figure of Cotton Mather, a brilliant New England theologian who became embroiled in the
witch hunts of Salem.   As he began to perceive in the American press and among some members of Congress a trend
toward new witch hunting, Feuchtwanger wrote a play, *Wahn
oder der Teufel in Boston*, 1946 [*The Devil in Boston*].
Again, while reading on the French Revolution in preparation
for *Proud Destiny*, he had been attracted to the tragic
figure of Marie Antoinette.   The unfortunate French queen
was to appear in no fewer than four of his works in the
late forties and early fifties.   Yet again merging the historical setting with a contemporary issue, Feuchtwanger now
wrote the play *The Widow Capet* (1949), which, like *Success*
many years earlier, dealt with the anatomy of a political
trial, in which "the accused was subjectively in the right
and the accuser objectively so."[8]   Still drawing on his
knowledge of the French Revolution, Feuchtwanger next examined the effect of that revolution on feudal neighboring
Spain.   *This Is the Hour* (1948–50) recounts the evolution
of the painter Francisco Goya.   But the novel also concerned
itself with the dynamics of the historic process and, in a
real sense, represents Feuchtwanger's literary testament.
The artist acquainted with higher notions of social justice
cannot remain silent in the face of visible inequities in his
own environment or nation.   He cannot stand on the sidelines
in times of terror or grievous wrongs; he cannot, Feuchtwanger felt in exile, escape into art for art's sake, feel
himself above the melee, take pleasure only in private de-
lights.   The Goya novel was followed by one on Rousseau,
*'Tis Folly to Be Wise or Death and Transfiguration of
Jean-Jacques Rousseau*, in which the philosopher, appearing but briefly at the beginning, is the foil for demonstrat-
ing two aspects of Feuchtwanger's own experience in his
post-German years: revolution is costly in its own time, but
perhaps ultimately rewarding (a thesis apparently of particular import to those suffering the "pangs of revolution" in
Eastern European countries); a man with a public will be
understood, or more often misunderstood, differently by various segments of this public and at different times.
     When the Rousseau novel was published in 1952, Feucht-
wanger was approaching seventy.   For some reason, possibly
compassion for Jewish suffering—possibly, too, because his
story explored further the notion of progress—the author
returned in part to themes and characters of *Jud Süss*
(1921–22), his first great success.   *Raquel, the Jewess of
Toledo* (1952–54) has the same brutish ruler but also a Jewish minister who is sensitive and incorruptible, whose daughter, like that of Süss, is violated by the ruler, and again
the Jewish community is ambivalent about the man so close
to the seat of power.   They fear him and they admire him;
they hope for his protection and, anticipating his fall, pray
that they will escape its consequences.   It was another in
a series of novels about Jews in which the perennial insecurity of the Jews is described poignantly, but not emphasized.
For there is little evidence that Feuchtwanger, although a

victim of Hitler's anti-Jewish measures, expressed himself
in paranoid terms or even consciously about the permanently
insecure status of the Jew.   In fact, in an article on "The
Jew's Sense of History,"[9] he referred in strongly positive
terms to a specific Jewish historic memory that had held Jews
together through two thousand years of exile and that had
enabled them, in his own time, to establish a third common-
wealth.   "No other people has felt so deeply the flow, the
dynamics of what they experienced as a community, nor has
any other people experienced as intensively the ever enduring, the permanence within this eternal change."   For him
Jews were now people who did not merely let things happen;
they caused them to happen.

It was this view of Jewish destiny that led him, cau-
tiously, toward greater endorsement of Zionism.   Sympathetic
from the first to the idea of a Jewish homeland, a refuge
for Jews who were threatened anywhere, it was only the Hitlerite experience that persuaded him to offer further support
--to recognize that if a people were to be a people, it could
not live, as Yohanan ben Zakkai in *Josephus* had hoped,
on books, memory, morality, and traditions.   Soil and land,
the concrete, were equally essential.   It was as a Jew that
Feuchtwanger comprehended the craving for Zion and that
he could not accept the solution of territory in Africa when
the Palestine problems became increasingly serious.   Thomas
Mann, when visited by the same committee, found the solution
acceptable.   But Zion was indeed academic for the great
Olympian.   For Feuchtwanger, who knew Jewish traditions--
though he observed them little--an African homeland seemed
a poor substitute.   Yet despite his increasing support for
Zionism, his comprehension of needs, and his general sympathy and support even for the terrorist Irgun, it would be
wrong to label Lion Feuchtwanger an avid Zionist.   His distrust of anything that even hinted at modern nationalism may
have served as the inner rein.

In 1903, at age nineteen, Feuchtwanger abandoned his
parental home because of excessive bickering, much of it
over the observance of Judaic traditions.   Yet despite this,
Feuchtwanger's interest in these traditions, in the language
that nurtured them, the culture that sprouted them, the Bible
that served as their foundation, had remained strong, and
his interest in the Judaica collection in the parental home
only increased with age.   Was it sympathy for the nascent
Jewish state, or, with the approach of death, a yearning
for his roots and childhood, that made him turn for his last
novel to a Biblical topic, the story of Jephta and his daughter?   Throughout Feuchtwanger's work, fathers losing their
daughters--as he had lost his own in 1911--abound, and perhaps subconsciously the theme had an additional attraction
for him.   But basically, to judge from his letters, biblical
research gave him such satisfaction that the scholar in him
threatened to gain control over the artist.   It was this
relationship between scholar and artist, history and fabulation or myth, and their respective natures and power that
formed the topic of Feuchtwanger's last and unfinished book.

For years, every time he was criticized for taking liberties with historical facts, which he knew with uncanny accuracy, he had been tempted to write this book, *The House of Desdemona* (1956-58). But again and again he had shelved it, despite extensive notes and preparations, in favor of another fabulation. It was ironic that Feuchtwanger, more sparing of time than most humans, should not have completed the work for which, again and again, he had expressed the most urgent of needs.

*   *   *

The mature Lion Feuchtwanger was the same man in and out of exile. Inevitably, exile affected him, although not in any deleterious, permanently debilitating fashion. It created moments of anguish and often petty impatience with endless bureaucratic annoyances. But in a man now solidly formed, firm in his belief in his talent, convinced that free will existed along with the necessity, at times, to bow to the inevitable, exile barely dented the personality. Exile did, of course, affect the outer life, and this in time left its mark on the literary landscape. For an author who employed the past to shed light on the present and, when writing of the present, viewed it from the vantage of the future--that is, as an aspect of the past--the contemporary scene was, of course, all-important. But because Feuchtwanger was persuaded that human nature did not change, that human problems often had a common base of sameness, topicality for him was not really rooted in time. It was timeless and universal. In this unique approach to universality may be found one strength of Feuchtwanger's oeuvre: in the combination of narrative talent, flesh-and-blood characterization, and plot development lies another; in a mature philosophy that mixed cautious optimism with irony resides a third; finally, in his quiet wisdom and humor, yet a fourth. These were his literary trademarks in exile and before. Feuchtwanger's work needs to be taken out of mothballs, studied once more and enjoyed, and perhaps nowhere more than in his own, often humorless land.

Notes

[1] Lion Feuchtwanger, *Moscow 1937: My Visit Described for My Friends*, trans. Irene Josephy (New York: Viking, 1937), p. viii.
[2] In virtually all references to the Soviet Union, from *Moscow 1937* (pp. viii ff.) to "An meine Sowjetleser" ["To My Soviet Readers"], in *Centum Opuscula* , ed. Wolfgang Berndt (Rudolstadt: Greifenverlag, 1956), p. 534, Feuchtwanger alludes to the rational society, rational planning, etc. now going on in the Soviet Union.

3Jean Améry, "Ein Romancier der reinen Vernunft: Erinnerung an Lion Feuchtwanger," a lecture delivered over the Hessischer Rundfunk, Frankfurt/M, 30 May 1971.   Uncorrected mimeographed text in the Lion Feuchtwanger Memorial Library.

4 *The Devil in France* , trans. Elizabeth Abbott (New York: Viking, 1941), p. 15.

5"Exiles" (Books), *Time*, 36, No. 20 (11 Nov. 1940), 80, 82.   I have discussed this episode and other aspects of Feuchtwanger's stay in the USA in my essay: "Lion Feuchtwanger," in *Deutsche Exilliteratur seit 1933: Band I, Kalifornien*, ed. John M. Spalek and Joseph Strelka (Berne: Francke, 1976), pp. 331-51.   See also my biography *Insight and Action: The Life and Work of Lion Feuchtwanger* (Rutherford,   N.J.:   Fairleigh-Dickinson   University   Press, 1975).

6Term used in a communication to the author.

7Letter to his publisher, Ben Huebsch, 8 May 1942. See Lothar Kahn, *Insight and Action*, p. 275.

8Letter to Huebsch, 17 May 1948.   Translation mine.

9Lion Feuchtwanger, "The Jew's Sense of History," *Jewish Heritage*, 1, No. 1 (Fall/Winter 1957), 13.

Oskar Maria Graf: Exile in Permanence

Helmut Pfanner[1]

Although Graf's literary reputation was established through his autobiographical novels, *Prisoners All*[2] and *The Life of My Mother*,[3] it is more than likely that future generations will first mention his name, not in connection with belletristic writings, but in a primarily politico-historical context. In 1933 Graf received worldwide recognition through a spontaneous act with which he took a public stand against the cultural policies of the Third Reich. While on a lecture tour in Vienna, he read in the *Berliner Börsen-Courier* of 7 May 1933 that all his books, with the exception of *Prisoners All*, had been recommended by the Nazis. Taking this as a personal insult, especially in view of the banning of such well-known authors as Heinrich Mann, Alfred Döblin, Franz Werfel, Bertolt Brecht, and Kurt Tucholsky,[4] and the burning of their books on 10 May, Graf immediately wrote his famous protest, which appeared in the Viennese *Arbeiterzeitung* of 12 May 1933 and was soon reprinted either totally or in part by the world press.[5] In his article "Verbrennt mich!" ["Burn Me Too!"], Graf condemned the Nazis for having tried to arrest him in Munich and, having failed to find him there, for destroying a large part of the books and manuscripts they had found in his apartment.

Now they wished to make him an exponent of that "new" German spirit. What had he done to earn this disgrace, he asked, and then continued:

> The Third Reich expelled almost all German literature of significance and disavowed all genuine German writing; it has driven the majority of our best writers into exile and made it impossible for their works to be published in Germany. The ignorance of a few arrogant, opportunistic scribes and the unrestrained vandalism of the present dictators are trying to stamp out everything of international stature in our literature and art, and to replace the concept "German" with a narrow-minded nationalism. . . .

The advocates of this barbaric nationalism, which has nothing, absolutely nothing, to do with being German, have the audacity to claim me as one of their "intellectuals" and to place my name on their so-called "white list"--which can only be a "black list" before world conscience.

I did not deserve such a disgrace!

The life I have led and all the books I have written give me the right to demand that my books be consigned to the pure flames and not fall into the bloody hands and the perverted minds of the murderous brown hordes.

Burn the works of the German spirit! The spirit itself can never be extinguished, nor can your own disgrace! [6]

The consequences of this letter can easily be imagined: within a few days Graf's books were also burned by professors and students at the University of Munich, and a few weeks later his German citizenship was revoked.

The unique courage of Graf's protest is beyond question. If one remembers that, unlike the majority of artists and writers whom the Hitler regime drove into exile, Graf was not a Jew, and also that his writings, at least to the superficial reader, showed some resemblance to the blood-and-soil literature that the Third Reich advocated,[7] it would have been understandable if Graf had let himself be courted by the Nazis. However, his rejection of any such association and his outspoken opposition to the fascist rule were the direct expression of his character and personal convictions. Graf's keen sense of political justice and social fairness can be traced throughout his work. It had been kindled in his early childhood and was intensified by his experiences as a young writer during World War I and the Weimar Republic.

Oskar Graf was born in the little Bavarian village of Berg on Lake Starnberg in 1894. He was the youngest son among eleven children of a baker and a farmer's daughter. Because of the father's early death, the oldest son Max took over as head of the family. Max was a tyrant who mistreated the apprentices in the family bakery, including young Oskar, beating them and demanding unusually hard work. These childhood experiences gave Graf an early taste of dictatorship and developed his aversion to all forms of human oppression. Nevertheless, he endured his brother's rule until he became sixteen years old. Then one day Max suddenly discovered that Oskar was secretly reading the works of the German classic authors, which he had purchased with his own money. For this "offense" Oskar received such a savage beating that he decided the time had come to leave. He withdrew his small savings from the bank and fled to Munich. In his naiveté, Oskar rented a room in a hotel and paid the rent for three months in advance, spending the major part of his savings on the first day. He then tacked a sign to his door that read "Oskar Graf, Author," and started to write poems and plays, which he submitted to

publishers. The cover letters that he enclosed with his manuscripts reflect the state of his mind as well as his grasp of
economics at that time:

> Dear Sir: I have completed a play and am ready to
> let you have it for publication. It is a tragedy. I
> would accept a thousand marks. If you are not pre-
> pared to pay so much, we can discuss the matter. It
> ought to be published promptly and is sure to be
> accepted for the stage at once, for it is highly dra-
> matic. Yours faithfully, Oskar Graf, Author, Crown
> Prince Hotel, Zweig Street, Munich.[8]

Of course, success left him waiting, and as he had soon
spent all his money, he had to look for some source of income. For several years Graf worked at low-paying odd
jobs, such as elevator operator, mail carrier, baker, factory
worker, and billposter. The experiences that he encountered
during this time left additional imprints on his social conscience and made him question a political system in which
people enjoyed unequal amounts of financial privileges and
various degrees of personal freedom.

During these years in Munich, Graf also got to know
the activist groups around Gustav Landauer and Erich Müh-
sam. Inspired by their utopian programs, in 1912 he and
his friend, the painter Georg Schrimpf, tramped into Switzerland to join an anarchist colony in the Tessin region. Having
personally met the legendary Prince Kropotkin and many
other anarchists, Graf was deeply disappointed in the con-
formist and basically bourgeois tendencies of these so-called
revolutionaries and soon made his way back to Munich. When
the war broke out in 1914, he was again disappointed--this
time by the enthusiasm that many of his bohemian friends
displayed for a nationalistic cause. Later he was drafted
into the army, but with his strong aversion to all military
practices, Graf could not become a useful soldier. As one
can read in his autobiography,[9] he became the nightmare
of his officers from the very first day of his military training. He reacted to their orders by laughing out loud, and
when he was asked to take part in a cavalry parade, Graf
spoiled the show by intentionally letting himself be thrown
off his horse. Consequently, he was one of the first from
his unit to be sent to the Eastern front. There he was
thrown into solitary confinement when he again refused to
obey a command. He went on a hunger strike and had to
be taken to a hospital where he made the medical personnel
believe that he was insane. Graf played his role so well
that even his visiting relatives and friends were fooled.
After one and a half years of life in a mental hospital, he
was released and also dispensed from further military service. Graf had thus carried into action his conviction that
it is possible for one man to oppose the military machinery
of an entire country.

Upon his release from the military, Graf resumed his
Bohemian life in Munich, and later participated in the revolution of 1918. He was temporarily imprisoned by the

government troops who suppressed the short-lived Soviet
Republic of Bavaria, but, thanks to an affidavit by Rainer
Maria Rilke, he was soon set free again. The harsh treatment that many of his friends received from courts exerted
a decisive influence upon Graf's political thinking. In the
final chapters of *Prisoners All*,[10] he recounts how large
numbers of workers and civilians, regardless of their degree
of participation in the revolution, were shot to death, and
how the ruling aristocracy rewarded these brutal acts. Had
he had any doubts about his own class affiliation before wit-
nessing these events, from then on Graf identified his rebellion against war and injustice with the proletarian cause
in general: "I knew once and for all where my place was,
and with whom."[11]

During the turbulent times marking the end of World
War I, Graf began to establish himself in his literary
career. He had previously had a number of poems published
in such journals as *Die Aktion*, *Sturm*, and *Simplicissi-
mus* and had reviewed books for a Munich newspaper. This
activity as a reviewer led to Graf's changing his name, for
it had repeatedly been confused with that of a Munich art
critic and author of patriotic essays, a certain Professor
Oskar Graf. The latter did not want to be confused with
the young revolutionary author and offered a sum of 500
marks if Graf would assume a new name. Gladly accepting
such an offer, Graf inserted "Maria" into his signature, a
name suggested by the painter Carlo Holzer, a Stefan George
enthusiast who, as Graf says, had developed a good feeling
for sound effects.[12]

In 1918 Graf's first book was published--a small volume of expressionistic poetry. It appeared in the Dresdner
Verlag series, "Das Neuste Gedicht," and carried on its cover
the very timely title, *Die Revolutionäre* [*The Revolutionaries*].[13] After a few other attempts at poetry and also
at art criticism, however, the young writer discovered his
real strength, which was in autobiographical novels and fiction in which the peasant life of upper Bavaria as well as
the proletarian atmosphere of the city were treated. Altogether Graf published some twenty-five books between 1918
and 1933. If one judges their reception by the critics, one
must conclude that, at least toward the end of the twenties,
he was regarded as one of the most promising young writers
of the Weimar Republic.

With *Prisoners All* (1927) Graf's reputation became
firmly established. The impact of his confessions, which
have frequently been compared to those of Rousseau, upon
their readers was so great that within twelve months a second and a third edition had to be printed. One of the
book's chief themes, the individual's suppression by tyranny
and war, was taken up by a number of other writers.[14]
The book was soon translated into the major literary languages of the world, and the favorable reception of the latest edition (1965) by contemporary readers was a great joy
to the author. Not only is this unusual autobiography a
key to the life and work of the young Graf; it also provides

the reader with an historical appreciation of the turbulent times of World War I and the ensuing revolution in Germany.

Among Graf's other publications from this period are the *Kalendergeschichten* [*Calendar Tales*],[15] a collection of short stories treating the life of the peasants of upper Bavaria and of the poor people of Munich, and *Das bayrische Dekameron* [*The Bavarian Decameron*],[16] a series of erotic tales, which has become the most frequently reprinted of all his works. Another book, which, next to his auto- biography, serves most clearly to express Graf's Weltanschau- ung, was published only months before the collapse of the Weimar Republic. As suggested by the title, *Einer gegen alle* [*The Wolf*],[17] its theme is the hostile confrontation between the individual and society.

The plot of *The Wolf* consists of a soldier's return from World War I and his inability to adapt to the life of a peacetime citizen and farmer in his native village. He voluntarily gives up his rightful inheritance to his younger brother and chooses instead to make a living by roaming through the countryside, beating and robbing the people he encounters. For a short time the vagabond becomes a ser- vant on a farm near his home, but he is finally arrested. During his trial he consistently denies his identity as well as any responsibility for the crimes he has committed. He is sentenced to death, but hangs himself before the execu- tion. On the wall of his cell is found the inscription: "War over, no use for peace,"[18] an indication that the prisoner had not been able to make the transition from being an irres- olute tool of his wartime superiors to being a useful member of the society at peace. What the author himself had suc- cessfully resisted, though not without enormous effort, namely the unquestioning subordination to the will of a military com- mander, the hero of his novel has accomplished to perfection: on account of the war, he has learned how to kill and rob so well that he cannot live differently thereafter. But Graf and his hero have both come into conflict with the accepted social norms and, therefore, have to retreat into a state of inner exile.

In addition to its psychological significance, this novel is one of the most convincing antiwar statements published in Germany during the Weimar Republic. The hero Loeffler is a living symbol of the cruelty and brutality of war, which appears particularly inhuman against the background of the poverty-stricken German society of the twenties. The realistic nature of the work has been underscored by the author by interspersing a number of historical events, such as the gathering of Germany's first democratic parliament at Weimar, the brutality of the government troops in their fights against the Communists, the beginning of inflation, and the rising unemployment, into the fictitious action. To connect Loeffler's inhuman acts to his military training, Graf has equipped his character with some positive features, which are gradually stamped out by the war; an example of the negative effect of the war on Loeffler's character is his dis- continuation of the voluntary support payments he had made to his girl friend and child at home.   War in this book has lost all the romantic associations it had for earlier generations.

Graf's political protest and voluntary exile in 1933 thus came as no surprise to anyone who had read his works. During his stay in Vienna, he was soon joined by his companion Mirjam Sachs (a cousin of the Nobel Prize-winning poet Nelly Sachs), who had remained in Munich a few weeks longer than Graf so that she could cast her vote once more against Hitler.   The couple stayed in Austria for less than a year, for in February 1934 Graf joined the ranks of the Austrian workers in their rebellion against the Dollfuss regime; and when the attempted uprising failed, he and Mirjam were forced to flee.   They went to Czechoslovakia, where they lived for a relatively calm and productive four years in Brno.   The only major interruption occurred in the summer of 1934 when Graf traveled as an invited guest to the First Congress of the Union of Soviet Writers held in Moscow.   On this occasion he personally met many internationally known authors, including the Russians Gorki and Pasternak, and he also renewed his contacts with several other exiled German writers, notably Klaus Mann, Ernst Toller, Theodor Plievier, and Johannes R. Becher.   Graf has described the many interesting experiences at the Congress as well as during the following six-week journey through the southern parts of the Soviet Union in a vividly written travelogue.[19]

One of the two major works that Graf wrote in Brno is *Anton Sittinger*,[20] the satirical novel of a petit bourgeois government employee who represents the mentality of those politically passive Germans who made possible Hitler's rise to power.   In another novel, *Der Abgrund* [*The Abyss*],[21] Graf strongly attacked the German and Austrian socialist parties for their petty rivalries and the basically bourgeois interests of many of their officials, factors that had contributed to Germany's political downfall.   During his years in Vienna and Brno, Graf was also a coeditor of the *Neue Deutsche Blätter*.   In this important German expatriate periodical, he was able to continue his fight against National Socialism and to publish excerpts of his works before they could appear in book form.

In 1938 Graf saw clearly that his life was not safe much longer in Czechoslovakia.   Together with Mirjam he fled to Holland and from there to New York.   Immediately after his arrival in the United States, Graf joined the other exiled writers in their battle against Nazi propaganda.   The newly founded branch of the Schutzverband Deutscher Schriftsteller in Amerika, or German-American Writers' Association (GAWA), elected Graf president.   In this function, he expressed his condemnation of the Nazi atrocities and fascist ideology in general through speeches held at cultural events in the major American cities and over the radio.   His political essays on the same subject also appeared in the German-language press of America, and Graf became a regular contributor to the New York Jewish newspaper *Aufbau*.[22]   Unlike other German expatriates, for example Emil Ludwig,[22] Graf did not condemn all German people and Germany's cultural heritage, but always pointed out the humanistic and also democratic tradition in German history.   Indeed, he became a highly respected spokesman for that other Germany that the world had known and that was in danger of being forgotten.   This objectivity in Graf's political outlook did not win him friends among Germany's enemies, and it even made him politically suspect to some German-Americans; at one point he had to defend himself against accusations of being a Stalinist agent.[23]

All this time, however, Graf wrote productively, completing the second part of *The Life of My Mother*[24] and working on several other new books.   Aroused by World War II and especially by the threat of an all-out atomic war, he was moved to write the novel *Die Eroberung der Welt* [*The Conquest of the World*], or as a later edition has been entitled, *Die Erben des Untergangs* [*The Survivors of the Holocaust*].[25]   In this work Graf envisaged a new human society based upon the principles of democracy and socialism.   Any nationalistic or imperialistic tendencies of the people are immediately erased and corrected by a world government.   In another novel, entitled *Unruhe um einen Friedfertigen* [*Agitation around a Peaceful Man*],[26] the story of a Jewish cobbler in a Bavarian village, who as a former refugee from Russia has become completely assimilated into the life of his community.   He manages to live in peace for some time after the Nazi terror has started to spread from the cities into the country; but one day, when he inherits a large sum of money, his Jewish background is revealed to a small government official.   Although the cobbler Kraus disproves all Nazi prejudice by showing no interest in his suddenly inherited wealth—he even gives it away—he soon becomes the object of malicious attacks and is finally cruelly killed by some Nazi rowdies.   Graf's sympathetic character portrayal of Kraus has turned this unassuming man into a lasting symbol through which suffering and sacrifice are seen as the fate of a minority under the rule of a tyrannical power.   *Unruhe um einen Friedfertigen* was first published by Aurora in New York, a firm founded by Graf and several other German exile writers.   Supported by the voluntary subscriptions of German-American workers, Graf had previously reissued several of his own out-of-print works in facsimile editions.[27]

The various problems of the exiled writer and of political expatriates in general are treated as the central theme of Graf's novel *Die Flucht ins Mittelmässige: Ein New Yorker Roman* [*Escape into an Average Life: A New York Novel*].[28]   Here the reader meets a whole group of exiled Germans living in a state of Diaspora in New York City. Although the war is over, emotional reasons keep them from returning to Germany; but what is even worse, they are still farther removed from the life that surrounds them—the American society.   The author himself, although he is disguised in name and his character is split into at least two figures, plays a dominant role in this novel; and, as in his earlier autobiographical works, he antagonized some people who found themselves mirrored in this book.   The many conversations between the German and Austrian expatriates sound as realistic as if they had been recorded verbatim.

The chief protagonist is Martin Ling, who finds unexpected fame when one of the many stories with which he had amused his German friends is published and translated into English.   In the course of the novel Graf shows how the sudden literary success gradually estranges the hero from his former compatriots, and since he also lacks a binding relationship with any of his new acquaintances, he finally finds himself in a complete social vacuum.   He therefore understands the warning in the words of one of his friends: "You, Mart, . . . you have decided in favor of Diaspora, where a person will perish if he gives up his belief in man! And you will admit yourself that, unless he retains this belief, he is no longer good for anything.   Not for real life or for an idea, not for any society, and least of all for friendship or even love.   He can't return home, you understand?   Sooner or later he will go to the dogs."[29]   Ling, like Graf himself, never learns the English language during the many years of his American exile, and although he is temporarily blinded by his professional successes, he comes to the realization that life in isolation from the everyday experiences of simple people is not worth living.   At the end of the novel, the hero burns his manuscript of an unfinished book and flies to Germany.   There he settles in a city where he is completely unknown, thereby accepting the state of exile as his way of life.

Unlike some other exiled writers, Graf did not return to Germany immediately after Hitler's defeat in 1945.   But as an expression of his feeling of solidarity with the German people and as a visible form of help, he took up a collection of food, clothing, and money among his American friends to send to suffering German writers when the war had ended. He was prevented from going to Germany himself on account of his special immigrant status.   Although he had repeatedly applied for American citizenship, Graf was not successful because he had refused to sign the naturalization papers, which contain the clause about a person's willingness to "bear arms on behalf of the United States when required by law."   Finally, in 1958 the Office of Immigration and Naturalization made an exception and removed the clause from Graf's papers.   Now that he possessed an American passport and could travel freely, Graf returned to Germany; but despite the fact that he had always consciously upheld his German heritage, his first visit to his homeland was not entirely the happy "homecoming" that he had perhaps expected.   He caused somewhat of a sensation when in the course of the 800th anniversary of the city of Munich he was invited to read from his works in the newly reconstructed Cuvilliés-Theater, for he appeared in the Lederhosen that he had worn on his departure from Munich thirty-five years earlier.   This native Bavarian costume, which Graf had worn during the Congress in Moscow and on many occasions in New

York City and for which he was never criticized, now became the object of fierce attacks by the conservative press in the city that he considered his home.   In Frankfurt, the bellboy who carried his American suitcase insisted on speaking only English, although Graf tried to explain to him that he could not understand what he said.   Graf was also less than pleased by the materialistic lifestyle in the land of the "economic miracle" and did not approve of either East or West German politics.   Thus Graf decided to keep his permanent home in New York, although he later made several more visits to Germany.   The thought of a permanent move to Munich again became more attractive to him during the last few years of his life.   His changing attitude in this respect becomes evident from Graf's correspondence with some of the city officials of Munich and has been confirmed orally by his widow.[30]   Graf died in 1967 in New York City, very close to his seventy-third birthday, after a long illness with emphysema and asthma.

Literary historians and critics have tried to find Graf's place in the wide spectrum of modern literature.   Both naturalistic and expressionistic elements can be found in his works, as well as some characteristics of *Neue Sachlichkeit* ("new objectivity").   A much more decisive influence on Graf's thinking and style was probably exerted by certain significant writers of the nineteenth century rather than by any particular period in literary history.   He himself considered Leo Tolstoy his intellectual father, and the close relationship between the thinking of the two writers becomes immediately evident upon comparing their works.   For example, the problem of an unhappy marriage, which is central to Tolstoy's *Kreutzer Sonata*, received similar treatment by Graf in his novel *Bolwieser* [*The Station Master*].[31] Beyond mere thematic resemblance, Tolstoy influenced Graf's social conscience and pacifistic Weltanschauung.   This can be seen not only in the reverence for simple people found throughout the works of both writers, but even more directly in Graf's novel *Die Erben des Untergangs* [*The Survivors of the Holocaust*], in which a semireligious sect, the *Stillen* ("Quiet Ones"), as the author's mouthpiece, advocate the Tolstoyan principle of nonresistance against the forces of evil.   It is indeed a pity that all the research material and notes that Graf had collected in preparation for a book on the great Russian author and pacifist were among the items that fell into the hands of the Gestapo in 1933 and were thus irretrievably lost.   The only extant piece of writing by Graf on Tolstoy is that published in his collected essays;[32] it is also a good source for an understanding of Graf's thoughts on other writers and on literature in general.

With regard to the form of his works, the models can also be found in the literary tradition of the nineteenth century.   The Swiss writer Jeremias Gotthelf must be mentioned as having had a major influence on the structure of Graf's short stories and novels.   Another Bavarian writer, Ludwig Thoma, whom Graf himself had known personally, was

probably the closest connection in this line of literary ancestry.   Those critics, however, who try to identify the spirit
and style of these two Bavarian authors must be reminded
that Thoma's stories are no more than the result of exact
observation of Bavarian peasant life, whereas Graf's own
works reflect much more the thinking and feeling of a person
who considers himself an integral part of the people about
whom he writes.   Consequently, although the reader can
laugh with Thoma about the comical characters of his books,
in Graf's works he receives a more direct "inside view" of
the joys and problems of simple people everywhere.

Graf's admiration of a simple existence has also been
carried over into his description and evaluation of other
literary figures.   In the continuation of his autobiography,
Gelächter von aussen [*Laughter from Outside*],[33] which
was the last work published during his lifetime, he tells
of his personal acquaintance with Rainer Maria Rilke during
the days of the Munich revolution.   Rilke, whose personal
status and style of writing differ diametrically from Graf's,
used to attend some of the loud, turbulent mass meetings of
the Bavarian revolution, and after one such meeting they
both walked home together.   In their conversation, they
reached a mutual understanding that the revolution would
not succeed as long as those who made it did not establish
closer contact with the people.

Although Graf had been living in political exile since
1933, and after 1938 even in a country whose language he
never learned to speak, he did not lack recognition.   Bertolt
Brecht, whom he had known since the early twenties,[34] wrote
the poem "Die Bücherverbrennung" ["The Book Burning"] in
his honor, and a group of friends arranged the publication
of *Der ewige Kalender* [*The Eternal Calendar*],[35] a collection of Graf's poems treating the yearly cycle of nature, for
his sixtieth birthday.   Another honor, one received by only
a few other German writers, was the awarding of an honorary degree from an American university.   It was bestowed
upon Graf by Wayne State University in 1960.   Two years
later, in 1962, he received the prize of the city of Munich,
a cash award in the amount of DM 5000.   Graf's wide recognition and influence are further reflected in the many newspaper articles that appeared in 1964 on the occasion of his
seventieth birthday and in the congratulatory letters he
received from fellow writers and other public figures on similar occasions.   While listing these honors, however, it is
important to note that fame did not alter Graf's outlook on
life or his very personal style of living.   Not only did he
maintain a close relationship to common people, but he also
continued to refer to himself ironically as *Provinzschrift-
steller* ("provincial writer").   As a kind of joke for his
friends and to puzzle the critics, his last volume of poetry
was anonymously published in 1962 under the unassuming
title *Altmodische Gedichte eines Dutzendmenschen* [*Old-
Fashioned Poems by an Average Man*].[36]   It clearly was
the work of an author who considered himself no more than
an ordinary man.

Just as he never abandoned his independent lifestyle, Graf was not in full agreement with either of the world's major political systems.   He saw the future of the world in its development away from the great-power structure, and as a positive alternative to the ideological competition between the present superstates, he advocated a political decentralization whereby all parts of the world would again be directly controlled by the people and yet coexist in a natural harmony with the unified whole.   Such a human society, foreseen by Graf in a longer and still unpublished essay under the title "Der Moralist als Wurzel der Diktatur" ["The Moralist as the Root of Dictatorship"] and also depicted in the form of a poetic vision in the final chapter of *Die Erben des Untergangs*, would not be free of all problems; but in it man would have lost his present fears of war and an uncertain future, because the world's natural resources would be used to the best advantage of all mankind.   In a fine check-and-balance system characterized by man's maximum control over the elements and simultaneous individual freedom, a lasting peace for all human beings would finally be attained.   But whereas this ideal is still far from realization, Graf's battle against the threats to personal freedom is carried on today by younger writers, thus bearing witness to his words: "Burn the works of the spirit!   The spirit itself can never be extinguished."

Notes

[1] I am grateful to the Alexander von Humboldt Foundation as well as the University of New Hampshire (Central University Research Fund) for their financial assistance.

[2] Oskar Maria Graf, *Wir sind Gefangene: Ein Bekenntnis aus diesem Jahrzehnt* (Munich: Drei Masken Verlag, 1927); trans. into English as *Prisoners All* (New York: Alfred A. Knopf, 1928); latest German edition: *Wir sind Gefangene: Ein Bekenntnis* (Munich: Süddeutscher Verlag, 1978).

[3] Oskar Maria Graf, *The Life of My Mother* (New York: Howell, Soskin & Co., 1940); first published in English. Subsequent editions in German, under the title *Das Leben meiner Mutter*, appeared in both the FRG and GDR (among others, Munich: Kurt Desch, 1946, and Weimar: Gustav Kiepenheuer, 1951).

[4] For a listing of the authors whose books were burned on 10 May 1933, see Dietrich Strothmann, *Nationalsozialistische Literaturpolitik* (Bonn: H. Bouvier, 1960), p. 74.

[5] For example, *Der Sozialdemokrat* (Prague), No. 112, 13 May 1933; *Volksstimme* (Saarbrücken), 15 May 1933; and *New York Times*, 13 May 1933.

[6] Based upon the German text in *An manchen Tagen: Reden, Gedanken und Zeitbetrachtungen* [*Incidentals: Speeches, Thoughts, and Observations*] (Frankfurt/M:

Nest, 1961), and the partial English text in *New York Times* (see n. 5). All translations of quotations from German originals in this article are mine.

7As indicated by their titles, several of Graf's books are set in his rural Bavaria, but they are entirely different from the blood-and-soil literature on account of their realistic style: *Bayrisches Lesebücherl: Weissblaue Kulturbilder* [*White-Blue Sketches: A Bavarian Cultural Reader*] (Munich: Gunther Langes, 1924); *Die Heimsuchung: Roman* [*The Affliction: A Novel*] (Bonn: Verlag der Buchgemeinde, 1925); *Die Chronik von Flechting: Ein Dorfroman* [*The Chronicle of Flechting: A Village Novel*] (Munich: Drei Masken Verlag, 1925); *Finsternis: Sechs Dorfgeschichten* [*Darkness: Six Village Tales*] (Munich: Drei Masken Verlag, 1926); *Im Winkel des Lebens* [*In Life's Corner*] (Berlin: Büchergilde Gutenberg, 1927); and *Dorfbanditen: Erlebnisse aus meinen Schul- und Lehrlingsjahren* [*Village Bandits: My Experiences as Schoolboy and Apprentice*] (Berlin: Drei Masken Verlag, 1932).

8Oskar Maria Graf, *Prisoners All*, p. 37. Translation revised by me.

9Ibid., pp. 114 ff.

10Ibid., pp. 409 ff.

11Ibid., p. 418.

12Ibid., pp. 237 f.

13Oskar Maria Graf, *Die Revolutionäre* (Dresden: Dresdner Verlag von 1917, 1918).

14For example, Erich Maria Remarque in *Im Westen nichts Neues*, 1928 [*All Quiet on the Western Front*], Ludwig Renn in *Krieg*, 1928 [*War*], and Theodor Plievier in *Des Kaisers Kulis*, 1930 [*The Kaiser's Coolies*].

15Oskar Maria Graf, *Kalender-Geschichten* (Berlin: Drei Masken Verlag, 1929). New, though greatly altered, editions have been published in the GDR (Rudolstadt: Greifenverlag, 1957) and in the FRG (Munich: Süddeutscher Verlag, 1975).

16Oskar Maria Graf, *Das bayrische Dekameron* (Vienna: Verlag für Kulturforschung, 1928). A new, expanded edition was published in the FRG (Munich: Willi Weismann, 1951), with several more editions following in East and West Germany.

17Oskar Maria Graf, *Einer gegen Alle: Roman* (Berlin: Universitas Deutsche Verlags-Aktiengesellschaft, 1932); trans. into English as *The Wolf* (London: Lovat Dickson, 1934). The only new edition since the war, which soon went out of print again, was published in the GDR (Potsdam: Märkische Druck- und Verlags-GMBH, 1950).

18Oskar Maria Graf, *Einer gegen Alle*, p. [223].

19For a description of this work, see my article "Oskar Maria Graf's 'Russlandsreise': An Unpublished Manuscript," *Modern Language Quarterly*, 30 (1969), 564–81. Meanwhile Graf's work itself has been published posthumously: Oskar Maria Graf, *Reise in die Sowjetunion, mit Briefen von Sergej Tretjakow*, ed. Hans-Albert Walter (Darmstadt:

Luchterhand, 1974), and *Reise nach Sowjetrussland 1934*, ed. Rolf Recknagel (Berlin: Verlag der Nation, 1977).

[20]Oskar Maria Graf, *Anton Sittinger: Roman* (London: Malik-Verlag, 1937).

[21]Oskar Maria Graf, *Der Abgrund: Ein Zeitroman* [*The Abyss: A Novel of the Times*] (London: Malik-Verlag, 1936). A revised edition of this novel was published under the title *Die gezählten Jahre: Roman* [*The Days Were Numbered: A Novel*] (Munich: Süddeutscher Verlag, 1976).

[22]For Ludwig's hostile attitude toward Germany, see Joachim Radkau, *Die deutsche Emigration in den U.S.A.: Ihr Einfluss auf die amerikanische Europapolitik 1933-1945*, Studien zur modernen Geschichte, 2 (Düsseldorf: Bertelsmann Universitätsverlag, 1971), pp. 205-10; and Helmut Kreuzer, "Von Bülow zu Bevin: Briefe aus dem Nachlass Emil Ludwigs," *Rice University Studies*, 55, No. 3 (Summer 1969), 43-114.

[23]See Siegfried Sudhof, "Leopold Schwarzschilds 'Neues Tage-Buch' im Winter 1939. Eine Korrespondenz Berthold Viertels mit Oskar Maria Graf," *Jahrbuch der Deutschen Schillergesellschaft*, 17 (1973), 122.

[24]Graf had written the first part of *The Life of My Mother* during his stay in Czechoslovakia. He finished it, with the help of an American stipend, in Yaddo near Saratoga Springs, New York. The colorful family history that this work presents is set in a wide historical panorama that extends from the Thirty Years' War to the takeover of Germany by Hitler. *Das Leben meiner Mutter* has received high praise from many critics and other writers, including Thomas Mann.

[25]Oskar Maria Graf, *Die Eroberung der Welt: Roman einer Zukunft* (Munich: Kurt Desch, 1949), and *Die Erben des Untergangs: Roman einer Zukunft* (Frankfurt/M: Nest, 1959).

[26]Oskar Maria Graf, *Unruhe um einen Friedfertigen* (New York: Aurora, 1947); new editions were published in the GDR (Berlin: Aufbau-Verlag, 1948, and Verlag der Nation, 1952) and in the FRG (Munich: Süddeutscher Verlag, 1975).

[27]Invitations to subscribe to these books can be found in several issues of German-American newspapers and journals, such as *Volksfront*, *Aufbau*, and *Solidarität*.

[28]Oskar Maria Graf, *Die Flucht ins Mittelmässige: Ein New Yorker Roman* (Frankfurt/M: Nest, 1959).

[29]Ibid., p. 388.

[30]Graf's literary estate, including his correspondence, is located at the University of New Hampshire Library in Durham, New Hampshire. I gratefully acknowledge the biographical information I received from Mrs. Gisela Graf (New York), the author's widow.

[31]Oskar Maria Graf, *Bolwieser: Roman eines Ehemannes* (Munich: Drei Masken Verlag, 1931); trans. into English as *The Station Master: A Novel* (London: Chatto & Windus, 1933); the latest German edition is entitled *Die Ehe des Herrn Bolwieser: Roman* (Munich: Süddeutscher Verlag, 1976).

[32]"Tolstoj als weltgeschichtliches Ereignis: Kleine Notiz zu seinem fünfzigsten Todestag" ["Tolstoy as an Event of World-Historical Importance: A Note on the Occasion of the Fiftieth Anniversary of His Death"], *An manchen Tagen*, pp. 162-67. (See note 6.)

[33]Oskar Maria Graf, *Gelächter von aussen: Aus meinem Leben 1918-1933* (Munich: Kurt Desch, 1966).

[34]The humorous story of their first encounter, in connection with the first performance of Brecht's play *Trommeln in der Nacht*, has been told by Graf in *Gelächter von aussen*, pp. 152 ff.

[35]Oskar Maria Graf, *Der ewige Kalender* (New York: Oskar Maria Graf, 1954). The limited edition of this work in 5,000 copies was set in special type and illustrated by the New York artist Anne-Marie Jauss, who is herself a political refugee from Germany.

[36]Anon., *Altmodische Gedichte eines Dutzendmenschen* (Frankfurt/M: Nest, 1962). A selection from these poems was published in English translation: Oskar Maria Graf, *Old-Fashioned Poems of an Ordinary Man*, trans. Elisabeth Bayliss (New York: Oskar Maria Graf, 1967).

Thomas Mann, Bertolt Brecht, and the "Free Germany" Movement

Herbert Lehnert

Among the many poems Brecht wrote during his years of exile there is one, dated 1944, that is remarkable for the hostile contempt it shows toward a fellow expatriate who is named in its title:

ALS DER NOBELPREISTRÄGER THOMAS MANN DEN AMERIKANERN
UND ENGLÄNDERN DAS RECHT ZUSPRACH, DAS DEUTSCHE
VOLK FÜR DIE VERBRECHEN DES HITLERREGIMES
ZEHN JAHRE LANG ZU ZÜCHTIGEN[1]

I
Züchtigt den Gezüchtigten nur weiter!
Züchtigt ihn im Namen des Ungeists!
Züchtigt ihn im Namen des Geists!

Die Hände im dürren Schoss
Verlangt der Geflüchtete den Tod einer halben Million
    Menschen.
Für ihre Opfer verlangt er
Zehn Jahre Bestrafung. Die Dulder
Sollen gezüchtigt werden.

Der Preisträger hat den Kreuzträger aufgefordert
Seine bewaffneten Peiniger mit blossen Händen
    anzufallen.
Die Presse brachte keine Antwort. Jetzt
Fordert der Beleidigte die Züchtigung
Des Gekreuzigten.

II
Einen Hunderttausenddollarnamen zu gewinnen
Für die Sache des gepeinigten Volkes
Zog der Schreiber seinen guten Anzug an
Mit Bücklingen
Nahte er sich dem Besitzer.

Ihn zu verführen mit glatten Worten
Zu einer gnädigen Äusserung über das Volk
Ihn zu bestechen mit Schmeichelei
Zu einer guten Tat
Ihm listig vorzuspiegeln
Dass die Ehrlichkeit sich bezahlt macht.

Misstrauisch horchte der Gefeierte.
Für einen Augenblick
Erwog er, auch hier gefeiert zu werden, die
    Möglichkeit.
Schreib auf, mein Freund, ich halte es für meine
    Pflicht
Etwas für das Volk zu tun.   Eilig
Schrieb der Schreiber die kostbaren Worte auf, gierig
Nach weiterem hochblickend, sah er nur noch den
    Rücken
Des Gefeierten im Türrahmen.   Der Anschlag
War missglückt.

III
Und für einen Augenblick auch
Stand der Bittsteller verwirrt
Denn die Knechtseligkeit
Machte ihm Kummer, wo er immer sie traf.

Aber dann, eingedenk
Dass dieser verkommene Mensch
Lebte von seiner Verkommenheit, das Volk aber
Nur den Tod gewinnt, wenn es verkommt
Ging er ruhiger weg.

The poem is formed around a scene in which its writer tries to enlist the Nobel Prize winner in the cause of the suffering German people. The scene is presented in the middle part of the poem. Parts I and III are dominated by judgments: part I by Mann's judgments concerning Germany as presented by Brecht, part III by Brecht's own judgment. Using the triptych as a simile, we may call parts I and III the wings, part II the centerpiece. Both wings make effective use of plays on very strong words like *züchtigen* and *Verkommenheit--verkommen*.

Part I presents Mann's opinion (that is, the opinion voiced by Brecht's figure of Mann) that the German people ought to be punished.   Strophe III of part I juxtaposes Mann as *Der Preisträger* ("the prize winner") with the Germans by the collective singular *Der Kreuzträger* ("the crossbearer").   The Germans become Christ, and Mann, the prize winner, absurdly asks them to attack their tormentors (the Roman soldiers in the image, the Nazis in reality) with their bare hands.   The poem refers to Mann's radio speeches to his former countrymen over the BBC. Specifically, in his radio address of 27 July 1943, Mann had indeed asked the Germans to shake off the yoke of Nazism.[2]   This strophe suggests that Mann felt offended because the Germans did not respond.   Mann is denoted by the past participle *"der Beleidigte* ("the offended one").   The absurdity of the situation is increased by the fact that Mann can speak to the Germans, but they cannot speak to him.   The press did not publish an answer from the Germans.   Because he is not obeyed, the offended Mann demands the castigation of the crucified Germans.   *Züchtigung*, "punishment," is the main motif--now interpreted by the Christ-passion image--of part I.   Part I presents Mann's demand, which is made to sound absurd and is condemned by the use of the crucifixion image.

Whereas part I is mainly Mann's satirically presented argument, the centerpiece is a scene in which the choice of words suggests a twisted morality.   The speaker of the poem introduces himself as the writer who masks and humbles himself to win a name worth a hundred thousand dollars for the sake of the tormented people.   The writer tries to deceive Mann into believing that honesty pays.   The poem suggests that Mann, who is here called *der Gefeierte*, "the celebrated one," associates honesty with pay in fame and money. Only for a moment does Brecht's Mann consider how much more renown he would win by doing what he is asked to do: to say something gracious about the German people.   Mann withdraws, leaving the writer with a meaningless statement of good intentions.   The implication of the scene is that Mann's morality is so distorted that he can be reached only by deceptive seduction, whereas Brecht's morality is straightforward.

The third part fortifies this judgment.   It has, like part I, a scenic element.   The petitioner, as the writer calls himself with irony, stands confused.   But he finds comfort in his own words.   First he calls Mann's attitude *Knechtseligkeit*, approximately, "slave happiness," a word that suggests an image of a lackey happy in his dependency. Mann is presented as dependent on fame and money.   The Nobel Prize stands for both.   But the image reaches further. The world that guarantees fame and money to the Nobel Prize winner is characterized by the capitalist system.   Mann is called "dieser verkommene Mensch," the most libelous statement in the poem.   *Verkommen* literally refers to someone who has lost the right track, a degenerate.   Mann had associated himself with the foremost capitalist power; in America he could continue to be celebrated and affluent.   Thus he lives "von seiner Verkommenheit" ("by his degeneracy"). The German people, however, if it perishes--an idea also expressed by *verkommen*--wins only death.   The implication is that, in contrast to Mann, the people preserves its moral integrity.

What Brecht means by "people" cannot be separated from his hope for a socialist future in Germany.   The poem never mentions Russia as a power that might also want to punish the Germans after the war.   This omission must be understood as a statement of hope for a German future with socialism, a hope incompatible with the notion that the leading socialist power might be a potential tormentor of the people. The words *verkommen* and *Verkommenheit* are informed by socialist ethics.

Mann and Brecht were introduced in this interpretation by their real names regardless of the degree of historical truth that the poem expressed. The poem clearly is aimed at Mann, and the writer clearly is Brecht. In other words, the reader is to see Mann and Brecht before his inner eye. The figure Mann is subjected to Brecht's language. The result is a representation of Mann's opinions and attitudes that we must not take as historical truth but as an interpretation of history by Brecht. He effectively suggests his judgment to the reader through the language of his poem. Insofar as the poem is telling a story, Mann becomes a fictional person it. Like all poems, this one tries to persuade the reader to accept its language as an expression of his own sentiment for as long as the poem lasts.

We are able to investigate the historical or biographical background of Brecht's poem. In so doing, we deal with two different value systems, one aesthetic, the other historical, which we must not allow to interfere with each other prematurely--in a short circuit, as it were. On the other hand, I do not suggest that the power of the language and the historical truth, as far as we can determine it, must always be considered separately. In our evaluation, both the aesthetic qualities of the poem and a value judgment about both Brecht's and Mann's attitudes in their controversy of 1943 and 1944 should enter and be balanced. We should not say the poem is bad because it is poisoned and unjust, nor should we allow ourselves to be persuaded by the power of its language into the belief that we have finally exposed the real Mann as a lackey of the capitalist system.

The background of the poem is Thomas Mann's refusal to become the figurehead president of a Free Germany Committee in the fall of 1943 and his subsequent refusal to sign the manifesto of the Council for a Democratic Germany in the spring of 1944. The events leading up to this refusal will be presented in chronological order.

On 1 July 1943, Mann wrote to Agnes Meyer about planning a lecture on Europe, a highly personal statement of what he knew of the countries and cities of Europe, beginning with his home town of Lübeck but extending to the spirit and destiny of the continent.[3] Agnes Meyer, wife of the publisher of the *Washington Post*, who frequently wrote reviews of Mann's books in the paper and, for a time, planned a biography of Mann, was always his host when he delivered his yearly lectures at the Library of Congress. The lecture-essay that was actually written during the summer of 1943 (interrupting the work on *Doctor Faustus*) contains more political statements than personal experiences. Its German title became "Schicksal und Aufgabe" ("Destiny and Commitment") when it was first published in 1944, after it had served as the basis for several speeches Mann gave in late 1943, among them "The War and the Future,"[4] his Library of Congress lecture of 1943, and "The New Humanism," a lecture delivered in New York. In May 1944 the

essay was published in English by the *Atlantic Monthly*
under the title "What Is German." We shall have to come
back to this lecture. At this point we note only that Mann
was at work on *Doctor Faustus* while considering a lecture
on Europe and Germany in the context of the political situation of the time, the war against fascism. We further note
that the essay had originally been planned to be more autobiographical than it turned out to be. The fact that it
became more political, that it discussed democracy and communism as well as the relation between Nazism and the German character, shows the influence of events that were to
follow.

On 8 July 1943, Mann, in another letter to Agnes Meyer,
declared that any intention to make him a head of government in exile was nonsense, especially because Germany, after
the war, would not be in possession of its political independence and would not need a "head." A few weeks later
he assured the same recipient: "Only under the greatest pressure would I consent to play a political role, and if I did
I would feel I were sacrificing myself."[5] These passages
show that there had been talk in some circles of a political
role for Thomas Mann.

On 12 July 1943, the Free Germany Committee in Moscow
was formed. German Communist refugees and prisoners of
war in Russian hands, who had formed a German officers'
league, published a manifesto in which they drew a line
between Germany and the Nazi regime. On 26 July 1943, the
organ of this committee published a statement by Thomas
Mann in which he linked the manifesto with a Western initiative directed toward Italy. Referring to his own radio
addresses to the German people, he stated that only a genuine and sincere turnabout could purge Germany of the forces
of evil and rehabilitate her.[6] The choice of the word *Um-
kehr* ("reversal," "return") rather than "revolution" and the
reference to an unrelated initiative of the Western powers
was intended to counteract a possible accusation of Communist leanings. On the other hand, he did respond to the
request for a statement from Moscow.

In his radio speech to the Germans dated 27 June 1943,
he had spoken of the resistance against the Nazis in all
European countries. In this connection he reminded his lis-
teners of the German resistance against the Nazis, quoting
a figure of 200,000 political inmates of concentration camps
at the outbreak of the war. He mentioned the death sentences handed down daily in Hitler's Germany, and especially the sacrifice of the students in Munich who died for
handing out anti-Nazi leaflets. In this context Mann said:
"Honor and sympathy to the German people too! The argument that says that we must not differentiate between the
German people and Nazism, that German and Nazi are one
and the same, is presented now and then in the allied countries eloquently and intelligently; but it is an untenable
view and will not prevail. Too many facts speak against
it. Germany has defended itself and continues to defend
itself as others do" (Mann, XI, 1076). The passage gives

an opinion, not a personal commitment. Mann was, as we shall see, not so certain whether the theory of the homogeneity of Nazism and the German people was really untenable. He was susceptible to the *Geist* ("intelligence") in this theory. The next radio speech, dated 27 July 1943, asks the Germans for action after the Italians had removed their fascists from power. It is probably this speech that occurs in Brecht's poem. Mann might have mentioned it in a meeting with Brecht in California soon afterward, on 1 August. We know about this meeting from Brecht's "working diary" (*Arbeitsjournal*). On 1 August 1943 a group of eight German refugees met in the house of Berthold Viertel, a writer and movie director and refugee from Austria. Besides the host and Brecht and Mann, they were Mann's brother Heinrich, an essentially bourgeois writer who sympathized with socialist and, to a degree, Communist causes; Lion Feuchtwanger, another writer-refugee and friend of both Brecht and Mann; Bruno Frank, a writer-friend of Mann's; the critic Ludwig Marcuse, who taught German literature at the University of Southern California; and Hans Reichenbach, originally a physicist, who taught philosophy at the University of California, Los Angeles. After long consideration the following statement was drafted:

> At this moment when the victory of the allied nations draws nearer, the undersigned writers, scholars and artists of German origin consider it their duty to state the following publicly:
> We welcome the manifesto of German prisoners of war and exiles in the Soviet Union in which they call on the German people to force its suppressors to unconditional surrender and to fight for a strong democracy in Germany.
> We, too, consider it necessary to distinguish clearly the Hitler regime and the social groups associated with it from the German people. We are convinced that there can be no lasting peace in the world without a strong German democracy.[7]

Although Mann had worked on the declaration, agreed to it, and read it to the wives that were present, he changed his mind the next day and withdrew his signature. He called Feuchtwanger, not Brecht. Consequently, Brecht's notes about what he said are at least secondhand. This is the relevant passage from Brecht's note on Mann's reasoning for withdrawing from the statement: ". . . this was a 'declaration of patriotism' that represents in effect an attack on the Allies 'from the rear' and he could not find it unjust if the Allies punished Germany for ten or twenty years." Brecht added a furious comment complaining about the misery of champions of German culture like Mann ("die entschlossene Jämmerlichkeit dieser 'Kulturträger'"). Two key concepts of Brecht's Mann poem appear here: *Knechtseligkeit* ("slave happiness") and *züchtigen* ("punish"). For a moment, Brecht writes, he considered how the German people could justify not only tolerating Hitler, but having tolerated Mann even without SS to suppress them.[8]

In a passage from a letter to Agnes Meyer of 9 August 1943, Mann commented on the Moscow manifesto and on his refusal to sign the statement. He informed Mrs. Meyer that he had stopped the movement of a group of German writers. This was his way of describing the event. He related the context of their declaration obviously from memory because there is one discrepancy. Whereas the declaration endorsed the distinction between the "Hitler regime and the groups associated with it on the one side and the German people on the other," Mann speaks of a distinction between "Hitler und Deutschtum" or "Deutschtum und Nationalsozialismus." The former distinction is in terms of class; the latter puts it in Mann's terms. *Deutschland* and *Deutschtum* are, for Mann, mythical entities that he dealt with at length in his World War I essay *Betrachtungen eines Unpolitischen* [*Reflections of a Nonpolitical Man*]. After 1933 he planned to write another essay on Germany that would have had different evaluations but similar substance. The plan finally was converted into fiction and became *Doctor Faustus*. Accordingly he wrote to Mrs. Meyer: "Moreover, the distinction between 'Deutschtum' and 'Nationalsozialismus' is a very broad field that could hardly be dealt with adequately in a book, let alone in a declaration." He tended to see the connections rather than the distinctions between Germany and the Nazi Weltanschauung because Germany for him was represented by the educated middle class, that is, the *Kulturbürger* or *Bildungsbürger*.

In the same letter Mann gave more reasons for his detachment from the Moscow Free Germany manifesto. He did not believe in the spontaneity of it but suspected a sinister Russian intention on which he did not elaborate. He probably meant that the Russians toyed with the idea of using the Germans against the Western Allies. Mann did not like the participation of German military men in the Moscow committee. Turning to his own position again, he expressed the reluctance he felt as a German exile to speak on behalf of his former country in the middle of a war against it. The following passage from the letter of 9 August 1943 verifies some of Brecht's notes on Mann's telephone conversation with Feuchtwanger, although the tone is certainly milder:

And finally, I think that one must leave it up to the liberal faction of America to warn against total destruction of Germany; in my opinion it is improper for us as emigrants to give America suggestions for the treatment of our country after a difficult and still distant victory. Among the left wing of the German socialists there exists a sort of patriotic fashion to demand that "nothing must happen" to Germany. That is not my feeling at all. After everything that has happened, I could hardly tear my hair over anything the Allies might undertake against Germany when she is finally brought to her knees. Naturally, one hopes that no

irreparable follies are committed that would unduly
jeopardize the future. But from a purely moral and
pedagogical viewpoint, the fall and penitence can
scarcely be great enough after the wanton insolence,
the vile megalomania, and the delusion of power in
which the nation intoxicated itself. Moreover, I believe that this time Russia will be the protector of
Germany, just as England was after 1918.

Instead of the word *züchtigen*, used by Brecht, we find the
word *Busse* ["penitence"]. Germany is obviously treated as
a mythical entity, like a person who has to pay for misdeeds
committed in a state of intoxication. This passage, incidentally, has a close parallel in the text of "Schicksal und
Aufgabe" ["Destiny and Commitment"].[9] What Mann meant
by "left wing of the German socialists" was Brecht and his
friends. As we have seen, it is a misunderstanding, although a revealing one, to call their concern patriotism.
Mann can see Germany only as an entity without class distinctions. This entity is equivalent to its culture and, therefore, to that layer of the population that produces and con-
sumes the culture. The *Kulturbürger*, that is, the educated
member of the middle class, is then mythically personified,
and individual ethics are applied to him. The last sentence,
finally, expresses the suspicion raised by the Russian action
of permitting and publicizing a Free Germany Committee.

From Brecht's point of view, Mann was simply bought
by the establishment. Mann would have furiously denied
that this was so. He had a natural inclination toward those
who read his works, who were friendly to him and helped
to provide the comfortable circumstances that he felt were
necessary for the accomplishment of his daily work. He felt
that he secured his freedom by not catering to their points
of view, by trying to extend the point of view of his readers, by telling them something they would prefer not to hear.
He must have felt that he did just that in the essay "Schicksal und Aufgabe," which Mrs. Agnes Meyer, a member of the
establishment, translated and from which the lecture "The
War and the Future" was taken.

This lecture is directed at an American conservative
middle-class audience. It warns of the dangers of fascism,
particularly of two fascist traps the existence of which Mann
recognized in America. One is the contempt of highbrow
intellectuals for traditional liberal, middle-class values like
freedom and progress; the other is irrational anticommunism.
In this respect he continued his former political admonitions
to his German readers. They are manifest as early as 1925
in the revised version of the essay "Goethe und Tolstoi," in
which he demanded that Karl Marx read Hölderlin (Mann,
IX, 170), and are continued in the essay "Kultur und Sozia-
lismus" of 1928 (Mann, XII, 639-49), in which he added that
there must be a *mutual* relationship between the conservative
idea of intellectual culture and the revolutionary idea of
society. In his essay of 1943-44 on destiny and commitment,
he conveyed to the American or Western Allied social scene

what formerly had been seen in the German political context. He specifically declared social democracy an unavoidable necessity and called anticommunism "the fundamental mistake of our time," because it fostered the rise of fascism (Mann, XII, 934), and, consequently, he detached himself from communism wherever he mentioned it.   What he really wanted was "a balance of socialism and democracy" (Mann, XII, 932).   While writing the lecture, he jokingly referred to it in a letter to his former secretary, now in an army basic training camp: "Frequently I utter shockingly 'leftist' statements, but I hope to neutralize any scandalous effect with a generous sprinkling of conservative and traditionalist powdered sugar."[10]   Writing to Agnes Meyer, he was more serious: "A significant tendency in the essay is my belief in the basic need for balance ('Natur und Geist' ['nature and intelligence']) that informs my whole outlook: I move to the *high* side of the sailboat and not to the side that already threatens to draw water, the side on which the conformists of the day are crowding."[11]   The reference to "Natur und Geist," a dichotomy he always liked to toy with, and which, though vague, is indispensable for our understanding of Mann's fiction, shows how much more Mann's thinking is dominated by manipulation of intellectual generalities that may be used in fiction, than by delving into political facts. This is further demonstrated by the simile he used in the essay to show that adaptation of bourgeois society to socialism is possible.   This simile is the adaptation of the public to new music.   Mozart, Beethoven, Verdi, Wagner, and Mahler were felt to be scandalous at first, just as communism is now.   In this essay, Mann proposed to coopt socialism to the present organization of society.   Although this may be the only real way to social progress in countries with a functioning constitutional government, to a Marxist like Brecht such a prospect was anathema.

Music serves as an example in the most conservative statement in "Schicksal und Aufgabe."   Mann believed democracy to be goodness and sympathy from above, from the leading cultured circles, as shown by Beethoven when he set Schiller's *Ode to Joy* to music with the line: "Seid umschlungen Millionen," instead of insisting on the right of genius to be esoteric (Mann, XII, 933).

In this context it is not surprising that Mann's attitude remained ambiguous on the question of whether a distinction was to be made between Germany and Nazism. "Schicksal und Aufgabe" makes use of the radio speech of 27 June 1943.   It mentions the German resistance against Hitler and the execution of the students of Munich.   But on the other hand, Mann is not prepared actually to pronounce a distinction between Nazism and Germany: "The case of Germany is so confusing and complicated because good and evil, the beautiful and the ominous, are mixed in the most peculiar manner."   Richard Wagner's music is his demonstrative example.   After initially being scandalous, it was enthusiastically received in Europe.   It was Germany's contribution to nineteenth-century greatness, and yet it was a modern archaism.

Wagner's music dramas were not concerned with the society; his work displayed contempt for the Enlightenment and was steeped in the spirit of romanticism--in a word, it was pre-fascist (Mann, XII, 924-26). This is certainly not far from the truth; the point is only whether this analysis concerns the German people or rather a part of the educated bourgeois layer of the population, the *Bildungsbürger*. Mann could not help seeing Germany as an entity identified by its culture. He had done so in 1941 in an essay entitled "Germany's Guilt and Mission"; he would do it again in his speech "Germany and the Germans" of 1945. The evil Germany was also the good one, and vice versa. Germany's sins had to be punished, because the people as a whole was guilty.

Mann was not entirely unconcerned about the fate of the individual as a result of such a punishment. To Wilhelm Herzog, who had responded to the radio speech of 27 June, Mann wrote on 20 August 1943: ". . . Germany cannot survive much longer; I cannot believe it. The people are suffering too much--one can hardly endure it from this great distance; how are they to bear it for a long time? But it must be admitted: never was history more just" (*Briefe*, p. 330). The last sentence switches from the German individual who suffers from the Allied bombing raids to the mythically personified Germany, which was sinful and is therefore punished.

Once in the essay, Mann went so far as to call for a revolution in Germany:

> What must be destroyed is the unfortunate power complex, the world-threatening coalition of the landed aristocracy, the military establishment, and heavy industry. One should not prevent the German people but assist them in breaking the rule of this coalition once and for all, in executing the long overdue land reform, in short, in setting the genuine, true, and purifying revolution in motion that alone can rehabilitate Germany in the eyes of the world, of history, and in her own eyes, and can open the way to the future, to a new world of unity and cooperation; to serve such a purpose, the German spirit, by virtue of its higher tradition, is thoroughly prepared. (Mann, XII, 928-29)

Parts of this statement could have been embraced by Brecht, who also wrote an essay in 1943 intended for American readers in which he tried to explain why "the other Germany"--the title of the essay--the non-Nazi Germany, did not make itself known. In this essay Brecht explains Hitler's rise to power by the weakness of the divided working class: "To complain that the German people allows its government to wage a frightful war of aggression is actually to complain that the German people does not rise in a social revolution."[12] But it is quite clear that the context is different. For Brecht the social revolution was a class struggle. Had the German workers, which for Brecht means the Communists, been in power, Brecht is convinced Germany would have

remained peaceful, because he believed that workers under
Communist leadership do not have any interest in war.   It
is foreign to Mann's thoughts to refer to groups such as
noblemen, generals, and industrialists.   He was probably
influenced by Brecht, Viertel, and Feuchtwanger during their
discussion on 1 August 1943.   Soon enough he returned to
mythical personifications.   This happened already in the passage quoted above when he spoke of the German *Geist*. Mann
continued this idea by explaining what he had called the
higher tradition of the German *Geist*.   It is universalism.
"We wish to be psychologists to the degree that we can recognize that the monstrous German attempt to subjugate the
world, the catastrophic failure of which we now witness, is
nothing but a twisted, wretched expression of that very universalism inherent in the German character, that previously
had a much loftier, purer, and more noble manifestation,
and won for this important people the affection, even the
admiration of the entire world" (Mann, XII, 929).   The same
intellectual quality that would make the new Germany ready
for international cooperation has made the present Germany
belligerent.   Mann referred to a German political tradition
that is explained by its peculiar history stemming from the
Holy Roman Empire.   The idea of a distorted universalism
is a motif in Mann's *Doctor Faustus*.   It is certainly an
idea that is restricted to interpretations of intellectual history or, as the Marxists would say, to bourgeois ideology.
Mann does have a point here, however, because universalism,
the relative weakness of a sense of national community in
Germany, and the need for a compensation, are factors in
the political orientation of Germans.   Although such considerations and attitudes are indeed more prevalent in the educated
classes, they do influence the people as a whole through
teachers, newswriters, and media commentators.

On the other hand, Brecht's socialist commitment kept
him from identifying with his American environment.   This
is demonstrated by a number of poems written at that time.
Naturally this alienation increased his allegiance to his homeland.   Thomas Mann, on the other hand, did integrate himself much more into American society.   On 30 October 1943
Mann addressed a Writers' Congress at the University of
California, Los Angeles.   In his lecture, "The Exiled Writer's
Relation to His Homeland," he speaks of the problem of being
a German exile when the very name of Germany is synonymous with horror and fear.   However, his radio speeches to
the Germans have renewed his old contact.   They have broken his almost complete isolation from Germany, where his
books are banned.   Nevertheless, he is determined not to
return to Germany:

> The idea of returning to Germany, to be reinstated into
> my property, and to regard these ten years, or how
> many they may be, as a mere interlude, this thought
> is far from me and appears to me quite impossible.
> It is now too late for me, and I say to myself that
> at my age it is of no consequence in what place one

completes the life's work which, on the whole, is already established and which in a certain sense is
already history.   I am now on the point of becoming
an American citizen just as my grandchildren, who were
born here and are growing up here, and my attachment
to this country has already progressed so far that it
would be contrary to my sense of gratitude to part
from it again.13

Brecht probably knew of this utterance because his (and
Mann's) friend Lion Feuchtwanger was also a speaker at the
conference.   Mann's willingness to have himself integrated
into American society while he was speaking to his former
countrymen seemed to predestine him to be the symbol of the
Free Germany movement, which had become more active in
exile circles in the fall of 1943.   Brecht, who in the meantime had gone to New York, participated in their delibera-
tions.   The movement was encouraged by some native Americans like Reinhold Niebuhr.   An Association of Free Germany,
Inc., a discussion group consisting of German-Americans and
exiles, had existed in New York since 1940.14   One of its
leaders in the East was the theologian Paul Tillich.   Mann,
on the other hand, was uneasy about these activities.   His
wavering attitude on the occasion of the meeting of 1 August
1943 showed this.   He did not want to be associated with
Communists, nor did he want to endanger his future status
as an American citizen.   He was to show the same ambiguous
attitude when asked to be the figurehead president of the
movement.   Mann left California on 9 October; he gave his
lectures "The War and the Future" and "The New Humanism"
in Washington and New York, respectively.   While in Washington, he might have discussed a possible impending request
by the exile group with Mrs. Meyer because, according to
unpublished correspondence,15 Mrs. Meyer had arranged for
Mann's later contact with Mr. Adolf Berle, assistant secretary of state.   First Mann tried to evade the issue.   In *Die
Entstehung des Doktor Faustus* [*The Genesis of a Novel*]
he reported, on the basis of his diaries, that he did not
attend the funeral of the director Max Reinhardt in New York
in part because of a cold, but also to avoid the exile circles that wanted him as head of their committee.   A conference did take place later, though, and everyone present
agreed that Mann should contact the State Department.   He
went to Washington, and according to his report in *Entstehung*, he found his expectation realized that the State
Department had no favorable inclination toward any Free
Germany Committee that even remotely resembled a government
in exile.   This result he reported back to the New York group
and thus escaped--with considerable relief--the uncomfortable
role of a semiofficial exile politician (Mann, XI, 184).

This version of the event, as told by Mann, is essentially correct, but somewhat simplified.   Mann's letter to
Adolf Berle, dated New York, 18 November 1943, is preserved
in the State Department files.   In it he stated the intention
of "the politically interested groups of the German émigrés"

to form a Free Germany Committee. Such a committee could influence the Germans "in support of the political warfare" and advise the American government "in view of its knowledge of the German mind." But after describing the possible usefulness of a Free Germany Committee for American war policy, he went on to say that he lacked any ambition to play a political role now or in a future free Germany, where such a role under an occupation force must be a precarious and thankless one. He mentioned his impending naturalization and stated "the essential condition," which "would be that the formation of such a committee would meet with the approval of the authorities in Washington."[16] On the basis of this letter Berle could only have advised Mann to take the honorary leadership of the committee if the State Department had wished to endorse it. There was no such active interest. Adolf Berle invited Mann for lunch on 25 November. He filed a brief "Memorandum of Conversation" on the same date. Its essential text follows:

> I had lunch with Mr. Thomas Mann. . . . He stated that he had difficulty in accepting the chairmanship of any committee designed to intervene in German politics because he had applied for American citizenship and expected to spend the rest of his life here. I told him I thought indeed that would place him in a difficult position.
> I told him also that his own name was very highly regarded in German circles and that I rather felt that he might not wish to enter the tangled and controversial field until the issues became considerably clearer. With this he agreed.

> A. A. B., Jr.

From memory Berle gave this somewhat more detailed account in 1961:

> I said that this was a free country and he was entirely free to enter into this activity if he so desired. I added, however, that his was perhaps the greatest single name outside Nazi Germany and that he might therefore wish to be very careful when and how he used it. At that time it was impossible to say what forces would appear when Hitler was conquered and clearly impossible to determine what intra-German forces were represented by any committee functioning outside. He might very well wish to maintain an independent position until he could be more certain, but it was entirely his decision whether to enter the somewhat sterile complexities of exile politics, or await better opportunity.
> Mann said he also was undecided. He was indeed contemplating taking out American citizenship, and since he did have that in mind he was unclear whether he had a right to take a position purporting to represent internal German forces.

As you are aware, he finally decided not to enter the movement.[17]

The State Department's hands-off policy may also be explained by the fact that its files on the Free Germany movement show the Moscow Free Germany Committee as its prominent source.   However, the records are consistent in stating that Berle advised Thomas Mann on personal grounds only.   We also know that this was known to Brecht.   In the Brecht archive there are minutes of meetings of the Council of a Democratic Germany, which was founded in 1944.   In one of them a report of a conversation of Berle with the exile politician Paul Hagen is found in which Berle denied that he had told Thomas Mann not to participate in the Free Germany Movement; "Mann only was warned not to use up the value of his name prematurely."[18]

With minor variations, all reports point in the same direction: Berle addressed himself mainly to Mann as a person and to the value of his name, and thereby diplomatically avoided stating an official position on the movement itself. Mann took this advice as a negative attitude and reported it back to the New York exile group together with his refusal to figure as president of the Committee.

This meeting must have been a rather unpleasant affair. In a letter to Agnes Meyer of 5 December 1943, Mann quoted Tillich: "He said that I pronounced the death sentence on Germany."   Mann also described Brecht's face as "scornful and bitter."   He saw Brecht as a "party liner who, if he is placed in a position of power by the Russians in Germany, will hurt me in any way he can."[19]

We know that no one had any intention of giving Brecht political power, nor is there any indication that he sought it.   However, the history of Brecht's relationship to Mann justifies Mann's distrust.   Brecht had attacked Mann repeatedly in no uncertain terms before 1933.   He insisted that the kind of literature Mann wrote was hopelessly dated and should better remain unpublished.   The center of attack was *The Magic Mountain*, a book successful with both the critics and the reading public.   After 1933 the common fate of exile did not soften Brecht's contempt, perhaps because Mann's books continued to be sold in Germany until 1936, a privilege for which Mann had had to pay by withdrawing his name from the list of contributors of the emigrant journal *Die Sammlung* edited by Mann's son Klaus.   In 1934 Brecht included the following stanza in his "Ballade von der Billigung der Welt" ["Ballad on Approving of the World"]:

Der Dichter gibt uns seinen Zauberberg zu lesen.
Was er (für Geld) da spricht, ist gut gesprochen!
Was er (umsonst) verschweigt: die Wahrheit wär's
    gewesen.
Ich sag: Der Mann ist blind und nicht bestochen.
                              (Brecht, IX, 472)[20]

Drafts of this stanza, extant in the Brecht Archive, suggest that what is denied in its last line, that Mann is bribed by the bourgeoisie, is really insinuated.   This interpretation is confirmed by the context of the *Ballade*.[21]   It is not known whether Mann saw this text, but it is unlikely that it remained unknown to him.   If he did see it he might not have understood more than its unfriendly intention.   Brecht, although he never read *The Magic Mountain* thoroughly, aimed at the difference between his own and Mann's political thinking.   From Brecht's point of view, Mann was hiding the truth, which was economic oppression of the lower class by the upper class.   In *The Magic Mountain* Mann was toying with ideas that disregarded what Brecht considered reality.   Even though there is a chance that Mann might not have known these lines, Brecht apparently was unable to hide his true feelings during their meeting.

That Brecht's distrust of Mann had remained in 1943 can be demonstrated by many passages from his *Arbeitsjournal*.   On 9 September 1943, Brecht wrote that he heard from a direct source that Mann had expressed the opinion that leftists like Brecht were acting on orders from Moscow if they tried to make him sign statements about a difference between Hitler and Germany.   Brecht added his own opinion to this report.   Mann, whom he called "Reptil" in this diary passage, could not imagine that a person could do anything for Germany and against Hitler without having been given orders "and that a person entirely on his own, let's say out of conviction, can see in Germany something else than a paying reading public."[22]   It seems quite clear here that Mann's suspicion of Brecht's party discipline, if this is the true core of the rumor (see the passage from the letter to Agnes Meyer of 5 December 1943 quoted above), is as wrong as Brecht's view on Mann's complicated relation to Germany, which he simplified here to the point of nonrecognition, according to his way of thinking along the lines of economic interest.   Any real understanding between these two geniuses of German exile literature was hopelessly impossible.

Nevertheless, Brecht made another attempt.   When Mann returned home to California in December 1943, a letter by Brecht was waiting for him.   This letter, dated New York, 1 December 1943, expressed concern that Mann's public utterances would increase American doubts about the existence of considerable democratic forces in Germany.   The victims of the Nazis, the concentration camp inmates, all the resisting non-Nazis who--as Brecht believed--were tying down fifty SS divisions in Germany, deserved Mann's support.[23]   Mann's answer expressed astonishment at first that no member of the New York group, which had met with him, went to listen to his New York lecture.   He then continued with a summary of the content of "Schicksal und Aufgabe."   Mann felt, and from his point of view probably had a right to feel, that he had said as much as he could, that he had even met the leftists more than halfway.   Brecht, from his vantage point, could not have been satisfied with a lecture containing some statements that looked similar to his kind of thinking, as long as they were balanced by others.   Mann's lecture qualified for what Brecht called "Tuism" in the language of his unfinished Tui-novel, which poked fun at intellectuals.

Our story has a postlude.   In the spring of 1944 the New York group under the leadership of Paul Tillich formed the Council for a Democratic Germany and published a manifesto that was signed by German exiles and sympathetic Americans.   Mann did not sign.   Asked by the writer Clifton Fadiman to disavow the Council publicly, Mann refused also (*Briefe*, pp. 366–69).   Mann defended his position in two long letters.   To Ernst Reuter (29 April 1944) he explained his refusal to join the Council; to Clifton Fadiman (29 May 1944) he justified his refusal to disavow it.   Both are moving statements from a man who struggled to preserve his freedom: "For reasons of conscience and tact I am resisting a kind of German émigré patriotism . . . ."   Such an attitude, he believed, lacked any sentiment for the suffering of European peoples under German domination.   Heavy sacrifices were still to be made by the Allied forces.   In this situation, Mann felt unable to take a German political position. The future peace with Germany could turn out to be an unwise one, although he hoped it would not, "but there is no such thing as an unjust peace with Germany after all that has happened."   And yet he was also conscious of his inability to integrate himself completely into his host country: "And although I am about to become an American citizen, I am and will remain a German, whatever questionable honor and sublime misfortune that might mean" (*Briefe*, p. 365).   For this reason, he wrote to Fadiman, it would be ugly and self-destructive ("unschön und selbstzerstörerisch") "if a German like myself--who intends to remain faithful to the German language and to complete his life's work in it even as an American citizen--arrogates to himself before the tribunal of the world the role of the accuser of his misled and guilt-laden people, and, by his possibly influential testimony, induces the most extreme and destructive measures against the land of his origin" (*Briefe*, p. 367).

Thus it is clear that Mann did not suggest the punishment of the Germans; he only felt that it was not his proper role to try to prevent such a punishment when it happened. Brecht's accusation does not reach the real person Thomas Mann; it is directed against a figment of his imagination. His poem is something like symbolic patricide, as much of Brecht's writing is, blaming the sufferings of the common people, and especially war, on the need for the upper-class bourgeoisie to maintain their standard of living, which is based on exploitation.   If we follow his accusing finger in spite of its injustice, we nevertheless are given a perspective that lets us see an ideology in Mann's political orientation.   This ideology influenced his works, especially *Doctor Faustus*.   To treat a group of people as a mythical entity subjected to an individual ethic of retribution is really to disregard the fate of the individual victim.   Mann was encouraged to think along these lines by his romanticist background.   The forming of mythical entities was also encouraged by a tendency to see his own fiction in a representative

fashion.   Hans Castorp in *The Magic Mountain* and Adrian
Leverkühn in *Doctor Faustus* represent Germany; Joseph represents Mann's educational ideal of a balance of nature and
spirit, which he conceived as a Goethean ideal.   His mode
of representation is socially confined.   Mann's representatives of Germany or its ideals are *Bildungsbürger*, to use
his own term referring to the educated middle class.   Even
Joseph, although growing up in a tent, is the son of a rich
man.   Common people appear in Mann's work as reflections
of the upper class, as their background.   They usually
admire the upper-class representatives, as in *Buddenbrooks*
and *Joseph*.

Brecht, although more critical toward generalities, was
not without an awareness of the problem of guilt and punishment that had become associated with the Germans in World
War II.   His poem "An die deutschen Soldaten im Osten" ["To
the German Soldiers in the East"] of 1942 speaks of dying
German soldiers.   Their guilt consists of attacking the great
socialist country:

> . . . das friedliche Land der Bauern und Arbeiter
> Der grossen Ordnung, des unaufhörlichen Aufbaus . . .

The suffering German soldiers are not seen in the Christ
image.   Their guilt is that they had allowed themselves to
be subjugated:

> Nur weil ich ein Knecht war
> Und es mir geheissen ward
> Bin ich ausgezogen zu morden und zu brennen
> Und muss jetzt gejagt werden
> Und muss jetzt erschlagen werden.
> (Brecht, X, 839)

There is a different biblical allusion in the same poem:

> Der Fuss, der die Felder der neuen Traktorenfahrer
>   zertrat ist verdorrt.
> Die Hand, die sich gegen die Werke der neuen
>   Städtebauer erhob ist abgehauen.
> (Brecht, X, 843)[24]

The words *verdorren* and *abgehauen* allude to grass and
flowers, frequently used biblical images for transitoriness.[25]
Brecht wants to convey the idea that what happens to the
German soldiers in Russia is something like tragic necessity,
almost a natural law, a fate that befalls those who turn
against the call to liberate themselves.   Brecht's German
guilt does not consist in intoxicated intellectual hubris, as
does Thomas Mann's.   The guilt originated before the war
and consisted in withdrawal from the class struggle.   A
short poem from Brecht's *Kriegsfibel* [*War Primer*] demonstrates the point again.   The verses of the *Kriegsfibel*
were written as comments on pictures clipped from newspapers,
this one apparently on the picture of a grave of a German
soldier in the Caucasus:

> Ihr Brüder, hier im fernen Kaukasus

> Lieg ich nun, schwäbischer Bauernsohn, begraben
> Gefällt durch eines russischen Bauern Schuss.
> Besiegt ward ich vor Jahr und Tag in Schwaben.
> (Brecht, X, 1041)[26]

In these poems the speaker seems to identify with the German soldiers, inviting the reader to do the same. But then he makes the reader feel guilty and absurdly agree to the necessity of perishing. An imaginative identification that is to be checked by a critical attitude of the reader is also the perspective of Zeitblom in Mann's *Doctor Faustus*. The limitations of Zeitblom's perspective are an important part of the message of *Doctor Faustus*. Zeitblom is a typical representative of the educated middle class, as Adrian Leverkühn is a typical artist. Fulfilling their typical roles, they have made the German catastrophe possible. Mann assumes that the intellectual leaders of the nation should have done better, but he does not question the title of the educated upper class to leadership. Such a title is denied by Brecht and the catastrophe explained solely by the failure of the lower class to wrest the privilege of leadership away from the exploiters. The dangers of both views are apparent: Mann's can disappear into vague generalities and substitute ideas discussed in small circles for orientations of the people as a whole. Mann tends to disregard economic forces and social stresses (although not entirely), while Brecht's view is so dominated by the concept of class struggle that it can become simplistic and therefore unrealistic, as his allegiance to the Soviet Union (where he did not, however, want to spend his exile) often is.[27]

On the other hand, Mann was justified in wondering about Brecht's patriotic blindness, even though his patriotism was really the result of a socialist hope. Brecht's class consciousness made him more aware of the sacrifices of Russians and his comrades in Germany than of members of Western nations. Sympathy with *all* who suffered is really a comprehensible justification for Mann's refusal to take a pro-German stand. His torn feelings appear in a passage from a letter to Agnes Meyer of 11 July 1944, together with a real concern for the fate of individuals. She had written him about the death on the battlefield of a mutual American acquaintance. Mann answered: "I confess that the pity that I feel by now for the unfortunate people in Germany is mixed with a strong personal bitterness over losses of this kind."[28] Mann went on to express sadness over the loss of writer friends in Holland and Czechoslovakia. Brecht must have felt that the Americans fought for the preservation of capitalism. Mann combined hopes of a social democracy with his support of the American war effort. In the end, Brecht's hope for a better, socialist Germany was just as illusionary as Mann's hope for a fundamental reform of the system. In West Germany the old upper class was restored to power by the Americans. In East Germany a bureaucracy of the Russian type, combined with Prussian traditions, stifled socialist hopes. America, although coopting a larger segment

of the population into the affluent society, developed urban
ghettos together with an anticommunist ideology that drove
Brecht (who had toyed with the idea of staying) and Mann
into a second emigration.

Both Mann and Brecht were informed but also victimized
by their ideologies. Mann had a pluralistic viewpoint limited by a romantic heritage and bourgeois class perspective.
Brecht's viewpoint was extended as well as limited by his
forced effort to replace the bourgeois perspective of his own
upbringing with Marxist ideology. And yet both Mann and
Brecht have much more in common than ideological orientation. They were both deeply concerned with the German problem during their years of exile. Both translated this concern into literature and approached each other in the process.
Mann's Adrian Leverkühn conceived of a new art in the service of society, although he does not enter into it; and Zeitblom, the narrator of his biography, does not even understand it. Brecht, on the other hand, was capable of dis-
carding his theories and asking the spectator of his plays
for sympathy with a bourgeois victim of the bourgeois system.
An impressive example is the scene of the Jewish woman in
Furcht und Elend des dritten Reiches [*The Private Life
of the Master Race*], which incidentally was played by
Brecht's wife Helene Weigel in the Berlin performance of
1957. Much common ground could be found by a comparison
of Brecht's principal play of his exile years, his *Galileo
Galilei*, and Mann's *Doctor Faustus*. Both works contain
autobiographical elements; both must be described in terms
of ambiguity; both end with the self-accusation of an intellectual. Mann and Brecht are not actually worlds apart,
as some critics would have us believe; they are more like
hostile brothers. It is in Brecht's language but also in the
conciliatory spirit of Mann's later years that Brecht asks
in his poem "An die Nachgeborenen" ["To Those Born Later"]:

> Ihr aber, wenn es so weit sein wird
> Dass der Mensch dem Menschen ein Helfer ist
> Gedenkt unser
> Mit Nachsicht.[29]

Notes

[1]Bertolt Brecht, *Gesammelte Werke in 20 Bänden*, Werkausgabe edition suhrkamp (Frankfurt/M: Suhrkamp, 1967),
X (*Gedichte* III), 871-73. Future references are given in
the text as: Brecht, with volume and page numbers. The
title in translation: "When the Nobel Prize Winner Thomas
Mann Acknowledged the Right of the Americans and the English to Punish the German People for Ten Years for the
Crimes of Hitler's Government." A paraphrase of the poem
is included in the interpretation. The following additional
notes may be helpful: a key word is *züchtigen*, "punish."
In German *züchtigen* is a stronger word than the usual
strafen; it is somewhat old-fashioned, bearing the connota-

tion of corporal punishment.   A prize winner in German is called *Preisträger*, literally prize bearer; Brecht associates this with an unusual, but easily understood word: *Kreuz- träger*, "cross bearer," which the reader will associate with Christ.   Brecht refers to Communist workers in the concentra- tion camps representing the Germans.   The poem makes much use of past participles functioning as nouns: *der Gezüchtig- te*, "the punished one" (Brecht's Germans); *der Geflüchte- te*, "the refugee" (Mann); *der Beleidigte*, "the offended one" (Mann); *der Gefeierte*, "the celebrated one" (Mann); *der Gekreuzigte*, "the crucified one" (normally reserved for Christ; again Brecht means Germans under Hitler).   Mann is called *der Besitzer*, "the owner"; Brecht refers to him- self as *der Schreiber*, "the writer," and *der Bittsteller*, "the petitioner."   In III Brecht uses the word *Knechtsselig- keit*, approximately "slave happiness," to describe Mann's mental state and uses a pun on *verkommen*, which means "degenerate," but also "suffer" and "die" (the former of Mann, the latter of Brecht's Germans).   *Verkommenheit* means only "degeneracy."   Mann's degeneracy is dependence on capitalism.

   [2]Thomas Mann, *Gesammelte Werke* (Frankfurt/M: S. Fischer, 1960), XI, 1077-79.   Future references are given in the text as: Mann, with volume and page numbers. Unless indicated otherwise, all English translations from German are mine.

   [3]The letter is unpublished.   Original in Beinecke Li- brary, Yale University.

   [4]The speech published under the same title in *Deci- sion*, I, No. 2 (Feb. 1941), 11-18 is a different one.   Mann used the same title again.

   [5]Both letters unpublished; see n. 3.

   [6]*Freies Deutschland*, No. 3 (6 Aug. 1943), p. 3; quoted by Günter Hartung in "Bertolt Brecht und Thomas Mann: Über Alternativen in Kunst und Politik," *Weimarer Beiträge*, 12 (1966), 407-35; the quotation is on p. 430, n. 60.   The article by Günter Hartung presents a very intelli- gent Marxist view of the Mann-Brecht controversy.

   [7]German text in Bert Brecht, *Arbeitsjournal 1942-1955* (Frankfurt/M: Suhrkamp, 1973), p. 597.

   [8]Brecht, *Arbeitsjournal 1942-1955*, p. 599.

   [9]Mann, *Gesammelte Werke*, XII, 928.   The letter to Agnes Meyer is unpublished; see n. 3.

   [10]Mann, *Briefe 1937-1947* (Frankfurt/M: S. Fischer, 1963), p. 329, 19 Aug. 1943.   Future references are given in the text as: *Briefe*, with page numbers.

   [11]The relevant passage in *Briefe 1937-1947*, p. 331, is omitted because a similar wording occurs elsewhere in the letters.   Original in Beinecke Library, Yale University.

   [12]The essay was translated by Eric Bentley.   The Ger- man original is lost.   Brecht, *Gesammelte Werke*, XX, 285- 86.

   [13]*Writers' Congress: The Proceedings of the Con- ference Held in October 1943 under the Sponsorship of the Hollywood Writers' Mobilization and the University*

of California (Berkeley: University of California Press, 1944), p. 343. My colleague Ehrhart Bahr of UCLA has kindly brought this text to my attention.

[14] Michael Kuehl, "Die exilierte deutsche demokratische Linke in USA," *Zeitschrift für Politik*, n.s. 4 (1957), 282.

[15] Letter by Mann to Mrs. Meyer, dated Kansas City, Missouri, 5 Dec. 1943; in Beinecke Library, Yale University.

[16] A copy of the letter was made available to me by G. Bernard Noble, Director, Historical Office, Bureau of Public Affairs, Department of State, in 1961. I wish to thank Mr. Noble for this and other valuable information.

[17] Letter by Adolf A. Berle to the author of this essay, Washington, D.C., 6 July 1961.

[18] Hartung, "Bertolt Brecht und Thomas Mann," p. 431, n. 65.

[19] Original in Beinecke Library, Yale University.

[20] English version in: Bertolt Brecht, *Poems*, ed. John Willett and Ralph Manheim with the cooperation of Erich Fried (London: Eyre Methuen, 1976), p. 198: "The author has us read his Magic Mountain / What he wrote there (for money) was well thought up. / What he suppressed (for free): that was the real thing. / I say that he is blind; he's not been bought up."

[21] Cf. Hartung, "Bertolt Brecht und Thomas Mann," pp. 425–26. Hartung prints the drafts from the Brecht Archive. In an earlier version of the stanza the author of *Der Zauberberg* was compared with an old prostitute (because he was bought by the bourgeoisie, an allusion to the success of the book).

[22] Brecht, *Arbeitsjournal 1942–1955*, p. 621. See also Hans Bunge, *Fragen Sie mehr über Brecht: Hanns Eisler im Gespräch* (Munich: Rogner & Bernhard, 1970), pp. 60–63.

[23] Brecht, in *Sinn und Form*, 16 (1964), 691–92. Also in his *Gesammelte Werke in 20 Bänden*, XIX, 478–80.

[24] English version in Brecht, *Poems*, p. 374: "The peaceful land of peasants and workers / With its great order, its ceaseless construction"; p. 374: "Merely because I was a menial / And was ordered to / I set out to murder and burn / And must now be hunted / And must now be slain"; and p. 377: "The foot that trampled the new tractor drivers' fields / Has withered. / The hand that was raised against the new city builders' works / Has been hacked off."

[25] Among others: Psalms 90.5–6; Isaiah 40.6–8; I Peter 1.24 (cited from Isaiah), in the Luther translation. The text from Isaiah is used in Brahms's *German Requiem*.

[26] "You brothers, here in faraway Caucasus / I, a Swabian farmer's son, now lie buried / Felled by a Russian farmer's shot, / But defeated long ago in Swabia."

[27] See John B. Fuegi, "The Exile's Choice: Brecht and the Soviet Union," in this volume.

[28] Original in Beinecke Library, Yale University.

[29] English version in Brecht, *Poems*, p. 320: "But you, when the time comes at last / And man is a helper to man / Think of us / With forbearance."

Thomas Mann and His Friends before the Tolan Committee (1942)

Erich A. Frey

Thomas Mann's plea before the "Select Committee Investigating National Defense Migration, U.S. House of Representatives" stands out as a significant example of his readiness to be a spokesman and advocate for all anti-Nazi refugees in the United States during World War II. We are referring here to Mann's testimony during a hearing of that committee (known as the "Tolan Committee" after its chairman, Representative John H. Tolan), which met in the State Building in Los Angeles on 6 and 7 March 1942.[1]

The Tolan Committee hearings, which took place in Los Angeles and other cities along the West Coast,[2] were a direct result of Executive Order No. 9066, signed by President Roosevelt on 19 February 1942, authorizing the Secretary of War or his military designate to establish "military areas" and to exclude or intern any suspicious persons, that is, "enemy aliens."[3] This order, which the president (who usually favored the émigrés) had issued under pressure from the military, some California members of Congress, and the California press, caused great unrest among the German refugees. It brought about all the more uneasiness because it involved stricter registration, evening curfews, and the threat of evacuation from the West Coast. Last but not least, the order recalled feelings of insecurity and harassment in the minds of many weary refugees who had escaped from Nazi persecution a short time before.

In a telegram to Roosevelt dated several days before the president's order, Thomas Mann had already initiated his plea for the pro-American émigrés from Germany and Italy.[4] Mann happened to be exempt from the effects of this order by virtue of his status as a Czechoslovakian citizen, but the "public handling" ("öffentliche Handhabung") of the security measures did not please him one bit. In fact, he wrote to his friend Agnes Meyer, the influential publisher of the *Washington Post*: "[This handling] causes me real concern on America's account. The California press is agitating in an atrocious manner, and there are restaurants around here that are beginning to display signs saying 'enemy aliens keep out'--which is alarmingly reminiscent of 'non-Aryans keep out.'"[5]   The subsequently published direc- tives of the overzealous military commander on the West Coast, General J. L. DeWitt, bear out the fact that Mann's concern was indeed justified.   Before the hearings of the Tolan Committee took place, DeWitt had made preparations to evacuate all German, Italian, and Japanese "enemy aliens," although the German and Italian aliens ranked as classes three and four (behind Japanese and Americans of Japanese descent).[6]   It also seems significant that the general's chief of civilian staff and coordinator concerned with the evacua- tion problems, Mr. Tom Clark of San Francisco, was invited to appear as a witness in Los Angeles on the very same day that the spokesmen for the German, Italian, and Japanese "enemy aliens" were making their pleas before the same com- mittee.[7]

The invitation extended to Thomas Mann and his friend Bruno Frank was undoubtedly connected with the preceding telegram to Roosevelt, which had been drafted by Thomas Mann and cosigned by Bruno Frank, Bruno Walter, Einstein, Borgese, Sforza, and Toscanini.   The Tolan Committee, inci- dentally, was independent of the military and was charged by Congress with probing the effect of the evacuation order on refugees from the Axis countries, based upon the evidence of the depositions made during its hearings.   Because the committee was empowered to forward the proposals resulting from the hearings directly to the Executive in Washington, it may be concluded that the pleas of Thomas Mann and his associates contributed substantially to preventing the evacua- tion of the Germans living in California.

The chief argument of Mann's deposition, which was delivered in English during the committee's morning session on 7 March 1942, lay in the assertion that the categorical and arbitrary evacuation of all German exiles, even if it should later be revoked, was not only unjust and demoraliz- ing for those concerned, but also that America's own moral fiber would necessarily suffer thereby.

Because the original wording of Thomas Mann's testi- mony has remained practically unknown and is still unlisted in previous Thomas Mann bibliographies, the full text of his and Frank's testimony is made available on pages 207–15 of this article.   The committee record shows clearly that the long middle part of Mann's deposition was previously pre- pared and that Mann read his remarks from a manuscript. The German draft of that middle part, like so many German drafts of his English letters, seems to have been lost, al- though one paragraph of the original draft is preserved in Thomas Mann's letter of 27 March 1942 to Ludwig Marcuse.[8] It is in this middle part that Mann informs the committee members about the telegram that he and his prominent fellow émigrés had sent to President Roosevelt in February.

Thomas Mann seems to have been quite pleased by his appearance before the Tolan Committee.   He wrote to Marcuse two weeks later: "I would like to believe that the bark will prove to be worse than the bite.   We have warned most strongly against sweeping measures at the outset, pointing out that they can do a great deal of irreparable harm."9 He was particularly impressed with the receptiveness of the committee members, as can be seen from the enthusiastic remarks to his confidante Agnes Meyer: "The hearings yesterday in Los Angeles before the Washington Committee were extremely interesting. They represented a regular public court session and one of the most heartwarming American experiences since I came here."10

An interesting sidelight is his evaluation of Frank's testimony. Mann writes of it to Mrs. Meyer with characteristic irony: "Frank was unfortunately too emphatic and *larmoyant*, but the congressmen nevertheless seemed to enjoy the hors d'oeuvre very much."11

Besides Mann and Frank, two other German-born witnesses pleaded the cause of their fellow refugees before the Tolan Committee during the Los Angeles hearings on 7 March 1942. One of them was Felix Guggenheim, representing the Jewish Club of 1933, Inc., Los Angeles. He explained to the committee the British treatment of "enemy aliens," which he considered exemplary, and also submitted a prepared statement on behalf of the German-born "anti-Nazi refugees" (*Hearings*, pp. 11733-737). The other witness was Hans F. Schwarzer, who characterized himself as "a simple example of a simple citizen" and described his personal fate as a refugee from Hitlerism, who was now trying "in every way to get Americanized" (*Hearings*, pp. 11806-807).

A third émigré writer, Lion Feuchtwanger, although he did not give evidence in person, submitted a written statement to the Tolan Committee while it was holding its hearings in Los Angeles. Feuchtwanger's statement, dated 5 March 1942, was accepted for the record as "Exhibit 22." Having been classified as an enemy alien upon his arrival in the United States, he now felt that he was "menaced [sic] to be removed from [his] home in West Los Angeles" (*Hearings*, p. 11879). His plea strikes a primarily personal tone, recounting his early fight against Nazism, his close connections with government leaders of England, France, and the Soviet Union, and the unfair treatment accorded him by the Vichy regime in France. However, he ended his appeal for special consideration by pleading for "almost all of those Germans who have immigrated into the United States since 1933 and were not yet able to acquire their American citizenship," and by suggesting three major exemption categories that included virtually all of the above-mentioned German immigrants (*Hearings*, p. 11880). (See below, pp. 215-17.)

With so many representative spokesmen and prominent personalities having such political weight as Thomas Mann and his friends, the American government and the public in general took an increasingly sympathetic position toward German aliens during the weeks following the Los Angeles hearings. Several scholars who have reexamined the entire "War Relocation" program of those years repeatedly stress the effectiveness of the "politically important leaders of German and Italian descent" who "pleaded for the aliens of their nationality," and they cite this as one of the main reasons why these two ethnic groups were spared from evacuation.[12]

Aside from the racial discrimination against Asians, which undoubtedly also played a role, a research report mentions the following point in conclusion: "The Japanese aliens [in contrast to the German and the Italian aliens] had no mature leaders of their ancestry in high political, social, and financial circles applying pressure."[13]

In the end, Japanese nationals and United States citizens of Japanese ancestry were the only population groups that found no positive responses from the Tolan Committee and other United States authorities and who were evacuated from the West Coast in 1942 under extremely discriminatory circumstances.

Notes

[1] Mann was accompanied by his friend Bruno Frank, who testified after Mann. The next witness was Felix Guggenheim. See *Hearings before the Select Committee Investigating National Defense Migration*, House of Representatives, 77th Cong., 2nd sess. Part 31, Los Angeles and San Francisco Hearings, 6, 7, and 12 March 1942: Problems of Evacuation of Enemy Aliens and Others from Prohibited Military Zones (Washington, D.C.: U.S. Government Printing Office, 1942), pp. 11725-732. Cited hereafter as *Hearings*.

[2] The Portland and Seattle hearings took place on 26-28 Feb. and 2 March 1942, respectively. Cf. *Hearings*, Parts 30-31.

[3] *WRA: A Story of Human Conservation*, by the U.S. Department of the Interior (Washington, D.C.: U.S. Government Printing Office, 1946), p. viii.

[4] Thomas Mann, *Briefe 1937-1947*, ed. Erika Mann (Frankfurt/M: S. Fischer, 1963), pp. 236-37. Cited as *Briefe*.

[5] Unpublished letter of Mann to Agnes Meyer, 16 Feb. 1942, Beinecke Library, Yale University. Permission to quote is kindly acknowledged. Mrs. Meyer and her husband, Mr. Eugene Meyer, were Mann's closest American friends, and they helped him establish many valuable contacts with high government officials in Washington. (English translations mine.)

[6] Edward H. Spicer et al., *Impounded People* (Tucson: University of Arizona Press, 1969), p. 37.

[7] *Hearings*, p. 11773.

[8] Mann to Marcuse: "Before the Tolan Committee I said: 'I am by no means thinking only of the emigrants; I am also thinking of the fighting spirit of this country. I have the terrible example of France in mind. A nation that takes pleasure in victories over its most intimate enemies does not seem in the best psychological condition to defeat those enemies!'" See *Briefe*, p. 251, and *Hearings*, p. 11726.

[9] *Briefe*, p. 252.

[10] *Briefe*, p. 247.

11*Briefe*, p. 247.
12 Spicer, p. 38.
13 Spicer, p. 38.

TESTIMONY OF DR. THOMAS MANN, 1550 SAN REMO DRIVE,
PACIFIC PALISADES, CALIF., AND DR. BRUNO FRANK,
513 NORTH CAMDEN DRIVE, BEVERLY HILLS, CALIF.

MR. ARNOLD. Dr. Mann, you and Dr. Frank need, of course, no introduction, but for the record the committee would like to have you give your name, address, and occupation so that the record might be complete.

DR. MANN. My name is Thomas Mann. I am living now in Pacific Palisades, No. 1550 San Remo Drive.

MR. ARNOLD. Doctor, will you give us for the record your occupation and a little background?

DR. MANN. I am a writer, sir; author, novelist, essayist, and lecturer.

MR. ARNOLD. Are you a native American?

DR. MANN. No, sir. I was born in Germany. I lived a long time in Munich where I studied and married. I left Germany in the year 1933 just before Hitler came to power. Then I lived 5 years in Switzerland before I came over to America.

I came over to America first in the year 1934 for a short visit and I visited America each year after that. I came over to settle definitely in this country in the year 1938.

I followed my vocation of lecturing at the University of Princeton. I did that for two winters. It was only for 1 year first, but it was prolonged for the second year.

Then I made the acquaintanceship of California and came out here to settle. We have our home in Pacific Palisades.

MR. BENDER. Dr. Mann, I would like to ask you about the Munich conference, but I won't.

One of the questions which has come to our attention during our hearings in San Francisco, Portland, and Seattle, has been the effect of the evacuation order on refugees from Axis countries. We are interested in hearing from yourself and Dr. Frank your views and observations.

The committee would like to have you proceed in your own way, Dr. Mann, and then we will hear from Dr. Frank. We understand that you happen to be a Czech.

DR. MANN. Yes.

MR. BENDER. And are not yourself affected by the recent alien-control regulation.

DR. MANN. Correct.

MR. BENDER. Would you proceed in your own way.

DR. MANN. Thank you very much.

I really feel highly honored to have the opportunity to take part in this meeting, the subject of which has been close to my heart since the problem arose. It is close to

my heart not only because it is of so vital, moral, and material importance for the people it concerns, but also because
only a fair solution would be worthy of this great Nation
which is fighting for freedom and human dignity.

I would like to add that, certainly, the behavior of
a war-waging nation against her emigrees has something to
do with the good fighting spirit of that nation.   It is the
frightening example of France I had in mind.   A nation
which seeks and enjoys victory over the most intimate and
most natural enemies does not seem to be in the happiest
psychological condition to meet these enemies.

I realize, of course, that in times of crisis no natural
inclination to generosity and kindness can be allowed to
imperil the safety of the country, and certainly it is not
easy to find a general solution which does justice to both
sides, the refugees and the interests of the country at war.
As a matter of fact, we have to face an absolutely paradoxi-
cal situation, such as perhaps never existed before. We have
to deal with people who by their birth and descent, if their
case is treated mechanically, fall under the category of
"enemy aliens," but who are in fact the most passionate
adversaries of the European governments this country is at
war with, and who left their native lands in protest against
the political systems ruling there, or were forced to leave
it.   Most of them lost the citizenship of their original countries, and even formally cannot be regarded as nationals
of a country with which they do not have the slightest connection.   So in this war, the idea and characteristic of "enemy alien" has lost its logical justification in the case of
the German and Italian emigrees.

Perhaps it is not superfluous to add that I, personally,
am not affected for the reason that when I was deprived of
my German citizenship, President Benes of Czechoslovakia was
generous enough to make me a Czech citizen; so I am a
friendly alien, even technically, but only by chance.   And
I have imagination enough to understand the feelings of
these victims of national socialism and fascism who were seeking refuge and freedom to breathe in this great democracy,
and would be only too happy to do their share in the work
of defense, but now find themselves under suspicion and subjected to special regulations which, for many of them, would
mean a deadly catastrophe, the collapse of their newly and
painfully rebuilt existence.   For that reason, just some
weeks ago I decided to join a few prominent emigrants from
Italy and Germany in sending a telegram to the President
of the United States, in which we expressed the same feelings
and ideas I am trying to develop today.   I give you the
names of the signers of this telegram; they were the Italians,
Arturo Toscanini, Count Carlo Sforza, and Professor Borgese,
and the Germans, Bruno Walter, Albert Einstein, my friend
Dr. Frank, and myself.   With the exception of Toscanini,
all these men are either already American citizens or friendly
aliens, but all of them felt obligated to act for their countrymen, and to ask the President to bring about, in some
way, a clear and practical distinction between potential

fifth columnists and people who are the victims and proven opponents of the powers with which America is at war today.

I really do not feel that the difficulties for establishing such a distinction are insurmountable. Other groups of aliens like the Austrians, Czechs, and so on, have already been excepted. It is certainly not my intention to say anything against the loyalty of these groups, but so much may be said that in no other group so many reasons speak for a passionate desire for Hitler's defeat, as in the case of German and Italian refugees. So I think that where it can be incontestably proven that a person is a refugee, a victim of Nazi oppression, an exception should be made, and the questionnaire of the registration form has already given, by its point 15, the authorities the necessary material for clarification. Moreover, there can be no doubt that the Federal Bureau of Investigation has carefully observed all aliens for quite some time, and has proven to be very well informed about their behavior and intentions. Whoever is individually suspicious will doubtless be taken care of, and it should not be difficult to find out all cases needing clarification. In my opinion it would be worth while to investigate a number of cases, which certainly would not be very considerable, instead of taking radical measures against the entirety of the refugees. All of us know that the burning problem on the west coast is the question of the Japanese. It would be a great misfortune if the regulations, perhaps necessary in their case--it is not my business to talk about the Japanese problem--would be applied to the German and Italian refugees, even with the intention of revising single cases later. For, as I have already mentioned, in many cases irreparable harm would be done to perfectly harmless and loyal persons. I think this should and could be avoided, and I am certain that other members of this meeting will make more concrete and practical propositions. In speaking for the refugees it is not only their interests I am visualizing. Every day it becomes more urgent that all available forces be put into the service of the country, and there are certainly many of the refugees who instead of becoming a burden to themselves and the country could be of valuable help in the struggle until victory.

MR. BENDER. Doctor, I am appreciating that your position is rather delicate by virtue of your Czech citizenship. I would like to ask you a number of questions and if you desire to answer all right, and if not it will be perfectly all right.

Are you acquainted personally with a Dr. Fritz Baum?

DR. MANN. No; I don't know him.

MR. BENDER. Who is the husband of the daughter of Albert J. Berridge?

DR. MANN. Sorry; I don't know.

MR. BENDER. Are you acquainted personally at all with Dr. Frank Zigmund, who is a scientist and inventor? He is a Czech citizen.

DR. MANN. It seems to me that I remember the name but surely I never met him.

MR. BENDER.   Do you know the Czech language, Doctor?

DR. MANN.   No; I don't.

MR. BENDER.   In regard to this question of alien enemies, your impression is that everybody who is labeled that way is not necessarily an enemy?

DR. MANN.   No; surely not.

MR. BENDER.   And you believe, from your observation, that possibly we might have additional facilities for handling that problem?

DR. MANN.   I think so.

MR. BENDER.   In expediting the just treatment of these cases?

DR. MANN.   Yes; I think so.   I am sure that some way will be found.

MR. BENDER.   You believe that there are many alleged enemy aliens incarcerated in detention places that might be of service in this war effort in the event that this could be expedited?

DR. MANN.   That is very probable; yes.

MR. BENDER.   What percentage of the Jewish refugees are classified as enemy aliens?   For example, from Germany, Czechoslovakia, Rumania, and other places.

DR. MANN.   What percentage?

MR. BENDER.   What percentage of them?

DR. MANN.   Of Jewish descent?

MR. BENDER.   Yes; that are now being held by the United States Government who might be extremely useful in this war effort in the event of such expediting?

Dr. Frank, would you care to answer that question?

DR. FRANK.   Well, perhaps I can.

MR. BENDER.   Doctor, before you speak, I wish you would identify yourself.   It is the committee's understanding that you are an officer of a refugee organization and are deeply concerned with alien-control rulings and that you have given the problem some thought.

DR. FRANK.   Yes, I have.

MR. BENDER.   First, for the record, will you identify yourself?

DR. FRANK.   My name is Bruno Frank.   I am by profession a writer.   I live at 513 North Camden Drive in Beverly Hills.

MR. BENDER.   Under what circumstances did you come to this country?

DR. FRANK.   I left Germany in February 1933 the very first day after the legal government was overthrown, because very probably I wouldn't have survived the second day.

MR. BENDER.   We would like to have you discuss the problem that we are particularly interested in at the moment, as it affects anti-Axis refugees who happen to be citizens of enemy countries.

DR. FRANK.   Yes.

MR. BENDER.   Will you proceed in your own way?

DR. FRANK.   I am appearing before your committee, most thankful for the honor bestowed upon me, and let me add this at once, with a deep feeling of confidence:

Ever since the question of the evacuation of enemy aliens arose, there has been much consternation and fear among the German and Italian refugees out here. Many of them remember how, in a moment of frantic confusion, the Government of France treated the exiles, and they are afraid the same things might happen again. They already see their last and only hope gone.

May I frankly say that I personally could never share these dreads for a single moment. No, the victims of that hateful oppression won't be confounded with the oppressors. The bitterest and most consistent foes of nazi-ism and fascism won't be treated the same way as Nazis and Fascists themselves. Not in this country. Not under the great President of this Republic; not under its Congress, which is the strongest remaining fortress of constitutional freedom in the world; not under its Department of Justice, whose humane and enlightened utterances we have heard; and not, certainly not, under its military men. For these are not Prussian generals shaped after the pattern of some unspeakable "Fuehrer." They are American citizens proudly wearing their uniforms in defense of the same liberties, the loss of which has driven the refugees out of their homeland.

Thus my confidence was greatly strengthened when I saw the registration questionnaire, which so clearly indicated the intentions of the American Government. For here the fullest opportunity was offered to each German or Italian refugee for stating whether he left his country because of racial, religious, or political persecution and for naming such trustworthy persons who could vouch for his loyalty. This, I feel sure, was not done without good reason and purpose.

And there is still stronger evidence. Before the war, about a year and a half ago, a number of refugees, then trapped in defeated France, were saved by a magnanimous action of your Government. Among them were eminent statesmen, scientists, artists, writers. Under the auspices of the Presidential Advisory Committee, emergency visas were granted to them, and so they were, in the nick of time, snatched from immediate peril. How then could anyone imagine that these same people, who by the American Government were recognized as stanch democratic fighters against the Nazis, should now be branded as enemy aliens by the same Government?

But, sir, I am not so much concerned about those outstanding men, when, for instance, I read that Arturo Toscanini, before going from New York to Philadelphia in order to conduct a concert for the War Relief Fund or the Red Cross, has to ask for a permit because he is technically an enemy alien--then I think this an odd story. But I am not afraid for Signor Toscanini. Not much will happen to him. A great name, or even a well-known name, shields a man from hardship.

I am concerned about the so-called average man or woman, the little fellow who, after long and terrible sufferings, having lost situation, property, and, more often than

not, those dearest to him, has finally found here a haven
of rest and ultimate hope.

As it is always more instructive to give a concrete and
living example than to speak in generalities, let me present
to you, sir, an average case among many, nothing particularly striking, but typical for those refugees who now live
in deadly fear to be branded as enemies.

In a family I happen to know they have a housemaid,
a Jewish girl, kind, honest, hardworking.   She alone of her
kin has escaped from Germany, and it is her only longing
to save and to bring to these shores her old parents she
was forced to leave behind.

She comes from a small town in northern Germany, where
80 Jewish families have been living for more than 600 years.
It was one of the oldest communities.   Now the Nazis have
uprooted these people, they have burnt their synagogue to
the ground, trampled underfoot and swinishly soiled their
sacred books, and desecrated their graveyard.   Of the 80
families 3 are left.   The rest have been exterminated, dispersed, or have been "removed to Poland."   What this expression means, sir, you most certainly know.   It was perfectly
illustrated by those horrid pictures in last week's Life magazine, showing heaps of naked, emaciated corpses, piled upon
one another like so much rubbish, ready to be flung into
the common pit.

The two old people over there live under the constant
threat of being carried away to that hell.   Get the money
for leaving the country--or else--they are told.   Their daughter saves every penny she makes for their passage and for
the bribes--for every single one of those Nazi gangs has to
be bribed separately.   But each time she offers her savings,
she is told it is not enough.   Transportation costs have gone
up, and so have the bribes.

The girl knows what a life her parents have over there.
They live in one windowless room.   They are not allowed
to go out in the daytime.   They are not allowed to burn
light at night.   They are not allowed to use a phone or a
radio, or to ride on the train, or to sit on a bench in the
park.

Don't lose patience, writes the girl (or, rather, she
wrote, because now of course she cannot write any more).
Don't despair.   One day my money will be enough.   Then
you will come here.   This is heaven.   One lives among
friends here.   I shall work for you, and you will live peaceful years.

Well, sir, what should she write now, if write she
could?   I am no longer among friends?   I am branded as
an enemy now, just as the beasts who are torturing you.
Forget all about it.   It was but a dream.   Go to Poland,
and die.

No, sir, she won't have to write thus.   Not here.

Your Government, sir, is acutely aware of the gulf that
separates the victims from the oppressors.   They have already
exempted different groups from being classified as enemy
aliens, for instance, the Czechs and the Austrians.   Nothing

could be more justified, more appropriate. And though, when exempting these groups, the Attorney General most certainly realized that among the holders of Czech passports are those so-called Sudetens, who plotted with the Nazi aggressors; and that among the holders of Austrian passports are those Austrian Nazis who opened the gates of Vienna to Hitler. These facts, most fairly, were not considered a reason for impairing the rights of the enormous majority of loyal Austrians and Czechs. If any of the suspect elements were to be found in this country, the F.B.I., I am sure, would make short shrift of them.

But, sir, the only group where even such loathsome exceptions are most unlikely to be found, are the refugees from Germany, the very victims and proven opponents of Hitler.

Nearly all of them have been deprived of their nationality, either by individual decree or by groups. This means they have been outlawed and officially robbed of all they possessed. All of them, or next to all, have, under their oath, declared that they will sever allegiance to the debased land of their origin as soon as the American law will allow them to do so. There is absolutely no relationship left between them and the Nazis, none but bitter, implacable hatred.

Never, as far as my knowledge goes, has there been one single case of a refugee conspiring with or working for the enemy. In France there have been at least 20 times more refugees than in the United States. Not a single case has occurred. And the same goes for England.

In England, as I take it from the excellent information furnished by our expert in this matter, Dr. Felix Guggenheim, examination boards were set up, which exempted all genuine refugees from restrictions. However, when the Nazis came within 20 miles of England's shores, restrictions were suddenly tightened. But, under the very bombs of the aggressors, public opinion and the House of Commons protested violently and they did not give way until the position of the refugees had been restored. Today all these exiled scientists, physicians, workers, and industrialists enthusiastically contribute to the British war effort against the common foe. And in their registration certificates, in order to identify them as allies, these words are stamped, "Victim of Nazi oppression."

Now, as I pointed out, the number of refugees in this country is very much smaller. In the Los Angeles area, for instance, where accumulation is relatively dense, there are about 4,000--that is one-fifth of 1 percent of the population. The number of 4,000 individuals is equivalent to 1,000 or 1,200 family units. The task of investigating this number, and so to avoid the tragic consequences of wrong classification, would not be a heavy one.

For, since the registration, which in my opinion came as a godsend, the exact data about any single one of these cases are in the hands of the F.B.I. The vast majority of them will be clarified at once. There might be a few border cases, especially among gentile refugees who left Nazi Germany out of sheer horror and disgust, and who, being gentiles, were not honored by the Hitler regime with expatriation.

An examination board, sir, should be set up at once. I cannot presume to suggest how such a board should be composed. The only thing I feel allowed to propose is that, in an advisory capacity, one or several aliens with a sound knowledge of the matter, and enjoying the confidence of both the authorities and their fellow refugees, should be associated to it.

Pending final regulation, a licensing system could be established in the military zone No. 1, not in any contradiction but in fullest accordance with General DeWitt's proclamation. The spot zones, naturally, designated as such, would be excluded.

But now, sir, here comes my plea, and most ardent it is. Please don't delay. Take the anguish off the minds of those harassed people as soon as ever possible.

The idea has been proffered, I am told, that at first the refugees should be evacuated as enemy aliens, and that later on, by and by, individual readmission might be granted. Sir, that would never do. Such a procedure would spell disaster. Once removed, these people would be lost. The frail roots they have taken in this soil would be cut off. They would lose their jobs, their small businesses, and, most important of all, the friendly contact they have established with their American neighbors. Should they ever come back, perhaps after many months, they would be unwelcome strangers again, looked at with suspicion as people who once have been stigmatized and taken away as potential enemies.

Not all of them, sir, would have the strength for starting afresh, not many of them. They have been through too much. I don't want to dramatize, but I know that, if such steps were taken, there would be suicides before long.

May I add one final word, sir? I could imagine some people saying: All this may be true, but this is a world war. Our country faces the gravest crisis in her history. We are sending our husbands and sons to distant shores to fight and, maybe, to die. Why should we care for a handful of foreigners?

I don't know whether anybody in this country speaks like that. I'd rather think not. But, if so, this would be the answer:

These foreigners have fought against the same hideous foe as your boys. They still bear the scars on their bodies and souls. There is hardly anyone among them who has not lost relatives and friends by the same brutish hands. No group, by its hatred of evil and its love of freedom, could be closer united in spirit to the American soldier than these very people.

MR. BENDER.   Doctor, is the United States Government making sufficient use of your services, and Dr. Mann, of yours, and your associates who were in similar positions or are in similar positions to yours? Is there anything that you could assist with further that we might suggest to the

United States Government that they might call on you for additional services other than those which you have already been called upon to render?

DR. MANN. Well, I am only awaiting a call from the Government. I would be absolutely at the service of the government. At present my defense work is more or less personal because I am going over the country and lecturing in many cities about the problems of the war and of the coming peace. That is my moderate contribution to the public service.

MR. ARNOLD. Dr. Mann, I might say that in my district in Illinois, about one-third of my constituents are of German descent, mostly American citizens, but several of whom, prior to Pearl Harbor, were sympathetic, apparently, with Mr. Hitler. I might utilize your services this fall in the campaign.

MR. BENDER. Recognizing the condition that you speak of, Dr. Frank and Dr. Mann, do you not think that for one of these alleged enemy aliens or any of that group to be incarcerated in these immigration detention centers, or in any other place, even in their plight, is like Heaven, compared to the alleged freedom of their existence over in Europe under Axis domination?

DR. FRANK. Yes; I certainly would prefer the life in an American prison to free life in Germany or even in France today. This, I admit. But I don't wish it for them. They wouldn't survive.

MR. ARNOLD. Thank you very much, gentlemen. We appreciate having you come here before the committee. We will take a 2-minute recess. (*Hearings*, pp. 11725-732)

EXHIBIT 22. STATEMENT BY LION FEUCHTWANGER,
1744 MANDEVILLE CANYON, WEST LOS ANGELES,
CALIFORNIA

March 5, 1942

According to the regulations I had to register as enemy alien, and now, being considered an enemy alien, I see myself menaced to be removed from my home in West Los Angeles. Therefore I beg to apply to the Honorable Chairman John H. Tolan and his congressional committee by making the following statement:

Since the year 1922 I have been fighting against the spread of naziism. I have written a number of novels dealing with the rise of the Nazis and the threat to civilization by naziism. I have published articles against the Nazis in the leading reviews, magazines, and newspapers all over the world. I broadcasted against the Nazis in the capitals of the world. My anti-Nazi books have been translated into many languages, their circulation amounts to millions of copies. My material is copiously used by the underground movement against fascism in Germany, in Italy, and even in Japan. Leading papers in this country, of England, of the

Soviet Union, and even of China have repeatedly declared my literary activity an efficient weapon in the struggle against the Nazis. My plays and my pictures against the Nazis have been shown to millions of people. British pilots over Germany dropped leaflets quoting from my books. The Soviet Government spread my books and my films in order to spur the fighting spirit against Nazi Germany. The President of the French Republic before the collapse, English Cabinet Ministers, the Soviet Prime Minister, and members of the Government of this country asked to meet me and to hear my opinions on the struggle against naziism.

The Nazis themselves consider me as a very dangerous enemy, according to the public speeches of the German Minister of Propaganda. Hitler himself, many other Nazi leaders and Nazi papers attacked me. I was abused in numerous Nazi broadcasts. Thus, by the threat of the Nazis, I was forced to leave Germany in November 1932 already. My Berlin home was looted as one of the first in February 1933, my library was destroyed, my books were burnt, my fortune was confiscated. Albert Einstein and I were the first to be warned by the German Government that we would lose our German citizenship. In fact, on August 23, 1933, the German Government announced officially that I, together with twenty-odd others, had lost my German citizenship.

At the outbreak of this war I lived in France and was interned on account of general measures.

This fact aroused astonishment everywhere, especially in the United States, and many newspapers elaborated their reports on my internment with ironical comments on the French authorities. And the Nazis gloated over it in their newspapers and in their broadcasts. I just published a book on my experiences in France and how I was involved in French red tape. This book, *The Devil in France* , met with much interest in this country.

Should I definitely be classified as an enemy alien and removed from my home in West Los Angeles, the consequences would be rather critical for my future work. For months, I would have to interrupt my present work on an anti-Nazi novel, and my planned activities for anti-Nazi pictures would be frustrated. There is no question that the Nazis would be pleased if they heard about such measures against me.

Many others, probably almost all of those Germans who have immigrated into the United States since 1933 and were not yet able to acquire their American citizenship, are in a similar situation. Most of these people, however, have not only nothing in common with the political structure of today's Germany, but they are the natural enemies of the present German Government. Among three groups at least of these immigrants (since 1933) the percentage of potential Nazi sympathizers is by no means higher than among the average inhabitants of this country. Those groups of the so-called German enemy aliens could be classified rather easily:

(1) All those who lost their German citizenship by edict of the German Ministry of the Interior before September 3, 1939. These people are listed by name on lists published by

the German Reichsanzeiger. Only such people are named in these lists who, according to the opinion of the present German Government, have impaired the interests of the German Reich. In every single case it could easily be demonstrated how far these people proved to be Nazi enemies.

(2) All those people who could not obtain a German passport so that they were forced to travel on other identification papers.

(3) All those who can produce actual evidence of their activities against the Nazis before America's entrance into the war.

Outstanding immigrants of German descent would gladly be willing to assist the American authorities in the possible inquiry of anti-Nazi activities.

It seems obvious that the reclassification of the so-called German enemy aliens according to such or similar principles would be fair and useful. (*Hearings*, pp. 11879-880)

Robert Musil in Switzerland: Aphorism and Pragmatic Tradition

Wolfgang Freese

In what way exile during the recent history of fascism affected a writer's literary production has long intrigued critics of this period. Some hypothesize that the conditions of exile prompted writers to prefer specific literary genres such as the historical novel and the sonnet. The reasons for this shift have also been set forth, often and persuasively. Alfred Döblin, for example, mentioned the "absence of the present" as the crucial element in the case of the historical novel;[1] Theodore Ziolkowski accounts for the peculiar popularity of the sonnet by citing conscious commitment to a strong formal tradition, which can serve both as a foothold and as compensation for decaying values and relationships, accords and communities of interest.[2] For many reasons a similar shift was to be expected in the case of Robert Musil and his novel *The Man without Qualities*. In fact, a cursory look at his years of exile in Switzerland would indicate that this does seem to have happened. Exile placed the usual burden on the work, obstructing and eventually jeopardizing it, and the break caused by Musil's sudden death on 15 April 1942 did no more than give abrupt expression to what might have been expected to occur in the normal course of events. The external situation served to aggravate an internal one that manifested itself as early as the 1920s in the form of severe writer's block. This circumstance has been analyzed in numerous dissertations[3] dealing with the aesthetic problems of the novel's ending, the possibly unavoidable fragmentation, or simply Musil's waning power to assert mastery over the complex structure of what he had already created.[4] Depending on the thesis, stress is placed either on the inevitability of the intrinsic development or on the effects of the arbitrary external situation. Always, however, attention remains wholly focused on the single object, the great novel fragment. Everything hinges on analysis, commentary, and discussion of the work.

During the last ten years of his life Musil made little significant progress in his work, writing no more than a chapter and a half a year. Although he was clearly unable to arrive at the desired final version, a tendency toward a particular form becomes overt in conjunction with the time of his exile. Although this tendency was noticeably embedded in Musil's earlier work and thought, it was only during his final years that it gained conscious artistic expression, thus exerting some influence on reworkings of earlier sections of the novel and interacting with all of it. This is the tendency to the aphoristic, to the form of the aphorism.

It is not clear whether this impulse to aphoristic expression is to be seen primarily as an escape from the difficulties presented by the work or as a breakthrough to a preference long adumbrated in Musil's work and thinking. We cannot lightly dismiss the argument that such external requirements as the restrictions on continuity occasioned by exile or the desire of the aging writer to arrive at conclusions, even if only in isolated thoughts, led to the almost accidental formulation of ideas in maxims. But it is a remarkable fact in itself that during Musil's time of exile the aphorism as a form gains in stature. We may also assume that in the case of a writer working as consciously as Musil such a development is not accidental.

But once we accept the importance of this observation, bewildering consequences follow. The concurrence or sequence of long epic writing and aphoristic terseness is by no means random. On the contrary, each extreme refers back to the view expressed by Friedrich Schlegel, according to which the essence of art consists in unending reflection. The extensive weight of the novel—that is, the multitude of words—corresponds to the intensive weight of the aphorism. Abridgment and omission to the point of obscurity in the aphorism lead to a state in which language becomes conscious of itself and correspondingly renounces the illusion of cut-and-dried "all-expressing" statements, gaining instead the depth of unending reflection. What is surprising is to find these two tendencies immediately adjacent, interwoven, and in sequence. The great aphorists did not write novels. In this instance Musil takes his place in the German tradition from Lessing by way of Lichtenberg through Schopenhauer and Nietzsche to Karl Kraus. Except for Schopenhauer, Musil had a direct relationship with all of these, based on exhaustive knowledge of their work. But there is one other aphorist, whose work radicalized the tradition in various ways and to whom Musil also seems related, both by contemporaneity and by cultural background—Wittgenstein.[5]

From Lichtenberg to Wittgenstein there is a confrontation of German thinkers and writers with the contradiction— already present in the *lingua characteristica universalis* of Leibniz and Jakob Böhme's *lingua adamica*—between a language of quantitative or quantifiable concepts and one of poetic sensibility, between calculation and intuition, between logical sequence and semantic significance, or, to use Musil's own designation of what he called "the polarities of the day," between "rationality and mysticism" (*T*, 237).[6] Thus Musil can be seen as heir to two different traditions. One is represented by the linguistic reflections of Lichtenberg and Wittgenstein, grounded in mathematical foundations. In this tradition the linguistic problem will always focus on the inexplicable remnants--the "beautiful," the "individual," the "phenomenal," and the like--unities that are not quantifiable and can only be comprehended aesthetically. At the same time Musil can be seen to be in the tradition of Nietzsche and Karl Kraus, carrying on a concept of language with an ethical and satiric cast, whose rhetorical tools seek to exploit rather than inhibit the blurred relationships and metaphorical elements of ordinary language.

About the biographical details of Musil's emigration not much can be said here. Once in Zurich (2 September 1938) he found himself not only without a publisher but soon also without a readership. On 20 October 1938 he was notified that "your novel *The Man without Qualities* has been declared inadmissible for the entire area of the German Reich."[7]   Early in July 1939 he moved from Zurich to an older residential quarter of Geneva, where to his great delight a police ordinance forbade the roosters to crow--he always found noises of any kind intolerable. The correspondence of the final years, until Musil's death on 15 April 1942, consists almost entirely of petitions to government officials, requests for extensions of his residence permit, and more or less covert references to his financial situation.

Under the circumstances it is no wonder that Musil's total production--that is, work on *The Man without Qualities*--amounted to "fourteen chapters, a chapter and a half per year," between 1932 and 15 April 1942, according to Karl Corino's calculations.[8]   Not only money worries, weariness, nervousness, occasional total exhaustion, but also fears about the work itself led to blockages. In addition, Musil had been forced to leave his entire library in Vienna, because he continued to maintain his apartment there (at 20 Rasumofskygasse, where he had moved in 1921), if only to fulfill Swiss immigration requirements.

A comparison Musil makes in a letter of 20 January 1942 to his friend Rolf Langnese is typical of his state of mind:

> Try to imagine a buffalo with two ridiculously sensitive "corns" growing in place of mighty horns. This creature with the mighty brow, which once bore weapons and now bears corns, is the man in exile. If he has been a king, he speaks of the crown that once was his, and he senses that others have begun to wonder whether it might have been nothing more than a hat. He himself comes to question whether a head still surmounts his shoulders. It is a sad, but almost equally ridiculous, and therefore doubly sad situation. (*PD*, 829)

But he is not always able to give metaphoric expression to his own suffering in order not to burden the recipient with "sick humor" or "endless money worries which, if expressed, turn one into a Willie the Weeper."[9] When no one took note of his sixtieth birthday, bitterness did come to the fore for once. In his only thank-you note, to Lejeune, he writes, "It looks as if I were already gone. . . ."[10]

The struggle against failure--against the "feeling of uselessness," as he once put it--is a typical attitude for Musil; in this context he sees himself as altogether "heroic." Thus the question concerning political focus and literary involvement, which arises in all exile literature, is also put in this light.

How has Musil been ranked within groups of other exiled writers, according to his political and philosophical bent? Some of these subordinations into groups are false to an exemplary degree, and I should like to go into greater detail in one case. Jost Hermand has rightly rejected the thesis of clear alliances among the émigrés after 1933: "A common front can hardly be expected from a group that is so disturbed, terrorized, and ideologically disparate. During the early years of exile, therefore, there was neither a 'humanistic' nor an 'antifascist' front, as was claimed after 1945."[11] According to Hermand, the dominant elements of this period were "first of all scattering, schismatization, overall chaos. Both the committed left-wing writers and the nonpoliticals simply had not believed that such a change of power could occur" (p. 15). Hermand's theory was fed by, among others, Lion Feuchtwanger in his novel *Exil*, 1940 [*Paris Gazette*]. How, then, can these writers be classified, subdivided, categorized? Hermand proposes three groupings: "resigned-escapist," "culturally conscious-humanistic," and "active-antifascist tendencies" (p. 16). In the first group he includes writers who withdrew in various ways-- into Zionism or Catholicism (he cites Döblin and Werfel as examples of the latter); "into themselves" like Tucholsky; and into their "poetic interior chambers" even before 1933, like Beer-Hofmann and Schaeffer. Hermand also mentions those scholars "who claim that this literature has no exile characteristics whatsoever" and adds, "in the case of writers who continued writing without a break, this thesis might be tenable" (p. 17). But continuing this line of thought, that is exactly what is so particularly remarkable about Musil-- that he "continued writing without a break" on *The Man without Qualities* . Does this make Musil an exponent of this group? As far as Hermand is concerned, certainly not, if for no other reason than that there is no evidence of philosophical escapism in Musil, but especially because he considers Musil paradigmatic for the second, "culturally conscious-humanistic tendency," the "new Weimar types of humanistic representatives of culture": "It is widely composed of solidly and highly bourgeois authors whose emigration was accomplished with aristocratic reserve and who chose for the place of their exile such bourgeois-harmonious countries as Switzerland, Sweden, and Holland. They like to refer to the myth of the 'country of poets and thinkers' and stand for the theory that good art is 'the best politics'" (p. 17). This group, claims Hermand, is characterized by "Musil's speech in 1935 in Paris at the first Writers' Congress in

Defense of Culture, which has a distinctly moving ring in its apologia for the apolitical" (p. 13).

According to Hermand, Thomas and Klaus Mann, Ernst Cassirer, Ludwig Marcuse, and Oskar Maria Graf also belong to this group to varying degrees, by virtue of the fact that all of them remain "primarily caught up in the realm of the unpolitical-metaphorical--that is, the demonic, sickly, satanic, mad, or bestial" (p. 18) when they mention the Nazis. That is, they demonize out of an attitude arrested in tradition, guided by Goethe's cosmopolitanism and Kant's idealism.

This is not the place to discuss whether Switzerland was a "bourgeois-harmonious" host country. Other documentations and exhibits have revealed much of what applies also to Musil's special situation.[12]   Musil devoted considerable thought to the "choice" of exile.   For years he literally toyed with the thought of emigrating to the United States, but as for the literary compromise of hack work, such as Hollywood might offer, he claimed to possess no flair for it, being "unsuited to Broadway plays, bestsellers, or talking pictures."[13]

Was Musil a "solidly and highly bourgeois" writer? Apparently this question depends on the evaluation of his total writings.   It cannot, at any rate, be answered by reference only to his background or his professional career. His father, the engineer Alfred Musil, who was given a professorship in 1890 and was raised to the nobility in 1917, no more determined his membership in the bourgeoisie than his subsequent poverty and unemployment made him a proletarian.   In this and many other aspects, as can be easily documented, Musil is more closely related to Brecht than to Thomas Mann, whose status as the "archexile" opened all doors to him, even in Switzerland.   Musil did not think much of the "land of poets and thinkers," and he was no less annoyed than Brecht by the "intellectuals' parade" at the Paris conference.[14]   Musil, with his little subsidiary lecture, hardly fits the atmosphere of this congress, with its grand sentimental moments (such as the appearance of the masked man or Heinrich Mann on the stage of the Mutualité).   His language--ironically cool as usual, aiming at precision and at a distance from the addressed problems--lends a markedly different tone from that of the other papers, even, or especially, where his themes coincide with those of others--for example, Heinrich Mann's speech on "Problems of Creativity and the Dignity of Thought."   Brecht notes with great amusement that Mann had previously submitted the paper to the Sûreté.[15]

Does Musil belong to the "new Weimar types or humanistic representatives of culture"?   Does he take his direction from Goethe or Kant?   The only allusions to "Goethean man" ("der goetheide Mensch") in his work are satirical.   Weimar as a cultural tradition was relatively foreign to him--even if Wolfgang Leppmann did deal with the topic.[16]   "Historically," Musil noted in his 1931 essay "Literat und Literatur" ["Literature and the Man of Letters"], "the humanistic type began with classical and Biblical quotations, and although such quoting may have gone out of fashion outwardly, it simply went underground, and all of belles lettres is like a pond of quotations (*Zitatenteich*) where the currents not only continue visibly but also sink to the bottom and rise again" (*T*, 701).   Reading one of Lichtenberg's aphorisms, he mentions the "wholly platitudinous heritage of our literature" (*T*, 581).   The fact that Musil's concept of culture is entirely keyed to the requirements of the present means that he also criticizes the legendary era of classicism: "When Goethe or Lessing are taught as self-contained, unique entities, what is exemplary in these major figures may have 'cultural value.'   But teaching them in isolation is basically no different from a physics teacher lecturing only on the biographies of Kepler and Newton" (*T*, 639).   Musil's approach is rooted, not in Weimar, but in a European intellectual tradition that was more likely to be scorned in Weimar: "It is well known that 'our great classical intellectual heroes,' if I may be allowed the expression, see red when this intellectual tendency comes to the fore" (*T*, 629).   He is speaking of pragmatism.   The engineer and mathematician in Musil also cared more for the empirical tradition than for almost all the rest of literature, and this circumstance allows him a specific mode of criticism of German classicism: "Classicism was not open to English looms, to mathematics, to mechanics, nor, if memory serves me right, to Locke and Hume, whose skepticism (if we may call it that) they rejected.   It seems to have been only a form of the spirit of positivism, which arose along with natural science, mathematics, and industry, and which classicism instinctively sensed as destructive" (*T*, 630).   And Musil's criticism of the classical epigones went far beyond the history of ideas and extended into aesthetics and the consideration of closed forms and adopted entities: "If my conception of our great humanists is correct, they were--even including all possible commotions in the human heart--somehow concerned about a cosmos, a steady order, a closed set of laws . . ." (*T*, 630).   If the pragmatic tradition made him critical of Weimar,[17] Musil had an equally complex reaction to Kant and especially to Kantianism.   It is largely positive when Kant is seen in the context of the Enlightenment and Lessing.   He always felt especially close to any evidence of enlightenment at any time when it has a spiritual component, as in Euripides,[18] the Encyclopedists, or Lessing.   Only with this in mind can one contemplate how "apolitical" Musil was.

His lecture in Paris simply addressed itself to the topic of the meeting ("In Defense of Culture").   It can be called "apolitical," if only because Musil does so himself at the outset: "What I am about to say is apolitical.   All my life I have stayed away from politics, because I feel I have no talent for it" (*T*, 889).   This seems indeed revealing and moving in its naïveté--an attribute that Corino, for example, also bestowed on Musil.   But Musil is simply questioning the political talent of writers as he had done in the days of expressionism.   His naïveté is skepticism, for by politics he means political action.   Musil himself was never short on political theory.   When a group of expressionists embraced mankind, Musil wrote in a little-known essay, "Politisches Bekenntnis eines jungen Mannes" ["Political Confession of a Young Man"]: "And I ask myself quite innocently: who will clean my shoes, cart off my excrement, crawl into a mine for me at night?   My brother?   Who will perform those labors for whose completion it is necessary to spend a lifetime standing at the same machine, doing the same thing?"[19]

Many of Musil's concepts are scattered throughout his sketches and essays, lectures and diaries.   They include his extraordinarily precise and acute analysis of political romanticism and its survival in the twentieth century, the theories of the organic corporate state, and modern conservatism in law and theology; his comments on German nationalism and such specific movements as the Austrian home guard; his criticism of mythologizing philosophies of life such as the agrarian-feudalist ruling forms in "Kakania," as represented, for example, by Alois Prince Lichtenstein (Count Leinsdorf in *MoE*); his basic attitudes toward capitalism and imperialism; and his biting unmasking of anti-Semitism.   He wrote: "The fully developed anti-Semite represents a wholly paranoid intellectual constitution.   He sees confirmation in everything, he cannot be contradicted. . . . We must not let it get to that point!   The roots of anti-Semitism are: Ignorance of the concept of objectivity.   The belief that all higher concerns are false or corrupt (lack of respect of the ignorant).   Lack of cultural inhibition" (*T*, 582).   Consequently when Musil says that he feels no talent for politics, he is not talking about political consciousness but about political action, about the kind of activism for which Hermand provided his third group, the "active-antifascist" category.   Even Georg Lukács--who counted Musil among the leading representatives of "decadence," "avant-gardism," "antirealism," and "formalism" and who succeeded in having his misinterpretation determine the initial reaction to Musil in the Communist countries --admitted that "everyone knows that personally Musil was an antifascist" and he was prepared to recognize this as a "direct political stance."[20]

Brecht once proposed that the approach of antifascist literature intended to be effective within Germany itself should be "propaganda for thinking," at the same time stressing the "changeable, transitory, inconsistent," without any allusions to ultimate destiny.[21]   In this sense Musil used the method proposed by Brecht to practice the literary resistance that sufficed to make his publications "illegal."   Perhaps it was his fascination with the typical--especially the "intellectually typical," as he described it in a 1926 interview (*T*, 785)--that bestowed on him a certain immunity against typical behavior both before and during his emigration.   Especially on the private level of Musil's exile situation the observer time and again encounters a political dimension where normally the full focus is on existential questions. David Bronsen, discussing Joseph Roth, has tried to show that emigration means a "marginal situation" in the existentialist sense: "Especially in the life of the émigré, it means the loss of native country, of social standing, possibly of family, profession, livelihood, as well as ties with friends, community, and religious concepts. It implies the surrender of protective routines, powerlessness against depression, and decrease in self-esteem."22 In Musil's case these considerations apply only minimally or to a limited degree. If there is one unifying concept in all the complaints that links the exiles of various times and countries, it is probably the loss of the "native country" (Heimat). The longing for home has not changed from Ovid in Toma to Solzhenitsyn in Zurich and Vermont. In Musil, the term "native" exists primarily in the phrase "native novel" (Heimatroman), and this distance remains during the time of exile. Nor is it any different in the "moving" Paris speech: "Thus, for example, my native country expects its writers to be Austrian native writers [Heimatdichter], and there are cultural historians who can prove that Austrian writers have always been different from German ones" (PD, 899). He remains conscious of the political dimension of the term, and even in a time of "existential need" he is more likely to note the national narrowing of the concept, thus coming into closer contact with the historical situation and the history of the concept than many others before or after him. Musil refuses, as it were, to let exile influence his work. He did not make himself available, he did not join, he was not programmatic. There is hardly a mention of Musil in any of the lists of publishers of and contributors to particular exile periodicals. When his name does appear in such groupings, one hardly knows why, and it may be that the critic does not know either. Thus Ulrich Weisstein takes the occasion of an analysis of the periodical Das Wort, published in Moscow at the time of Musil's exile, to include Musil in a grouping of contributors: "As progressive representatives of the bourgeoisie, Alfred Döblin, Lion Feuchtwanger, Arnold Zweig, and Alfred Kerr cut a relatively good figure (better, in any case, than Heinrich Mann, the 'granddaddy' of the popular front in literature), whereas more conservative writers--such as Thomas Mann, Hermann Broch, Robert Musil, Bruno Frank, Joseph Roth, and Stefan Zweig--seldom or never appeared."23 But what does he mean by "seldom" and "never"? And if never, as is the case for Musil, why include him in the context of an émigré journal that, as Weisstein writes, was against "reasoning" (p. 39)? And then, the "group" itself! I have tried elsewhere to counter the quasi-automatic coupling of Musil and Broch, and I have spoken of the relationship between Musil and Thomas Mann.24 Had he found himself grouped with Stefan Zweig, especially under the rubric of "conservatism," Musil would have considered it an occasion for acute satire. "It is not possible," Musil noted with some bitterness in 1938, "to polemicize individually against Emil Ludwig, Stefan Zweig, and Feuchtwanger. It would seem like petty bickering. But all three together, these three beneficiaries of the emigration who became darlings of all the world while good writers were barely able to save their lives--all three of them together are a colossal symbol of our time. President Roosevelt, the

man with the Brain Trust, who allows Emil Ludwig to listen
in on government in the disguise of a portraitist!" (*T*,
402).25

Somewhat later, in the series of notes "Aus einem
Rapial,"26 arranged as a collection of aphorisms, Musil
wrote:

> In the course of long experience, it has become clear
> that I am a perfect touchstone for everything that is
> half-good when it is paired with a certain refinement:
> it rejects me.   Kulturbund, Verlag Zsolnay, Concordia
> [the Viennese Association of Journalists and Writers],
> Frau [Alma] Mahler, the Akademie [the Prussian Acad-
> emy of Arts, which refused membership to Musil be-
> cause, as Musil once delightedly stated, he was 'too
> intelligent'], Stefan Zweig . . . a prognosis can be
> made for such creations. (*T*, 567)

Such statements go far beyond simple egocentric and opinion-
ated polemic; they are based on Musil's self-knowledge as
a writer as well as his general aesthetic and ethical convictions.   In this they are like his acid comments on Broch and
Thomas Mann.

Beginning in the mid-1930s and with increasing force
until the end of his life Musil felt that his novel was primarily an obligation to be discharged.   The diary entry for 29
January 1940 reads: "I . . . have a duty to perform toward
myself and my work.   It is serious" (*T*, 529).   This sense
of obligation—combined with the uncommon "passion . . . for
correctness, exactness" (*MoE*, 1640), even under the conditions of exile and of a world that had changed considerably
since the early 1920s, when he had begun to write the novel
—became a burden.   On 23 December 1940, he wrote to Victor
Zuckerkandl: "There is nothing more to be said about me
except that *The Man without Qualities* weighs on me like
a pair of handcuffs."27   The restrictions imposed on him by
the novel consisted primarily in the need to complete what
had been conceived so long ago, but also in the self-imposed
attempt to integrate changes, new experiences, realizations,
and insights into the novel.   It was precisely this dimension
of the present and the future that would not be relinquished,
and Musil sometimes gave expression to a feeling of "stifling"
in the novel without "this kind of breadth" (*T*, 521).

This aspect—the concrete political and social conditions
and the conditions of exile—explains much of what has complicated scholarly explications of Musil during recent years.
It does not mean that we have to give up the larger context
of the general meaning of the utopian ideal for Musil's intellectual existence, of his grand principle of opposition to all
causal claims of inevitability and to everything that is simply contemporary, in the Hegelian sense of the real but not
the actual.   Nevertheless, attempts at psychoanalytic explanations of the problems posed by the novel's ending—like those
of Karl Corino, who tried to bare the "psychoanalytic basis
of Musil's mysticism" and of his inability to complete the
project as well as the causes of his slowness—remain inade-

quate.   Musil was thoroughly conscious of his everlasting textual emendations and joked about it in a letter to Zucker-kandl: "But you need not be afraid that I am suffering from some sort of laundering compulsion of the text; I am proceeding quite properly."[28]

Musil regarded his work on *The Man without Qualities* as the artistically "more objective" part of his literary creation, shaped by many questions that no longer pressed on him personally as they had twenty years earlier.   This attitude is revealed particularly in his notes and plans for the publication of a collection of aphorisms during the final years of his life.   And since Musil demonstrably ran into difficulties with his great novel, it might be interesting to ask whether these aphorisms deserve more attention than has been paid to them until now.   Like plans for an edition of the essays,[29] the aphorisms naturally were not an undertaking entirely separate from work on the novel.   The positive or negative relationship with *The Man without Qualities* always remains more or less directly apparent.

As early as 1937 Musil wrote some aphorisms for a yearbook, *Die Rappen*, published by Bermann-Fischer.   This led to the plan to undertake a larger collection under the title *Ein Rapial* ("or something similar").[30]   The principal topic is soon revealed to be the writer's own attitude in and to his time.   The historical obligation of the novel oppressed Musil, and he clearly tried to free himself through aphoristic concern with his era.   In a letter to Lejeune of 28 July 1939, he writes about *The Man without Qualities*: ". . . in any case, the book gets bogged down, as it were, step by step, and the execution often revolves for months around the same difficult details, so that at times the need becomes almost unbearable once again to have a free spirit and to be able to move freely in any direction, so that versatility will protect me from malformation.   Such, in a word, is the origin of the *aphorisms*" (*PD*,747).   Nevertheless, Musil approaches the composition of his aphorisms with his usual systematic circumspection.   He asks himself whether they should be viewed as "notes and fragments" or as "genuine, crafted aphorisms" (*T*, 558); he questions "who" is saying all this-- the old problem, equally important for the narrative perspective of his novel--and answers, "A person, not only the author!"   Thus "the author as person" (*T*, 558).   Who, then? Obviously Musil, but not in his character as author of *The Man without Qualities*.   And yet his intention ultimately transcends the purely subjective stance.   It leads to the assumption that the state of the world demands the aphoristic form, which in turn leads back to the problems of the novel. Because Musil stresses thematic groups, even though or perhaps especially because they refer to current reality, the common interests result almost compellingly, and Musil sees this himself very clearly.   His notes for the conclusion of the novel, he writes, "and the aphorisms show the same resistance to being worked out.   Neither is controlled by a will, a determination, or an affect that determines the choice. An idea follows from the previous one; they lead in many

directions.   They are notions; continuity over the long run
inheres only in the object" (T, 558).   The only distinction
is that the collection of aphorisms allows a relatively loose
organization whereas the novel remains tied to the design
of its whole.   But thematically the transitions flow into each
other, the notes for the novel reveal the same observations
as some of the aphorisms, both contain reflections on aesthetics, philosophy, and art, on psychology, on science and
technology, on the future of literature, on dramatic forms
and theories of fiction, Musil's thoughts on sexuality, "mathematical morality," the particular themes of his final years
such as individualism versus collectivism, eclecticism and
literary evaluation, popular success, the problems of the
"unreality of films," stupidity from the moral point of view,
and so on.   The parallelism of the thoughts, the necessity
of making the novel more topical, finally also lead to the
consideration of a formal connection: "Novels in aphorisms,"
Musil wrote in 1940; "Considered something similar once
before.   Outlines of figures and problems" (P, 701).   It is
known that according to one of these sketches Ulrich, the
hero of *The Man without Qualities*, is to appear as the
narrator of an epilogue.   In this manner Musil intended to
integrate into the novel the mental work of his final years:
"The aged Ulrich of today, who lives through the second war
and on the basis of these experiences provides his history,
and my book with an epilogue.   This makes it possible to
combine the plans regarding the aphorisms with the actual
book.   It also makes it possible to consider the story and
its value for contemporary reality" (*MoE*, 1651).   As far as
the novel is concerned, Musil writes probably three days
before his death in a draft letter to his American patron
Henry Church: "It is difficult to tell the story well without
skimping on either its being or its meaning, either its origins or the future."[31]   In fact this is Musil's dilemma.   If
the novel tends to work through the past--itself to become
more and more a part of the past--the aphorisms make an
attempt to direct themselves to the present and the future.
At the moment Musil decided to place an aphoristic, future-
oriented epilogue at the end of his novel, he acted atypi-
cally within exile literature.   Where others went out of their
way to find the form of the "historical novel," Musil tried
in every possible way to avoid it, to prevent his novel's
slipping into that genre.   The aphorisms of his final years
were formal weapons in the struggle.   These and other notes
confirm the assumption that he was wholly concerned with the
reality of his times, that mysticiam as a solution was very
far from his mind.   It was not mystical experiences by the
principal characters that were to make up the end, but an
intellectual overview, possibly ordered somewhat like trains
of thought such as we find in Wittgenstein's work.   In any
case Musil had something similar in mind when he made a
note on the "Form for Aphorisms," suggesting "even for a
separate publication numbered (or unnumbered, as the case
may be) subdivisions of several problem areas" (T, 579).
He also made entries for "group[s] of aphorisms" (T, 580).

Even if we do not need to believe absolutely in a reference to Wittgenstein's classification, an intention to systematize is nevertheless indisputable.

From this point of view, it seems that Musil waited until near the end of his life to allow himself the freedom of the aphoristic form, which is amenable to every literary intellectual trend and which is therefore particularly appealing to the author of *The Man without Qualities*. But this freedom grew out of necessity. And this necessity of the contemporary situation--the "adequate expression" of which Musil considered a trait of realism (*T*, 435)[32]--turned the novel into a loose sequence of sketches and Robert Musil the novelist into an "author as person," an aphorist. But in this way the Musil of the exile period gained a special and sharper outline as an artist than the fragmentation-process of the novel would lead us to believe at first glance.

Translated by Ruth Hein and the author

Notes

[1] Alfred Döblin, "Der historische Roman und wir" ["We and the Historical Novel"], *Das Wort*, 1, No. 4 (1936), 56-71. Rpt. in Alfred Döblin, *Aufsätze zur Literatur*, ed. Walter Muschg (Olten/Freiburg: Walther-Verlag, 1963), 163-86. Klaus Schröter has argued that emigrants after 1933 cannot lay any particular claim to the form of the historical novel. See "Der historische Roman: Zur Kritik seiner spätbürgerlichen Erscheinung," in *Exil und innere Emigration: Third Wisconsin Workshop*, ed. Reinhold Grimm and Jost Hermand (Frankfurt/M: Athenäum, 1972), pp. 111-51. On the problem of literary criticism and the historical novel in exile, cf. now Hans Dahlke, *Geschichtsroman und Literaturkritik im Exil* (Berlin: Aufbau-Verlag, 1976). This is primarily an attempt to review the pertinent discussion of the thirties in a historical perspective.

[2] Theodore Ziolkowski, "Form als Protest: Das Sonett in der Literatur des Exils und der Inneren Emigration," in *Exil und innere Emigration*, pp. 153-72. Ziolkowski's thesis that the sonnet constitutes protest through form has also been opposed. See Alexander von Bormann, "'Wer heut Sonette schreibt . . .,'" in *Literaturwissenschaft und Geschichtsphilosophie: Festschrift für Wilhelm Emrich*, ed. H. Arntzen, B. Balzer, K. Pestalozzi, and R. Wagner (Berlin: Walter de Gruyter, 1975), pp. 146-59.

[3] Cf. Elisabeth Albertsen, *Ratio und 'Mystik' im Werk Robert Musils* (Munich: Nymphenburger Verlagshandlung, 1968). This question is closely related to problems concerning the edition of Musil's novel *The Man without Qualities*, and therefore most studies in this field must address themselves to it.

[4] Most convincing is Eithne Wilkins's argument that Musil created anomalies of plot and especially of the novel's

chronology already in early drafts and structural plans in the middle twenties. This was partly caused by his publisher's (at that time Ernst Rowohlt, Berlin) request to rewrite and shorten the first volume. See Eithne Wilkins, "Musils unvollendeter Roman *Die Zwillingsschwester* auf Grund einer Arbeit von Ernst Kaiser†," *Colloquia Germanica*, 10, No. 3 (1976/77), 220–36 (published posthumously).

5For a recent analysis of Musil's relationship to Wittgenstein see J[anos]. C. Nyíri, "Zwei geistige Leitsterne: Musil und Wittgenstein," *Literatur und Kritik*, No. 113 (1977), pp. 167–79. The author works primarily with analogies.

6Quotations are taken from Robert Musil, *Gesammelte Werke in Einzelausgaben*, ed. Adolf Frisé, as follows: *Der Mann ohne Eigenschaften* (Hamburg: Rowohlt, 1952; 4th ed. 1958), cited as *MoE*; *Tagebücher, Aphorismen, Essays und Reden* (Hamburg: Rowohlt, 1955), cited as *T*; *Prosa, Dramen, späte Briefe* (Hamburg: Rowohlt, 1957), cited as *PD*. In addition, I have quoted from the following collections: *Robert Musil: Leben, Werk, Wirkung*, ed. Karl Dinklage (Vienna: Amalthea-Verlag, 1960), cited as *LWW*; *Robert Musil: Studien zu seinem Werk*, ed. Karl Dinklage, with Elisabeth Albertsen and Karl Corino (Reinbek bei Hamburg: Rowohlt, 1970), cited as *Studien*. The new edition of Musil's diaries by Frisé was not available prior to completion of this article. It contains a substantial number of documents, letters, previously unedited diary entries, and also extensive footnotes by the editor laying the groundwork for a Musil biography. See Robert Musil, *Tagebücher*, ed. Adolf Frisé, 2 vols. (Reinbek bei Hamburg: Rowohlt, 1976), cited as *T I, T II*. The first complete edition of Musil's works was published in May 1978: Robert Musil, *Gesammelte Werke*, ed. Adolf Frisé, 9 vols. (Reinbek bei Hamburg: Rowohlt, 1978); this is a paperback edition. A two-volume hardcover edition has the same pagination and is cited here as *GW I* and *GW II*. Unless otherwise indicated, all English translations in this article are by the translator and the author.

7Unpublished letter by Hahn, government administrator for Bermann-Fischer Verlag. (My thanks to Professor Otto Rosenthal, Philadelphia, for allowing me access to the correspondence of Martha Musil and other materials.) Cf. now *T II*, 751–54. Frisé does not mention Hahn's letter, but seems to assume its existence by chronological inference. He maintains that Musil always considered the suppression of his novel "a sort of rumour" (p. 751). Dinklage reports that "Claasen [sic] called on Musil on orders of the Reich propaganda ministry" (*LWW*, 252). This somewhat daring assertion may be read against the entry in *Die deutsche Exilliteratur 1933–1945*, ed. Manfred Durzak (Stuttgart: Reclam, 1973), p. 563: "[Musil] represented an apolitical view of culture. Courted by National Socialism." Frisé finds such assumptions completely unfounded, and quotes from a letter of Musil's to Hahn, in which he indicated his interest in different publishers in Germany and Switzerland (see *T II*, 753 f.).

[8]Karl Corino, "Probleme des späten Musil," *Literatur und Kritik*, No. 66/67 (1972), p. 337. However, Corino himself contradicts this reckoning in his essay "Reflexionen im Vakuum: Musils Schweizer Exil," in *Die deutsche Exilliteratur*, ed. Durzak, p. 261, n. 22, which states: "Actually he first made clear copies of fourteen chapters in a timespan of barely four years. Given the same rate of speed, he would have required exactly those twenty years that in his estimate made up the time he had left to work in completing the novel."

[9]Letter to the Wotruba family of 3 April 1940, *PD*, 773.

[10]Letter of 11 Nov. 1940, *PD*, 784.

[11]Jost Hermand, "Schreiben in der Fremde: Gedanken zur deutschen Exilliteratur seit 1789," in *Exil und innere Emigration*, p. 15. Cf. now also Dahlke, pp. 20–22.

[12]See Hans–Albert Walter, *Deutsche Exilliteratur 1933–1950*, Band II: *Asylpraxis und Lebensbedingungen in Europa* (Darmstadt: Luchterhand, 1972), pp. 106–31; or the catalogue of the 1973 exhibit on exile in Zurich.

[13]Robert Lejeune, "Gedenkrede für Robert Musil," *LWW*, 421; cf. *T II*, 754 f.

[14]Klaus Völker, *Brecht-Chronik: Daten zu Leben und Werk* (Munich: Hanser, 1971), p. 63. See also a second, previously unpublished, version of Musil's Paris speech in *GW II*, 1259–65.

[15]This is not to say that Musil did not wholeheartedly agree with the mobilizing and organizing character of this antifascist meeting as Dieter Schiller has described it recently in ". . . *von Grund auf anders*": *Programmatik der Literatur im antifaschistischen Kampf während der dreissiger Jahre* (Berlin: Akademie-Verlag, 1974), pp. 30 ff.

[16]Wolfgang Leppmann, "Zum Goethebild bei Robert Musil, Hermann Broch und Ernst Jünger," *Monatshefte*, 54, No. 4 (April/May 1962), 146–55.

[17]Hans–Wolfgang Schaffnit, *Mimesis als Problem: Studien zu einem ästhetischen Begriff der Dichtung aus Anlass Robert Musils* (Berlin: de Gruyter, 1971), devotes eighty pages to the influence of Hume's "empiricist argument" on Musil.

[18]See Ervin Hexner, "Musils Interessenkreis," *LWW*, 143–44, where the author states that Musil felt related to Euripides: "He more or less identified with him" (p. 144), among other reasons because he considered Euripides's end in Macedonian exile rather like his own. Much more could be said about this point. One need only consider rationalistic psychologizing, the relationship to tradition (myths), the interest in the facts of science, the study of religion and ecstasy, the female figures in the works of both, the "great spiritual restlessness" (cf. Albin Lesky, *Geschichte der griechischen Literatur*, 2nd ed. [Bern: Francke, 1963], p. 396), the conflict between represented myths and their critical annihilation in Euripides, and the equivalents of all these in Musil.

[19]Robert Musil, "Politisches Bekenntnis eines jungen Mannes," *Die weissen Blätter*, 1 (1913), 242.

[20] Georg Lukács, "Die Gegenwartsbedeutung des kritischen Realismus" ["The Present Meaning of Critical Realism"], in *Essays über Realismus* (Neuwied: Luchterhand, 1971), p. 518.

[21] Bertolt Brecht, "Fünf Schwierigkeiten beim Schreiben der Wahrheit," *Versuche* (Berlin: Aufbau-Verlag, 1959), p. 98.

[22] David Bronsen, "Der Sonderfall als exemplarischer Fall: Joseph Roth und die Emigration als Grenzsituation," in *Exil und innere Emigration II. Internationale Tagung in St. Louis*, ed. Peter Uwe Hohendahl and Egon Schwarz (Frankfurt/M: Athenäum, 1973), p. 69.

[23] Ulrich Weisstein, "Literaturkritik in deutschen Exilzeitschriften: Der Fall *Das Wort*," *Exil und innere Emigration II*, p. 32.

[24] See Wolfgang Freese, "Vergleichungen: Statt eines Forschungsberichts; über das Vergleichen Robert Musils mit Hermann Broch in der Literaturwissenschaft," *Literatur und Kritik*, No. 54/55 (1971), pp. 218-41; Wolfgang Freese, "Satirisches Fragment und 'heilige Form': Anmerkungen zu Robert Musil-Thomas Mann," *Literatur und Kritik*, No. 66/67 (1972), pp. 372-86.

[25] In his new edition of Musil's diaries Frisé does not leave out the remaining sentence of the manuscript entry: "Das Glück, von dem der Ns. begünstigt ist, hat ihn diese Leute entfernen lassen" (*T I*, 903). ("The luck that favors Ns. [that is, national socialism] made him expel these people.") This certainly sounds compromising, and Frisé's decision to suppress this line in his first edition, together with the entry headline "Der Auswurf der Demokratie" (literally "the scum of democracy," but also a play on words via *Hinauswurf*, ejection), seems to have been caused by his generally protective attitude in that earlier edition. However, the context proves that Musil's long-standing feud with some writers of great success is the correct point of reference here. (Cf. also *T II*, 674 f., with further references.) Exile conditions and the necessities of an antifascist or popular front did not change any of his categories with regard to literary criticism.

[26] The title is difficult to translate because of the allusions it contains. The word "Rapial" may be a play on "Rapier" (rapier, a slender two-edged sword used mainly for thrusting) and the ending, as in "Futteral," suggests a sheath for the blade of the sword. Hence the meaning of the title seems appropriate for a collection of polemical remarks. See also n. 30.

[27] Fritz Wotruba, "Robert Musil: Unveröffentlichte Briefe," *Wort und Wahrheit*, 22, No. 4 (April 1967), 297.

[28] Wotruba, p. 290.

[29] See, for example, the letter to Lejeune of 13 July 1939, *PD*, 745.

[30] See *T*, 557-86. Musil had published a selection of eleven aphorisms in *Die Rappen: Jahrbuch 1937*, a yearbook published by Bermann-Fischer in Vienna (now reprinted in *GW II*, 819-23), five of which Musil had already included in

a collection of twelve notes (*Notizen*) in *National-Zeitung* (Basel), 17 Nov. 1935 (see now *T II*, 670). Eight further aphorisms, only recently rediscovered, had appeared in *Der Wiener Tag*, 31 May 1936 (now: *GW II*, 816-19). Musil had begun to take notes for his *Rapial* (now: *GW II*, 917 ff.) in 1940/41. He asks himself: "What is a *Rapial*? (History of a naming/title)," and he mentions having found the word by chance while reading in a dictionary. The word means "waste-book," "note-book," or "pad," Low German *Kladde* (which was first used by merchants in the early eighteenth century). But Musil likes an additional "militant" ring to it. *Rapial* reminds him of Latin *rapio* (see *GW II*, 935), "to seize and carry off," to snatch, tear, drag, draw, or hurry away, but also "to lay hold of quickly" (as in a waste-book) and "to strive for" in purchasing (perhaps as indicated in *Rapial* for *Kladde*, account-book). In a further allusion to his own plans for a "Rabenbiographie" (biography of the raven; *Rabe* is Musil's cipher for his wife Martha) and an autobiography, both in connection with the idea of aphorisms ("I decided to mix it in a *Rapial*," *GW II*, 918), the emerging complexity indicates Musil's general problem (and strategy) of putting maximum weight on a relatively small basis. The systematizing is also pursued in notes like "The systematic order of the *Rapial* and the liquidation of vol. I in vol. II work hand in hand" (see: *T II*, 736).

[31]See Dinklage, in *Studien*, p. 116.

[32]Concerning this problem, see my article "Robert Musil als Realist: Ein Beitrag zur Realismus-Diskussion," *Literatur und Kritik*, No. 89 (Oct. 1974), pp. 514-44.

Theodor Plievier's Double Exile

Dieter Sevin

Considerable interest and scholarly investigation have been directed toward authors who left Germany during the thirties and eventually spent the war years in the United States. Less attention has been paid to those German men of letters, such as Johannes R. Becher and Theodor Plievier, who for one reason or other spent those years in the Soviet Union.[1] Becher's decision to stay in Russia is easily understood; he was, after all, a member of the Communist party. Less obvious, however, is the choice of the non-Communist Plievier. Why did he spend eleven years of his life in Soviet Russia? Why did he return to East Germany in 1945, only to flee to the West two years later? And finally, what effect did these years of exile have on his literary career?

Theodor Plievier was a rebel all his life. Born in Berlin in 1892, he left his family at the age of seventeen after a disagreement with his father, a simple working man who had no sympathy for the literary interests of his son. The young Plievier traveled and worked throughout Europe, while continuing his education by reading every book available to him. He also worked as a sailor on various ships and spent considerable time in South America exploring the continent, supporting himself with odd jobs. Returning to Germany shortly before the war started in 1914, he was forced to serve in the German navy until 1918; in November of that year he participated in the Kiel mutiny, which contributed to the ending of World War I.

In the early twenties, Plievier became involved in journalistic activities. He wrote political essays in which he attacked social injustices and warned against the dangers of a new war. During these years he also read extensively: "My inner, almost metaphysical revolt taught me to read, and helped me to select authors full of social dissatisfaction and revolt; I began with the prophets of the Old Testament and the mystics of the Middle Ages, continued with Lao-Tse and the old Chinese writers, and ended with philosophers such as Friedrich Nietzsche and authors such as Heine, Ibsen, Gorki, Dostoevski, and Tolstoy as well as the contem-

porary writers."[2]   Plievier was maturing intellectually during these years, yet his youthful feeling of revolt did not
diminish, but was transformed into an intense belief in
man's right to individual freedom.   This transformation explains Plievier's attraction toward socialism during these
years; through a new socialist order he hoped to find a solution to the economic enslavement he saw all around him.
Also, his belief in individual freedom explains his later opposition to communism after he had seen its reality in Russia.
      Plievier achieved his first major success as a novelist
with *Des Kaisers Kulis* [*The Kaiser's Coolies*].   Translated into ten languages, this novel portrays the German
navy during World War I and contains many autobiographical
elements.   It is an outcry against the abuse man has to suffer from man, a concern that remained a major theme throughout Plievier's literary career.   The novel *Des Kaisers Kulis*
also became a major reason why the Nazis intensely disliked
Plievier; in their view, he had slandered the German military in the eyes of the world.   But there were other reasons
for the Nazis' hatred of Plievier.   He had openly expressed
his pacifistic and anti-National Socialist views in various
speeches before Hitler's ascent to power.   It is not surprising, therefore, that Plievier had to leave Germany in 1933,
like so many others.   Narrowly avoiding arrest by the SA,
he escaped to Paris via Prague and Vienna.   In the French
capital he lived on a rather meager advance from a publisher.   Many of his notes and even two completed manu-
scripts--a novel *Demokratie* [*Democracy*] and a play *Koka*
for which he had received the advance--were lost as a result
of his sudden departure.   Thus serious financial problems
plagued Plievier during these early days of his exile.
      In this depressing situation, the invitation of the
Soviet Union to attend the First Congress of the Union of
Soviet Writers in Moscow in August 1934 seemed especially
attractive to Plievier.   Not only did he appreciate the interest expressed in his work and person, but this invitation to
visit Russia with all expenses paid also seemed to offer a
welcome temporary solution to his financial dilemma.   He was,
however, without a valid passport, because the Germans
refused to renew his old one.   Efforts to have a French passport, a *titre de voyage* for foreigners, issued to him were
unsuccessful, which reflects the reluctance of the French
authorities to accommodate political refugees in their country
during this time.   Finally, the Russian consulate stamped the
visa into Plievier's old, invalid passport.   During his stop-
over in Sweden, he again tried to get a passport, but there,
too, it proved impossible to obtain one in time for the Moscow convention.   Furthermore, Plievier was low on funds and
could not afford to remain in Sweden any longer.
      A decision had to be made.   The Soviet government had
already purchased a ticket for him and his wife Hildegard
to go by boat to Leningrad.   In addition, Plievier was promised considerable sums in Russian currency for his books.
These promises and the attention he received--he had experienced nothing but hardships and had felt ignored by the

world ever since leaving Germany--finally persuaded him and his wife to accept the Russian offer even without a valid passport and without a guarantee of return to the West.   Perhaps his lifelong dream of visiting Russia--Tolstoy was one of his favorite authors--helped to suppress the apprehensions he might have had.

The convention itself was a disappointment for Plievier. Maxim Gorki presided as official host.   Every facet of the convention had to follow a strict order of business.   Only once did Gorki break the prescribed routine, when he personally welcomed Hildegard Plievier.   He had met her in Berlin during the twenties, while visiting her first husband Erwin Piscator.   Thus, except for a few stimulating discussions with Oskar Maria Graf, the convention turned out to be rather meaningless, and soon the Plieviers had to adjust to everyday Russian life.   Unable to find a reasonably priced apartment in Moscow, because the purchasing power of the money he had received was less than expected, he and his wife moved to Leningrad.

In the beginning of their stay in Leningrad, the Plieviers were preoccupied with getting settled and learning about Soviet life.   They had received two rooms instead of the usual one as living quarters from the Union of Soviet Writers, whose guests they were.   Plievier spent much time trying to find furniture in second-hand stores, because he disliked the style of those provided by the state.   All his efforts, however, could not conceal the drabness of Soviet life, and the Plieviers soon had the feeling of being trapped in a country and under circumstances quite different from what they had imagined.   At an early point in their residence they therefore decided that every effort should be made to obtain a passport so that they could leave Soviet Russia.

The true character of the Soviet political system surfaced, however, after Plievier had contacted the Swedish ambassador.   Soviet authorities made it clear to Plievier that such contacts with foreign dignitaries should not be continued, and Plievier had no choice but to abide by this "wish." There appeared to be no legal way to leave Russia.   With the beginning of the great purges in early 1935 and the feeling of personal danger to their lives, Plievier felt persuaded to take a desperate step: he prepared to leave the Soviet Union illegally across the Finnish border.   He obtained the necessary maps, clothing, and other supplies in shops for foreigners for the long march across the border to escape what he called "a new Soviet edition of the rule of terror by Robespierre." 3   He considered himself and his wife particularly endangered, because they were not members of the Communist party.   As it turned out, however, the fact that he was not affiliated with the party probably saved him, for the brunt of the purges was directed against party members. Nevertheless, the Soviet secret police probably found out about the hoarding of food and supplies in his rooms; he was, at any rate, politely but firmly asked to move to a tiny village, Pavelskoye, in the Republic of Volga Germans to help in the development of an indigenous culture for the

Volga Germans. The pretense of this request was all too obvious, but the move there was probably a blessing in disguise as far as their safety was concerned. The Russian rural areas were at that time relatively safe. Many of the other immigrant Germans living in Leningrad eventually fell victim to the purges.[4]

Any attempt to leave the Soviet Union had now been made impossible, and Plievier made an honest attempt to adjust to the new situation and environment. In the remote village of Pavelskoye, Pliever became a farmer; he raised horses and his wife bred dogs while living in one of the cottages provided by the village Soviet. In contrast to many other exiled authors in the West, the Plieviers still received sufficient funds in royalties from their books in the Soviet Union to live comfortably. With respect to Plievier's literary endeavors, however, this period was for all practical purposes lost to him. He did work on a novel entitled *Schwarzbart* [*Blackbeard*] and made notes for another one concerning the history and fate of the people around him, the Volga Germans. These efforts had to be destroyed, however, for security reasons when the terror of the purges reached even these remote areas of the USSR. The only larger novel from this period is *Das grosse Abenteuer* [*The Great Adventure*],[5] which represents a withdrawal into his past adventures in South America as a young man. Although this book contains some excellent adventure scenes, Plievier himself realized the great deficiencies in continuity and congruity of this volume and planned a complete and enlarged revision. The fact that this revision never materialized is further evidence of his artistic paralysis at this time. As a matter of fact, except for a few autobiographical sketches, Plievier did not write anything new from 1936 to 1940, and we may conclude that his literary talents were completely stifled during these years, mostly by the danger of the purges, but also by the unavailability of a German-speaking market for his books. His *Das grosse Abenteuer* had been published in Holland in 1936, but was not at all successful, which must be attributed at least in part to the fact that the book was not sold in Germany proper.

Life in Pavelskoye became unpredictable for the Plieviers. According to Harry Wilde, Plievier's friend and biographer, little is known about this period,[6] except that Plievier continued his efforts to leave the Soviet Union by trying to obtain an official invitation from an organization or publisher in the West. This was Plievier's only hope of leaving the country legally at this time.

No invitation to visit the West was forthcoming,[7] but the Plieviers were permitted to return to Moscow in 1939. Johannes R. Becher had interceded with the authorities on their behalf. In the suburbs of the Russian capital, Plievier built a small house almost completely by himself, and for a short time--the purges had receded in the big cities by then--he was able to write. His subject matter, however, was far removed from Russian realities, again tapping his experiences in South America. He still did not feel free to

write about his real concerns.   This contention is supported
by the fact that he did not dare to ask Bertolt Brecht, whom
he had met in Moscow in 1940, to intercede in his behalf for
an exit visa.[8]
     With the German attack and advance on Russia in June
1941, Plievier again felt paralyzed.   And, indeed, his stay
in Moscow was interrupted shortly thereafter.   He and his
wife, together with other foreign authors, had to leave for
the remote city of Tashkent.   The special train was overflowing with foreign refugees; all their actions and thoughts centered on the fear of a German victory.   What would happen
to them then?   Life in Tashkent, with a population more than
twice as large as it had been before the war, was extremely
difficult.   Hildegard Plievier writes in her book *Flucht nach
Taschkent* [*Escape to Tashkent*] that most of their possessions were sold on the black market during their early stay
there.[9]   Plievier even here looked into the possibilities for
escape, but the high mountain ranges to Asia were impas-
sable.   After the German army was repulsed before Moscow,
life normalized in Tashkent, and in February 1942, Plievier
celebrated his fifty-second birthday with a party to which
Johannes R. Becher and the Hungarian literary critic Georg
Lukács were invited.
     In May of the same year, Johannes R. Becher obtained
for Plievier the commission to examine various letters of
German soldiers that had fallen into Russian hands in order
to deduce from them the mood in the German armed forces
and among the people in Germany.   For this purpose, the
Plieviers were moved to Ufa, a city in the foothills of the
Urals, where they stayed until March 1943.   The number of
letters he was to examine increased steadily, and soon he
received the first letters of German soldiers who were fighting or had fought at Stalingrad.   He soon began to take a
personal interest in the tragic plight of these men and to
feel compassion for their suffering.
     The capitulation of the German Sixth Army at Stalin-
grad signaled the turning point of the war, and most foreign
authors, among them Plievier, were allowed to return to the
Russian capital.   He now prepared many radio broadcasts to
be transmitted to Germany.   Many of these speeches, urging
the Germans to stop this senseless war, were also broadcast
by British and American stations.   Plievier's main concern
at this time, however, was the fate of the German army at
Stalingrad, a fate he had been permitted to witness almost
firsthand through the many letters he had read.   His dor-
mant creative powers were aroused, and he felt the urge to
write a novel about the tragic events at Stalingrad.   Johannes R. Becher, to whom he expressed this wish, immediately
and enthusiastically agreed.   The difficulty was to obtain
the consent of Walter Ulbricht and Wilhelm Pieck.   These
arch-Communists and appointed future leaders of the "new
Germany" urgently desired a literary work on Stalingrad;
they no doubt reasoned that a successful novel about the
defeat of the National Socialist armies at Stalingrad could
have considerable political impact in Germany after the war.

However, because Plievier was not a party member, they thought it improbable that he would achieve this, their main objective.

No one else was found, however, who could handle the complex events at Stalingrad, and in September 1943 Plievier received permission to write the book. Plievier himself commented to his friend and biographer Harry Wilde on how *Stalingrad* came into being and the problems he encountered: "The novel was finished before I wrote even the first line. None of my other books did I see so clearly in front of me as *Stalingrad*. The immense number of letters was just begging to be utilized. My problem at this time was not so much to obtain permission to begin writing while still in Moscow instead of having to wait until after my return to Germany; my problem was rather to be granted permission to visit the prisoner of war camps in order to obtain the fresh and unfaded impressions of the men who fought at Stalingrad."[10]

In the fall of 1944, one year after he had been granted permission, the manuscript was finished. *Internationale Literatur* published it first as a serial. In 1946, *Stalingrad* was published as a book by El Libro Libre in Mexico. Soon thereafter, it was translated into many languages and became an international success. *Stalingrad* is the narrative account of the decisive battle in and around that city, which began in November 1942 and ended with the unconditional surrender by General Paulus and the remnants of his German Sixth Army on 31 January 1943. Plievier incorporates into his novel the belief that this catastrophic German defeat could probably have been avoided during the initial stages of the encirclement if the 300,000-man German army had been permitted to make an effort to break through the Russian lines. Hitler's orders, however, defying all military logic, were to stay and defend the encircled positions. He persisted in this militarily untenable directive until it was too late and thus sealed the fate of the encircled army. Besides the description of the battle, the suffering of the soldiers, and their attitudes toward the war and National Socialism, Plievier deals with the problem of absolute military obedience demanded of the ranking German officers in the face of a militarily senseless sacrifice of thousands of men. They obeyed Hitler and refused to heed the Russians' repeated summons to capitulate, even though they were aware that their men were dying not only from Russian bullets but from hunger and disease and that there remained no hope of escaping the encirclement. Plievier's novel encompasses this desperate three-month struggle in which 200,000 German soldiers lost their lives for a meaningless cause.

There is a clear indication in the writings and remarks of Plievier that he intended to achieve a convincing and authentic portrayal of this tragic and probably most decisive battle of the war. This confronts the reader and critic, however, with the question: how was it possible for Plievier to write a book about the events at Stalingrad with the consent of the Soviet regime without being influenced by the prevail-

ing political opinions and pressures of the Russian government?   Plievier addressed himself to this problem when he
wrote in his "Mein Weg" ["My Path"]: "I was able to write
Stalingrad in Moscow under the condition of Soviet censorship   because   my   portrayal   of   the   German   defeat   appeared
to be useful for the literary politics of the day.   Nevertheless, nothing is to be changed or added to the book *Stalingrad*."11
     These words by the author indicate that he was not com-
pletely   free   while   writing   his   novel;   Soviet   censorship   did
exist   and   posed   a   problem.   Therefore,   he   obviously   had   to
avoid   any   critical   remarks   concerning   the   Soviet   Union,   and
he had to be careful about any positive comments on Germany.   Considering   this   situation,   how   can   we   explain   Plievier's   insistence   that   he   managed   to   portray   the   events   at
Stalingrad   authentically?   How   was   he   able   to   circumvent
Soviet   propagandist   wishes   and   censorship   in   such   a   way
that "nothing was to be changed or added" to the work?
     The   answer   must   be   sought   in   the   text   itself,   in   the
way   the   material   was   selected,   in   what   was   actually   presented   and   what   was   omitted.   *Stalingrad*   does   not   start
with   the   successful   German   advance   toward   the   Don,   but
rather   with   the   Russian   counteroffensive,   with   the   turning
point   of   the   war   in   1942.   Plievier   thus   covers   only   a   portion   of   the   military   aspects   of   the   campaign;   however,   it   was
this   final   battle   of   the   German   Sixth   Army   that   was   to   him
most   pertinent   and   deeply   moving.   Indeed,   it   was   the   overwhelming   amount   of   firsthand   information   and   the   varied,
manifold   impressions   collected   while   interviewing   the   prisoners   of   war   that   had   impelled   him   to   write.   In   doing   so,   he
relived   the   fate   of   the   entire   army.   His   concern   and   interest   almost   naturally   led   him   to   concentrate   on   the   German
side   of   the   battle   of   Stalingrad.   The   sequence   of   events   is
not   subdivided   by   chapters,   but   presses   on   with   increasing
momentum   and   carries   the   novel   toward   its   climax,   as   in   a
Greek   tragedy.   The   victorious   Russian   advance,   on   the   other
hand,   is   hardly   mentioned.   Nowhere   in   the   more   than   500
pages   of   the   novel   does   the   author   try   to   glorify   Stalin   as
a   brilliant   strategist,   nor   does   he   praise   the   bravery   of   the
Soviet   soldier.   The   Red   Army   remains   faceless--it   has
merely the function of nemesis.
     In   limiting   the   novel   to   the   fall   of   the   German   Sixth
Army,   the   author   is   able   to   reproduce   the   historic   events   as
he   heard   them   from   the   prisoners   of   war   and   read   about
them   in   the   letters.   No   propagandist   additions   were   needed,
because   the   mere   presentation   of   the   facts   was   so   horrifying
that   Russian   censorship   was   satisfied.   Without   doubt,   the
reader   can   easily   detect   a   deeply   felt   and   penetrating   criticism   of   the   German   military   leaders.   Throughout   the   novel
Plievier   decries   the   senseless   sacrifice.   His   denunciation   of
those   he   regarded   as   responsible,   however,   is   motivated   by
a   profound   and   unshaken   love   for   the   abused   German   people
and should not be interpreted as ideological propaganda.
     Plievier's   denunciation   of   an   event   that   had   degraded
man   in   a   most   shocking   and   appalling   fashion   reveals   his

innermost convictions. Thoroughly alarmed by the total disregard for human beings, Plievier considered it his duty to
let his warning voice be heard, thus creating a monument
for all those who were forced to participate. We agree with
R. Haerdter, who believes that "Plievier wrote *Stalingrad*
guided by a moral and political sense of responsibility, with
complete intellectual freedom."[12] In this respect, Plievier's
attitude corresponds to that of the majority of German authors
in exile. Like them, he followed his conscience as an author
above all and refused to submit to the political pressures of
the day. Plievier's awareness of intellectual responsibility
toward the German people links him to one of the paramount
and deeply ingrained concerns of most German authors in
exile.[13]

In spite of the intellectual freedom maintained by Plievier, one cannot help but be aware of the circumstances
under which *Stalingrad* was written. This holds true particularly if one compares this novel with *Moscow* and *Berlin*,
which were written in retrospect after Plievier's return to
the West. The immediacy of the events at Stalingrad and the
author's involvement with those tragic events can be sensed
by the reader throughout the entire novel. Hermann Pongs
concludes that Schiller's statement concerning the "naive
poet" may be applied to Plievier: "The subject matter has
total control over him."[14] Certainly, this is the case with
respect to the author's powerful style and his dramatic and
most effective use of language. Furthermore, the interpretation of the events is influenced by the author's nearness to
them and his personal involvement with them. This personal
proximity explains certain scenes that are difficult to document in spite of Plievier's sincere interest in historical accuracy. Nevertheless, they are within the realm of possibility
and are convincing in the framework of the novel. The devil-
ish fanaticism of Goebbels, for example, gives the reader an
insight into the thought pattern of the Nazi minister of propaganda: "They must all die, from the field marshal to the
last man. . . . A corpse has to be a real corpse. We cannot
profit from a partly dead body. Everyone who manages to
find a hole to escape through and who succeeds in staying
alive acts against the enterprise, against the gigantic effort
to stir the entire nation to fight to its utmost capacity. They
must die. All of them!"[15] Here Plievier makes use of his
poetic license in depicting the evil intentions of the minister
of propaganda and the highest German leaders: the whole
Sixth Army was to be sacrificed for political purposes. The
German high command wanted a total defeat like that in the
Nibelungenlied. No other explanation could be found by
the author in view of the shocking and senseless suffering
and dying. Indeed, a military purpose was no longer detectable, particularly not in the last two weeks of the battle.

The structure of the novel is supported by an exact
historical frame in which the fictional characters are introduced and developed. By skillfully and artistically utilizing
modern film technique with the sometimes rapid sequence of
short scenes, Plievier succeeds in interweaving a large vari-

ety of analyses, monologues, and dialogues into the story. In this way, he is able to combine the multiplicity of facts and events into an artistically balanced whole that portrays convincingly the panorama and human tragedy of modern war. The fictional characters also play a significant role. They often appear at decisive points in the story, and through them the author frequently interprets the events. The fate of the common soldier August Gnotke, which is developed throughout the entire trilogy, allows the reader an insight into the deep tragedy the war has inflicted on one man. Moreover, the thorough delineation of this character refutes any cursory remarks such as: "Individuals rarely appear in the foreground. Plievier lacks any interest in the fate of private individuals or psychology."[16] Such superficial statements do grave injustice to the author, because it is precisely through his main characters that he demonstrates his excellence as a writer.[17]

At this point, we want to touch briefly upon another question: to what extent did Plievier succeed in dealing with the voluminous amount of material and still write what might correctly be called a novel? Are we really dealing with a novel or possibly with a different genre, such as an eyewitness account, a running commentary, a documentary, a montage, or reportage? Applying the term reportage to *Stalingrad* would be too one-sided and would not do justice to Plievier's creative power. Such a technique would have been unsatisfactory for him as an author. Also, it is important to consider his intentions in this connection. What did he hope to accomplish? According to his own account, Plievier wanted to achieve an authentic and convincing, as well as historically exact, analysis and portrayal of those very complex events; at the same time, he wanted to create a novel, not just a historical account.[18] Plievier was convinced that fiction and historical fact had to go hand in hand to accomplish this dual objective. He compressed this tenet of his creative writing into one sentence: "Pas de vérité sans fiction!"[19] Indeed, he succeeds in smoothly combining and blending documentation and fiction, a noteworthy achievement that may, without doubt, be considered his outstanding narrative characteristic.[20]

Although Plievier believed that he had achieved his objective of rendering a valid account of the historical events, he was aware that he was not writing the absolute or "transcendental" truth.[21] He recognized that the ultimate truth depends on the philosophy and creative power of the author as well as on the milieu in which he writes. These limitations he also acknowledged for himself. On the other hand, precisely these limiting factors give Plievier's *Stalingrad* its unique character and legitimate this novel as a powerful and relevant commentary. In the words of Hermann Pongs, this volume of the trilogy ranks as the "one achievement in the German language that successfully managed to portray the tragedy at Stalingrad in the form of a novel."[22]

In the fall of 1944, *Stalingrad* was completed. The following spring, shortly after the collapse of the Third

Reich, Plievier was flown back to Germany. With him were seventeen German Communist leaders, including Walter Ulbricht, Wilhelm Pieck, and Johannes R. Becher, who constituted the nucleus of the new East German government. Plievier's presence in Berlin was not desired, for he was not a party member. Transferred to Weimar, he became a member of the Thuringian parliament. Financially, he was very well taken care of by the state. He was furnished with a villa and even a car and chauffeur. His experiences and impressions of this period are reflected in the second half of his novel *Berlin*.

East Germany, however, did not provide Plievier with the freedom he had hoped for; he still felt inhibited in his creativity and decided to take advantage of the first opportunity to leave for the West. His adventurous flight on 28 July 1947 created an uproar in East Germany, where he was accused of selling out to the West. This accusation was of course entirely unfounded. After all, he sacrificed the luxury of a plush villa for a rather uncertain future. Indeed, the fact that the East Germans tried twice to kidnap him and return him against his will to the East indicates how much they were embarrassed and annoyed by his escape.[23]

His arrival in the West signaled a new creative period for Plievier, although he lost some time in trying to get settled. Free from any censorship, Plievier reactivated his plan to write a novel about the German invasion of Russia. Furthermore, the plan for the third part of his trilogy crystallized in his mind. This novel, *Berlin*, was finished by the author in 1954, one year before he died. The plan for *Moscow*, written in 1951, goes back to the year 1941 when the German invasion of Russia took place. However, Plievier had been unable to write it in Russia or in the German Democratic Republic because he intended to include the Russian side as well. Plievier himself explains: "They would never have given permission to depict the Red Army in its state of confusion and disorganization, nor would they have allowed the description of the Russian people in their passive resistance against the regime."[24]

Once in the West, Plievier felt free to write *Moscow* as well as his last novel, *Berlin*. No censorship limited him in his freedom of expression. He had gained the necessary distance to plan retrospectively the organization of the last two parts of his trilogy. Indeed, the three novels together were intended and should justifiably be considered as a unit, a trilogy depicting the war on the Eastern front. The unity of the three volumes is accomplished by the historical frame as well as the characters, who are traceable through the whole trilogy and thus contribute greatly to its continuity. *Stalingrad* is structurally as well as historically the high point, the climax of the gigantic struggle of the war that the trilogy portrays. *Moscow* constitutes the rising action of the three novels, depicting the German invasion of Russia and advance to the gates of Moscow, whereas *Berlin*, portraying the final defeat of Germany with the Russian

invasion of the German capital, constitutes the denouement.[25]
In spite of this basic unity of Plievier's trilogy, there
are important differences among the three volumes. When
Plievier wrote *Stalingrad*, the immediacy of the historical
events dominated his style and composition; by contrast,
after going to the West, he had sufficient distance to have
complete control in the arrangement of *Moscow*. Characteristic of this control are a skillful organization into three parts
and an eloquent, clear style. Furthermore, Plievier felt free
not only to include the chaos of the Russian army in retreat,
but also to criticize the Communist regime itself. Whereas
Plievier condemned National Socialism and its leaders in
Stalingrad, he now extended his critique to the Soviet leadership. Both political systems are rejected by Plievier,
because both reveal in this deadly confrontation their total
disregard for individual human life.[26] Human beings are
reduced to numbers and evaluated only in terms of their
usefulness to the regime. Any opposition is ruthlessly
crushed. In addition, Plievier portrays the Russian people,
their customs and traits, their hopes and melancholy. During
his eleven years of exile, Plievier had learned to love and
feel compassion for the simple people of this vast country,
who for centuries had been exploited by autocratic and totalitarian systems and had suffered from wars and famines.
Now war was sweeping across their country again, and
although they had little loyalty to the regime, they wanted
to defend their homeland against the invaders. All this is
reflected in the novel *Moscow*.
In contrast to the first two volumes of the trilogy,
Berlin encompasses a much longer period. Even though a
large portion of this novel, its first three parts, is devoted
to the actual invasion and occupation of Berlin in 1945, the
last two parts deal with postwar East Germany up to the Berlin workers' rebellion in 1953. Plievier shows great empathy
for the city in which he grew up. He particularly bemoans
the destruction of irreplaceable art treasures. In vivid and
very realistic language--although sometimes the delineation
of events becomes blurred by too many parallel scenes--the
reader sees how the Russian armies slowly move into the
heart of the city, how teenagers and old men are pressed
into defense units by the Nazis, and how the dictator in his
bunker continues to sacrifice these, his last troops, only to
commit suicide in the end. The last two parts of the novel,
somewhat incongruous in the context of the trilogy as a
whole, reflect Plievier's own years in East Germany after the
war. A keen observer, he portrays how the Communists
gained control by using methods similar to those the Nazis
had used before them. The workers' rebellion of 1953 in Berlin appeared as the logical outcome of Communist political
methods and served to affirm Plievier's belief in the judgment and integrity of the common man.
In conclusion, it is the contention of this paper that
the whole trilogy, especially *Stalingrad*, is without question
the literary product of Plievier's involuntary stay in the
Soviet Union. The portrayal of the Russian army and the

Russian people in *Moscow* would not and probably could not have been written had he not observed and learned about them firsthand.   Certainly, *Stalingrad* could not have been written with the same intensity without the immediacy of Plievier's experiences, impressions, and particularly the letters and interviews available to him during his residence in the USSR.   On the other hand, he felt inhibited and stifled, restricted and confined in his creativity during the eleven years he spent in Russia.   Life in a foreign country, the lack of a ready market for his books, and especially the continuous threat of Soviet censorship suppressed his literary talents for many years to such an extent that for all practical purposes they were nonexistent.   Indeed, we are tempted to coin the term "double exile" for Plievier's involuntary stay in the USSR.   "Double exile" seems to describe Plievier's situation, because he not only had to cope with the problems of residing in a new country and culture, but in contrast to exiled writers in the United States, he was also limited in his freedom of expression by Soviet censorship. Only once, that is, when he wrote *Stalingrad*, did he succeed in overcoming this dual restraint, which was possible because he was able to satisfy the wishes of the state and still write about what concerned him in his innermost being. That one year in which he wrote *Stalingrad* was the exception, however, to the many years lost to his literary career. Nor did his return to East Germany remove his inhibitions and unleash his creative power; he still felt unfree.   We may conclude, therefore, that Plievier's exile did not really end until his successful flight to the West, which signaled a new and final creative period.   The fact that his last two novels, *Moscow* and *Berlin*, continue to deal with events and impressions from his last years in exile confirms how decisive this time was for the man and writer Theodor Plievier.

Notes

[1]This essay was first published in *Colloquia Germanica*, No. 2 (1976/77), pp. 154–67.

[2]Theodor Plievier, "Mein Weg" ["My Path"], in *Haifische* (Munich: Kurt Desch, 1953), p. 310.   All translations of quotations in this article are mine.

[3]Harry Wilde, *Theodor Plievier: Nullpunkt der Freiheit* (Munich: Kurt Desch, 1965), p. 354.

[4]Ibid.

[5]For a detailed bibliography of all of Plievier's writings during his exile, including essays, speeches, and poems, see Marc Schreyer, "Theodor Plievier im Exil, Bibliographie seiner Schriften (1933–1945)," *Recherches Germaniques*, No. 2 (1972), pp. 163–203.

[6]Wilde, *Theodor Plievier*, p. 366.

[7]The two short novels *Im letzten Winkel der Erde* [*In the Last Corner of the Earth*] and *Haifische*

[*Sharks*] did appear in Moscow (1941/42) according to Marc Schreyer, "Theodor Plievier im Exil," p. 183.

[8]Brecht showed no interest in staying in the Soviet Union and left for the United States soon after his meeting with Plievier. One of the major reasons for this departure was the limitations put on the artistic freedom of émigrés in Russia during these years, as emphasized in the Fuegi article in this volume, "The Exile's Choice: Brecht and the Soviet Union."

[9]Hildegard Plievier, *Flucht nach Taschkent* (Frankfurt/M: Heinrich Scheffler, 1960), p. 67.

[10]Wilde, *Theodor Plievier*, p. 400.

[11]Plievier, "Mein Weg," p. 317.

[12]Robert Haerdter, "Der Chronist von Stalingrad," *Gegenwart*, 10, No. 6 (26 March 1955), 202.

[13]I am indebted to Professor Robert Kauf for calling my attention to this point.

[14]Hermann Pongs, *Im Umbruch der Zeit: Das Romanschaffen der Gegenwart* (Göttingen: Göttinger Verlagsanstalt, 1952), p. 166. The original of Schiller's phrase is: "Das Objekt besitzt ihn gänzlich."

[15]Theodor Plievier, *Stalingrad* (Munich: Kurt Desch, 1947), p. 344.

[16]Klaus Betzen, "Deutung und Darstellung des Krieges in der deutschen Epik des 20. Jahrhunderts," *Deutschunterricht*, 14, No. 1 (March 1962), 59.

[17]For an analysis of the main characters of the trilogy see: Dieter Sevin, *Individuum und Staat: Das Bild des Soldaten in Plieviers Romantrilogie* (Bonn: Bouvier, 1972).

[18]See Theodor Plievier, "De Stalingrad à Moscou," *Documents: Revue des Questions Allemandes*, 12, No. 4 (1957), 562-74.

[19]Plievier, "De Stalingrad à Moscou," p. 569.

[20]This thought likewise goes back to a remark by Professor Kauf.

[21]Plievier, "De Stalingrad à Moscou," p. 573.

[22]Pongs, *Im Umbruch der Zeit*, p. 160.

[23]According to Harry Wilde, *Vom Proletarier zum Staatsbürger* (Ottobrunn: Privately published by the author, 1967), p. 17.

[24]Plievier, "Mein Weg," p. 317.

[25]For a study of the structure of the trilogy, see Ingrid E. Lotze, "Theodor Plieviers Kriegstrilogie *Moskau Stalingrad Berlin*," Diss. Columbia University 1969, pp. 100-140.

[26]Plievier reaffirms this rejection of totalitarianism in "De Stalingrad à Moscou," p. 564: "In *Moscow* and *Stalingrad* I described that which characterizes the totalitarian state in times of war and peace. . . . In one as well as the other, we shall meet Germans and Russians, who have to undergo an unspeakable fate and who, in the hands of their leaders, are no longer human beings, but rather a very pliable material that one sacrifices en masse."

Erich Maria Remarque: Shadows in Paradise

Hans Wagener

When the German edition of Erich Maria Remarque's novel *Schatten im Paradies* [*Shadows in Paradise*]¹ was published posthumously in the spring of 1971, it skyrocketed to the German bestseller list as most of his previous novels had done. Once again the name Remarque proved to be a trademark for exciting, readable, and appealing adventure stories dealing with war or with refugees from Nazi Germany, garnished with a touch of sentimental romance. In short, his popular bestsellers reflected and shaped the taste of millions. Yet unlike his highly acclaimed previous novel, *Die Nacht von Lissabon*, 1963 [*The Night in Lisbon*], the professional critics, with only few exceptions, did not find his last novel up to par: "Nothing New from Ascona," a pun on the title of *Im Westen nichts Neues*, 1929 [*All Quiet on the Western Front*], was the headline of Werner Ross's review in the German weekly *Die Zeit*,² and Friedrich Luft, highly acclaimed critic of *Die Welt*, called it "Elegant Pain That Does Not Move Us," concluding: "Remarque, who died in the winter of last year, will remain a phenomenon. *Shadows in Paradise* adds nothing or little to our knowledge about him and his capabilities. This novel does not click any more. It shows an author, shortly before his death, who has lost his old powers of writing and his undisputed preferences."³

Although verdicts like these may be too harsh, they no doubt contain some truth. But such shortcomings in the work of an author who strove throughout his literary career for perfection and was his own severest critic are obviously not accidental. It is my conviction that *Shadows in Paradise* is not just a skillfully concocted story about some imaginary refugee hero, but in essence the story of Remarque himself, the writer in exile. It is furthermore my opinion that most of the novel's flaws can easily be accounted for if one takes into consideration Remarque's own existence as an author in exile, his image of the successful author and bon vivant on the one hand and the reality of the melancholic writer in exile on the other--in short, his own double existence.

247

To be sure, the "hero," a former journalist by the name of Robert Ross, does not have the same fate as Remarque, but in his physical environment he mirrors the writer's own life. Many of his feelings, his hopes, and his impressions are those of the author. Only at a superficial glance does there seem to be a striking contrast to Remarque's own life.

Let us take a closer look at the writer's past and his situation in exile--the spectacular personal and literary career of a man who, as a member of the "lost generation," rose to fame and an existence like that of a movie hero, although a refugee. Then we will be able to bring the actual man behind the façade more clearly into focus, and perhaps better understand his emotional dichotomy.

Returning as a simple soldier from World War I, Remarque had worked in numerous jobs, such as headstone salesman, copywriter for a tire company, racing driver, and editor of a sports magazine. Success came in 1929 with the publication of *All Quiet on the Western Front*, which in Germany alone sold 1,200,000 copies during its first year. Fame and fortune helped the young author enjoy life in Berlin, the roaring city of the Weimar Republic. But shadows were soon cast upon this short-lived happiness. When the movie version of *All Quiet* was shown in Berlin in 1930, the Nazis set white mice loose in the theater, threw stink bombs, and had uniformed men stage a demonstration outside the theater. After 11 December 1930, the movie was not permitted to be shown in theaters throughout Germany. The signs of the times were clearly readable. In view of the political tensions of the time and an imminent coup d'état, Remarque's presence in Berlin endangered his life. At 4:00 one morning in January 1933, his literary agent found him in a Berlin night club and begged him to leave the country immediately: "There was fantastic luck again. I considered, should I order another drink and then go home to bed, or should I order another drink, get into my car and drive to Switzerland."[4] The next morning found him in Switzerland. This was just days before the Nazis' seizure of power in 1933. Luckily, he had acquired a villa several years earlier in Porto Ronco in the vicinity of Ascona in Tessin, overlooking the scenic Lago Maggiore, as far south as possible. He also had been able to get his money and his collections of works of art out of Germany before the Nazi takeover. Therefore, he could stay in Switzerland until 1939 without suffering financial hardship. During this time, Remarque worked on his third novel, *Drei Kameraden* [*Three Comrades*], which was published in 1938 by Querido in Amsterdam (the English edition, *Three Comrades*, appeared in 1937), the publisher of many German exile writers. His second work, *Der Weg zurück*, 1931 [*The Road Back*], had still been published in Germany. In Switzerland Remarque enjoyed the lifestyle of a financially independent gentleman. He collected paintings, particularly those of French impressionists, antique sculptures, Chinese bronzes, and Persian rugs, and drove a much-admired Lancia.[5]

At the end of March 1939, Remarque came to New York aboard the *Queen Mary*, accompanied by his literary agent and friend, Otto Clement. Although he traveled on an international card of identification issued by the League of Nations --his German citizenship had been revoked by the Nazis in 1938--he did not come as a homeless refugee. He came to the United States primarily to pay a private visit to Marlene Dietrich, whom he had befriended in Berlin in 1931. Therefore, he continued on to Hollywood, staying in New York for only a few days. During the summer of 1939 he even went back to Europe, in the company of Marlene, spending eight weeks in Paris and on the French Riviera. At the beginning of September 1939 he returned to New York, again aboard the *Queen Mary*. Remarque came to the United States as the world-famous author of three novels with sales totaling 5,500,000 copies in thirty-five languages, with a reputation already firmly established in the United States, where the sale of his books and movie rights guaranteed him more than sufficient funds for a comfortable existence. His art collections were sent to him later, complete and unharmed. Throughout his stay in the United States, he kept his villa in Porto Ronco, Switzerland, complete with housekeeper and gardener.

From 1939 to 1942 Remarque stayed primarily in Hollywood, except for several trips to New York and Mexico City. At first he lived in a bungalow in the park of the exclusive Beverly Wilshire Hotel, still one of the most elegant hotels in Los Angeles. Later he rented a home in Westwood.

Remarque never had to complain about a lack of friends, although he was more shy than outgoing. Handsome, admired by women, a connoisseur of fine restaurants, an expert in wines and spirits, he was to be seen in the company of Marlene Dietrich, a friendship that lasted, with interruptions, until about 1946. Greta Garbo was also among the prominent female friends of the author. Remarque had numerous friends and acquaintances among actors and film makers-- interestingly enough, mostly Austrians rather than Germans. Among the numerous exile writers who had found refuge in Los Angeles, Remarque was on friendly terms with Franz Werfel, Lion Feuchtwanger, Bruno Frank, and Curt Goetz. Among the American writers, he had close contact with F. Scott Fitzgerald.

Remarque did not buy any stocks and never owned any home or other real estate in the United States. He always traveled light. He invested the considerable royalties that he received from his books, serializations, and movie rights only in works of art. Occasionally he lent his impressive collection of impressionist paintings, which included paintings and drawings by van Gogh, Matisse, Renoir, Degas, and Cézanne, to local museums or distinguished art galleries, for example to the Los Angeles County Museum, where it was exhibited at the beginning of 1942, or to the Knoedler Galleries in New York, where the "Collection Remarque" was exhibited in the fall of 1943.[6]

After 1942 Remarque spent more and more time in New York, where for years he had a suite in the Ambassador Hotel on Park Avenue, and, after the summer of 1953, an apartment at 320 East 57th Street, with a superb view of Manhattan Island.   "He writes longhand at a desk where he can see the view or, when he chooses, a framed letter of Goethe," wrote a reporter who visited him there in 1957.   "In the room are his spinet-style piano and a number of small and choice works of art, including a Degas and a bevy of exquisite Chinese bronzes."7   He had left Hollywood because he simply disliked the sprawling character of Los Angeles:

> He said he'd go out for walks and break them off and hurry back to his hotel and go to the bar and have a drink.   "There always was someone in the bar, but the streets out there [in Hollywood] are deserted.   No one walks.   You know, that's ugly.   In the country I take it for granted that I won't meet anyone, but there are animals, the life of the country. But to walk in a city where there are rows upon rows of buildings and sidewalks extending for miles and people nowhere to be seen, only buildings and automobiles--ah, ghastly. Hollywood is ghastly anyway.   I had nothing to do with pictures, never went near a studio, but the ghast-liness of it crept into me and I had to come away."8

Although Remarque may be overstating his dismay a bit--after all, many of his friends, both male and female, were in the movie business, and he actually fit in very well--New York was certainly more to his liking than Los Angeles.   By comparison, New York appeared to him like a European city, a real metropolis.   Los Angeles could not deny its transient, centerless character.   "I now think of New York as my home," he admitted in the *Newsweek* interview quoted above.   "It is an unbelievable city.   There is virtually everything here. I am very happy to have become an American. [He had acquired American citizenship in 1947.]   I have met exceedingly cultivated people in America.   Americans have an innate sense of freedom, whether they realize it or not.   They act toward each other that way.   It is so easy to mix with others.   This freedom is something it is very hard for a European, who has not observed it, to conceive of."   He liked New York so much that even after returning to Switzerland he periodically returned to his New York apartment during his later years to work there and to enjoy the social and cultural life of the city.   Although he worked hard in New York, writing and perfecting his novels, constantly rewriting them, always in neat, precise longhand, he also built quite a reputation as a nightowl who, in the company of celebrities, frequented "21," the "Stork Club," and other fashionable night clubs.   He tried desperately to play to the hilt the part of a jet-setter, with all its innate superficiality.

However, this kind of life was a role, a grand pose; otherwise neither his books nor personal impressions of his friends can be accounted for.   The works and the man suggest that he had a much more introverted and serious nature

than his lifestyle indicated.   "He is essentially a very serious man," one of his friends is quoted as saying, "like all
good writers, a moralist at bottom.   His night club pose
appears to be almost carefully cultivated, a kind of bravado.
Writing and nightlife exist in him, all right, but there's a
good deal less of the man-about-town these days."9   And his
translator and friend Denver Lindley tries to play down the
author's nightlife in a public relations article in the *Book-
of-the-Month Club News* by calling it "One of the most widespread literary legends of our day."10   Yet facts cannot be
denied: Remarque led a kind of double existence, which, in
my view, is the key to the self-contradictory style of his
novels, particularly the weaknesses of *Shadows in Paradise*.
It is the two-sidedness of a man who wants to be a glamor-
ous star, yet cannot conceal his vulnerability.   On the one
hand Remarque was the frequenter of night clubs, on the
other hand the sensitive, contemplative author whose books
about war and exile never lack philosophical conversations
and romance.   Behind the pose of the grand seigneur, somewhere deep inside he was still the son of a bookbinder from
the provincial city of Osnabrück in Westphalia, a school-
teacher from a small town close to the Dutch border, who as
a young man was yearning for real life, for action: "I was
so hungry for life," he later recalled, "I was starved for it,
and sitting alone, writing, was almost a waste of life, as
it seemed to me."11   His sudden rise to world fame with *All
Quiet* changed all this, but--noblesse oblige: Remarque felt
throughout his life that he had to live up to his first success and fulfill expectations placed upon him.   His striving
for perfection, his constant rewriting in an attempt to create
and live up to his image, reveal that it was indeed an
image--a pose that had to be always established anew and
maintained at all costs.   "His great worry at that time
[while still in Switzerland] was that of the holder of a
world title," remembers Victoria Wolff, "who is afraid not
to be able to keep his title. *All Quiet on the Western
Front* had been the great hit.   Would he be able to make
the same hit again with a second and a third book?   The
critics would use the first book as a yardstick for each new
one."12
      Remarque had been surprised by the tremendous success
of *All Quiet*, in which he had intended only to describe his
personal war experiences and feelings, the feelings of a generation that had been termed "lost."   The book was indeed
pacifistic in spirit, showing the dirty side of war without
nationalistic, pseudoheroic glorification, and after the publication of the novel he was not willing to take on any political role, not willing to become the outspoken mouthpiece of
pacifistic, antimilitaristic liberal or leftist forces at a time
when National Socialism was gaining in strength in Germany.
He wanted to stay in the background, shy, by himself.   He
refused to speak at rallies and was drawn into the arena of
political forces against his intentions.   He had the chance
to become the spokesman of pacifism in Germany; he rejected

it, but could not escape the impact of his first book and the interpretation given to it by others.

Life in Switzerland seems to have been pleasant, if one judges from appearance only. Emotionally and, in the last analysis, financially, it was the life of a refugee writer: "A writer without a home country?" Remarque asked himself later, "What is he supposed to write about? How is he supposed to make a living? When Hitler drove me out of Germany, my third novel, *Three Comrades*, was almost finished. Having to leave Germany was such a shock for me that it took me four years to finish the book. Without my country I was like an animal that was not being fed any more."[13] Because his books were banned in Germany in 1933--they had been publicly burned with those of other liberal authors--he did not receive any further royalties from Germany. But apart from the financial aspect, we have to believe the author's serious emotional shock arising from the situation, his isolation, his consciousness of being cut off, being severed from his reading public.

In the United States Remarque continued his privately oriented existence, his policy of noncommitment--except in his books. He was a member of neither any club of German exile writers nor the Screenwriters' Guild nor any other professional organization. He never gave formal or informal talks, claiming that what he had to say was all in his books. He did not write for emigrant periodicals or newspapers, just as he never published any essays of any kind.

However, that does not mean that the seemingly nonchalant writer of the forties was untroubled by the reality of the war and of Nazi rule in Germany. Not only do all his books of this time center on the theme of exile, he himself, although financially secure, was very conscious of being a refugee. His situation certainly became very clear when on 29 October 1943 the Nazi "People's Court" sentenced his sister, Elfriede Scholz, née Remark, to death by beheading for making "incitive defeatist remarks toward the wife of a soldier."[14] They had not been able to get Remarque, so his sister had to suffer for him. In 1942, when he took out his immigration papers, and in 1947, when he became an American citizen, he was deeply moved, according to his friends. In his 1946 interview, quoted above, he even gave rules for refugee living: ". . . have a phonograph and books if possible; take a room as near the center of a great city as you can get; be on friendly terms with a large number of people who are not refugees and who do not speak your native language; avoid the temptation to write an autobiography."[15]

This is the "other Remarque," not the "man of peace and plenty," as he had been called,[16] but Remarque the human being. Without the pose of the jet-set swinger, he was a man troubled by exile. He was a hard-working, self-critical, and self-analytical enigma.

Having viewed the two-faceted portrait of the writer, the flaws of *Shadows in Paradise* become, if not excusable, perhaps explainable. The two extreme sides of Remarque himself, namely playboy and introvert, are mirrored in his "hero," and it is this dichotomy of spirit that accounts for the novel's inconsistencies.

Although Remarque did not write an actual autobiography, *Shadows in Paradise* is full of autobiographical features. The "hero," Robert Ross, lives on 57th Street, just as Remarque did. He works illegally for an art dealer, who specializes in French impressionist paintings; he is an expert on Chinese bronzes similar to those that Remarque owned himself. He loves the night clubs and the fine restaurants of New York, where he takes his beautiful girl friend, a model by the name of Natascha. He accompanies his boss to Hollywood, where he encounters the superficial world of the movie industry. At this point, one of the liveliest parts of the entire book, the novel widens and becomes almost a satire on Hollywood life. To be sure, Remarque describes the United States entirely from the viewpoint of his hero, a practice he always liked to follow in his novels, but the picture he draws here is identical with the one he painted in the interview quoted above:

> Reality and fake were fused here so perfectly that they became a new substance--just as copper and zinc became brass that looked like gold. It had nothing to do with the fact that Hollywood was filled with great musicians, poets, and philosophers; it was just as filled with phantasts, religious nuts, and swindlers. It devoured everyone, and whoever was unable to save himself in time, would lose his identity, whether he thought so himself or not. The commonplace about selling the soul to the devil had become reality here.[17]

Like his "creator," Robert Ross returns to New York because he despises the fake spirit of Hollywood. As previously noted, the book is full of the usual Remarque conversations with their sadness, melancholy, and sentimentality, an expression of the writer's most private side. The love relationship is doomed from the very beginning because of the "hero's" fear of committing himself. His general feeling of impermanence, his personal defensiveness, his insecurity, and his jealousy, which incidentally seem to have been character traits of Remarque himself, are far from conducive to a stable relationship. In Robert Ross we meet an observer of life, someone who can identify neither with his homeland, nor with the exiled Jews, nor with his new environment. He truly remains a "shadow in paradise." Like Remarque, he plays the hedonist who loves good eating and drinking in exclusive restaurants, although one wonders at times where all the money for these escapades comes from or why a refugee spends his last dollars on such extravagances. Robert Ross, therefore, has the same two-sidedness that we found in Remarque himself. But in the hero of the novel, these traits do not convince us; they are neither believable in this exaggerated concentration, nor do they make for good reading. The reason is simple: Remarque had been convincing when he created the haunted refugee in an environment far away from the reality of his own exile, for example, when the setting was France, Austria, Switzerland, or Portugal. It was plausible when he wrote about his Dr. Ravic in Paris in *Arc de Triomphe*, 1946 [*Arch of Triumph*, 1945], about his Steiner in *Liebe Deinen Nächsten*, 1941 [*Flotsam*], or about his Josef Schwarz in *The Night in Lisbon*. But when he endowed Robert Ross with his own features and placed him in his very own environment, the clash between the reality of his own life and the yarn about the former inmate of a German concentration camp caused the story to fall apart. Remarque's feelings may have been identical with those of his hero, but the experience of his own financially secure exile and the fictitious story about a refugee who came to the United States, practically penniless, do not mix.

The deep effect of Remarque's exile, to be sure, can be seen in the attitude he later developed toward Germany, in interviews as well as in his writings, particularly in *Shadows in Paradise*. In September 1939, he had stated upon his arrival in New York: "There is no reason for war. Think what you will. This will be a war on women and children." Although in disfavor with the Nazis, he could not fight against "poor Germany."[18] This compassionate attitude was going to change in the course of the years. Although not intended as a documentary on German concentration camps, his *Spark of Life* (1951) contains a fervent denunciation of the crimes and cruelties committed not just by a minority of criminals but also by petty officials, who, under the influence of a spirit of order and a sense of duty and obedience that had been misdirected, fulfilled their gruesome duty with the precision of machines. As he wrote in *Shadows in Paradise*: "The Germans were not revolutionaries. They were a people who took orders. Orders were their substitute for conscience. How could a man be held responsible for what he had done under orders?"[19] The sympathetically drawn Dr. Gräfenheim in *Shadows in Paradise* even expresses serious doubts that the Nazis have no future in Germany after the war, adding: "I heard the roaring on the radio, the fat, bloodthirsty screaming in the political campaign rallies. That was not one party any more. That was Germany."[20] Because of these views, Remarque was very concerned with the political reeducation of the Germans after the war. Most interesting in this connection is an article in the *Los Angeles Times*, dated 10 February 1946, stating that Remarque had made recommendations to the Office of Strategic Services of the United States Army about methods of reeducating the Germans.[21] If that task were not undertaken correctly, he considered it likely that some day the Germans would wage a third world war. The prime objective of his reeducation plan would be to destroy the belief, which he considered still prevalent in German minds, that the guilt for the war rested upon the Allies. The Germans had to be shown that Hitler started the war; they had to be made to realize that Hitler went far beyond his initial program of reclaiming German minorities abroad. Second, the myth of the "invincible German soldier," the German superman myth, would have to be destroyed, and third, the myth that Germany was beaten only by a superiority of matériel and production would have to be seen as the myth it was: "By pointing out their own limited resources, it can be demonstrated to them that the German general staff should have known they would be beaten by matériel and production; that this 'super body' was at fault in not knowing it; that due to their geographical position in Europe they will always be beaten."22

It was this fear of a reawakening of the militaristic spirit in Germany--in particular, a deep estrangement from the country of his own cultural background--that prompted him not to return to Germany permanently.   To be sure, he made frequent trips to Germany from his Swiss home, but he always returned.   The Germany he had known, the Berlin of the twenties with its cultural and social life, had been bombed out.   When militant and nationalistic tones were heard again in the early sixties, he expressed his worries in an interview with the German newspaper *Die Welt*: "I am worried," he said; "Can a nation change completely in twenty years?   You certainly have to be alert, you have to impose controls.   I am convinced that the old Nazi spirit does not exist any more [in 1962], but here and there sparks are flickering and you have to watch out that they are extinguished in time."23   After living abroad for thirty years Remarque was viewing Germany not only as a German, but also as a Swiss and as an American.   In short, he saw himself as a writer whose view had been sharpened by his exile, who had become a cosmopolitan, a citizen of the world. He had become distrusting, watchful, and alert toward a Germany that had proved its destructive and self-destructive tendencies in two world wars.

Remarque also takes up the question of the refugees' returning to Germany in *Shadows in Paradise*.   When peace seems in sight, Kahn, a kind of escape artist among the refugees, predicts that it will represent a great letdown for the refugees: "Up to now we've been sustained by the thought of the injustice that was done to us.   And now all of a sudden the injustice is gone.   We'll be able to go back. What for?   Where?   And who wants us?   How *can* we go back?"24   And later in the novel, Kahn declares at a refugee party:

> . . . I'm leaving.   I can't take any more of this atmosphere, this mixture of excitement, sentimentality, and uncertainty.   All these people make me think of blind birds that keep dashing against the bars of their cage; then one day they discover that the bars are not made of steel but of cooked spaghetti.   And they don't know whether to sing or weep.   Some have started to sing.   They'll soon find out that there's nothing to sing about, that they've only been deprived of their last possessions: romantic nostalgia and romantic hatred.25

These quotations, to be sure, provide several reasons why Remarque himself did not go back to Germany.   In addition, they point to another feature of *Shadows in Paradise*:

in this novel the author is guilty of the very romanticism
mentioned in the above passage by applying it to the life of
a German refugee in the United States. His Robert Ross is
not a realistically drawn refugee, but a refugee such as
Remarque imagined by projecting a romanticized image of his
own inner self. Autobiographical sentimentalism blurred his
view and consequently led him to write an unconvincing
story. The narrative powers that he displayed when he
wrote about the haunted existence of the refugees in his
other novels were impaired by personal sentimentalism when
dealing with his own life. Thus *Shadows in Paradise* suffers from the incongruity of Remarque's own successful life
in exile and the struggles of his fictional refugee hero.

Notes

[1] German edition: *Schatten im Paradies* (Munich:
Droemer/Knaur, 1971), cited as *Schatten*; American edition:
Shadows in Paradise, trans. Ralph Manheim (New York: Harcourt Brace Jovanovich, 1972), cited as *Shadows*. Quotations
cited from *Schatten* only when missing from *Shadows*.

[2] Werner Ross, "Aus Ascona nichts Neues: Erich Maria
Remarques nachgelassener Roman," *Die Zeit*, 20 Aug. 1971,
p. 17.

[3] Friedrich Luft, "Eleganter Schmerz, der uns nicht
berührt," *Die Welt der Literatur*, 6, No. 15 (22 July 1971),
5. All translations of quotations in this article except quotations from *Shadows in Paradise* (see n. 1) are mine.

[4] "Erich Maria Remarque, the Violent Author . . . A
Quiet Man," *Newsweek*, 1 April 1957, p. 108.

[5] See Griffith Borgeson, "A Lancia Goes Home: A Memoir,"
Road & Track, 23, No. 9 (May 1972), 53–56.

[6] Compare the catalogue: *Loan Exhibition of the Col-
lection of Pictures of Erich Maria Remarque, October 19–
November 13, Knoedler Galleries . . . New York* (New
York: William Bradford, 1943).

[7] "Erich Maria Remarque," *Newsweek*, p. 108.

[8] Robert van Gelder, "Erich Maria Remarque Lays Down
Some Rules for the Novelist," *New York Times Book Review*,
27 Jan. 1946, p. 3.

[9] Bernard Kalb, "A Man of Peace and Plenty," *Saturday Review of Literature*, 22 May 1954, p. 15.

[10] Denver Lindley, "Erich Maria Remarque," *Book-of-the-
Month Club News*, May 1954, p. 4.

[11] van Gelder, "Erich Maria Remarque Lays Down Some
Rules," p. 3.

[12] Victoria Wolff, "'Die herrliche Unruhe des Lebens':
Erinnerungen an Erich Maria Remarque," *Aufbau* (New York),
37, No. 25, 18 June 1971, p. 13.

[13] Heinz Liepman, "Erich Maria Remarque: So denk' ich
über Deutschland: Ein Interview," *Die Welt*, 1 Dec. 1962.

[14] The documents of the trial are quoted in *Der laut-
lose Aufstand: Bericht über die Widerstandsbewegung des*

deutschen Volkes 1933-1945, ed. Günther Weisenborn (Hamburg: Rowohlt, 1953), pp. 263-65.

[15] van Gelder, "Erich Maria Remarque," p. 3.

[16] Kalb, "A Man of Peace and Plenty," p. 15.

[17] *Schatten*, p. 277; missing in *Shadows*.

[18] "Queen Mary Docks with 2331 Aboard," *Los Angeles Times*, 5 Sept. 1939, part 1, p. 8.

[19] *Shadows*, p. 304; *Schatten*, p. 399.

[20] *Schatten*, p. 88; missing in *Shadows*.

[21] "Remarque Would Bring War Guilt Home to Nazis," *Los Angeles Times*, 10 Feb. 1946.

[22] Ibid.

[23] Liepman, "Erich Maria Remarque."

[24] *Shadows*, p. 268; *Schatten*, p. 351.

[25] *Shadows*, p. 289; *Schatten*, p. 379.

The Experience of Exile in Joseph Roth's Novels

Curt Sanger

The historical novel holds an important place in the literature of exile from 1933 to 1945. Although this genre has been criticized for its escapism--as expressed in the exiled writer's apparent avoidance of his duty to oppose Nazism--the frequent use of allegories, parallels, and veiled allusions to the contemporary period in works of this kind leaves no doubt of their authors' intent to confront the situation of exile. Thomas Mann's *Joseph* novels, Heinrich Mann's *Die Jugend des Königs Henri IV* [*Young Henry of Navarre*], Lion Feuchtwanger's *Josephus* trilogy, and Alfred Neumann's *Neuer Caesar* [*Another Caesar*] are but a few of the more salient examples. Mathias Wegner in his pioneer study of the literature of exile sees a definite need for the study of the historical novel: ". . . the historical novel . . . portrayed the difficulty of the emigrants in a nutshell. The significance of this literary genre for exile literature should one day be thoroughly examined, especially the depiction of actual events after 1933 that appear in historical disguise."[1]

One exile writer who shows a preoccupation with the past in his novels, but is inexorably involved in the present, is Joseph Roth. This is particularly true of his last two works, *Die Kapuzinergruft* [*The Crypt of the Capuchins*] and *Die Geschichte von der 1002. Nacht* [*The Story of the 1002nd Night*].

If one is to grasp clearly the specific motifs of exile as they appear in these novels, a short description of Roth's unique experience of exile is necessary. On 31 January 1933, the day of Hitler's appointment as chancellor of Germany, Roth was in Paris, where he had maintained a permanent residence since 1927. He was never a German citizen, and even though he had been employed by German newspapers since 1921, he felt no special loyalty toward Germany, but rather aversion. By 1925 he had come to consider France, and especially Paris, his intellectual and cultural home.[2] As a roving reporter for the *Frankfurter Zeitung* from 1923 to 1932 Roth was constantly on the road, lived regularly in hotels, and never owned an apartment or other property.   Because he had no family, he did not share the usual worries of the writer in exile who had been forced to abandon his relatives upon leaving Germany.   In contrast to most of the emigrants who came to France after 1933, Roth was familiar with the French language and mode of life and was in no danger of losing his residence permit.

Nevertheless, after Hitler's rise to power Roth had a much smaller market for his books, like most of the writers in exile whose books were blacklisted or burned in Germany, and in consequence his financial difficulties grew.   At the same time his precarious state of health was further weakened by his continual and excessive drinking, which grew chronically worse during exile.   Poverty and poor health also restricted his travels, which were vital for him, indeed an escape from himself.

Above all, his relationship to Austria was decisive for Roth's life in exile.   From 1925 on, his letters and writings convey a gradual transformation from a left-wing, revolutionary postwar author to a conservative Austrian monarchist,[3] a transformation that appears complete by 1932 with the publication of *Radetzkymarsch* [*Radetzky March*].   At this time Roth writes: "My strongest experience was the war and the fall of my fatherland, *the only one* I ever had: the Austro-Hungarian Monarchy."[4]   In subsequent years Roth's allegiance to the defunct Hapsburg Monarchy and the Catholicism traditionally and ideologically bound to it symbolizes his longing, in an age of instability and inhumanity, for a stable, humane, and transcendental order.

Keenly aware of Austria's dilemma, Roth foresaw the threat to the Republic by the Nazi government.   In many of his letters he nourished hope for the restoration of the Hapsburg Monarchy, which he saw as the sole guarantee of Austrian independence.   With this in mind he wrote numerous articles for exile journals (such as *Das Neue Tagebuch* and *Die Österreichische Post*, as well as for the *Christlicher Ständestaat*, published in Austria) calling attention to the cultural and historical uniqueness of that nation.   The downfall of Austria in 1938 had a decisive effect on Roth.   A study of the exile elements in *Die Kapuzinergruft* and *Die Geschichte von der 1002. Nacht* reveals the indelibility of this experience.

Roth began *Die Kapuzinergruft* in 1937, perhaps affected by the precarious political situation of Austria, which he observed at first hand during a stay in Salzburg.[5] The novel, apparently planned as a sequel to *Radetzkymarsch*, follows the destiny of the narrator Franz Ferdinand Trotta--a cousin of the hero in *Radetzkymarsch*--from the immediate prewar period to the fall of the Austrian Republic.

The fact that *Die Kapuzinergruft* is a first-person narrative in which the hero relates episodes of his life from memory lends an air of authenticity to the story.   This impression is borne out by the fact that the narrator's account of certain incidents from his life--for example, his army career, his disillusionment and despair as a returning soldier, and his growing consciousness of the loss of the

Danube Monarchy—all coincide with Roth's own experience, about which he constantly spoke and wrote. The shared experience of author and fictional character points to the possibility of an intended identification. As Käthe Hamburger observes in her analysis of an author-character relationship, the relationship between the two can "be so narrow . . . that we cannot distinguish with certainty whether we are dealing with an authentic autobiography or a fictitious creation."[6] In *Die Kapuzinergruft* it is the mutual Austrian experience that unites author and character: the belated love both feel for the Monarchy and the political ideals ensuing from this love. The title *Die Kapuzinergruft* in itself characterizes Roth's experience of exile. Not only is it the loss of the Hapsburg Empire, but also the dissolution of the Austrian Republic, with which the hope for restoration of the Monarchy vanishes also. The twilight atmosphere in which the action takes place, the melancholy mood, the despondency and apathy of the narrator and his friends, and the leitmotifs of death produce the funereal mood that pervades the book and anticipates the fall of Austria.

The political ideologies expressed in *Die Kapuzinergruft* are a reconstruction of the exiled Roth's political attitude toward the Austrian problems of his immediate present. Thus Count Chojnicki, representing the monarchist view of Austria, describes what he terms the lack of the proper appreciation for the future of Austria on the part of the Social Democratic and Christian Socialist parties:

> Austria is not a state, not a homeland, not a nation.
> It is a religion. The clerics and the clerical fools
> who are governing are making a so-called nation out
> of us; out of us, who are a supranation, the only
> supranation to have existed in the world. . . . The
> Social Democrats have proclaimed Austria a component
> of the German Republic, they who are after all the dis-
> gusting creators of the so-called nationalities problem.
> The Christian Socialist fools from the Alpine hinterlands
> follow in the footsteps of the Socialists. (I, 422)

That the fictitious character Chojnicki functions as spokesman for the author can be seen in the following excerpt from a Roth letter:

> Yes, the empire of our forebears, I worry anew about
> it . . . will it come to pass? . . . I am apprehensive
> for the following reasons: . . . It was destroyed by
> this loathsome nationalistic socialism [= National Social-
> ism]. . . . The new rulers strike me as too provincial.
> They are too much part of the Alpine region; they are
> not capable of grasping the all-embracing physiognomy
> of the Empire, but only the limited one. Can Austria
> rise again out of that which is geographically limited
> even though its essence lies in what is geographically
> unlimited?[7]

Although Chojnicki's statements apparently refer to past events, they come to have direct bearing on the present through Roth's interpretation of Austrian problems at the time he wrote *Die Kapuzinergruft*. The author refers to the parallel between the prewar agitation of the German Nationals and the annexation politics of the Socialists in 1921 and 1931, and to the inner weakness of the current Christian Socialist government, whose inability to understand the transcendent mission of the Monarchy and to work for its restoration exposes Austria to the threat of the Nazi state.

Typical of Roth's attitude in exile is his deep-seated animosity toward Germans. It is not accidental that the villain in *Die Kapuzinergruft* who cheats the Trotta family out of their last possession is a German--more specifically, a Prussian. The stark portrayal of this type reveals an antagonism that could have derived only from recent events:

> A new personality came into our life, a certain Kurt von Stettenheim . . . He looked like one of those men nowadays considered to be racially pure. . . . Such persons come from the Baltic Area, from Pomerania, even from the Lüneberg Heath. Comparatively speaking, we were still relatively fortunate. Our Mr. von Stettenheim was only from the Mark Brandenburg.
>
> He was tall and sinewy, blond and freckled; he wore the inevitable dueling scar on his forehead, the distinguishing mark of the Prussians, and also a monocle, so inconspicuous that one could not help but notice it. . . . There are faces from Pomerania, from the Baltic, from the Mark Brandenburg, in which the monocle gives the impression of being a third, unnecessary eye, no help to the natural eye, but its mask of glass. (I, 403-04)

In contrast to this portrait are the sympathetic ones of Jewish characters and their humane temperament, contradicting the Nazi representation of Jewish types. The visit of the Jewish driver Manes Reisiger prompts the narrator to express his views on anti-Semitism: "At that time I knew a few Jews, Viennese Jews naturally. I by no means hated them, precisely because at that time the patronizing anti-Semitism of the nobility and the circles that I associated with had come into fashion among caretakers, the petty bourgeoisie, chimneysweeps, paperhangers" (I, 328). Reisiger's physical appearance too makes an impression on the narrator and denies the Nazi concept of a specific Jewish type: "As I entered the anteroom, I saw a man who not only contradicted entirely my usual conceptions of a Jew, but could even have been capable of completely destroying them. He was something uncannily black and colossal. . . . The man was strong and tall" (I, 328-29). The character sketch of the Jewish lawyer Dr. Kiniower, in whom Old Testament wisdom combines with genuine concern for his clients, is aimed at Nazi propaganda about the dishonesty and maliciousness of Jews. Although Roth, who outwardly professed Catholicism during his exile period, was reared a Jew, he nevertheless vigorously opposed Nazi anti-Semitism on purely humanitarian rather than sectarian principles.[8]

The structure of the novel, too, reveals a relationship to the present. The loose, unorganized construction of the plot, especially the scrambled succession of episodes in *Kapuzinergruft*, contributes to the vagueness of events as they appear to manifest the decadence and disorder of society. Narrative and social disorder in the novel thus reflect the inner disintegration of the Austrian state.9 The novel proceeds at a relatively slow pace through the longer episodes of the postwar period and then abruptly converges upon the events of February 1934. It appears as if the pressure of contemporary events upon Roth's consciousness was responsible for the present overtaking of the past. The death of Trotta's mother coincides with that of Ephraim Reisiger. Both incidents symbolize the impending doom of Austria. With the death of the mother, who with her aristocratic character and elegant manners is the last representative of old Austria, hope for the restoration of the Monarchy dies too. The death of young Reisiger, a victim of the bloody suppression of the Social Democratic Party by the Dollfuss government, is one of the causes for the actually impending downfall of the Austrian Republic.

The capitulation of the Austrian government to Nazi power on 11 March 1938 caused Roth to write the last chapter of *Die Kapuzinergruft*. 10 The concluding action demonstrates his inner compulsion to come to terms with the lowest point of his experience of exile. In the traumatic final scene, which begins with a nostalgic recollection of the Viennese prewar nights, the brutal reality of the Nazi annexation and the triumphant proclamation of the storm trooper shatter the hero's consciousness: "Fellow Germans! The government has collapsed. A new German people's regime has come into existence!" (I, 428). Trotta's realization that Austria no longer exists has a devastating effect on him, as it had on his literary creator, who likewise could not bear the loss of his homeland. The hope of the protagonist, who does not become fully aware of the pointlessness of his existence until the downfall of Austria, together with the hope of the author himself for a new Austrian monarchy, is buried forever as Trotta despairingly seeks refuge in the Kapuzinergruft--the burial place of the Hapsburgs. For him, living as he does completely in the memory of the past and the isolation of his existence, shying away from the reality of the present, as well as for Roth, who by contrast could not dissociate himself from the reality of the present, Austria's fall constitutes the nadir of his life.

Die Kapuzinergruft is the literary transfiguration of Roth's exile agony. The author shares with his hero not only despair for Austria but also guilt for their initial sceptical indifference to the Monarchy while it still existed. Both realize the tragedy of its loss only after it ceases to exist. Roth, like Trotta, confronted by the harsh reality of his time, nostalgically recalls the Empire, a utopia that lives only in his memory. Finally, the loss of the last vestige of this supranational entity, the Austrian Republic, destroys Roth's personal and literary raison d'être. In the final analysis, *Die Kapuzinergruft* becomes a requiem for both Austria and Joseph Roth.   The despairing question with which the novel ends, "Where should I, a Trotta, go now?..." (I, 430) is an expression of the writer's own despair.

In a letter of 20 June 1937, Roth writes: "A new book has already gone to press, *Die Geschichte* [*von*] *der 1002. Nacht*, but not proofread and worked through."[11]   Stefan Zweig believes, in the summer of 1938, that Roth must now be finished with the novel.[12]   In any case, the work was published only posthumously, in 1939.   Thus Roth worked on his book at a time when his despair for Austria, together with his failing health, brought his emotional and physical crisis to its ultimate phase.

At first glance, the title—*Die Geschichte von der 1002. Nacht*—indicates the possibility of a thematic relationship with the original Persian *Arabian Nights*.   The impression is strengthened by the oriental frame narrative in which the actual plot is enclosed.   The frame stories of the nineteenth century (for example the *Novellen* of Theodor Storm and Conrad Ferdinand Meyer) had lent a certain degree of authenticity to their narratives.   In contrast, the frame of Roth's final novel serves a purely ironic purpose, behind which the exile experience is concealed.   Roth employs the fairy-tale-like frame to create the expectation that the story will be completely removed in time and space from his present, an expectation that he then shatters by allusions to contemporary events.   He opens the narrative in the traditional style of a fairy tale: "In the spring of the year 18.. the Shah-in-Shah, the holy, exalted, and eminent monarch, the absolute ruler and emperor of all the states of Persia, began to feel an uneasiness he had never known before" (I, 633).

In designating some indefinite period of the nineteenth century as the time of the action, Roth consciously situates the events of the narrative at a distance from the present. Yet as soon as the introduction is over and the actual narrative begins, the author abolishes the apparent disparity in time with the following commentary:

> Just barely two hundred years had passed since the cruelest of all Mohammedans had advanced toward Vienna.   At that time a true miracle had saved Austria. Far more dreadful than the Turks had been, the Prussians now threatened the old Austria—and although they were almost more heathen than the Mohammedans . . . God did not perform any miracles. . . . Now another, more frightful epoch commenced, the era of the Prussians, the era of the Janizaries of Luther and Bismarck.   On their black and white flags—both colors denoting deep mourning—there was certainly no half-moon to be seen; rather a cross, but it was an iron cross.   (I, 640-41)

In identical language Roth mourns the fall of Austria in "Requiem Mass," a polemic written in 1938: "The Prussian boot trudges over the oldest European seed.   The tower of St. Stephan's Cathedral, which was spared from the half-moon for a couple of centuries, will soon be transformed into a symbol of falsehood by the swastika. . . . and over the Kapuzinergruft flutters the old black, white, and red foe" (III, 616). The similarity of content and style between the two passages and the deliberate absence of the Austro-Prussian conflict from *Die Geschichte von der 1002. Nacht* suggest Roth's intent to express his reaction to the annexation of Austria in allegorical terms.

One of the author's leitmotifs in the novel is the illusion of tranquillity: "At that time a profound and supercilious peace prevailed in the world" (I, 689). This description is repeated later in the novel: "Far and wide a profound, almost frighteningly profound peace prevailed" (I, 715). By defining this state of peace as "supercilious," however, and therefore inauspicious and "frightening," Roth alludes to the inertia that characterized the Western powers in the face of the Austrian annexation. Essentially it is the same sentiment, or rather resentment, that prompted his protest elsewhere: "A world has been relinquished to Prussia. A world? *The world* has been handed over to Prussia: for better or for worse. . . . The world meanwhile negotiates with Ribbentrop" (III, 618).

The central character of this novel, who emerges from the frame of the story, is a certain Baron Taittinger. Taittinger, an aristocratic member of the officer class with his studied indifference and inborn casualness, may be regarded as a figure symbolic of the decline of the Austrian Empire. Like his antecedents in Roth's works in particular and in Austrian fin-de-siècle literature in general, he is a passive hero alive in a world of his own.

The plot centers on the Shah's passionate desire to possess, for one night, a countess whom he has seen during a banquet given in his honor at the Viennese court. The imperial courtiers, perplexed by the unexpected wish of the oriental ruler, substitute a double hastily fetched from a brothel on the advice of Baron Taittinger, who knows of the resemblance between the two ladies. Taittinger's role in this so-called "affair" leads to his transfer from the Viennese court to a remote garrison, his eventual resignation from the Army, and finally his suicide. This tragic denouement results from his failure to perceive reality until it is too late. The reality that Roth has created in this, his last novel, to affect the protagonist so harshly lies in both the nature of the state that confronts him and the character of the people who individually and collectively contribute to his ruin. Like the hero in *Die Kapuzinergruft*, Taittinger experiences the ultimate futility of his existence. As a true Austrian, he has lost his time and place.

Significantly, in this novel Roth fashions the state, not into a patriarchy headed by an emperor, as in his earlier works, but into an anonymous power, estranged from the individual. He describes a bureaucracy of a Kafkaesque character, whose officials--"Minute little wheels in incomprehensible service to the incomprehensible state . . . instruments of fate . . ." (I, 787)--sacrifice the protagonist to the

interest of the state.   In this portrayal of a despotic authority, selfish and indifferent to the fate of the individual, the
sense of alienation in Roth's own exile is revealed.

Roth's perspective on contemporary events unquestion-
ably influenced his creation of characters who alone and
together bring down the hero.   Although Roth, in accordance
with Austrian literary tradition, portrays the common people
in his early novels as decent and loyal, he perceives these
types in *Die Geschichte von der 1002. Nacht* with caustic
irony, etching their vices with vitriol.   Taittinger's proletarian friends exploit his naive trust, his basic benevolence
and willingness to make amends, thereby destroying his
career and any chance he may have of rehabilitating himself.   Their vulgar manners and grotesque appearance are
matched only by their mutilation of the German language.
The wax figures these characters use in the puppet theater
that they have induced the protagonist to purchase for them
symbolize their heartlessness.

In creating such character types, Roth was undoubtedly
motivated by his knowledge of the events transpiring in
Vienna during and after the Nazi annexation of Austria,
which belied the widespread reputation of Viennese *Gemüt-
lichkeit*.   The traumatic effect of the barbaric present upon
such a sensitive artist as Joseph Roth may have caused him
to conclude *Die Geschichte von der 1002. Nacht* with the
epilogue of the puppet maker: "I could perhaps produce pup-
pets that have heart, conscience, passions, feelings, morals.
But no one in the entire world asks for such.   They want
only sideshow freaks in this world; they want monsters.
Monsters are what they want!" (I, 795).

In *Die Geschichte von der 1002. Nacht* the author
shows more narrative objectivity than in *Die Kapuzinergruft*, whose first-person narrator unfolds the story.   The
apparent detachment and the setting of the former novel in
the distant past reflect Roth's desire to escape from the reality of his time.   Conversely, the writer's habitual references
to the present and the scathing irony by which he unmasks
the characters and their actions express his suffering resulting from contemporary events.

An Austrian writer steeped in the Viennese literary tradition, Roth exhibits in his life and works the typical dichotomy of the Viennese, an experience that Grillparzer depicted
in his cathartic play, *Der Traum ein Leben*, 1834 [*A Dream
Is Life*].   Roth, too, would have liked by means of his literary art to seek refuge from the dismal reality of the late
nineteen-thirties, but his active concern with the problems
of his day denied him this possibility.   With respect to such
ambivalence, Heinrich Schnitzler's opinion about the Viennese
and their writings offers great insight:

> It is another characteristic of the Viennese that they
> have always been perfectly aware of the game they
> were playing with reality; they always knew that they
> were trying to fool themselves; that this life of frantic
> escape was a delusion and that it was doomed.   This

. . . awareness . . . had various effects on Viennese
literature.   It sometimes led to complete acceptance of
the Catholic creed . . . or it might cause a mood of
complete resignation . . . or, again, it might cause
unrelieved despair; while in other instances it might
result in bitterness and cynicism.[13]

During the last two years of his life, Roth could not
elude the impact of the present either in his life or in his
writing.   Reality was so barbaric that Roth, like his protagonist in *Die Geschichte von der 1002. Nacht*, was
unable to survive.

Notes

[1]Matthias Wegner, *Exil und Literatur: Deutsche
Schriftsteller im Ausland 1933-1945* (Frankfurt/M: Athenäum, 1967), pp. 144-45.   This and all translations from German in this article are by me.

[2]See *Joseph Roth: Briefe 1911-1939*, ed. Hermann
Kesten (Cologne: Kiepenheuer & Witsch, 1970), pp. 45-46.
Cited as *Briefe*, followed by page nos.

[3]*Briefe*, p. 65.   See also "Seine k. und k. Majestät,"
in Joseph Roth, *Werke in drei Bänden*, ed. Hermann Kesten
(Cologne: Kiepenheuer & Witsch, 1956), III, 328.   Hereafter
references to this edition appear in parentheses in the text;
the volume is indicated by Roman numerals and the page number by Arabic numerals.

[4]*Briefe*, p. 240.

[5]Cf. Friderike Zweig, *Spiegelungen des Lebens* (Vienna: H. Deutsch, 1964), p. 189.

[6]Käthe Hamburger, *Die Logik der Dichtung* (Stuttgart:
E. Klett, 1968), p. 248.

[7]*Briefe*, p. 388.

[8]*Briefe*, p. 260.

[9]See Blanche Gidon, "Die Kapuzinergruft," *Joseph Roth,
Leben und Werk: Ein Gedächtnisbuch*, ed. Hermann Linden
(Cologne: G. Kiepenheuer, 1949), p. 204.

[10]It appeared as "Der schwarze Freitag" in *Das neue
Tagebuch*, 6, No. 17 (23 April 1939), 403-05.

[11]*Briefe*, p. 495.

[12]*Briefe*, p. 521.

[13]Heinrich Schnitzler, "Gay Vienna," *Journal of the
History of Ideas*, 15 (1954), 98.

Flight and Metamorphosis: Nelly Sachs as a Poet of Exile

Ehrhard Bahr

> How shall we sing the Lord's song in
> a strange land?
> If I forget thee, O Jerusalem . . .
>
> Psalm 137

Nelly Sachs (1891–1970) has generally been recognized and acclaimed as a poet of the Holocaust. The *laudatio* at the award of the Nobel Prize in 1966 characterizes her work as such: "With moving intensity of feeling she has given voice to the world-wide tragedy of the Jewish people, which she has expressed in lyrical laments of painful beauty and in dramatic legends."[1] In a similar vein, the citation reads: "For her outstanding lyrical and dramatic writings, which interpret Israel's destiny with touching strength."[2] Calling her "the voice of . . . the suffering of Israel," Marie Syrkin says that "her work is measured by the magnitude of her theme,"[3] and the Swedish critic Olof Lagercrantz writes that "the name Nelly Sachs will always be connected with the great Jewish catastrophe."[4]

But Nelly Sachs is also, and perhaps foremost, a poet of exile, not only because of the circumstances of her life, but also because exile is one of the central themes of her poetry. When she was awarded the Nobel Prize, she recited in lieu of an acceptance speech one of her poems on the theme of exile rather than on the Holocaust.

It was in exile that Nelly Sachs began the poetic work that earned her the 1966 Nobel Prize for literature, which she shared with the Israeli novelist Samuel Joseph Agnon. Nelly Sachs had escaped to Sweden in 1940. Through the intervention of Selma Lagerlöf she and her ailing mother had been able to flee Germany, where they had been under the constant threat of deportation to a concentration camp.[5] Nelly Sachs stayed in exile until her death in 1970, returning to Germany for visits only to accept the Droste-Hülshoff Prize in 1960 and the Peace Prize of the German Book Trade in 1965.

Her biography is not all that makes her a poet of exile. She wrote several volumes of poetry on the exile theme, grounded in Jewish tradition. It is Jewish literary tradition that provides the creative basis for her writings and supplies the images, the rhetoric, and the style of her work after 1940. The Bible and the literature of the Kabbalah and of Hasidism are the sources of her exile poetry. Judaism, in fact, is central to the understanding of Nelly Sachs's work, as has generally been recognized.[6] Thus the exile theme in her work must be interpreted in this light as well.

Exile is one of the oldest concepts in Jewish theological, philosophical, and poetic thought. Beginning with the expulsion from Paradise, the exile theme continues through the Books of Moses, the Babylonian exile, and the return to Jerusalem, until the last exile after the second destruction of the Temple. Many of the Psalms are lamentations about exile, as for instance the 137th Psalm: "By the rivers of Babylon, there we sat down, yea, we wept, when we remembered Zion." Not only does the theme of exile appear in Kabbalism, Messianism, and Hasidism, but it also dominates Jewish prayer and worship, as well as modern Jewish political and social theory, including Zionism.

Jewish mysticism, in particular--a profound influence on the poet--is permeated by the exile theme, in Hebrew *galuth*. As Gershom Scholem writes in his study of Jewish mysticism, "Life was conceived as Existence in Exile . . . and the sufferings of Exile were linked up with the central . . . doctrines about God and man." He also comments upon the "passionate desire to break down the Exile by enhancing its torments, savouring its bitterness to the utmost . . . and summoning up the compelling force of the repentance of a whole community." One of the most terrible fates that can befall man is captured in the symbol of the exile of the soul: "Such absolute exile was the worst nightmare of the soul which envisaged its personal drama in terms of the tragic destiny of the whole people." As Scholem summarizes, "absolute homelessness was the sinister symbol of absolute Godlessness, of utter moral and spiritual degradation."[7] Another dread fate is expressed in the image of God's exile from his creation, or the exile of the Shekinah, which represents the immanence of God in the totality of His creation. As Scholem concludes, "the exile of the *Shekhinah* is not a metaphor, it is a genuine symbol of the 'broken' state of things in the realm of divine potentialities."[8]

Though Nelly Sachs never uses the term *Exil* ("exile")-- the word occurs only in the English translations--a great number of key words related to exile are found in her poetry, such as *Auswanderung*, *Auszug* ("exodus"), *Flucht* ("flight"), *Flüchtling* ("refugee"), *Fremde* ("foreign land," that is, "exile"), *Heimat*, *Heimatland* ("homeland"), to mention only the most striking. Sinai and Israel, two proper names designating the specific tension between exile and homeland, are frequently used, Israel referring to the people as well as the land, whereas other proper names, such as Babylon, Jerusalem, Canaan, and Moses are less frequently

employed.   The word *Schechina* ("Shekinah") occurs only
once, but in such prominence as to indicate the importance
of the term for her poetry.[9]
    The poem Nelly Sachs recited when she was awarded the
Nobel Prize is included in her collection *Flucht und Verwand-
lung* [*Flight and Metamorphosis*], published in 1959.   The
poem does not have a title of its own, but is linked to the
title of the book.   It is a poem about flight and exile:

> In der Flucht
> welch grosser Empfang
> unterwegs--
>
> Eingehüllt
> In der Winde Tuch
> Füsse im Gebet des Sandes
> der niemals Amen sagen kann
> denn er muss
> von der Flosse in den Flügel
> und weiter--
>
> Der kranke Schmetterling
> weiss bald wieder vom Meer--
> Dieser Stein
> mit der Inschrift der Fliege
> hat sich mir in die Hand gegeben--
>
> An Stelle von Heimat
> halte ich die Verwandlungen der Welt--[10]

Flight is viewed not only as an ordeal, but also as a blessing: it is "a great reception" ("welch grosser Empfang")--a
reception by people who open their homes, but also a reception *of* people into one's inner self.   The exile is poor and
afflicted; he has no garment in which to wrap himself but
the "wind's shawl" ("der Winde Tuch"); he has no firm
ground under his feet, no secure place for his prayers,
because the sand is blown in all directions before the "Amen"
can be pronounced.
    "Fin" (*Flosse*) and "wing" (*Flügel*) are additional
metaphors of swift motion, images of flight.[11]   The sea is
also in motion--"the sick butterfly / will soon learn again
of the sea" ("der kranke Schmetterling / weiss bald wieder
vom Meer")--the waves come rolling toward the beach, but
they return again to the sea.   It is a fleeing, but not in
a straight line; rather it is a coming and a going, a fleeing and receiving.   The straight line of flight is turned into
an eternal circle.   The sea then becomes an image of constancy.   Its sight promises to strengthen the sick butterfly--
an image of the exiled soul.
    The waves bring stones from the depth of the sea,
stones of amber, left on the beach.   A fly is encrusted in
the stone of many hundred years ago; a fly that tried to
escape the dripping sap of a tree was caught by the resin
and its flight arrested by the yellowish gum, which turned

to stone, changing inconstancy and temporality into constancy and timelessness.

The fly leaves an "inscription" (*Inschrift*) on the stone: man can lose his homeland; he is subject to change; yet existence and identity are not lost during the flight through time and space. The persona of the poem is no longer in need of a homeland. In the language of the poem he preserved his identity through change.

This poem has often been interpreted in terms of Nelly Sachs's life, her flight to Sweden, her wandering along the beaches of the Baltic Sea, collecting amber.[12] It has also been read as expressing Nelly Sachs's trust in nature. The persona of the poem seems to derive comfort from the eternal laws of nature.[13] The poetic ambiguity of Nelly Sachs's images permits both interpretations, but taken as exclusive they reduce her poetry to merely autobiographical or escapist art. Her work is much more than confessional literature, escapism, or an expression of trust in nature in the tradition of Goethe.

Nelly Sachs's trust in nature is not that of the nineteenth-century nature poem, but trust in Shekinah, "the presence and immanence of God in the whole of creation."[14] The poem is about not only her own flight, but also the flight of all the people of Israel from ancient past to modern times, from the Biblical Exodus to the most recent persecution and flight of the Jews. On its flight the people of Israel are received by God—and they receive Him in the wilderness of Sinai, where the wind blows the sand in all directions.

But the sand is not only the sand of the desert; it is also an image of the people of Israel. In the Bible and in Jewish legends, Israel is compared to sand, to fish, and to a bird.[15] The sequence of "sand—fin—wing" in the poem is not only the sequence of modern evolutionary theory, it is also the flight and metamorphosis of Israel. According to Jewish legend, Moses wanted to be transformed into a fish or a bird in order to see the Promised Land.[16]

The sick butterfly is told that it will learn again of the sea. The soul in Jewish legends has the appearance of a butterfly.[17] In a passage elucidating the image of the exiled soul learning again of the sea, the *Zohar*, the most important book of Kabbalistic literature, says: "When the Holy One remembers His children, He drops them into the great Sea which is the Sea of Wisdom, in order to sweeten them, and He turns the attribute of Justice into the attribute of Mercy, and takes compassion on Israel."[18]

In the Bible and in Jewish legends stones are tokens of God's compassion. Precious stones are given to the pious. In the poem, the "inscription" on the stone is clearly an allusion to the Tablets of the Law given to Israel on Sinai. The people of Israel were led into desert exile in order to change their Egyptian way of life and to prepare for their return to the Promised Land.

The poem treats exile on different levels—autobiographical, cosmic, historical, and mystical—all complementing each other. Without an understanding of the several dimensions of exile, Nelly Sachs's poetry might be misunderstood as expressing simply an individual experience or a naive trust in nature.

The poet's relationship to nature emerges clearly in the following poem from her cycle *Sternverdunkelung* [*Eclipse of the Stars*]:

Wenn im Vorsommer der Mond geheime Zeichen aussendet,
die Kelche der Lilien Dufthimmel verströmen,
öffnet sich manches Ohr unter Grillengezirp
dem Kreisen der Erde und der Sprache
der entschränkten Geister zu lauschen.[19]

Judging solely by the first stanza, this appears to be a nature poem. But in the second stanza nature's neutrality becomes intolerable in the face of the historical reality of concentration camps:

. . . mitten in der Verzauberung spricht eine Stimme
    klar und verwundert:
Welt, wie kannst du deine Spiele weiter spielen
und die Zeit betrügen—
Welt, man hat die kleinen Kinder wie Schmetterlinge,
flügelschlagend in die Flamme geworfen—

und deine Welt ist nicht wie ein fauler Apfel
in den schreckaufgejagten Abgrund geworfen worden—

Und Sonne und Mond sind weiter spazierengegangen—
zwei schieläugige Zeugen, die nichts gesehen haben.[20]

Shock is voiced at the sun and the moon, which, having seen the horrors of concentration camps, continue on their course like "two cross-eyed witnesses" ("zwei schieläugige Zeugen") pretending to have seen nothing. Nelly Sachs seems to endow nature with human emotions, but her shock at nature's indifference is not an instance of pathetic fallacy; it expresses her fear that God may have withdrawn from His creation, and despair at the exile of the Shekinah.

It is the special symbolism and prominence given by Nelly Sachs to the single mention of the word *Schechina* that heighten its impact:

Immer hinter den Rändern der Welt
die ausgesetzte Seele Genoveva wartet
mit dem Kinde Schmerzensreich
im Heimwehgestrahl.

Auch *Schechina* kannst du sagen,
die Staubgekrönte,
die durch Israel Schluchzende

Und die heilige Tierfrau
mit den sehenden Wunden im Kopf,
die heilen nicht
aus Gotteserinnerung.
            (*Und niemand weiss weiter*)[21]

In full accord with the concept of Jewish mysticism, Shekinah appears here as a personification of the suffering and exile of Israel. She is the queen of exile (*Staubgekrönte*) and is being compared to the saint of Christian legends who was innocently accused and sentenced to exile with her newborn child without hope of return. Finally, Shekinah is appointed together with a pagan deity to protect the innocent creatures of nature that are hunted and killed by man. She appears blinded. Her wounds will not heal because she remembers God, who is hidden from man. This poem of 1957 from Nelly Sachs's collection *Und niemand weiss weiter* [*And No One Knows How to Go On*] reveals the centrality of the exile theme for her poetry.[22]

Even Nelly Sachs's Holocaust poetry is dominated by main concepts of the exile theme: flight and metamorphosis. The chimneys of the crematoria of the concentration camps turn into "the road for the refugees of smoke" ("den Weg für Flüchtlinge aus Rauch"); they become "ways of freedom for Jeremiah's and Job's dust" ("Freiheitswege für Jeremias und Hiobs Staub").[23] Dust is another key word of Nelly Sachs's poetic vocabulary originating in the Bible; it refers to human origin and destiny (see Genesis 3:19). Human life begins and ends in dust. Life in exile consists of dust, whereas transcendence is final metamorphosis, "journey into a dustless realm" (*Fahrt ins Staublose*), the title of her collected poetry of 1961.

A special cycle is dedicated to "Refugees and Flight" ("Von Flüchtlingen und Flucht"). This age is considered by the poet the age of refugees:

> Das ist der Flüchtlinge Planetenstunde.
> Das ist der Flüchtlinge reissende Flucht
> in die Fallsucht, den Tod!
> (*Und niemand weiss weiter*)[24]

Refugees are on all roads of the earth, whereas the streets of the city are free of fugitives:

> Auswandererschritte
> Pulsreise-Schritte
> betten sich in Landsflucht
> weit hinter dem Meilenstein,
> der verwaist im Tage wacht.
> (*Und niemand weiss weiter*)[25]

The roads of flight are mystically linked with the longing for God beyond madness and death:

> Flucht aus den schwarzgebluteten Gestirnen
> des Abschieds,
> Flucht in die blitztapezierten
> Herbergen des Wahnsinns,
>
> Flucht, Flucht, Flucht
> in den Gnadenstoss der Flucht
> aus der zersprengten Blutbahn
> kurzer Haltestelle--
> (*Und niemand weiss weiter*)[26]

In correspondence with the mystical value of language in Jewish mysticism, Nelly Sachs's poetry becomes "holy scripture in exile," returning to God:

> Dies ist die heilige Schrift
> in Landsflucht
> in den Himmel kletternd
> mit allen Buchstaben.
> (*Flucht und Verwandlung*)[27]

*　　　*　　　*

In her poetry Israel is the most frequently used proper name from the Bible referring to the people and the land, whereas in her collection *Sternverdunkelung* [*Eclipse of the Stars*] of 1949, the name Israel refers to the then newly founded State of Israel. The survivors of the Holocaust, burnt by the fires of the concentration camps, return from exile to their homeland:

> Land Israel
> nun wo dein vom Sterben angebranntes Volk
> einzieht in deine Täler
> und alle Echos den Erzvätersegen rufen
> für die Rückkehrer.
> (*Sternverdunkelung*)[28]

The exiled return to the Land of Israel "from the corners of the world." Their eyes are stained from the tears of suffering, but their new contact with the old homeland promises to be as significant and powerful as the psalms of David:

> Land Israel,
> nun wo dein Volk
> aus den Weltecken verweint heimkommt
> um die Psalmen Davids neu zu schreiben in deinen
> Sand. (*Sternverdunkelung*)[29]

Nelly Sachs never visited Israel.[30] The name of the state appears for the last time in her poetry in her collection *Und niemand weiss weiter* [*And No One Knows How to Go On*] of 1957. A distinct change now marks her concept of a home for the exiles: "Israel is not only land!" ("Nicht nur Land ist Israel!"). The continued suffering of the Jewish people is emphasized in the image of Israel as "the open wound of God" ("die offene Gotteswunde").[31]

Israel as a spiritual homeland is invoked in the poem "Jerusalem Is Everywhere" ["Überall Jerusalem"], from the collection *Noch feiert Tod das Leben* [*Death Still Celebrates Life*] of 1961:

> Verborgen ist es im Köcher
> und nicht abgeschossen mit dem Pfeil
> und die Sonne immer schwarz um das Geheimnis
> und gebückt die Sechsunddreissig im Leidenswerk

Aber hier
augenblicklich
ist das Ende--
Alles gespart für das reissende Feuer
Seiner Abwesenheit--

Da
in der Krankheit
gegoren zur Hellsicht
die Prophetin mit dem Stab stösst
auf den Reichtum der Seele

Da ist in der Irre Gold versteckt--
(*Noch feiert Tod das Leben*)[32]

The Biblical metaphor of quiver and arrow (Isaiah 49:2) sig-
nifies the utopian potential still hidden, the Messianic promise to be fulfilled in the name of Jerusalem.   The mystery
evolves in the form of dialectical metamorphoses.   The sun,
the light of hope and comfort, at its mystical point emerges
from its opposite.   The evil world is saved by the suffering
of the thirty-six just men who are unknown and not even
aware of their own mission.   Nelly Sachs employs here the
Hasidic legend of the thirty-six pious or just men for whose
sake the world is preserved and the Messianic promise of the
name Jerusalem will be fulfilled.[33]
     The dialectical paradoxes continue in the statement of
the final metamorphoses: the end becomes a new beginning;
the hidden God returns from exile, sickness leads to clear
vision, and treasures come to light in the barrenness of
exile.   The poem refers to a spiritual Jerusalem of the future,
where exile finally ends.   Unnamed but for the title of the
poem yet its major metaphor, Jerusalem is not specifically
mentioned in any of Nelly Sachs's other poems, a fact that
seems to point to its unique position in her writing and
thinking, as is the case with the term Shekinah.   Whereas
Israel is mentioned almost thirty times in her poetry, Jerusalem, the city on which for centuries the hopes of the exiled
Jewish people have been centered, appears to be singled out
by its very absence.   Yet Nelly Sachs seems to express these
hopes emerging, as they do, from exile in its absolute meaning.   In her poem lies the promise of an answer to the
annual prayer: "Next year in Jerusalem!"

Notes

[1] *Nobel Lectures: Literature 1901-1967*, ed. Horst
Frenz (Amsterdam: Nobel Foundation, 1969), p. 612.
     [2] *Nobel Lectures*, p. 610.
     [3] Marie Syrkin, "Nelly Sachs: Poet of the Holocaust,"
Midstream, 13, No. 3 (1967), 13.
     [4] Olof Lagercrantz, "Die fortdauernde Schöpfung: Über
Nelly Sachs," *Text und Kritik*, 23 (July 1969), 3.   The only
exception to this widely held point of view is Albrecht Hol-
schuh's article "Lyrische Mythologeme: Das Exilwerk von

Nelly Sachs," *Die deutsche Exilliteratur 1933-1945*, ed. Manfred Durzak (Stuttgart: Reclam, 1973), pp. 343-57.

[5] See Olof Lagercrantz, "In den Wohnungen des Todes," *Die Zeit*, 26 May 1970 (US edition); Walter A. Berendsohn, *Nelly Sachs: Einführung in das Werk der Dichterin jüdischen Schicksals* (Darmstadt: Agora, 1974), pp. 13 f.; Bengt Holmqvist, "Die Sprache der Sehnsucht," *Das Buch der Nelly Sachs*, ed. Bengt Holmqvist, 2nd ed. (Frankfurt/M: Suhrkamp, 1977), pp. 36 f. See also my forthcoming book on Nelly Sachs, to be published by C. H. Beck in Munich in 1980.

[6] See Beda Allemann, "Hinweis auf einen Gedichtraum," in *Das Buch der Nelly Sachs*, ed. Bengt Holmqvist, 2nd ed. (Frankfurt/M: Suhrkamp, 1977), pp. 291-308; Gisela Dischner, "Die Lyrik von Nelly Sachs und ihr Bezug zur Bibel, zur Kabbala und zum Chassidismus," *Text und Kritik*, 23 (July 1969), 25-40; Olof Lagercrantz, *Versuch über die Lyrik der Nelly Sachs* (Frankfurt/M: Suhrkamp, 1967), pp. 60-86; W. V. Blomster, "A Theosophy of the Creative Word: The Zohar-Cycle of Nelly Sachs," *The Germanic Review*, 44 (1969), 211-27; Dinah Dodds, "The Process of Renewal in Nelly Sachs's *Eli*," *German Quarterly*, 49 (1976), 50-58. See also my article on "Shoemaking as a Mystic Symbol in Nelly Sachs's Mystery Play *Eli*," *German Quarterly*, 45 (1972), 480-83.

[7] Gershom Scholem, *Major Trends in Jewish Mysticism* (New York: Schocken, 1961), pp. 249-50.

[8] Scholem, p. 275.

[9] See Paul Kersten, *Die Metaphorik in der Lyrik von Nelly Sachs mit einer Wortkonkordanz und einer Nelly Sachs-Bibliographie* (Hamburg: Lüdke, 1970), pp. 27a-143a.

[10] "Fleeing, / what a great reception / on the way--// Wrapped / in the wind's shawl / feet in the prayer of sand / which can never say amen / compelled / from fin to wing / and further--// The sick butterfly / will soon learn again of the sea-- / This stone / with the fly's inscription / gave itself into my hand--// I hold instead of a homeland / the metamorphoses of the world--." Quoted from *Fahrt ins Staublose: Die Gedichte der Nelly Sachs* (Frankfurt/M: Suhrkamp, 1961), p. 262. English trans. *O the Chimneys: Selected Poems*, trans. Michael Hamburger, Christopher Holme, Ruth and Matthew Mead, Michael Roloff (New York: Farrar, Straus & Giroux, 1967), p. 145. Wherever necessary, I have modified the existing translations.

[11] Horst Bienek, "In der Flucht . . . ," in *Doppelinterpretationen: Das zeitgenössische deutsche Gedicht zwischen Autor und Leser*, ed. Hilde Domin (Frankfurt/M: Athenäum, 1966), p. 159.

[12] Bienek, "In der Flucht," pp. 158-61; Paul Konrad Kurz, "Fahrt ins Staublose: Die Lyrik der Nelly Sachs," in *Über moderne Literatur: Standorte und Deutungen* (Frankfurt/M: Knecht, 1967), pp. 245-48.

[13] Bienek, "In der Flucht," pp. 158-61; Kurz, "Fahrt ins Staublose," pp. 241-48.

[14] Scholem, *Major Trends in Jewish Mysticism*, p. 216.

[15]Genesis 32.12; Louis Ginzberg, *The Legends of the Jews*, 7 vols. (Philadelphia: Jewish Publication Society of America, 1909–38), I, 228, 282, 284, 312, 382; II, 281; III, 70; V, 223. See also Kersten, *Die Metaphorik in der Lyrik von Nelly Sachs*, pp. 73–76, 99.

[16]Ginzberg, *The Legends of the Jews*, III, 442, 450.

[17]Ginzberg, V, 81.

[18]*The Zohar*, trans. Harry Sperling and Maurice Simon (London: The Soncino Press, 1933), III, 62–63.

[19]"When in early summer the moon sends out secret signs, / the chalices of lilies scent of heaven, / some ear opens to listen / beneath the chirp of the cricket / to earth turning and the language of spirits set free." Quoted from *Fahrt ins Staublose*, p. 153; English trans. *The Seeker and Other Poems*, trans. Ruth and Matthew Mead, Michael Hamburger (New York: Farrar, Straus & Giroux, 1970), p. 147.

[20]". . . in the midst of enchantment a voice speaks clearly and amazed: / World, how can you go on playing your games / and cheating time-- / World, the little children were thrown like butterflies, / wings beating into the flames--// and your earth has not been thrown like a rotten apple / into the terror-roused abyss--// And sun and moon have gone on walking-- / two cross-eyed witnesses who have seen nothing." Quoted from *Fahrt ins Staublose*, p. 153; Engl. trans. *The Seeker and Other Poems*, p. 147.

[21]"Beyond the borders of the world / exiled Genoveva still waits / with her child of Sorrow / in rays of longing to return home. // You may also call her Shekinah, / Crowned with dust, / who weeps for Israel // And the holy Lady of the Beasts / with wounds for eyes in her head / that do not heal / because they remember God." Quoted from *Fahrt ins Staublose*, p. 194; English translation is my own.

[22]See Kersten, *Die Metaphorik in der Lyrik von Nelly Sachs*, pp. 176–78. The concept of *deus absconditus* plays an important role in Jewish mysticism. See Scholem, *Major Trends in Jewish Mysticism*, pp. 11 f.; 110 f.

[23]*Fahrt ins Staublose*, p. 8; *Chimneys*, p. 2. The mystic interpretation is essential in this case; otherwise these statements might sound like the blasphemies uttered by the Doctor in Rolf Hochhuth's *The Deputy*.

[24]"That is the fugitives' planetary hour. / That is the fugitives' rending flight / into epilepsy, death!" Quoted from *Fahrt ins Staublose*, p. 160; Engl. trans. *O the Chimneys*, p. 99.

[25]"Immigrant steps / Pulsing journey steps / embed themselves far behind / the milestone on the road to exile, / which, orphaned, keeps vigil by day." Quoted from *Fahrt ins Staublose*, p. 166; *The Seeker*, p. 159.

[26]"Flight from the black-bled constellations / of farewell, / Flight into the lightning-papered / shelters of madness, // Flight, flight, flight / into the *coup de grace* of flight / from the short halting place / on the blown-up line

blood--." Quoted from *Fahrt ins Staublose*, p. 164; *The Seeker*, p. 157.

27"This is the holy scripture / in exile / climbing into the sky / with every letter." Quoted from *Fahrt ins Staublose*, p. 254; *The Seeker*, p. 255.

28"Land of Israel, / now when your people seared by dying / move into your valleys / and all echoes call the patriarchs' blessing / for those returning." Quoted from *Fahrt ins Staublose*, p. 126; *The Seeker*, p. 115.

29"Land of Israel, / now when your people / come home from the corners of the world with tear-stained eyes / to write the psalms of David anew in your sand." Quoted from *Fahrt ins Staublose*, p. 127; *The Seeker*, p. 115.

30Nelly Sachs had planned to visit Israel in 1967, but had to cancel her visits for reasons of health.

31 *Fahrt ins Staublose*, p. 199; *The Seeker*, p. 191. See also Kersten, *Die Metaphorik in der Lyrik von Nelly Sachs*, pp. 178-80, 388-89; Lagercrantz, *Versuch über die Lyrik der Nelly Sachs*, pp. 43 f.

32"It is hidden in the quiver / and not shot with the arrow / and the sun always black around the mystery / and the thirty-six bent in the work of suffering // But here / momentarily / is the end-- / Everything saved for the devouring fire / of His absence-- // When / in sickness / through ferment to clairvoyance / the prophetess strikes with the staff / upon the wealth of the soul // Gold is hidden there in the desert of wandering--." Quoted from *Fahrt ins Staublose*, p. 381; English translation is my own (cf. *The Seeker*, p. 377). See also Gisela Bezzel-Dischner, *Poetik des modernen Gedichts: Zur Lyrik von Nelly Sachs* (Bad Homburg v.d.H.: Gehlen, 1970), pp. 46-48.

33See Scholem, "The Tradition of the Thirty-Six Hidden Just Men," *The Messianic Idea in Judaism* (New York: Schocken, 1971), pp. 251-56; Naomi Ben-Asher, "Jewish Identity and Christological Symbolism in the Works of Three Writers," *Jewish Frontier*, 39, No. 9 (Nov. 1972), 12.

Anna Seghers: Between Judaism and Communism

Susan E. Cernyak

Netty Reiling-Radvanyi, better known as Anna Seghers, socialist writer of Jewish origin, left Germany in 1933 "after the police had already arrested me once and had kept me under surveillance,"[1] as she recalls in an article published in 1947. Her publications, including a novel that had been honored by the Kleist prize in 1928 on the recommendation of Hans Henny Jahnn, were included in the list of sequestered works of "undesirable authors" issued by the *Börsenblatt für den deutschen Buchhandel* of 16 May 1933, immediately after the government-instigated bookburnings.

She reached France via Switzerland and remained there for the next seven years. These years were highly prolific for Anna Seghers. In spite of precarious circumstances she managed to complete three novels during her stay in Paris: *Der Kopflohn* [*Headhunters' Bounty*] and *Die Rettung* [*The Rescue*], published by Querido, an exile publishing firm in Amsterdam, and *Der Weg durch den Februar* [*Passage through February*], by Editions du Carrefour in Paris, another exile publisher. Aside from completing three novels, Seghers was instrumental in establishing the periodical *Neue Deutsche Blätter*, published in Prague in collaboration with Oscar Maria Graf and Wieland Herzfelde. Though this publication was originally intended to be an antifascist propaganda organ, it included among its contributors such apolitical bourgeois authors as Hermann Kesten, Walter Mehring, and others. Kurt Batt, in his biography of Seghers, states that the periodical *Neue Deutsche Blätter* was the forerunner of *Das Wort*, published in Moscow between 1936 and 1939,[2] and dedicated to the struggle against fascism. Publication of *Das Wort* ended with the German-Russian non-aggression pact.

This event changed the tenor of Seghers's writing. From strident preoccupation with international communism and the fate of the worldwide proletariat, her work shifted into a minor key of mourning for the lost homeland. It seems doubly astonishing that Seghers should strike a nostalgic chord, for she faced persecution not only as a Communist

278

but also as a Jew. She was twice the enemy of the Reich. Furthermore, unlike the many German-Jewish emigrants without political commitment who remained in their new-found home- lands, Seghers returned to the German Democratic Republic, merely another dictatorship under a different flag, as early as 1947.

Two factors seem to contribute to this strong identifica- tion of a German-Jewish writer with Germany in the thirties. One is the political factor Martin Jay calls the color blind- ness that strikes the devout Marxist: "As has often been observed, Marxists, beginning with the founder himself and his controversial reply to Bruno Bauer on the Jewish question in 1843, have tended to deny the uniqueness of antisemitic oppression. That is, they have tended to subsume it under the more general rubric of the exploitation of the working class. . . . Or worse at times, they have condoned Judeo- phobia, implicitly and explicitly, as an expression of anti- capitalistic resentment."[3] This blindness to the Jewish trag- edy of the thirties and forties is particularly obvious in three of Seghers's exile works. Only one short story, "Post ins gelobte Land" ["Mail to the Promised Land"] in the col- lection *Der Ausflug der toten Mädchen und andere Erzäh- lungen* [*The Excursion of the Dead Girls and Other Short Stories*],[4] deals specifically with a Jewish milieu and car- ries religio-mystic accents. For this very reason the story was apparently considered unsuitable for inclusion in the collected works of Seghers, as published in East Berlin in 1951 and 1953.[5] Klaus Jarmatz, in his Marxist study of exile literature, does not list the collection at all.

The second factor is Seghers's overpowering homesick- ness. This yearning dominates the narrative in *Das siebte Kreuz* [*The Seventh Cross*], *Transit*, and especially "Der Ausflug der toten Mädchen." All three works reveal the major ideological shock for Seghers, the dedicated Communist, in the thirties: the nonaggression pact between Germany and Russia. Her ideological world had lost one of its mainstays. In 1929 the young writer had supplanted her Jewish religious beliefs with Marxist ideology. She had turned to communism as the result of an intellectual decision, but spurred on by emotion, in absolute trust and faith.[6] Concepts and ideas heretofore considered anathema to a follower of socialist real- ism (the credo preached by her mentor Georg Lukács) were now permitted to fill the void created by the betrayal of her faith.[7] Loss of faith in the principles of socialist realism is most strongly reflected in Seghers's works from 1939 to 1943. The novel *Die Toten bleiben jung* [*The Dead Stay Young*], begun in Mexico in 1944, already reflects her return to the Communist fold, under the increasing influence of her co-workers on the journal *Freies Deutschland*, a monthly periodical for antifascists, among them Ludwig Renn, Bruno Frei, and Alexander Abusch.[8]

Seghers clearly thought of herself first and foremost as a German. This was already evident in 1928, when she began signing her work "Anna Seghers," the name of one of her fictional heroines, instead of the foreign-sounding Netty

Reiling-Radvanyi.   Choosing such an earthy German name
was symptomatic of her attitude, which disregarded not only
her Jewish origin but also the tragedy of German Jewry as
a whole.   In 1933, replying to an invitation by Hermann
Kesten to contribute to an anthology of exiled writers, she
answers: "As for the anthology I must regretfully decline.
I have given the matter considerable thought.   If all authors
whose books were burnt were represented, I would not hesitate at all.   But a book containing only Jewish authors I
consider inappropriate, particularly at this time."9
    The three works in question reveal her nostalgia in
two forms: in the lovingly detailed descriptions of her native
landscape and its occupants as she wants to remember them,
and in the recurrent claim that the native roots are the only
source of strength and faith, regardless of the dangers
involved in clinging to them.   The latter is particularly
apparent in *Transit*.
    In *Das siebte Kreuz* as well as in *Der Ausflug der
toten Mädchen*, the unaltered beauty of the landscape, specifically the Rhine district around Mainz, Seghers's native
region, provides the background for the events of the narratives.   The earth appears as the one reliable constant from
time immemorial and the one promise of a brighter future:

> Along [these hills] the Romans drew their *limes*.
> . . . Here camped the legions, and with them all the
> gods of the world: city gods and peasant gods, the
> gods of Jew and Gentile. . . . There . . . the armies
> of the Franks were assembled when a crossing of the
> Main was attempted. . . . At the rivers' confluence
> lies the city of Mainz. . . . In this land something
> new happened every year, but every year the same
> thing: the apples ripened, and so did the wine . . . .
> The wine was needed by all and for all things: the
> bishops and landowners used it when they elected their
> emperor; the monks and knights when they founded
> their orders; the crusaders when they burned Jews . . .
> the Jacobins when they danced around their liberty
> poles.10

    Seghers lets the landscape and the people dominate her
stories.   History, in her view, has made this part of the
country a melting pot of races and ideas and has created a
special breed of men and women to whom love of their fellow
man and of the land has become the highest good.11   The
evil of the Third Reich has not taken root here.   Heisler's
last thoughts before leaving his native region for good
express Seghers's belief in the continuity of the country and
the unfailing compassion of its people: "The Rhine lay before
him, and beyond it the city . . . . Its streets and squares
. . . were fused into one great fortress that was reflected
in the river.   A flock of birds, flying in a sharply pointed
black triangle, was etched into the reddish afternoon sky
between the city's tallest spires, making a picture that
resembled a city's seal.   Presently, on the roof of the cathedral, between two of these spires, George made out the

figure of Saint Martin bending down from his horse to share his cloak with the beggar . . ." (p. 331).   The strength of the land is represented in the image of the fortress, and the image of Saint Martin is surely symptomatic of the innate solidarity of its inhabitants.

The short story, "Der Ausflug der toten Mädchen," was begun in Seghers's Mexican exile as a result of a traumatic experience.   She and other Communist emigrants had been offered asylum in Mexico.   After the publishing success of *The Seventh Cross* in 1941 she had gained fame as well as financial security.   She had also established a German-language publishing firm, El Libro Libre, in cooperation with several other antifascist exile writers.   The first German-language version of *Das siebte Kreuz* was published by this firm.[12]

In 1941, however, tragedy struck.   She was the victim of a hit-and-run driver in the Paseo de la Reforma in Mexico City.   In a letter addressed to her, Bodo Uhse, a fellow writer, raised the question whether it was really a hit-and-run accident or a political assassination attempt.[13]   During her convalescence Seghers began work on the short story. The first-person narrator, identified as Netty Reiling, Seghers's real identity, experiences a moment of quasi-hallucination prompted by her weakened condition after the accident. The hallucination begins during a walk through a dismal Mexican landscape.   She describes the landscape of exile as: "Greyish brown slopes . . . bare and rugged as a lunar landscape that denied by their mere appearance any trace of ever having harbored life."[14]   In the midst of this desolate setting her hallucination transports her back to the banks of the Rhine and "the mere sight of the softly rolling hillsides filled me with a light-hearted joy that replaced the deep melancholy within me, just as certain plants sprout only in their native light and soil" (p. 13).   The glowing landscape of the past imposed on the background of somber desolation sets the structural pattern for this short story. Marcel Reich-Ranicki describes this structure as a "kind of oscillation between the years of World War I and World War II almost like a combination of flashbacks and anticipation."[15]

Her waking fantasy recreates a class excursion from her school days, a steamboat trip on the Rhine.   As the steamer travels up the river toward Mainz, Seghers paints such a realistic and vivid image of the countryside that the reader sees and feels the soft light of late afternoon and smells the blossoms along the shore: "The slanting afternoon sun ruffled the pink and white blossoms of the fruit trees on the hills and in the vineyards. . . . We all waved to three little white houses that were as familiar to us as the pictures in our childhood fairy tale books. . . . likewise the village . . . its steep gables rising in a triangle of gothic proportion to the slim church steeple on the hill. . . . the three of us had linked our arms in . . . friendship that seemed to be part of the all-embracing bond of living things. . . . How was it possible that, at some time in the future, deceit, a madness . . . could infiltrate this bond" (p. 28). Just as in *Das siebte Kreuz*, the author stresses the inherent goodness of the land and its people.

Even in this strongly autobiographical story there is never any indication that the narrator herself is Jewish. Although one of the classmates and one of the teachers in the group are mentioned as being Jewish, their fate is considered merely a part of the tragic destiny that befell all of the school friends assembled on the class excursion. All these young women started out with the same promise and fell victim to the same antagonist: the Third Reich. Seghers puts the fate of the two Jewish characters, Miss Sichel, a teacher, and Sofie, a student, on the same level with that of the other German victims of the war, whether political dissenters killed by the regime or Germans killed by the wartime air raids. It is peculiar--and at the same time typical of Seghers--to equate the chances of survival in the gas chamber with that of free German citizens caught in an air raid.

The third work of nostalgia is the novel *Transit*,[16] published in Mexico in 1943. Seghers had begun writing it during her stay in Vichy-governed Marseille in 1940 and continued it in Santo Domingo, one of her several stopovers on the way to Mexico. This novel has an antecedent in an unpublished short story entitled "Die weisse Hochzeit" ["The White Wedding"]. The topic of the story is the kind of mock marriages entered into by many refugees in name only as a shortcut to obtaining emigration papers.[17] Like *Transit*, the story deals with the existential nightmare of refugees in a decidedly unfriendly France.

Seghers's emphasis on the importance of roots and a sense of belonging to a homeland stands in strange contrast to the title and topic of the novel: *Transit*, escape from Hitler-occupied Europe. From the outset, great pain is taken to establish the protagonist as an apolitical, uninvolved person. "I had managed [he says], party or no party, to get into a German concentration camp because I had refused to put up with all the dirty business around me" (p. 18). The lack of emphasis on Communist solidarity, coupled with an apolitical protagonist, relates this work to *Das siebte Kreuz* and "Der Ausflug der toten Mädchen"; all three grew out of Seghers's disillusionment with the nonaggression pact between Germany and Russia. In theme and atmosphere *Transit* suggests a leaning toward existentialism.[18] As in the other two works, the Third Reich is once more the antagonist. This time the Reich is not seen as the persecutor of the socialist comrades, as in *Das siebte Kreuz*, or as the destroyer of childhood promise as in "Der Ausflug der toten Mädchen," but as death personified, "still flaunting his lashing swastika flag" (p. 72), a merciless pursuer who has forced the fleeing masses to the edge of Western Europe, to Marseille, and who keeps pushing.

Having lived through just such traumatic experiences herself while in Marseille, Anna Seghers knew the horrors and frustration of the emigrants' existence firsthand.

In spite of her close acquaintance with the milieu, Seghers injects an astonishing point of view into the story. Observing the frantic scrambling of the refugees for exit papers, the narrator, Seghers's mouthpiece, speaks of them as *abfahrtssüchtig* (approximately "desperate for departure"). In his words, "I lived a quiet and rather solitary life surrounded by a frantic mob, intent on getting away from here" (p. 66).[19] *Abfahrt* is German for "departure," and *Sucht* approximates "a craze for" or "addiction" as in *rauschgiftsüchtig* ("addicted to drugs"). To speak of persons who try desperately to escape the camps and gas chambers of Hitler's regime as *abfahrtssüchtig* (or *süchtig* in any other way) is a denigration of the instinct for self-preservation of many thousands. The narrator observes these "addicts" in total detachment but does not hesitate to pose as a member of the group when that pose provides him with money. Through a strange coincidence he has come into the possession of a set of papers belonging to a German writer who had committed suicide upon the arrival of the Germans in Paris. With the help of these papers and a visa waiting for the dead man in Marseille, he now obtains money for living expenses from the local emigration organizations. Rather fortuitously he then falls in love with a woman whom he meets in a café; she just happens to be the wife of the dead writer under whose name he travels. Only his love for Marie, the dead writer's wife, moves the narrator to go through the motions of visa hunting, because the long lines of desperate applicants are repugnant to him. He is offended by "the wails and pleadings of the people [the original word used is *Winseln*—a pejorative term meaning the whining of a dog], all of whom believed they were threatened with imprisonment or death or God knows what" (p. 202). Such a remark about refugees in wartime Europe is at best unwarranted, at worst offensive. But Seghers lets her protagonist emphasize that in his opinion emigration equals cowardice and denial of one's duty to the homeland.

Prompted by his relation with Marie, the narrator begins to sympathize with the fears of the refugees. For himself, however, he sees no need to flee. He feels untouched by the rapidly spreading panic and therefore considers standing in line for visas or transits, which he does for Marie's sake, part of a game: "Everything had always passed me by. That was why I was still at large and unharmed—I knew my way about the world only too well" (p. 264). The old platitude "haste makes waste" never found truer proof than in the governmental offices and consulates of Europe in the thirties, if we accept Seghers's portrayal in *Transit*. The narrator, who feels neither pressure nor fear, is the one who achieves the goals (visa, transit, exit permit, and so forth) that the panic-stricken individuals cannot reach.

Marie departs for overseas, where she believes her husband is alive and waiting for her. Her departure ends the narrator's pose as one of those who are "desperate for departure." He gives up his papers, visa, and transit permit to another refugee and decides to go to the farm of a friend.   He wants to stay in Europe and defend the soil against Hitler's hordes: "If we shed our blood on familiar soil, something of us keeps growing there, just as it is with bushes and trees one tries to root up" (p. 311).   Marcel Reich-Ranicki terms the final lines of the novel "psychologisch völlig unglaubwürdig" ("psychologically totally unbelievable"),[20] and Mathias Wegner, in his book on exile literature, points to them as the only place where Seghers's relation to Communist ideology can be deduced.[21]   Neither of these readings acknowledges the guiding force behind *Transit*: Seghers's obsessive nostalgia for her lost homeland. The final lines of the novel are the logical conclusion of a writer paralyzed with homesickness.   For Seghers only the firm roots of *Heimat* ("home," "homeland"), of *Blut und Boden* ("Blood and Soil"), can give meaning to human existence.

Paul Rilla has called the setting of *Transit* "Kafkaesque."[22]   It is my opinion, however, that the term applies to the narrator instead.   In the Marseille of 1940 the scenario of Kafka's nightmares had become reality.   The narrator's pose of uninvolved disdain for the plight of the masses constitutes a peculiar distortion of the plot: "I didn't see anything threatening men . . .   How the time drags between . . . adventures" (pp. 202-03).   A character of equally distorted dimensions is the Polish refugee who wants to return "home."   When the German authorities deride his announced decision and bluntly outline what awaits him, he explains: "This isn't a question of my reception.   It's a question of blood and soil" (p. 292).   Finding this Nazi propaganda phrase used in a serious context by one of Hitler's victims in a book about the plight of those victims is indeed a Kafkaesque situation.

At that point in her career Seghers appears to have viewed all those who attempted to survive by leaving their homeland as deserters who evaded the responsibility of defending the land with which they were connected by ties of "blood and soil."   She exempted only the political émigrés from this duty.   The hunted majority, like the narrator's Jewish friends in the Café Source and all the other emigrants who supposedly are fleeing merely for economic or racial reasons, are referred to disdainfully as "people obsessed with a mania to get on a boat" ("abfahrtsbesessene") (p. 120).

Placing the three works within the chronological and historical context of their writing, it becomes obvious that, at a time when Communist ideology failed her, Anna Seghers filled the resulting emotional vacuum with another obsession: homesickness.

Notes

[1]Kurt Batt, *Anna Seghers: Versuch über Entwicklung und Werke* (Frankfurt/M: Röderberg, 1973), p. 81.   All

translations from German in this article, unless indicated otherwise, are by me.

2Batt, p. 88.

3Martin Jay, "Anti-Semitism and the Weimar Left," *Midstream: A Monthly Jewish Review*, 20, No. 1 (Jan. 1974), 42-50.

4Anna Seghers, *Der Ausflug der toten Mädchen und andere Erzählungen* (New York: Aurora, 1946).

5Marcel Reich-Ranicki, *Deutsche Literatur in West und Ost* (Munich: Piper, 1966), p. 377.

6Reich-Ranicki, p. 357.

7Georg Lukács, *Probleme des Realismus* (Berlin: Aufbau Verlag, 1955).

8Klaus Jarmatz, *Literatur im Exil* (Berlin: Dietz, 1966), p. 298.

9Hermann Kesten, ed., *Deutsche Literatur im Exil: Briefe europäischer Autoren 1933-1949*, Fischer Taschenbuch, 1388 (Frankfurt/M: Fischer Taschenbuch Verlag, 1973), p. 38.

10Anna Seghers, *The Seventh Cross*, trans. James A. Galston (Boston: Little, Brown and Co., 1942), pp. 6-8.

11More than ten years earlier, Carl Zuckmayer expressed similar thoughts about that particular area of Germany, its men and women, in *Der fröhliche Weinberg*. There was laughter in Zuckmayer's words, though the shadow of evil was already falling on the sunny landscape of his play.

12Batt, p. 170.

13Batt, p. 179.

14Seghers, *Der Ausflug der toten Mädchen*, p. 7.

15Reich-Ranicki, p. 337.

16Anna Seghers, *Transit*, trans. James A. Galston (Boston: Little, Brown and Co., 1944). For two recent articles on *Transit*, see Jörg Bilke in *Die deutsche Exilliteratur 1933-1945*, ed. Manfred Durzak (Stuttgart: Reclam, 1973), pp. 312-25; and Thomas A. Kamla in his book on novels in exile, "Anna Seghers: *Transit*; A Reassessment," *Confrontations with Exile: Studies in the Novel*, Europäische Hochschulschriften: Series I, German Language and Literature, 137 (Berne: Herbert Lang, and Frankfurt/M: Peter Lang, 1975), pp. 155-62.

17Batt, p. 154.

18Reich-Ranicki, p. 376. Cf. the present volume, p. 82.

19The published translation of this passage does not give a close enough approximation of the literal meaning of the original.

20Reich-Ranicki, p. 376.

21Matthias Wegner, *Exil und Literatur: Deutsche Schriftsteller im Ausland 1933-45*, 2nd rev. and enl. ed. (Frankfurt/M: Athenäum, 1968), p. 223.

22Paul Rilla, *Literatur: Kritik und Polemik* (Berlin: Bruno Henschel und Sohn, 1950), p. 233.

Ernst Waldinger: Between the Danube and the Hudson

Robert Kauf

It is an old axiom that criticism should precede theory, in other words that a literary work, or a period, or a movement, not be approached with too rigid theoretical preconceptions and that the theory should develop inductively from individual investigations, each of which follows the method it finds suitable for its particular subject. This holds true also with regard to the study of exile literature.[1]

I have chosen to analyze the work of a lyric poet because lyric poetry, properly understood, tends to provide us with the most concise and purest revelation of the literary psyche. It is revealed not only in a poem's explicit statements, but also, and especially, in the deeper structure, in that which T. S. Eliot has called "the pattern below the level of plot and character,"[2] which we can approach by paying attention to the general organization of the poem, to its imagery, figures, syntax, and lexicon.

Ernst Waldinger's work seems to have been neglected by Germanists and deserves to be better known. The first critical recognition came, interestingly enough, from the American author Ludwig Lewisohn, who met the young poet during a stay in Vienna in 1926, and was so impressed by his poetry that he devoted an essay to it in *The Nation*, an essay later reprinted in Lewisohn's collection *Of Cities and Men*. He predicts that "such work as his cannot go permanently unnoticed and unpraised."[3] A few years later, in 1933, the poet Josef Weinheber wrote in a similar vein: "It is characteristic that a lyrist, who, like Ernst Waldinger, is aware of the secret of form and the sweet nature of poetic structure and has applied this awareness in his . . . unopportunistic oeuvre . . . does not 'count' among the 'names.' . . . But because his art is genuine, it can afford to wait. And it is likely to survive the long-prophesied demise of poetry, which is proclaimed the loudest by those who have caused it."[4] And the contemporary Austrian critic Otto Breicha mentions Ernst Waldinger and Theodor Kramer, another neglected exile lyrist, as the two poets who have most strongly influenced the new generation of post-World War II Austrian poets.[5]

Born in 1896 of Jewish parents, Ernst Waldinger grew up in Neulerchenfeld, at that time a rather idyllic, quiet lower middle-class section of Vienna, away from the center of town and not far from the Vienna Woods. His lifelong love of nature, sympathy for the man in the street, and aversion to the hustle and bustle of the city may be due to the influence of this early environment. As a soldier in World War I he was seriously wounded, and his right arm and the right side of his face remained permanently paralyzed. In spite of this physical handicap, he enrolled at the University of Vienna and earned a Ph.D. in German. Then, in 1923, he married Beatrice Winternitz, a niece of Sigmund Freud's. His literary interests also date from these earliest years: he had been writing poetry since 1913 and in 1929 began translating American poets, including Santayana, Frost, Moore, Millay, Cummings, Tate, and Lowell. Waldinger proved himself a most skillful translator, with a protean ability to empathize with the styles and techniques of the various authors. In 1934, there appeared his first volume of collected poems, *Die Kuppel* [*The Cupola*]. It was followed three years later by *Der Gemmenschneider* [*The Cameo Carver*]. Just as he was beginning to establish his reputation as a poet, the German annexation of Austria in 1938 forced Waldinger, who was Jewish, to emigrate to the United States. The first decade in unfamiliar surroundings was extremely difficult for this gentle, unaggressive man who had to support a wife and two minor children while in frail health himself. Finally, in 1947, he found congenial work as Professor of German at Skidmore College. After his retirement in 1964, he moved to New York City, where he died on 1 February 1970. While in the United States, Waldinger published three volumes of poetry, *Die kühlen Bauernstuben* [*The Cool Rooms in the Peasants' Huts*], *Glück und Geduld* [*Happiness and Forebearance*], and *Ich kann mit meinem Menschenbruder sprechen* [*I Can Talk to My Brother*]. In addition, three volumes of collected poems appeared that were not edited by Waldinger himself and contained, in addition to poetry from the out-of-print volumes, some important new material. These are: *Musik für diese Zeit* [*Music for These Times*], *Zwischen Hudson und Donau* [*Between the Hudson and the Danube*], and *Gesang vor dem Abgrund* [*Song before the Abyss*].[6]

We can best discover Waldinger's central concern by looking at three poems, written at different times. The first, "Die Gestalt ist gerettet" ["The Form Has Been Saved"], is the lead poem in his first volume of verse, *Die Kuppel* (1934); the second, "Der Gemmenschneider," gives the second volume Waldinger published its name (1937); "Warum ich Sonette schreibe" ["Why I Write Sonnets"], originated in his American exile (around 1960):

Die Gestalt ist gerettet

Hat mich der Gott der Unterwelt beschworen,
Aus allen Kratern, aus der Glut der Hölle
Die Schlacke nur zu holen, das Gerölle
Porphyrner Worte mit zerrissnen Poren?

Die Verse, die das Chaos einst verloren,
Dass mir die Lava aus den Händen quölle?
Und zahlten wir dem Fährmann unsre Zölle
Und ziehn nur Schatten aus den Stygschen Toren?

Kein Nebelfetzen hängt an meinen Worten,
Wenn alle anderen Arme auch verdorrten,
Und Hohn von allen Wänden widerhallt,

Ich will den Meissel in den Marmor hau'n,
Mag spiegelnd die gerettete Gestalt
Den Himmel fangen und sich selbst beschau'n.

        (K, reprinted in Z, 58)[7]

Der Gemmenschneider

Indes rings um ihn her ein Reich verfiel,
Der Künstler Knecht nur war, dem die Tyrannen
Den Blutschein von den Blicken fortzubannen
Vielleicht befahlen, und ein Saitenspiel

Nur galt, weil Stunden ohne Sinn verrannen--,
Sass er, der Gemmenschneider, mit dem Kiel
Und schrieb ein Haupt ab, Nacken und Profil,
Und seine Finger zuckten schon und sannen,

Wie nachher sich aus eines Steines Funkeln
Der Umriss heben würde, kühl und gut:
Der Schönheit klare Grenze, die das Trübe

Nie überschwillt, ein Damm, zwar zart, doch Flut
Zerstört ihn nimmer . . . sein gedenk und übe
Im klaren Werk dich, wenn die Zeiten dunkeln.

        (G, reprinted in A, 28)[8]

Warum ich Sonette schreibe

Ich kehre zum Sonette stets zurück
In unsrer Zeit, die aller Helle bar,
Zur Form, die meine erste Liebe war,
Zur scharfen Schau und zum Gedankenglück.

Zerfällt die Welt auch, zeig ein Meisterstück
Und kein Gestammel meine eigne klar,
Die sich noch hält, trotz Chaos und Gefahr,
Und wie man seinen Abgrund überbrück,

Nicht gaukelnd über seinen Schatten spring!
Vollkommene Gestalt, Kristall, erkling,.

Gefüllt mit Wein und nicht mit Schlamm, der keimt,

Der gärt, wie trüber Urstoff und Verwesung!
Mir reimt es sich zur eigenen Genesung,
Wenn sich in dieser Welt auch nichts mehr reimt.
(A, 63) [9]

All three poems express one unwavering poetic purpose: to save by means of form, of the *Gestalt*, a world that is in danger of sinking into chaos.

In a lecture for an American audience, Waldinger explained his concept of *Gestalt* in the following manner: "[The poetic] experience must have a long period of incubation in the poet's soul before it is reborn in word, the glow of the soul. The primary flame of passionate emotion has to be purified in the mind and objectified by the molding strength of reason, in order to be cast into shape. It is the principle of form, *die Gestalt*, which has characterized the Western spirit since Homer and Virgil."[10] The vocabulary of the poems, too, provides insight into the poet's artistic ideology. Among positive words are those denoting cool reason, form, lucidity, and poetic craftsmanship: *kühl, Gedankenglück, Gestalt, Umriss, scharfe Schau, klare Grenze, Helle, Meisterstück*. Among negative terms are those associated with uncontrolled emotion, formlessness, opaqueness: *Glut, Hölle, gären, Schlacke, zerrissen, Chaos, Lava, Nebelfetzen, Flut, Schlamm, Urstoff, Verwesung, Trübe, dunkel*. The poems are essentially reflective and hortatory. The rhetorical figures are those favored by classical, or classicistic writers: rhetorical question, periphrasis, ornamental epithet, antithesis. The sentence structure at times becomes complex, as in "Der Gemmenschneider," yet it remains lucid and logical. There is also a tendency toward parallelism. These formal tendencies, for which we can find abundant evidence throughout Waldinger's work, coupled with his artistic creed, allow us to categorize his work as "classicistic." And, indeed, his work is deeply rooted in his Austrian homeland's tradition of Latinity.

When he left Austria, he did not abandon this tradition, nor his belief that the Western humanistic spirit can find its true expression only by means of such form and structure. If anything, it was strengthened by the general tendency among exile writers to regard themselves as guardians of a tradition betrayed by the barbarians in the homeland. Apostrophizing the German language in the opening poem of *Die kühlen Bauernstuben*, his first collection published in exile, he wrote:

Das Wolfsgebell, das lang die Welt erschreckte,
Und wenn's noch tausend Jahre widerhallt,
Hat nichts gemein mit deinem Wort, dem klaren,
Das mit uns flüchtete, das wir bewahren.
(B, 7)[11]

To Waldinger, the preservation of the humanistic tradition was tantamount to the preservation of the traditional lyrical forms.   Characteristically, three of the four poems in the opening section of *Die kühlen Bauernstuben* , headed "Treue zur Sprache" ["Fidelity to the Mother Tongue"], are sonnets. We thus find no radical formal break between his preexile and exile lyric, merely a tendency toward ever greater lucidity and simplicity in the latter.   He would not agree with Brecht—though he had high regard for his poetry—that the new situation necessitated a new poetic form, or that rhyming in these grim times would seem frivolous.12

To be sure, the explicit defense of traditional poetry is muted in the *Bauernstuben*, which contains primarily antiwar poems (its weakest section), nostalgic remembrances of Austria, and descriptions of New York and the poet's attempt to adjust to it.   The defense is, however, taken up with renewed vigor in later volumes, and the last collection devotes an entire group of fifteen short poems, "Das lebende Wort" ["The Living Word"], to it.   The very name of the last volume, *Ich kann mit meinem Menschenbruder sprechen*, proclaims the poet's belief in poetry as communication as opposed to poetry as an exercise in private, esoteric symbolism.   One might have expected that in the exile poems this thrust would take the form of a specific attack against the spirit of Hitler Germany, for there can be little doubt as to whom the poet refers in "Der Gemmenschneider" (published in 1937): here he alludes to tyrants and their subservient artists, emphasizing the servitude of the artist by the alliterative linkage of *Künstler* ("artist") to *Knecht* ("slave"). Contemporary parallels were *meant* to suggest themselves when the dying Marcus Aurelius laments the barbarian fog that is seeping in from across the borders ("Marc Aurel kehrt heim" ["Marcus Aurelius Returns Home"], *Z*, 50).13 But Waldinger does not avail himself of this opportunity to make the connection specific.   Though as an individual he was politically alert, there are remarkably few outright political polemics in his exile lyric.   He seems to have felt that he was fighting a more fundamental battle against a general trend of the time that transcended national boundaries and threatened the very foundations of our civilization.   In historical retrospect we perceive that Waldinger was battling against a new mannerism, a literary tendency that, as E. R. Curtius, Gustav René Hocke, and others have shown, threatens all the values held dear by the classical writer.   Mannerism rejects reality in favor of a causeless world of dreams, the fitting metaphor in favor of the unusual one, lucidity in favor of obscurity, the ordered humanistic world in favor of "paranoiac" distortion.14

Waldinger fought ceaselessly against this tendency. His fight focuses primarily on two targets.   The first and foremost, as will have become clear by now, is the man of intellect who, instead of opposing the pernicious new trend, has become its spokesman.   The enslavement of the artist by the tyrant, of which "Der Gemmenschneider" speaks, can now be interpreted in a context much wider than that of the immediate political situation.   In his essays, Waldinger minces no words: "The cult of ugliness, obtuseness and coldness of heart, the flaunting of nihilism or the overheated, explosive tension must not be the rule. As regrettable as the dehumanization and mechanization of our world are, no one forces the poet to go along."15 The word "mechanization" in this statement points to Waldinger's second target: technological civilization and its principal manifestation, the city. An early poem, "Musik für diese Zeit" (*K*, reprinted in *Musik*, p. 5), pictures the individual as an animal in the treadmill of technology—"das Tier, das blind am Göpel rennt." In his last volume, the poem "Winter der Technik" ["Winter of Technology"], using words almost identical with those of the early poem, gently chides Walt Whitman for his view that technology will bring about an age of brotherhood: "Was du nicht sahst, o mein Kamerad, war . . . / Dass wir an die Technik angespannt sind, wie das Tier am Göpel geht, / Dass sie, seelenlos selbst, uns die Seele stiehlt . . ." (*M*, 122).16

Waldinger's attitude toward America as the land of technology and New York as the metropolis par excellence is at first colored by his antitechnological and antibig-city prejudices, though he attempts to develop a fair view toward the land that had given him asylum. His position is equally far removed from Oskar Maria Graf's panegyric "New York! Zenith des Erdballs! Alles was ich bin und war, / hat sich in dich hineingesponnen!"17 and Brecht's cynical: "Ich / . . . / Finde, nachdenkend über die Hölle, sie muss / . . . Los Angeles gleichen." 18 Yet there seems to be a more compelling reason than his aversion to technology that will not allow Waldinger to feel comfortable within the American landscape, at least in the early years of his exile. In "Auf der Fähre" ["On the Ferry"], another poem addressed to Whitman, this time an homage, he observes that the old bard found his sanctuary in the limitless (*das Grenzenlose*), but that the nature of his, Waldinger's, poetic inspiration is different, and as if to underline this difference, he composes this homage in the form of a sonnet. The poet of the sharp outline and the clear boundary appears ill at ease in a country that suggests limitless expanse and in a city that seems amorphous. He tries new prosodic methods to get the new land into his poetic grip, but is not always successful.19 Thus, for example, "New York, von einem Wolkenkratzer gesehen" ["New York, Viewed from a Skyscraper"], the opening poem in a group of sixteen called "Blick auf New York" ["Looking at New York"], in *Die kühlen Bauernstuben* (*B*, 79–81), praises the gigantesque, rough-hewn beauty of this metropolis, which gives it a unique fascination unparalleled by that of any European city. Yet contrary to the expressed sentiments, the structure of the poem appears to betray mental reservations and general misgiving. The irregular rhymed free rhythms, unusual for Waldinger, suggest the chaotic nature of the metropolis, the forced rhyming (*hundertkarätiger/gewalttätiger*), incongruity. There are some trite phrases, such as "Und immer ist es ein Gipfel des Glücks, / Von den Wolkenkratzern niederzuschauen," 20 and synaesthetic images that are startling in the context of Waldinger's usual classical style: "Und überm Times Square, gleichsam als Echo von Schrein, / Steht des trunkenen Lichtes Widerschein, / Das Hymnen brüllt, orgiastisch tobend, / . . . ," and the poem ends with the clumsy line "Bis die fahle Frühstunde anhebt, lobend."21

Another poem in which the structure belies the professed sentiment is "Zwischen Hudson und Donau" ["Between the Hudson and the Danube"] (B, 18–19). It is intended as praise of both Austria and America. Written in nobly flowing hexameters, it appears to contrast objectively the principal rivers of the two nations as representative of the characteristic qualities of each country. Yet what the poet picks out in each case as characteristic for landscapes that in reality of course are quite varied, is revealing. He sees the Danube as bordered by cultivated vineyards, old castles, and cloisters: symbols of culture and civilization and images of aesthetic beauty; he perceives the American rivers as lined by factory smokestacks and plied by tugs and towboats: utilitarian highways of industrial society. Whereas the Danube is surrounded, embedded, and limited, as it were, by hilly slopes, the American landscape is described as ocean-like and infinite. Bearing in mind Waldinger's aversion to utilitarianism, industrial civilization, and that which cannot be delimited, we realize that the poet's imagery reveals what his words conceal: that despite a conscious effort to appreciate it, the immigrant writer finds the American landscape and the civilization it represents uncongenial.

There are also poems in which the optimistic pretense is dropped, and the poet is shown as a stranger in a strange land, as out of place as the horse on Forty–Seventh Street ("Ein Pferd in der 47. Strasse" ["A Horse on Forty–Seventh Street"] (B, 85) or the asters that grow wild in an empty lot in the big city ("Asternidyll in New York," A, 37).

The collections Glück und Geduld and Ich kann mit meinem Menschenbruder sprechen also contain groups of poems on America, which, however, is no longer a symbol of industrial civilization. The theme of technology plays only a minor part in the later poetry and a study of the deep structure no longer reveals any hidden resentments. The American countryside and the smaller towns replace New York as the principal topic. America is viewed with a great deal of sympathy, though not with the fervent love that is reserved for the old Austrian homeland.

The poetic ego no longer feels itself a stranger, and yet the poet is not completely at home either. Characteristically, "Fremde wird Heimat" ["The Foreign Land Becomes Home"], the first poem in a group of poems about America in Glück und Geduld, is composed in hexameters, suggesting an epic distance. There are, to be sure, poems that sing the beauty of the American landscape without qualification, such as "Herbst in Amerika" ["Autumn in America"] (M, 103), "Ulmen" ["Elms"] (M, 70), and "Am Strand von Santa Barbara" ["The Beach of Santa Barbara"] (M, 110), but there are others in which an ominous note makes the collective title for the group in Ich kann mit meinem Menschenbruder sprechen, "Aus dem Lande der Zukunft" ["From the Land of

the Future"], sound almost ironic.   For in a number of these
late poems, America becomes the melancholy landscape of old
age and of death.   The aging poet, by his own admission,
can no longer simply enjoy the beauties of nature, innocent
of all knowledge of mortality.   The thirty-one lines of "Banff
Springs, Canadian Rockies" (M, 113) contain scarcely any
description of the landscape at all.   Instead, the poet is
moved to reflect on the death of a journalist friend who had
written about that region many years before, and the poem
ends in a lament for his lost youth.

Each of the three collections of poetry published by
Waldinger during his years in America contains large groups
of poems dealing with Austria.   This is all the more remarkable because Austria plays no appreciable role in the poems
written before his emigration.[22]   Unlike his attitude toward
America, which is ambivalent and undergoes changes, his
feelings toward his former homeland that had driven him out
remain unequivocally positive.   Nostalgia alone cannot
account for this.   To understand fully why Austria is so
idealized, we shall have to turn once again to the poet's
preexile work.[23]

Throughout Waldinger's early poetry we encounter the
idea that the actual moment of experience is fleeting and
transitory--he touches here upon a problem that had also
occupied the Viennese impressionists--and that only our yearn-
ings and our memories are real: "Ach, zwischen Sehnsucht
und Erinnerung / Ist unser ganzes Dasein nur ein Nu."[24]
The last stanza of "Der Primelstrauss" ["The Primrose Bou-
quet"] (G, 33) states even more categorically: Life *is* memory, "Denn Leben heisst Gedenken, anders nicht!"[25]

This idea is applied to the concept of "Heimat" ["Homeland"] in the poem of the same name (K, reprinted in *Musik*,
11).   It opens, as do so many poems of Waldinger's, with
a rhetorical question: "Hat er [der Bauer] die Heimat mehr,
weil sie ihm zinst, / Weil ihm das Brot auf eignen Feldern
wächst?"[26]   The answer is given in the second stanza:

> Nur der hat Heimat, der die Sehnsucht hat:
> Der Strotter, der im Staub der Strassen zieht,
> Wer Sonntags früh hinaus ins Freie flieht
> Und heimkehrt und in nächtlich-stiller Stadt
> Vorm Haustor steht--wie einen Wiesenstrauss
> Trägt er sie mit ins dunkle Treppenhaus.[27]

There follows a catalogue of visual and olfactory impressions
that the city dweller has carried home with him from the
country; the last stanza sums up and reemphasizes:

> Der Bauer hat sie nicht, er hat die Erde;
> . . . .
> Nur der hat Heimat, der die Sehnsucht hat.[28]

It is not the person in daily physical contact with the soil
who has *Heimat*, then; only the person who is away from it
and has preserved it in his memory and longs for it.   An
ocean had to come between the poet and his native land

before the idea of the Austrian *Heimat* could develop out of memory and longing.

As the country that sheltered him in his boyhood, Austria is also seen as the poet's metaphorical mother who taught him how to speak and gave him a soul, as seen in this excerpt from "Von der Liebe zur Heimat" ["Love for the Homeland"]:

> Die Heimat ist wie eine Melodie,
> Ein Ammenlied, ins Herz dir eingesungen--
> Du nahst im Geist ihr wie der Mutter Knie,
> Das deine Kinderarme einst umschlungen.
>
> . . . .
>
> Die Heimat, die dir Wort und Seele lieh,
> Du atmest sie wie Bergluft in die Lungen.
>
> (*Gl*, 58)[29]

Austria is associated with the poet's boyhood and all the happy attributes that go with this time.   For youth still possesses the innocence and harmony of nature.   And for Waldinger, nature is a source of special strength.   Its contemplation raises him up when he despairs.   The little spider by his window, weaving its web humbly, patiently, and singlemindedly and thus following the dictates of the inner, timeless law of its being while empires crumble around it, encourages the artist to follow his inner voice patiently, unopportunistically, and unswervingly, regardless of literary fashions and political cataclysms ("Spinnennetz am Fenster" ["Spiderweb by the Window"] [*A*, 26]).

Existence in harmony with nature is for Waldinger authentic existence.   And in his mind he stylizes Austria into a land that still respects the rhythm of nature, a "Land der sanften Kraft" ["Land of Gentle Strength"] (the title of the group of poems on Austria in *Bauernstuben*), where city and country, *Natur* and *Kultur*, strike a happy, harmonious balance ("Acht Walzertakte" ["Eight Waltz Measures"] [*B*, 34]). A look at the poem "Die kühlen Bauernstuben" ["The Cool Rooms in the Peasants' Huts"] shows that an Austria thus stylized turns into a symbol of that which the poet artistically affirms; a similarly stylized Manhattan, into that which he rejects:

> In der Inselhitze von Manhattan,
> Wo das Hemd mir feucht am Leibe klebt,
> Steil sich Turm um Turm mit strengem Schatten
> In den glühenden Julihimmel hebt,
>
> Denk ich an der Bauernstuben Kühle
> Einer fernen Ferienzeit zurück;
> Ein Jahrhundert, das ich lasten fühle,
> Trennt dies Heut von jenem Knabenglück . . .[30]

The following four stanzas give a loving recollection of Austrian farm cottages.   Olfactory impressions, as so often in Waldinger's poetry, play a major role.   The last stanza again contrasts the idyllic memories to present realities:

All das kommt auf einmal zu mir heim,

Ist in mir, indes es ohne Pause
Fortlärmt, brodelnd, zwischen dem Beton,
Freundlich wirklicher,--da es zu Hause
Hass und Wahn gewitterfalb umlohn.

(B, 14)[31]

We note the association of boyhood and homeland by means of the explicit reference to *Knabenglück* ("boyhood happiness"). Austrian land and life is presented to conform to a Stifter-like ideal of a life in close communion and rhythm with nature. Contrasted to it is life in Manhattan, the prototype of the industrial hell: hot, chaotic, noisy. These attributes, as we know, are also used in connection with the kind of chaotic art Waldinger loathes, whereas the cool interiors of the farm houses suggest the coolness and clarity of the poetry he favors. Finally, the last stanza contains a timely--and for exile literature characteristic--variant on Waldinger's theme that only he has a homeland who recreates it in his mind. Although the physical homeland is tarnished by the political realities, the real homeland, the true Austria, is preserved pure in the mind and memory of the exile writer.[32]

Waldinger was well aware that he was drawing an ideal landscape ("mag . . . der Traum / Die Heimat goldner zeigen")[33] and that a return to the real Austria was going to bring disappointment. Though at times tempted to settle again in his former homeland, he ultimately decided, like so many of his fellow exiles, to remain in the United States, the country of his children and grandchildren. Still, Austria remained his *Orplid*, his island of dreams, and some of his happiest poems were inspired by it.[34]

Notes

[1] Cf. Karl O. Paetel, "Die deutsche Emigration der Hitlerzeit," *Neue politische Literatur*, 5, No. 6 (1960), 465-82.

[2] T. S. Eliot, "Hamlet," *Selected Essays* (London: Faber & Faber, 1932), pp. 141-46.

[3] Ludwig Lewisohn, "An Unknown Poet," *The Nation*, 123 (1926), 364.

[4] Josef Weinheber, *Sämtliche Werke* (Salzburg: O. Müller, 1954), IV, 370. All translations in the article are mine. I thank my colleague Robert R. Heitner for valuable suggestions in connection with the translation of the poems.

[5] Otto Breicha, "Die neue österreichische Lyrik nach 1945: Versuch einer historischen Skizze," *Wort in der Zeit*, 10, No. 2 (Feb. 1964), 4-5.

[6] For more detailed biographical information see Ernst Schönwiese's introduction to *Gesang vor dem Abgrund* (Graz: Stiasny, 1961).

[7] The following abbreviations will be used in the text: K for *Die Kuppel* (Vienna: Saturn, 1934); G for *Der Gemmen-*

schneider (Vienna: Saturn, 1937); *B* for *Die kühlen Bauern-stuben* (New York: Aurora, 1946); *Musik* for *Musik für diese Zeit*, ed. Ernst Schönwiese (Munich: W. Weismann, 1946); *Gl* for *Glück und Geduld* (New York: F. Ungar, 1952); *Z* for *Zwischen Hudson und Donau*, ed. Rudolf Felmayer (Vienna: Bergland, 1958); *A* for *Gesang vor dem Abgrund*, ed. Ernst Schönwiese (Graz: Stiasny, 1961); *M* for *Ich kann mit meinem Menschenbruder sprechen* (Vienna: Bergland, 1965). If a poem from a prewar volume has been reprinted in a later collection, reference will always be made to the latter, because the prewar volumes are not easily accessible. My translation of "Die Gestalt ist gerettet" ["The Form Has Been Saved"] follows: "Have I been charged by the god of the underworld / to gather merely the dross / from all the craters and fires of hell, / words once porphyry but now a debris of mangled pores? // Verses, long lost in chaos, / so that as lava they may now gush forth from my hands? / And did we then pay the boatman our tribute, / and are we going out through the Stygian gates as mere shades? // No shred of fog hangs from my words, / even though all other arms may have withered, / and though scorn resounds from every wall. // I want to hew the marble with my chisel, / then may the rescued form / catch Heaven like a mirror and contemplate itself therein." (Because of syntax, placement of virgules is sometimes only approximate.)

8 "The Cameo Carver": "While an empire crumbled round about him / and the artist was just a slave whom tyrants / might command to banish from their eyes the sight of blood, / and the sound of a lyre // Was valued only as a means of killing time-- / there sat the cameo carver / tracing a head, its neck and profile, with his quill, / and his fingers began to quiver in anticipation of // How by and by the outline would emerge, cool and good, / from the sparkling stone: / the clear boundary line of beauty, which turbid waters // Can never overflow, a dam, though fragile, that no flood / can ever penetrate . . . keep him in mind and practice / your lucid art when the times grow dark."

9 "Why I Write Sonnets": "In our time, which is so utterly lacking in brightness, / I keep returning to the sonnet form, / my first love, because of its sharp vision and its happy way of shaping thoughts. // Even though this world crumbles, let a masterpiece, / not something incoherent, clearly show forth *my* world, / which still holds together in the midst of chaos and peril, / and show how one may cross one's abyss, // *Not* how one may leap delusively over one's own shadow! / Ring out, perfect form, you crystal / filled with wine and not with germinating slime // Fermenting with turbid primeval matter and with putrefaction! / As for me, the rhyme restores *my* reason, / at a time when all rhyme and reason have fled the world."

10 Ernst Waldinger, "Tradition and Poetry," *Bulletin of Skidmore College* (Saratoga Springs, N.Y.), 46, No. 1 (Sept. 1960), 9.

11 Translation from "An die deutsche Sprache in der Zeit der Greuel" ["To the German Language in the Days of Hor-

ror"]: "The howling of the wolves that has been scaring the world, / though it were to continue for a thousand years, / has nothing in common with your lucid word, / which emigrated with us and which we preserve."

12 "Da das Instrument verstimmt ist / Sind die alten Notenbücher wertlos / Und so braucht ihr einige neue Griffe" ("The old musical literature has become worthless / because the instruments are out of tune / and therefore you need to learn some new touches"), Brecht, *Gesammelte Werke in 20 Bänden*, Werkausgabe edition suhrkamp (Frankfurt/M: Suhrkamp, 1967), IX, 624.   "In meinem Lied ein Reim / Käme mir fast vor wie Übermut," *Gesammelte Werke*, IX, 744; English version: "In my poetry a rhyme / Would seem to me almost insolent," Brecht, *Poems*, ed. John Willett and Ralph Manheim with the cooperation of Erich Fried (London: Eyre Methuen, 1976), p. 331.

13 In Waldinger's poetry many of its protagonists and images are taken from classical antiquity.   Marcus Aurelius, the Roman emperor who died in Vienna, is an especially appropriate symbol for the synthesis of the Austrian and the Roman spirit.

14 Cf. Gustav René Hocke, *Manierismus in der Literatur* (Reinbek bei Hamburg: Rowohlt, 1959).

15 Ernst Waldinger, "Tradition und Lyrik," *Wort in der Zeit*, 3, No. 5 (May 1957), 19.

16 "What you did not see, O my comrade, was . . . / that we are harnessed to technology like an animal to the treadmill, / that technology, being without a soul itself, steals *our* soul."

17 "New York!   Zenith of the globe!   All that I am and was / has entwined itself within you!" (Oskar Maria Graf, "Ode an New York," *Aufbau* [New York], 21, No. 52, 30 Dec. 1955, p. 13.

18 Brecht, "Nachdenkend über die Hölle," *GW*, X, 830; English version in Brecht, *Poems*, p. 367: "On Thinking about Hell": ". . . I / . . . / Find, on thinking about Hell, that it must be / Still more like Los Angeles."

19 Years later he admits in "Semmering: Gedanken an New York" ["Semmering: Thoughts of New York"]: "Fifth Avenue und Broadway, Mahlstrom des Gewimmels, / Von dem ich einst bei Poe als Knabe las, / Kalt, fremd und herzlos schien er mir wie ihm, / Als ich zum ersten Mal zu schlendern hier versuchte, / Nicht liess es mühlos sich in Reime fassen, / Nur der Hexameter mit seiner Meerflut, / Unendlich rollend, er war ihm gewachsen" (*M*, 94).   ("Maelstrom of crowds, Fifth Avenue and Broadway, / of which I read as a boy in the works of Poe, / cold, strange, and heartless did it seem to me as it did to him, / the first time I tried to stroll here. / I was unable to capture it effortlessly in rhymes; / the hexameter only, rolling unendingly like the sea, seemed equal to it.")

20 "And it is always the height of happiness / to look down from the skyscrapers."

21 "And over Times Square, like an echo of shouts, as it were, / stands the reflection of intoxicated light, / roar-

ing out hymns, raving orgiastically / . . . until the pale morning hour arises, singing praises."

22Waldinger admits in "Verschämte Liebe" ["Bashful Affection"]: "Es hat als Mann mir erst das fremde Land, / Das neue, drin so gut sich's hausen liess, / Und nicht die Heimat, die mich schnöd verstiess, / Die Zunge, die zu singen doch verstand, / So spät gelockert . . ." (*M*, 82). ("Only the new, the foreign land, / which was so good to me, / and not the homeland, which expelled me shabbily, / has loosed so late in life / my tongue, which after all knew how to sing.")

23The unequivocal praise of Austria does not always extend to the Austrian populace or to individual Austrians such as Josef Weinheber, the former friend, whom Waldinger never forgave for becoming a supporter of Hitler. These critical poems, though, are comparatively rare, as is "hate poetry" in general, which Werner Vordtriede considers one of the typical genres of exile literature. See "Der Josefsplatz" ["Joseph Square"] (*B*, 28), "Der falsche Prophet" ["The False Prophet"], "Bettel-Wien" ["Vienna, Beggar City"], "Der Narrenturm" ["Fool's Prison"] (*Gl*, 30, 66, 68); Vordtriede, "Vorläufige Gedanken zu einer Typologie der Exilliteratur," *Akzente*, 15, No. 6 (Dec. 1968), 571.

24 From "Ton in des Schöpfers Hand" ["Clay in the Creator's Hand"], in *K*, reprinted in *A*, 40: "Oh, between longing and memory our entire life is but a fleeting moment."

25"For life is memory, nothing else."

26"Has the peasant more homeland because he pays tribute to the soil, / because his bread grows in his own fields?"

27"Only he who knows longing has a homeland: / the hobo who walks on the dusty roads, / the person who early on Sunday flees the city for the country, / returning home at nighttime and stands before his door in the night-quiet town, / he carries it [the homeland] with him into the dark stairhalls of his apartment house / like a bunch of wildflowers."

28"The peasant does not have it [the homeland], he has the soil. / . . . / *He* only has a homeland who knows longing."

29"The homeland is like a melody, / a nurse's song sung into your heart-- / in your mind you approach it like your mother's knee, / which your child's arms once embraced. / . . . / The homeland that gave you language and soul, / like mountain air you breathe it into your lungs."

30"On the steaming island of Manhattan / where the shirt sticks moistly to my body / and towers with somber shade crowd / into the scorching summer skies, // I remember the cool rooms of the peasants' huts / of distant vacation days; / it seems as if a century--and how it weighs!-- / separates Today from those times of boyhood happiness."

31"All this suddenly comes back to me, // is *in* me friendly and more real, / while outside there is constant noise and hubbub, / and back home / hatred and insanity burn round about it in stormy colors."

32 See also "Der Josefsplatz" ["Joseph Square"] (B, 28), in which the poet addresses a traitor: "Doch hast du ihn [den Josefsplatz] verraten, wie dies Wien, / Das nimmermehr in Wirklichkeit besteht, / Obwohl du es durchschreitest, während ich, / Es in die Fremde, in die Wahrheit selbst, / Herüber in mein Herz gerettet habe." ("But you betrayed the Joseph Square as you betrayed Vienna, / which no longer really exists, / although you walk through it, while I / have rescued it into the strange land, into truth, / into my heart.") Similarly in "Hadersfeld bei Greifenstein" (B, 40): "Unwirklich scheint es, besser kann ich's retten / . . . / Und in den Schatten der Erinnerung betten." ("It seems unreal, I can rescue it better. / . . . / and bed it in the shadow of my memory.")

33"Heimweh" ["Homesickness"], M, 84: "The dream may make the homeland appear in a more golden light."

34Other frequent themes of Waldinger's poetry are nature and artifacts. The nature poems, mainly on flora and often in sonnet form, frequently portray a somewhat anthropomorphized nature--an early group of nature poems is characteristically called "Der verwandelte Hain" ["The Metamorphosed Grove"]. The poems on artifacts provide the defender of the humanistic tradition with an opportunity to celebrate the creations of the human spirit. There are remarkably few poems dealing with Hitler Germany. More important are the poems in which Waldinger affirms his Jewishness. The Jew is the symbol for the righteous man who is exiled and made an outcast in an unrighteous world ("Der fremde Jude" ["The Foreign Jew"] [M, 143]); Judaism is an attempt to order, hallow, and humanize our chaotic existence ("Sabbatausgang" ["The End of the Sabbath"] [M, 142]) and a sign of hope and promise that the humane spirit has not been completely obliterated in these days of darkness ("Siebenarmiger Leuchter" ["Seven-branched Candelabrum"] [M, 139]). See also my "Ernst Waldinger: Stiller Dichter in lärmender Zeit," *Wiener Bücherbriefe*, 6 (1966), 181-86.

Franz Werfel's Image of America

Lore B. Foltin

Franz Werfel, one of the most important German writers to find refuge from Hitler in the United States, produced the greater portion of his late and best-known works in California. The image of America in Werfel's works changed significantly during the course of his stay in this country (from 1940 to his death in 1945), and this change can be better understood if it is considered within the framework of America's reception in German letters. A comprehensive survey of the image of America in German literature was provided by Harold Jantz.[1] Other studies, confined mainly to the nineteenth century, are those by Paul C. Weber and Hildegard Meyer.[2] Finally, there is a substantial number of studies about America in the works of twentieth-century German authors, especially in the works of writers after 1945.[3] Many of the writers who experienced America as a land of exile and asylum after 1933 expressed their views and impressions of America in autobiographical works. Thomas Mann's *Die Entstehung des Doktor Faustus* [*The Genesis of a Novel*],[4] Carl Zuckmayer's *Als wär's ein Stück von mir* [*Part of Myself*],[5] and Salka Viertel's *Das unbelehrbare Herz* [*The Kindness of Strangers*][6] are representative examples. Werfel's antipathy toward such "outpourings of the heart" and his desire to let his work and the ideas contained in it speak for themselves account for the fact that he did not produce such autobiographical work himself. One is nonetheless able to trace Werfel's change of attitude toward America through his work.

Werfel had a special relationship to America from the very beginning of his literary career. When his first volume of poems *Der Weltfreund* [*Friend of Mankind*] appeared in 1911, his contemporaries and critics compared him to Walt Whitman. Ernst Stadler, for example, saw in these poems "a new and fervent intensity"[7] characteristic of Whitman. Werfel himself emphasized Whitman's influence and often discussed it with Johannes Urzidil and Willy Haas, friends of his youth from Prague. Thus he himself contributed to the myth of his poetic kinship with Whitman, although it was

many years before he wrote explicitly about this relationship.
    There were many parallels between the two poets: one
is the long metrical line with the slowly unfolding rhythm.
But despite such a formal similarity, the pantheism of Whitman's youth contrasts sharply with Werfel's own theology,
in which creation itself constitutes sin. The isolation of the
individual places man in a condition of sin that can be
expiated only by sympathy, compassion, and brotherly love.
Such emotions do not refer to some idealized, universal, or
abstract "mankind," but relate specifically to the Negro, the
acrobat, the servant girl, and other social and cultural
déclassées, as they are called in the poem "An den Leser"
["To the Reader"].
    In his article "Thanks" (1941) Werfel writes:

> I was seventeen or eighteen when Walt Whitman's *Leaves
> of Grass* fell into my hands. I can never forget those
> intoxicated days when my mind was inundated by this
> Mississippi of poetry. Until that time I had believed
> there was an aristocratic hierarchy of objects suitable
> for poetry. But Walt Whitman taught me and my genera-
> tion that in the realm of reality there is nothing com-
> monplace; that in the simplest word, the commonest
> designation, the most shopworn idea there lies hidden
> an explosive force surpassing a thousandfold that
> which is esthetically sanctified. Walt Whitman, this
> prophet of a cosmic democracy, taught us far more:
> that a mysterious, a divine stream of love fills the
> universe--a stream in whose embrace all creatures alike
> receive their religious value. And through his own
> mighty example he showed us that the poet can be the
> antenna of the stream. The example of this Homeric
> American continues to work upon a future yet unknown.[8]

In this same article Werfel further names Edgar Allan Poe as
an influence on his intellectual development. His contact
with Poe also dated back to his youth. For Werfel, Poe constituted the greatest architect of lyric poetry. Having called
Whitman the Mississippi of poetry, he saw Poe as one of the
"subterranean rivers whose melancholy water, winding through
caves and grottoes and rocky domes, have never been beheld
by mortal eyes." When one thinks of the sinister winter garden in Werfel's later *Stern der Ungeborenen* [*Star of the
Unborn*][9] with its cradle graves of retrogenetic humus, the
gruesome canal waters, the beastly expectant midwives, and
the lake of forgetfulness, then the line back to Poe is not
difficult to trace. Willy Haas, who notes Werfel's love of
reciting Poe's lyric, suggests a more direct line of influence
between Poe's *The Facts of the Case of M. Valdemar* and
Werfel's *Der Tod des Kleinbürgers*, 1927 [*The Man Who Conquered Death*]. Besides Whitman and Poe, Werfel came to
hold other American authors, such as Sinclair Lewis, Eugene
O'Neill, Ernest Hemingway, Pearl S. Buck, and Thomas Wolfe,
in high esteem. But in his youth his enthusiasm was for
Whitman and Poe.

Werfel's creative production during the period 1911–20 concentrated on poetry. *Der Weltfreund* had made Werfel famous overnight, and the poem cycles *Wir sind*, 1913 [*We Exist*], *Einander*, 1915 [*Each Other*] and *Gerichtstag*, 1919 [*Day of Judgment*] followed that volume. Only a small portion of this prodigious lyrical production was ever translated into English, and what was translated found little response. The husband and wife team of Avrahm Yarmolinsky and Babette Deutsch included nine of Werfel's poems in their anthology, *Contemporary German Poetry*,10 and individual poems appeared in translation in the periodicals *Poetry*, *The Nation*, and *Poet Lore*.

After the end of the war, Werfel wrote his first larger prose work, the *Novelle Nicht der Mörder, der Ermordete ist schuldig*, 1920 [*Not the Murderer*], whose overall theme is the conflict between generations. After the protagonist of the *Novelle*, Karl Duschek, has served his sentence in a military prison, he emigrates to America. How does this refuge, America, look to Karl Duschek? "After a ten days' voyage I beheld the great Statue of Liberty; across the bay the faint sound of music and traffic came to my ears. It was the first of August, nineteen hundred and fourteen."11 In the epilogue the narrator says: "I will give back my stock to the earth, the freed, limitless earth, that she may absolve us of all our murders, our vanities, sadisms, the corruptions born of our urban, huddled lives" (p. 692). Thus, in the end, it is not the America of the cities, but of the "freed, limitless earth" that is accorded the ability to liberate, indeed to "absolve." In accordance with his wish, Karl Duschek becomes a farmer in the West, marries an American girl, and begins a new life. America appears here in a positive light, idealized, free of the "dreams of cripples, the downtrodden, perverted, flippant, revengeful" souls of old Europe (p. 691).

It was not through his lyrics or his *Novelle* that Werfel's name became known to the American public, but through his drama *Bocksgesang* [*Goat Song*], produced by the Theatre Guild of New York on 25 January 1926.12 Judging by the reviews of the production, it is apparent that American critics ignored the figure of the American in the drama. Because they were mainly concerned with interpretations of the drama, especially concentrating on the goatlike creature of the title, it is quite understandable that they failed to single out the treatment of the American from among the characters. How does Werfel portray the American in *Goat Song*? According to the stage directions, Werfel has the American appear in ragged farm clothes, with long leather boots and a sombrero! Again, as in *Not the Murderer*, Werfel is portraying a rural America, not the bustling cities of a new continent, and an America he has not yet seen. The American in *Goat Song* is proud of his "wonderful country" (p. 54) where people from all over the world come together. He lauds the freedom in the New World and the absence of class structure: "They are free and obey no one. . . . No man thinks himself better than the rest, and the son of the hanged and the daughter of the whore have nothing to fear there" (pp. 54–55). One is reminded of Goethe's Faust in Part II who envisions himself standing "with free men on free ground." In his embodiment of both the possibility and actuality of such an ideal condition, the American becomes a spokesman for the homeless, just as Werfel himself became a spokesman for the exiles some twenty years later.

The historical drama *Juarez and Maximilian* was written in 1924.[13] As soon as the curtain rises, the first figure to speak is that of an American by the name of Clark, a war correspondent for the *New York Herald*. He considers himself an antimonarchist and democratic reporter; he talks of the "friendship and brotherly love" of the United States for Mexico. As depicted by Werfel with much irony, this newspaper reporter is intent on reporting "moving events" and giving "sympathetic accounts" even where none exist, since that is the wish of his editor and the American government. His democratic attitude soon reveals itself to be less than genuine, for he stresses negatively the assimilation of the Indian population by Mexico as opposed to their continued segregation in North America.

In *Not the Murderer* and *Goat Song* Werfel's image of nineteenth-century America remains vital and salutary, but a change in his attitude shows through in *Juarez and Maximilian*. The reporter Mr. Clark has no longer any connection with the Golden West that enabled failures to begin a new life; he is a modern and urban man full of ambivalence. He pays homage to democratic ideals in principle, but for him Indians are nothing but "Redskins," that is, second-class human beings.

Werfel was to become even more skeptical of America as political trends in Europe became clear. Seeking influence in influential quarters, Werfel engaged in public speeches, the first of which was entitled "Realismus und Innerlichkeit" ["Realism and Inwardness"], and was held on 6 May 1931 before the Kulturbund in Vienna.[14] In this talk, he refers more than once to America in an uncomplimentary tone, and he nearly always mentions America in the same breath with Soviet Russia. "The deadly mandibles of America and Russia," he states, threaten to seize the "superannuated culture of Europe" (p. 5). And again: "The United States and the Union of Soviet Socialist Republics are identical in their radical realism" (p. 6). What does Werfel understand by "radical realism"? He means a surrogate for the spiritual and intellectual values of the Western world, a materialistic world view that results in the loss of inner, subjective values, hence the title "Realismus und Innerlichkeit." Werfel sees the beginnings of this material way of thinking in the French Revolution, whose moral principle he describes as "the saving grace of the work ethic" (p. 12). Out of this material attitude arises the exaggerated ethical value placed on work and the overemphasis on physical culture—Werfel speaks sarcastically of "body worship" (p. 9). Though radical realism, according to Werfel, is most evident in the Soviet Union and the United States, other countries share in this cultural trait.   The Soviets have made it an official dogma of the state, according to which class consciousness is to guarantee human happiness; the American version of this ideology views man as determined by his functions and reactions, that is, behaviorism.   In the latter case, Werfel sees John B. Watson, whose book *Behaviorism* appeared in 1925, as partly responsible for the misery of the modern-day American.   He also blames American journalism, without which he believes there would be no underworld.   All of these value judgments fall in a period prior to Werfel's arrival on American soil.

Werfel came to the New World on 12 November 1935 on the occasion of the production of his biblical drama *Der Weg der Verheissung* [*The Eternal Road*].[15]   The play was intended to answer the wave of lies and hate that poured forth over the world from Hitler's Germany by showing the unchanging values of the Bible.   Werfel saw America as the ideal place for the premiere for two reasons: on the one hand was the strong American Bible tradition, and on the other was the dangerously superior role accorded the natural sciences in America.   The drama was meant to prove to scientifically oriented Americans that mankind can find salvation and redemption only in religion, not in science.   It need not be emphasized that Werfel had little success with this missionary undertaking.   His intention to attend the premiere of *The Eternal Road* was never realized.   The preparations for the production, directed by Max Reinhardt, consumed enormous sums of money and became so protracted that Werfel finally returned to Europe without having seen it performed on stage.

During his stay in New York, Werfel gave several interviews in which he expressed his opinions of America.   Edited quotations in newspapers cannot always be taken at face value, but one can nevertheless assume that serious reporters such as Agnes E. Meyer, a friend of Thomas Mann, offered in good conscience an accurate accounting of Werfel's views.[16]   It is clear from these interviews that Werfel's one-sided judgment of America has shifted, that he no longer maintains his recent wholesale condemnations.   His comments are best understood in the context of the times: Werfel's novel *Die vierzig Tage des Musa Dagh* [*The Forty Days of Musa Dagh*] was blacklisted in Germany and hailed as a great achievement in America.[17]

Werfel returned to America on 13 October 1940 as an exile.   He did not pause to recover from the hardships of his flight into exile.   During his ten-week stay in New York, he lectured and wrote an article "Unser Weg geht weiter" ["Our Path Goes On"] for the *Aufbau* in New York.[18]   In this article Werfel attempts to trace the causes of modern anti-Semitism, which by 1940 had broken out of its previous "provincial boundaries" to become the basis of a "religious war with global dimensions."   Werfel writes: "England is making the frontal assault in this holy war.   If England falls, American democracy falls."   American democracy!   Werfel assumes a priori that America is a democracy and represents the last bulwark against the forces of evil. Neither the image of a sparsely settled West of nineteenth-century America as portrayed in *Not the Murderer* and *Goat Song*, nor the image of an America with "deadly mandibles" as portrayed in "Realismus und Innerlichkeit" is evoked here, but America as the most reliable ally of those who are fighting "for the salvation of the entire world."

On 16 March 1941, Werfel delivered a radio address as guest speaker of the National Broadcasting Company over station KECA in Los Angeles. The program, "I'm an American," was arranged by the United States Department of Justice and took the form of a dialogue, in which William A. Carmichael from the Immigration and Naturalization Service in Los Angeles asked questions to which Werfel responded.[19] Werfel said: "As I sailed into the harbor of New York, the Statue of Liberty looked like an angel of Paradise. You can understand that being an American is a very sacred matter to one who knows what it means to be denied those liberties that are guaranteed by the American Constitution. Americans are lucky people!" Later in the program he said: "America is more than a country and more than a people. It is an enormous continent and a unique amalgam of strong races. America's greatness, its freedom, its way of life overwhelm me." These words show clearly Werfel's new attitude toward America, an attitude conditioned by the fact of his exile. Werfel became even more exuberant: ". . . in articles I wrote many years ago I stated my firm belief that America was destined to defend victoriously eternal values—Christian values, against the Blitzkrieg of Satan. I wrote that America will be the phoenix that arises triumphant from world conflagration. So you see, I have long been an American at heart through my faith in her." Perhaps Werfel was referring to his essay "Betrachtungen über den Krieg von morgen" ["Reflections About the Next War"], which appeared in 1938.[20] The main argument in that essay is that the wars of the future will be fought on an ideological rather than a nationalistic basis. However, direct comments about America and a reference to the radiant American phoenix do not appear there, and Werfel's comments are better taken simply as an avowal of the emigrant toward his country of refuge.

Werfel was one of the most successful of the exiled writers. His novels *Der veruntreute Himmel* [*Embezzled Heaven*], written in French exile, and *Das Lied von Bernadette* [*The Song of Bernadette*] were accepted by the Book-of-the-Month Club, making them accessible to a very large reading public. When the Bernadette story was filmed in 1943, he achieved financial as well as popular success. America offered him not only asylum but also recognition and honors—the University of California at Los Angeles awarded him an honorary doctorate on 9 June 1943. It is therefore quite understandable that he saw the country in an increasingly friendly light, as interviews held in the last years of his life reveal.

Werfel's last novel, *Star of the Unborn*, takes place in a California of the far distant future. He writes the book as a man marked for death, for he had experienced several severe heart attacks. Calling the book a *Reiseroman* ("travel novel") in conscious reference to that literary tradition, he spoke about its relationship to the *Divine Comedy* and *Gulliver's Travels* in an interview with the *Santa Barbara News Press*.[21]

The narrator in *Star of the Unborn*, whose initials F. W. emphasize the autobiographical character of many events of the novel, says of California:

> It is appropriately called a paradise, although certain snobs have been known to make disparaging remarks about this lovely spot and there are even some who claim to prefer the flat Florida landscape to the diversified West Coast. These snobs slanderously call California a desert covered with artificial luxuriance, whose rouged roses, bougainvilleas, poinsettias, and other flowers have no fragrance, whose fruits and vegetables have no savour, whose inhabitants are good-looking, but somehow "Lemurian." That is because long before the beginnings of mankind as we know it, California was part of the submerged continent of Lemuria. That may have influenced the character of the Californians. The Lemurians seem to have been a shadowy, trifling race, whitewashed gravestones, in a word, actors, who deceived the world with gay and false pretense devoid of true substance. There is a contemporary expression for this Lemurian characteristic, the word "phony." And so the snobs of today—I mean our own today or yesterday—turn up their noses at California, chiefly because a certain famous city in that state produces films, those fantastic photographic tales that have become the vogue of their time, although, or perhaps precisely because, they are Lemurian.[22]

The narrator F. W. then describes in words of rapture the rich variety of the California landscape, the snow-capped mountains and the Pacific Ocean: "Between them are broad valleys planted with fabulous orchards—oranges, lemons, grapefruit. They blossom year round with a fragrance that beggars description. And in April even the deserts bloom, pink and violet with their countless cacti. Wherever you turn the mountains tower in the blue distance" (pp. 16-17). When one reads these words of Werfel, one can, in my opinion, only partially agree with Alois Dempf, who writes that Werfel directed his piquant humor and wildly satirical fantasy *against* [my italics] California."[23]   Dempf's point is certainly debatable. For example, transposed, during a séance, from death into the "astromental" civilization of the year 100,000, F. W. learns that the Christian revival emanated from America after the Americans could no longer tolerate "high speed": "The Americans were suddenly not able to stand any degree of speed. In any form of locomotion that exceeded twenty-five miles per hour they fell victim to a critical cerebral anemia that assumed epidemic character." And so forth. A further symptomatic disease of this era was

the so-called "plutophobia," a skin disease, "a sort of aller-
gic psoriasis that was induced by the sight of drafts, stocks,
bonds, mortgages, but especially of long, complicated con-
tracts. . . . The Congress in Washington was obliged to
adopt an amendment to the Constitution by virtue of which
the economic law of supply and demand was declared null
and void" (pp. 187-88).

   This and similar passages in the book are full of exuberant parody.   They can be read as the judgment of an
author who knows the weaknesses of America and criticizes
them but does not reject the country.   It is not satire by a
despondent author, as is often claimed, but humor born of
the time and place.

   Werfel did not live to see publication of his book.   In
his last preserved letter, written from Santa Barbara on
18 August 1945 to the Austrian writer Friedrich Torberg, he
compares the work on his "travel novel" with the legendary
ride across Lake Constance and hopes he will not have to
share the fate of that rider.   But the rider's fate overtook
him too, for on 26 August, just a few days after completion
of the book, he died.

   Werfel's opinion of America swings like a pendulum
from positive in the beginning to negative later.   Then,
toward the end of his life, shaped by the experience of exile,
the positive and negative aspects neutralize each other.   Werfel, the friend of the world, was not a man to brood away
his time in bitterness and isolation.   On the contrary, his
last creative period in exile is mellow with humor.   America
was, for him, intellectually a mixed experience, perhaps as
it was for many exiles, but it was undeniably the environment that brought him great literary triumph and personal
recognition.   Especially with *The Song of Bernadette*, he
became a revered author to the mainstream of the American
public.   Even though Werfel could resort to polemics and
criticism, his love for his fellow man—and America's appreciation of him—triumphed.

Translated by Adrienne Ash

Notes

[1] Harold Jantz, "Amerika im deutschen Dichten und Denken," in *Deutsche Philologie im Aufriss*, ed. Wolfgang
Stammler, 2nd ed. (Berlin: Erich Schmidt, 1962), III, col.
309-72; see also Horst Oppel, "Amerikanische Literatur," in
Reallexikon der deutschen Literaturgeschichte, ed. Werner Kohlschmidt and Wolfgang Mohr, 2nd ed. (Berlin: Walter
de Gruyter, 1958), I, 47-60.

[2] Paul C. Weber, *America in the Imaginative Literature of the First Half of the Nineteenth Century* (New
York: Columbia University Press, 1926); Hildegard Meyer,
*Nord-Amerika im Urteil des deutschen Schrifttums bis
zur Mitte des 19. Jahrhunderts: Eine Untersuchung über*

Kürnbergers "Amerika-Müden"; Mit einer Bibliographie von Hildegard Meyer (Hamburg: Friderichsen, de Gruyter & Co., 1929). See also: *The German Contribution to the Building of the Americas: Studies in Honor of Karl J. R. Arndt*, ed. Gerhard K. Friesen and Walter Schatzberg (Hanover, N.H.: Published by Clark University Press and distributed by the University Press of New England, 1977); *Amerika in der deutschen Literatur: Neue Welt--Nordamerika--USA; Wolfgang Paulsen zum 65. Geburtstag* , ed. Sigrid Bauschinger, Horst Denkler, and Wilfried Malsch (Stuttgart: Reclam, 1975).

    3 *Die USA und Deutschland: Wechselseitige Spiegelungen in der Literatur der Gegenwart; Zum zweihundertjährigen Bestehen der Vereinigten Staaten am 4. Juli 1976*, ed. Wolfgang Paulsen, Achtes Amherster Kolloquium zur modernen deutschen Literatur (Bern: Francke, 1976). See also *Annalen des ersten Montrealer Symposiums Deutschkanadische Studien: 25.-27. März 1976* , ed. Karin Gürttler and Friedhelm Lach, *Deutschkanadische Studien / German Canadian Studies / Etudes Allemandes Canadiennes*, 1 (1976); Erich A. Frey, "Amerika in den Werken Thomas Manns," Ph.D. Diss. University of Southern California, 1963; *Deutschlands literarisches Amerikabild: Neuere Forschungen zur Amerikarezeption der deutschen Literatur*, ed. Alexander Ritter, Germanische Texte und Studien, 4 (Hildesheim: Georg Olms, 1977). This volume reprints twenty-nine formerly published articles and contains an extensive bibliography; Harold von Hofe, "Lion Feuchtwanger and America," in *Lion Feuchtwanger: The Man, His Ideas, His Work; A Collection of Critical Essays*, ed. John M. Spalek, University of Southern California Studies in Comparative Literature, 3 (Los Angeles, Calif.: Hennessey & Ingalls, 1972), pp. 33-50.

    4Thomas Mann, *Die Entstehung des Doktor Faustus: Roman eines Romans* (Amsterdam: Bermann-Fischer, 1949); English version *The Genesis of a Novel*, trans. Richard and Clara Winston (London: Secker, 1961).

    5Carl Zuckmayer, *Als wär's ein Stück von mir: Horen der Freundschaft* (Frankfurt/M: S. Fischer, 1966); English version: *Part of Myself* (New York: Harcourt Brace Jovanovich, 1970).

    6Salka Viertel, *Das unbelehrbare Herz: Ein Leben in der Welt des Theaters, der Literatur und des Films; Mit einem Vorwort von Carl Zuckmayer* (Hamburg: Claassen, 1970); English version *The Kindness of Strangers* (New York: Holt, Rinehart & Winston, 1969).

    7Ernst Stadler, "Deutsche Literatur," *Cahiers Alsaciens / Elsässer Hefte*, 2, No. 11 (Sept. 1913), 285. All translations from German in this article are by the translator, except where English sources are given.

    8Franz Werfel, "Thanks," *Decision*, 1, No. 1 (Jan. 1941), 43.

    9Franz Werfel, *Stern der Ungeborenen: Ein Reiseroman* (Stockholm: Bermann-Fischer, 1946); English version

Star of the Unborn, trans. Gustave O. Arlt (New York: Viking, 1946).

10 *Contemporary German Poetry: An Anthology*, chosen and trans. Babette Deutsch and Avrahm Yarmolinsky, The European Library (New York: Harcourt, Brace and Co., 1923), pp. 115-31.

11 Franz Werfel, *Nicht der Mörder, der Ermordete ist schuldig: Eine Novelle* (Munich: Kurt Wolff, 1920). This and the following quotations are taken from: Franz Werfel, "Not the Murderer," in *Twilight of a World*, trans. H. T. Lowe-Porter (New York: Viking, 1937), p. 690.

12 Franz Werfel, *Bocksgesang: In fünf Akten* (Munich: Kurt Wolff, 1919). The quotations are from the English version, *Goat Song (Bocksgesang): A Drama in Five Acts*, trans. Ruth Langer, The Theatre Guild Version (Garden City, N.Y.: Doubleday, Page & Co., 1926). A complete collection of the reviews of Werfel's American productions is available in the Theatre Guild Archives at the Beinecke Rare Book and Manuscript Library, Yale University.

13 Franz Werfel, *Juarez und Maximilian: Dramatische Historie in 3 Phasen und 13 Bildern* (Berlin: Paul Zsolnay, 1924); English version *Juarez and Maximilian: A Dramatic History in Three Phases and Thirteen Pictures*, trans. Ruth Langer, with a note on the play by Gilbert W. Gabriel, The Theatre Guild Version (New York: Published for the Theatre Guild by Simon and Schuster, 1926).

14 Franz Werfel, *Realismus und Innerlichkeit* (Vienna: Paul Zsolnay, 1931). The following quotations are translated from the German version. The English version, published much later, contains a number of changes and deletions that alter considerably the tone of the original; see "Realism and Inwardness," in *Between Heaven and Earth*, trans. Maxim Newmark (New York: Philosophical Library, 1944), pp. 45-75.

15 Franz Werfel, *Der Weg der Verheissung: Ein Bibelspiel* (Vienna: Theaterabteilung Paul Zsolnay, 1935); English version *The Eternal Road: A Drama in Four Parts*, English version by Ludwig Lewisohn, Text of the Max Reinhardt Production (New York: Viking, 1937).

16 Agnes E. Meyer, "Notes on Franz Werfel: Herewith a Brief Interview with the Author of *The Eternal Road*," *New York Times*, 22 Dec. 1935, sec. ix, p. 5.

17 Franz Werfel, *Die vierzig Tage des Musa Dagh: Roman* (Berlin: Paul Zsolnay, 1933); English version *The Forty Days of Musa Dagh*, trans. Geoffrey Dunlop (New York: Viking, 1934).

18 Franz Werfel, "Unser Weg geht weiter," *Aufbau*, 6, No. 52, 27 Dec. 1940, pp. 1-2.

19 The typescript of this interview is located in the Franz Werfel Archives at the University of California in Los Angeles.

20 Franz Werfel, "Betrachtungen über den Krieg von morgen," *Paneuropa*, 14, No. 3 (March 1938), 65-77.

21 "Franz Werfel: At Work on Latest Novel," *Santa Barbara News-Press*, 11 Feb. 1945, p. C6.

22Werfel, *Star of the Unborn*, p. 16.

23Alois Dempf, "Philosophie eines Romans: Franz Werfel: *Der Stern der Ungeborenen*," *Frankfurter Hefte*, 5, No. 4 (April 1950), 440–43.

Stefan Zweig

Donald Prater

"I sometimes feel," wrote Hermann Kesten to Paul Lüth in 1948, "that I was born in exile. Every original man of letters lives in his own, eternal exile."[1] The aphorism could well apply to Stefan Zweig, whose exile, first from his homeland and then from Europe, was in a sense no more than the natural continuation of the restless mobility of his earlier years. Born in bourgeois comfort, cosmopolitan by birth, environment, and instinct, he traveled Europe and much of the world during the first decades of the century and was as much at home in Paris or Berlin, Prague or Rome as in his native Vienna or his base after the first World War in the Salzkammergut. "The Flying Salzburger," as Romain Rolland called him, found that his craft as a writer prospered rather than suffered from this constant change of scene: the author's "exile" into his work, the intense concentration he needed, was as readily to be found in a hotel room in distant resorts like Boulogne or Ostende, or the bustle of a seaport like Marseille, as in the seclusion of the Kapuzinerberg --a seclusion that admittedly suffered in summer from the influx of visitors to the Salzburg Festival, necessitating escape to Gastein or Zell am See if no excursion further afield tempted him. When you met him, said Antonina Vallentin, there was always the feeling that a half-packed suitcase stood ready in the next room.[2]

That such a man should succumb to despair and take his own life when exile became a necessity and movement no longer his free choice was a paradox to his contemporaries, and even today seems at first hard to explain. His "dreadfully wakeful prescience"[3] warned him well before the actual events of what was to come, and his decision to give up his home and leave Austria was made a full four years before the Nazi annexation of Austria. Such prudent disengagement, coupled with the international success of his work, which obviated any substantial material loss for him in emigration, and his eventual acquisition of British citizenship, were the envy of those German and Austrian writers who, in 1933 and 1938, found themselves plunged unprepared into an exile that meant a bitter struggle for mere existence. Although England, where he settled first in London and later in Bath, was less familiar to him than the rest of Europe, his emigration seemed simply one more move in a life that had already been that of an affluent nomad. It was scarcely surprising that others who had been forced to emigrate regarded him not merely as a favorite of fortune (*Glückskind*) but also as a skilled operator in the business of life, and found the enigma of his suicide all the more baffling.

To many, of course, and especially those who preached the social responsibility of the writer, his savoir-vivre was too clever by half, and his whole life and final renunciation of a piece: the prudence simply fear, the mobility a flight from reality, and the suicide a crowning act of cowardly evasion. Arnold Zweig, studying many years later the portrait frontispiece to the 1930 edition of *Angst* [*Fear*], felt the title was mirrored in these eyes "full of fear, in a hunted countenance": "So must the course of his life have been--as though running away: the feeling kept in check by the strength of mind of the adult, well aware that only phantoms pursue him, but with their inescapable claws nevertheless at his back . . . always in flight from something."[4] In the Hitler years he had been contemptuous of his namesake's political quietism, which he stigmatized as the desire to remain "a man above party."[5] Similar reproaches had been leveled at Stefan Zweig's "revered master of an earlier century," Erasmus: in times of fanaticism the man who attempts to hold to the middle way is execrated from both sides. *Erasmus von Rotterdam*, which Zweig wrote in the first year of the Third Reich, was in his own view "a quiet hymn of praise to the antifanatical man, for whom artistic achievement and inner peace are the most important things on earth--in this work I have symbolized my own way of life."[6]

On the day in May 1933 after the burning of the books of those in disfavor with the regime, including his own, he wrote that it was now imperative to "wait, wait, keep silent, and silent again . . . . That festival celebrated with my books has unhappily attracted much more attention abroad than I could have expected. For my part I would gladly have done without such publicity. You know I am a man who prizes nothing more highly than peace and quiet."[7] His silence then, and the fact that he made no immediate move to break with his publisher in Germany, were naturally interpreted as spineless self-seeking; and the case was clinched in the eyes of the émigré opposition when, together with Thomas Mann, Alfred Döblin, and René Schickele, he withdrew his name from the list of collaborators with Klaus Mann's journal *Die Sammlung*. That this was from a genuine desire to avoid political engagement and to preserve his privacy was shown in the letter he wrote to his publisher, the Insel Verlag, on 26 September 1933. Ironically, however, when this was published in the *Börsenblatt für den deutschen Buchhandel*, without his knowledge or authorization, he was still forced to take the stand he had tried to avoid, and face the fact that his association of twenty-five years with Insel had to be ended.[8]   It was lucky for him that the Gestapo's view of his "splendid attitude" in 1934--"correct and politically unexceptionable"[9]--did not also become public knowledge at the time.   That he took no action to stop the 1935 première in Dresden of Strauss's *Die schweigsame Frau* [*The Silent Woman*], for which he had written the libretto, was, in the eyes of his opponents, evidence of similar cowardice.

To those who are politically committed to the overthrow of a regime, as most of the émigrés were, silence is of course tantamount to approval of the status quo, and thus, "objectively," support of the other side.   Kurt Kersten put it squarely in his article "Four Years of Exile" in 1937:

The main thing demanded of the émigré writer is . . . that he should maintain an upright bearing, that he should be conscious always of his responsibility as the representative of the living and future Germany of the spirit. . . . More and more it must be generally recognized that the day is over, once and for all, for the methods of the *juste milieu*. . . .

We watched writers who sought consciously to avoid all controversy abstaining from even the slightest allusion and pretending that the blows they too received were nonexistent, who adopted a studied, seemingly aristocratic demeanor as a cloak for the impotence of their capacity to react. . . . Into every writer's consciousness must penetrate more deeply the realization that we are in a state like that of war, that the fronts are clearly defined and recognizable to all, so that no one can wander around no-man's-land or fail to appreciate where the shooting is coming from and who is firing on whom.[10]

He might have been directly addressing Zweig, who three years earlier (of course, in a private letter) had described his own approach in exactly the opposite terms, as that of the noncombatant in the no-man's-land between the antagonists:

I was born a conciliator, and must act according to my nature. . . . I can work only from the connective, from the explanatory, but I cannot be a hammer, nor will I be an anvil.   We are a small handful whose post is the most thankless and most dangerous of all-- in the middle between the trenches: those whose hand is not on the trigger, but on the plough.   That which unites us is invisible, but perhaps for that very reason stronger than the bonds of slogans and congresses, and I have a secret feeling that we act rightly if we but rally to the standard of humanity and renounce that of party.[11]

But it is hard, if not impossible, to plough your lonely furrow in no-man's-land when the firing intensifies and sallies from both fronts cut you off.   Zweig, living in a country that was still an asylum for refugees from Germany, left it for good after the "February days" of 1934, when his Salzburg home was searched for hidden *Schutzbund*-arms. This invasion of his privacy was decisive for him, more compelling even than his instinctive forebodings of war: "I could not sleep there, at night I could always hear from the German border the rumble of tanks," he said to Zuckmayer in London. He warned Zuckmayer that he was returning to a trap that would sooner or later snap shut on him.12 Nevertheless, once established in London, there was nothing to prevent him from starting afresh in a new "private life"—retreating to an ivory tower, as his denigrators would have said, or, in his own view, to that "inner citadel" of which Goethe had spoken and which Montaigne had known how to defend against a world of chaos and brutality.

He was in his early fifties, and the world crisis coincided for him with "that typical crisis of the fifties, in which one feels one has lived one's life wrong."13 Already in 1930 he had confessed that his outward success seemed only a burden: "I seem to myself like a hunter who is actually a vegetarian and so takes no pleasure in the game he has to shoot," and that his one preoccupation was how to change his way of life. He felt that, because he lacked self-confidence, he also lacked the necessary toughness to defend himself and that "only flight remains . . . . Nothing preoccupies me more than this attempt to transform my way of life. I have sloughed off much . . . but the final formula for my freedom still eludes me. And without freedom I am without any real spiritual strength. . . . it is in fact a complex and I don't understand myself why I can't shake free. Somewhere in my disposition I lack a necessary shot of brutality and self-reliance."14 Like many men at this age, he had been seized by the idea of a fresh start, and it was significant that he had already come to regard his family ties, the marriage with Friderike, as restrictive. In 1930 he wrote to Victor Fleischer that because of "family obtuseness," he had been unable ever to spend more than three weeks at a time away from home for the past twelve years.15 The urge, at times verging on the pathological, to preserve his freedom of action and movement was the dominant note throughout his life; and at this time the threat of Hitlerism coincided with the feeling that Salzburg, his home since 1919, had been transformed from base and "springboard" into the ball and chain of a prison. Though he revisited Austria frequently between 1934 and its annexation by Nazi Germany, his growing irritability at Friderike's apparent reluctance to leave—her "Österreicherei"—showed that his flight had been motivated as much by the unacknowledged desire to break with her as by his political prescience or by the indignity of the house search. Typically evasive even here, however, he took three years to face up to the reality, and it was not until the end of 1937 that the Rubicon of divorce was crossed.

With Zweig, then, we must recognize exile as not only self-imposed—not only a remarkably well-timed reaction to the Hitlerite threat and the world crisis--but also as the attempt at a solution to his personal problems: to shake himself free of the "burden" of wife, family (her children, not his), house, and autograph collection.   He wrote to Rolland in May 1934 from London that he felt well and freer than ever before without the incubus of possessions.16   Already a year earlier, on the very day of the book burning, he had said goodbye to house, collection, books: he told Rolland that he did not care if all these were to be confiscated: "On the contrary, I shall be freer when all this life no longer weighs on my shoulders. . . . all that is for quiet years that go on at a snail's pace--in times like these it's better to have one's shoulders free."17   He seemed cheerful, and grateful for life in London and for the precious hours, unknown to youth, that the years of maturity could bring: he liked the French better than the Germans, he told Ludwig, and the English better than either.18   One is reminded of Döblin's feeling of excitement, his involuntary euphoria, when he found himself pitchforked overnight into exile: ". . . the detachment and isolation, the jolt out of the cul-de-sac, this plunge and sinking seemed to me a 'blessing.'   There was a song in my heart: 'It's pulling me to the surface.' I could not resist the feeling."19   Zweig, for all his pessimism, also thought at first that the crisis would be as salutary for him as that of 1914, which tore him loose from the soft and gentle life of Vienna; he said that it was "sometimes a good thing for old gentlemen like me if a great shock comes to jolt them out of their rut."20   Thrown once more, as he wrote to Roth, "into a student-like freedom, I've begun here to learn again like a schoolboy.   I'm all uncertainty once more, and curiosity.   And I have the love of a young woman--at fifty-three!"21   That only seven years later he should find life no longer worth living was a function as much of a failure to solve his personal problem as of his despair as a humanist over the future of the world.   He felt he could never achieve the personal freedom he sought, "and without freedom I am without any real spiritual strength"; better then, "to end a life in which the work of the mind was always the purest joy and *personal freedom* the finest thing on this earth." 22

The combination of political events with this personal crisis, as he put it to Erich Ebermayer,23 compelled him to flight; and his determination to steer clear of political involvement made it, as so often before, a flight into the refuge of work, "the purest joy on earth."   For him, unlike most of the émigrés, it should have been easy.   To Kesten, in the early days, on the news of Kesten's installation with Allert de Lange in Amsterdam, he had written: "So you have at least found an artistic home, at a time when they want to make us homeless; and the other homeland, of work, you can plant anywhere."24   He himself no doubt felt, as he settled in London and, with *Erasmus* completed, turned to *Maria Stuart* [*The Queen of Scots*], that his own plant could flourish as easily there as in Salzburg.   To René Schickele he wrote that he could only too readily understand the tragic sterility that lay in wait for the émigré writer, "a fearful thing, to feel obliged . . . to spend one's whole life *against* something. . . . To my mind, however, we should not waste our strength running our heads against the cell wall, but rather preserve them and, following Cervantes, write good books in this invisible prison."25 To write good books is one thing, but to get them published so that they can be read, another: here too his luck and business acumen were the envy of the less fortunate, for once the break with the Insel Verlag had been forced on him, he saw to it that Herbert Reichner set up a new publishing house in Vienna to take over his works, old and new. Thus, at least for a time, he was able to put off the émigré's hardest trial of all—exile from his own language.

In the conscious internationalism of his post-World War I years, he had still had a real homeland—the German language. In the early days of World War I he had written to the German Kippenberg that the Austrians' loss of Brody (a Galician town) to the Russians had left him unmoved, whereas the devastation of Insterburg, a town with a German name, had affected him deeply. This experience led him to comment that ultimately, "our language alone is our fatherland."26 Twenty years later, the thought was a compelling reason—or perhaps a convenient rationalization—for his instinctive political reserve. Only three months after Hitler came to power he had justified to Rolland his silence in the face of events: ". . . even now, true to myself, I am *determined* not to fall into hatred of a whole country: and I know that the language in which one writes means that one may not divorce oneself from a people, even in its madness, nor call down curses upon it."27 During the summer of 1933 he wrote to Erich Ebermayer: "I shall stay here over the summer, then will come a long journey . . . one must look elsewhere in the world to replace what one has lost in the homeland (for the German language is my homeland, indissolubly) . . . ."28 For all his foresight and astute maneuvering, however, he could not avoid, any more than the others, the step-by-step denial of his sphere of activity, the loss with each successive Hitlerite aggression of a further slice of his readership in German. "Poor fools!" said Roth of the émigré publishers, "they produce books in German at a time when that language is less common than Esperanto or Latin. I mean of course the German language in which a few of us are still writing. The other, in which the others write and speak, is regrettably only too widespread."29

For Zweig, the success of great editions in other languages, though financially advantageous, seemed to make the loss of his homeland of German unbearable. "Don't give up your inner homeland!" his friend Franz Theodor Csokor had written to him in London. "Don't copy your Erasmus! Don't leave the soil from which everything has grown for you!"30 But it was not the patch of earth, so much as the language, whose loss with the annexation of Austria plunged him into the pessimism from which he never recovered. "The Austrian affair has nevertheless hit me very hard. Not only that my mother is there, and my friends, not only that my whole work is once more reduced to pulp and must be started once again from scratch--it is also the loss of almost my last readership, a plunge into the void."[31] Of what use, he complained bitterly to Felix Braun, are a million readers of German in Switzerland?   Nor was Zweig consoled when Braun countered with his own earlier argument that it was the books themselves that mattered: "Don't say 'the million Swiss'!   All that matters is that the books themselves should exist.   After us it will be a long time before anything else follows."[32] "We are a lost legion," he wrote to Csokor.[33]

Zweig, fortune's favorite, seemed to take it harder than most.   What was his life worth now, condemned to write in German and thus finished for a world that belonged to "that other Germany?"[34]   In the final months, when his isolation in Brazil was at its most depressing, the sharpest twinge seemed to come not from lack of friends or books but from severing of his linguistic roots.   "I find it touching," he wrote from Petropolis to Viktor Wittkowski in Rio, "that, while we have to translate what we write into other languages so that it can be read, you carry on faithfully with the task of rendering foreign works *into* German . . . I hope we can soon go through your Valéry together and enjoy the game of weighing words. . . . Wonderful that you are able to read and work, true to yourself and true to the tradition that from the lips has penetrated to the blood, from which nothing can ever separate it."[35]   And after the attack on Pearl Harbor he wrote that, like Wittkowski, he was "in complete despair.   Our world is destroyed . . . . And what a curse it is to have to think, live, write in that very language! . . . What heroism on your part, to translate *into* German!"[36]   Emigration was easier, as Döblin said, for the businessman, painter, musician: for the writer, bound body and soul to his language, to give it up was not just to shed a skin but to commit hara-kiri.   "So one stayed as one was-- vegetating, eating, drinking, and laughing, but still just a living corpse."[37]

Linguistic isolation, as all the émigrés found, brings with it a crisis of identity and an overwhelming sense of rootlessness.   Even when physical existence is assured--and few could boast of such favorable conditions as Zweig's--the refugee feels he has merely exchanged one prison cell for another.[38]   In Berthold Viertel's words: "There were leave-takings, again and again a new start and a breaking off. One caught a glimpse of a way, but the road remained a Utopian dream.   Nowhere was I at home, I could not fit in . . ."[39] "The fall of Austria would be our spiritual extinction," Zweig had written to Roth two years before the annexation of Austria.[40]   Nevertheless, it was not until his refuge in Brazil in 1941 that the crisis for Zweig reached its peak: "I suffer intensely from the unnatural situation of being neither one thing nor the other: committed to both sides, a German writer with no books, an Englishman who is not really English, and on top of it all the feeling that I shall never again find a proper order and stability.   It is not only

plants and teeth that cannot live without roots--a man is in
no better situation."[41]   By November of that year, in the
remoteness of Petropolis, the feeling grew stronger that he
belonged nowhere, a nomad yet not free: "I can no longer
recognize my own identity . . . a return is unthinkable for
a long time to come, and it would no longer be a real homecoming anyway. . . . Still, most of the road is behind us,
cold and darkness are setting in . . . ."[42]   His work, to
which flight had always been possible, was now little more
than a drug.   A long-range enterprise seemed out of the
question: his material for the "great Balzac," assembled
over many years, had been largely left behind in Bath, and
for his dream of another "Austrian" novel he needed the
sources of the libraries of New York.   The autobiography
finished, he tinkered with the Balzac, sketched out the essay
on Montaigne, completed his *Schachnovelle* [*The Royal Game*]
--but it was all from habit, "without intensity."   To Wittkowski he described his "immeasurable longing for peace and
concentration in these times that pursue us with unremitting
violence--the work that once I used to approach with tenderness and reverence is now just a refuge for me.   Will it
think me ungracious that I use it now as opium and hashish,
instead of nectar?"[43]

Already in England the notion that his generation had
reached the end of its road had been uppermost in his mind.
"For us," he said to Joseph Leftwich in 1939, "the best is
over, and our only task is to testify truthfully for the day
that will come,"[44] and to Körmendi in 1940: "Today it would
be more sensible to make a quiet exit rather than stay to
witness what is coming to us."[45]   To Victor Fleischer he
wrote: "The good meat of life, we have eaten it up, now
pick at the bones . . . silly old chaps which speak of the
good old times."[46]   In New York he told Zuckmayer that
sixty years of age was enough; and when his friend replied
that they had to get to ninety or one hundred so as to see
decent times again, his response was ineffably sad: "Those
will never come again for us. . . . We shall be homeless
. . . . What is the sense of living on as one's own shadow?
We are ghosts--or memories. . . . However the war may turn
out--a world is coming in which we don't belong."[47]   Others
might burn their boats, Americanize themselves, even give up
their language: "I am too old for all that."[48]   *Die Welt
von gestern* [*The World of Yesterday*], completed just
before his sixtieth birthday, has an unmistakable air of
finality about it: the duty to describe the world that once
had been, before yielding the stage to the coming generation.
As he wrote in 1941: "The generation for which I was spokesman had no heirs."[49]   A letter from Roger Martin du Gard,
which reached him early in January 1942, expressed exactly
his own feeling that "we in our age have only the charge of
spectators in the great play (or better tragedy), that the
others, the younger one [*sic!*] have to play her [*sic!*]
part.   Ours is only to disappear quietly and in a dignified
way."[50]   Only one possibility remained for him, "the one and
only flight, that into the uttermost depths of the being."[51]

All his life he had shown the classic symptoms of the
manic-depressive. His "black liver," as he called it, would
cast him into depths of gloom contrasting sharply with periods of elation and euphoria--depths in which he was on two
occasions obsessed by the idea of a suicide like Kleist's,
and sometimes by the fear of madness (this was why, according to Friderike, he refused to have children by her).   At
these times too, flight had been the cure; but the under-
current of pessimism remained powerful.   Even at the end of
the twenties his hopes for the intellectual unity of Europe
were fading: "For him the signs were multiplying that Europe
was at the end of its mission.   Creative power was waning
catastrophically.   We were plunging headlong into a trough
of poverty in art and barbarism. . . . Despite the pipe that
lent such a comforting air to our company, his dark gaze
held an incurable pessimism."52   With the advent of Hitler
this pessimism gained and held the upper hand.   "I had a
beautiful library.   I had a fine house," he said to Max
Brod, in "prophetically gloomy words."53   He was apt to cite
Rilke's phrase, "to survive is everything," but by the time
of the annexation of Austria he doubted whether he could
find the strength: ". . . the constant starting again, one's
head bespattered with the thousand filthy ordures of outward
existence.   Passports, domicile, family problems, living problems.   One often gets very tired."54   The Munich Pact seemed
to confirm his despair.   One had almost forgotten that an
Austria had once existed: ". . . one wave overtakes the
other: we are already no longer alive, but consigned to the
coffin of history."55   It was folly to think that the new
regime in Germany might collapse.   "Let us have the courage
to admit that we (no less than our ideals) are finished, past
history."56
    It was ironic that the feckless Roth, whom he bombarded
with well-meant advice and whose straitened circumstances
contrasted sharply with his own favored situation, should
show a sturdy resistance to so pessimistic an outlook.   "I
don't see why, my dear friend, you say our situation is
'hopeless.'   If it is, then it is our duty, our *absolute*
duty, to show *no* signs of pessimism. . . . Our situation is
by no means hopeless. . . . You are a defeatist."57   The
accusation was justified, though hardly a fair one from
Roth, whose drinking was, as Zweig well knew, a form of
evasion worse than his.   Both men were politically naive to
a degree, and their renunciation of life, in their different
ways, resulted partly from despair that a political solution
could ever be found for the world's ills; but it resulted
even more from their lack of that fibre of optimism or faith
in the ultimate victory that could sustain someone like Zuckmayer through the harsh wartime winters on a farm in Vermont, or even the gentle Felix Braun in his bleak banishment in the north of England.
    "My nose for political mischief troubles me like an
inflamed nerve," Zweig said to Roth in 1936.58   In Austria
no one would listen to his warnings.   There was either
ostrich-like refusal to look at the danger, or naive belief in

the power of Vienna to tame the ogre if he came.   Vienna would moderate the brutality of the Nazis, predicted a theater director to Bertha Zuckerkandl two days *after* Austria had been annexed.[59]   To be proved right in forecasts of disaster is a thankless role, and, from one who has already left his own country, a voice of warning is even less likely to be heeded by his new hosts.   He becomes, as Csokor noted, "a highly unwelcome Cassandra," as he watches the storm he has just escaped move on remorselessly to overtake the haven he has reached.[60]   When Zweig first arrived in England, its "courteous and hateless atmosphere" and detachment from the affairs of the Continent seemed an unmitigated blessing: ". . . they have only one aim here, to keep out, and that is mine too as a writer."[61]   While he could work in the British Museum, far from the "stupidities of politics," the change was as beneficial as a sanatorium, and his forebodings of disaster were temporarily stilled.   But both in England and, after the war had begun, in America, it became painful to have to stand by and watch helplessly as the democratic powers relinquished their outer lines of defense and continued stubbornly to refuse to learn any lessons from Europe's experience of Hitler.   His innate aversion to publicity, however, and a strong feeling of the duty to be courteous to his hosts, kept him silent still.   "We remain foreigners, though 'distinguished,'" as Emil Ludwig wrote on the eve of his departure for the United States; "we can neither help, nor influence, nor better."[62]

There was a curious ambivalence in his attitude toward his fellow refugees, and especially toward the Jews among them.   He gave of his best in aid, both time and money, but often manifested irritation over their helplessness, and more than once gave voice to the thought that their troubles were largely of their own making.   "The people turning up now . . . are nothing but beggars, mostly the less able and weaker brethren who delayed too long," he wrote in 1939 after moving from London to Bath to escape the pressure of appeals for advice and help.[63]   "As with every process of decomposition, the emigration inevitably builds up poisonous and stinking gases."[64]   Like Ludwig, he abhorred the sterility of the émigrés' disputes among themselves, "people hopelessly lost, who will never get back to their own world but sink into oblivion like their Russian predecessors," as Csokor had put it in trying to dissuade him from leaving Austria in 1934.[65]   Dissension in public could only help the Nazis, and Zweig deplored the attacks on himself as much for this reason as for the more personal.   After Ludwig Marcuse, for example, had criticized *Erasmus*, in a review in the Paris *Neues Tagebuch*, as an appeal for neutrality on the part of the exiles, Zweig commented to Roth in a letter from Vienna that "the essay itself was shrewd and not formally malicious —but what actually *comes out* of such things you can see best in the enclosure: the Nazi paper here grins behind its muzzle and hugs itself with *immense* glee to see the Jews still at each other's throats in the year 1934."[66]   Though he was far from denying his Jewishness, he often showed acute distaste for what he perceived as the pushiness of his race, which to his mind was at the root of much anti-Semitism; he felt that it was "not by pushing forward, but by deliberately holding back, that a man reveals his moral strength."[67] The émigrés were gravely at fault, he considered, in harping on the theme of the persecution of the Jews, for the only result was "that they constantly bring the Jewish problem to the attention of countries where it has not hitherto existed, so that precisely the opposite effect is achieved."[68]

Early in 1940 he expressed the view that his hardest trial had been, not the enforced separation from people who meant much to him, like Hans Carossa or Ricarda Huch, nor the ravages of the Nazis among the Jewish communities of Europe, but the demeanor of those Jews who had escaped:

> . . . I am thinking of that other attitude . . . that I have been forced to remark in those who, with strident and often angry words, wish to claim me exclusively for their race and their political views. I mean the attitude of a number of (understand me right) studiously literary and journalistically active Jews, mostly from Berlin and Vienna, in regard to official and private persecution. This attitude, which is also to be seen among small and big businessmen, has completely abandoned all sense of dignity.[69]

These were, in Zweig's view, Jews whose families over generations had helped to shape the Germany they now attacked as such, in its bad as well as its good qualities, who had helped, in other words, to create the very anti-Semitism from which their people now suffered. In 1936 he had written to Roth: "Apart from yourself, I want to see of the Germans only Ernst Weiss. What a revolting conflict now--this campaign against Thomas Mann, Hesse, Kolb, and mostly by people who, if they had been able to get a quick loan of a foreskin, would now be sitting, silent or vocal, in Germany."[70]   He could see clearly the imbalance to which the refugee was prone. "Emigration is a loss of balance, because the individual no longer has the same weight, in the sense of standing, as before," he wrote to Thomas Mann soon after his arrival in America in July 1940; and he went on to say:

> . . . this leads like an epidemic to spiritual disorders. My experience has been little better than yours-- the unhappy Zarek suddenly wrote me that I was "preventing" the other German writers, and especially himself, from appearing in English, and such pathological nonsense; well, my reaction is one of pity for a mental disturbance, of course in Ludwig's case making no such allowances, for he, if anyone, with his international standing and his Swiss passport, has been able to escape for years all those troubles that for us have been crushing and devastating, because they destroy our concentration . . . .[71]

Zweig's Olympian detachment here reads oddly now when one considers his own lack of balance and his inability to see things through, compared with the staying power of the others.

A strong reason for his final withdrawal to Brazil--he had only a visitor's visa for the United States, but it is highly likely that he could have immigrated permanently had he so wished--was the pressure of demands for help, money, and affidavits from his fellow refugees and his growing contempt for their behavior. "I saw there pretty well all those who had fled from Hitler, and hardly any have benefited from the change. Most are trying to fit themselves totally into the American way of life, put up with everything and use their elbows more and more as the broth gets thinner in the pot... Whereas I myself maintain a dark determination not to change, on the contrary to do my utmost to remain the man I was . . . . "72 But to remain the man he was proved impossible for him. He had tried all he could to help others, but was unable to help himself 73 when, isolated by events from his homeland and from his language and isolated of his own volition from friends, books, and the intellectual stimulus that had been his lifeblood, no further flight was possible.

*   *   *

Considering Zweig's character, "relevance" is the last thing we would expect to find in his work of the exile years, but it would nevertheless be reasonable to seek some evidence at least of his deep spiritual unease and of his vicarious experience of the sufferings, not only of his own people, but also of those of the whole world in war. With all due allowance, however, for his relative comfort in the material sense, after his uprooting from Salzburg and during his peregrinations in England and the Americas, it is remarkable how closely the work to which he "fled" in those last nine years follows the tradition of that which preceded it. With *Erasmus*, *Maria Stuart* [*The Queen of Scots*], *Castellio gegen Calvin* [*The Right to Heresy: Castellio against Calvin*], *Magellan*, *Amerigo*, and the almost completed "great *Balzac*," there is the same eager enthusiasm, though often now without the superheated and repetitive style that marked the earlier biographies, the same diligence in distillation of the source material (he had accumulated 2,000 pages of notes for the *Balzac*). Four further studies were added to the collection of historical miniatures *Sternstunden der Menschheit* [*The Tide of Fortune*], entirely in the model of the earlier--"between the report and *Novelle . . .* a new epic-dramatic genre,"74 where "even the obvious . . . wears a mask of distinction."75 The legend of *Der begrabene Leuchter* [*The Buried Candelabrum*] followed that of *Rahel rechtet mit Gott* [*Rachel Arraigns God*]; he translated Pirandello's *One Does Not Know How* in 1934, and, with Richard Friedenthal, Irwin Edman's *A Candle in the Dark* in the early months of World War II, just as he had collaborated with Rolland and Barbusse in World War I. The *Kleine Reise nach Brasilien* [*A Short Journey to Brazil*], written after his 1936 visit, is reminiscent of the 1919 essays entitled *Fahrten* [*Journeys*].   The war found no reflection in his work, although in an interview for the *New York Times* in 1940 his concern was with its effect on literature--as it had been in the 1916 essay *Die Bücher und der Krieg* [*Books and the War*].76   The four *Novellen*,77 finally, are (with the exception of *The Royal Game*) typical of the Zweig whom one rare critic had castigated ten years before: "everything false, impure . . . no matter how amusing his chatter, in the last resort this is only railway-carriage reading."78

Surprisingly enough, in the United States and South America he was constrained for the first time in his life to write strictly for a living.   Although his royalties from the Viking Press for the American editions of his works were not insignificant, the greater part of his wealth at this time was in Britain, and the wartime currency restrictions meant that his pen had to supplement his income, if the comfortable lifestyle to which he was accustomed was to be maintained. The nomadic life in New York and New Haven hotel rooms was costly, and even the small villa he rented at Ossining, New York, for the summer months of 1941 far from cheap.   Therefore, whereas he continued in his own tradition with *Amerigo*, and prepared the reminiscences of *The World of Yesterday*, the *Novellen Fishermen on the Seine*, *Die spät bezahlte Schuld* [*The Debt*], and *War er es?* [*Jupiter*] were little more than potboilers to bring in dollars from *Harpers*, *Colliers*, and the *Chicago Sunday Tribune*.79   That this was their object is clear from his total lack of interest in their translation, which, by unknown hands, resulted in considerable alteration and even abbreviation of the originals--a thing he would never have countenanced in normal times.   He was not even above rehashing old material, as witness his essay on Rodin, "Great Lesson from a Great Man."80   The *Brazil* book, although the result of genuine enthusiasm for his subject as a land of the future, was written basically as repayment for government hospitality and to assure himself of a little local income.   His popularity on the lecturer's rostrum he also exploited in Brazil, Argentina, and Uruguay for the same purpose, although it is fair to note that the proceeds often went to refugee relief.   He had already contributed to the *Reader's Digest* before leaving England, and renewed the association now with two contributions to a series entitled "Profit from My Experience."81   The spectacle of Zweig, of all people, in such company is sufficient commentary on this, for him, unprecedented situation.

The short article "Hartrott and Hitler" was a piece of journalism to which he would scarcely have turned his hand in earlier years, and is of interest as one of the very rare instances in Zweig's case of direct public comment on Hitlerism, which he describes here as the expression of the Germans' eternal subconscious dream of world domination.   Typically, however, his theme is still a literary one: Julius von Hartrott, the caricature of the Pan-German, with strikingly Hitlerian views, is a minor character in Vicente Blasco Ibáñez' 1916 novel *Los cuatro jinetes del Apocalipsis* [*The*

Four Horsemen of the Apocalypse], and Zweig concludes as we would expect of him: "Blasco Ibáñez' fiction has shown again that it is the poet who understands his time and the future better than the professors of politics."[82]   On his arrival in America, after the fall of France, he had noted with alarm the same head-in-sand attitude that England had shown two years before: ". . . as we émigrés in England recognized the danger more clearly than the English did, so we Europeans can detect in America's present prosperity her coming hour of need, the problem unsolved here as it was there."[83]   But it was rare indeed that he ventured to speak out and try to identify the danger for his hosts, and apart from his speech at the opening of the European P.E.N. Club Center in New York, on 15 May 1941, printed in the next day's *Aufbau*, the little piece on Blasco Ibáñez was his only public condemnation of Hitlerism—to be published at a time when, after Pearl Harbor, the Americans needed no further persuasion of its evils.

Whatever he may have said of Blasco Ibáñez and the superiority of the poet over the professors of politics, however, his own concept of the literary artist's role remained essentially that of the golden age of his youth, to which he now harked back in *The World of Yesterday*; and his ideal of the moral and intellectual unity of Europe and the world was not to be striven for with the journalist's pen in the public arena. *Erasmus*, the nearest he could come to literature of "relevance," had been his profession of faith, the condemnation of fanaticism by depicting the tragedy of the "gentle, weak man in the middle," "mirroring something of my own destiny." The last of the *Tide of Fortune* episodes, on the death of Cicero, which he wrote in Bath in the summer of 1939, concerned "another who was killed by dictatorship, who dreamed of order and stood for justice"[84] but drew no lessons for the modern struggle against the dictators. In *Castellio against Calvin*, two years after Hitler's rise to power, he had even seen hope for the future, asserting that moderation must eventually prevail over fanaticism, however entrenched the latter may appear. If Erasmus showed Zweig as he was, Castellio is his portrait as he would wish to have been; and in *The Royal Game*, too, his only work whose theme relates directly to current events, and the last to be completed, there is perhaps something of wish fulfillment in the Austrian lawyer's power of resistance to Gestapo pressure.

But the problem stated in *Castellio*, "how to unite freedom with order," remained with Zweig when he turned, in his refuge in Petropolis, to his "brother in destiny," Montaigne. With the world torn apart, and war sunk to the uttermost depths of brutality, in the twentieth century as in the sixteenth, he was faced, like Montaigne, with the supreme problem: how to remain free, how to preserve the inner self against the onslaughts of a world in chaos. The fragment on Montaigne that he left, almost completed, at his death concentrates only on this aspect of the great skeptic's philosophy and does not follow in its form the earlier *Master*

Builders essays.   That he left it unfinished is symptomatic of his own failure to achieve the solution that Montaigne's stoic determination offered.

He had broken new ground in the novel *Ungeduld des Herzens* [*Beware of Pity*].   It had long been his dream to write the "great Austrian novel," and the attempt was his refuge during the years that saw the Spanish Civil War, the annexation of Austria, and the Munich Pact.   It is a sentimental theme, and its scene, the distant days of the Hapsburg Monarchy, is that of many of his earlier *Novellen*. The young Lieutenant Hofmiller, in fact, in his scarcely credible innocence, is strongly reminiscent of the student in *Verwirrung der Gefühle* [*Confusion of Feelings*].   Although the setting is that of the last years of Emperor Franz Joseph, as in Roth's *Radetzkymarsch*, Zweig's treatment concentrates on the narrower theme to the exclusion of the wider scene: Hofmiller's disastrous thoughtlessness remains a purely individual story, with 1914 significant only in the relief it offers from the burden of the tragedy he has brought about, and there is nothing of Roth's powerful evocation of the decay and collapse of a system.

Immensely long for its content, the book is no more than an expanded, overwritten *Novelle* of the Zweigian kind. Nevertheless, when it appeared in English translation in 1939, it sold as well in England and America as its shorter predecessors in Germany, and made a successful film in the immediate postwar years when such escapism was the mode of the day.   To write it had been an escape for Zweig, but it expressed something of his troubled spirit in exile--a deep nostalgia for his lost country, and the pity that played a large part in his regard for the woman who was to become his second wife.

The World of Yesterday was naturally also a new departure in his work.   He had always shunned the limelight and had never been, despite his renown, the busy author constantly before the public view; but his feeling, when the war he had foreseen finally broke out, that it represented the end of the road for his generation, impelled him to set down his memories of what that generation had been through. It is not an autobiography in the accepted sense, and contains nothing beyond the most general allusions to his personal life.   But the world of the mind, the historical picture of the Europe and the great Europeans he had known between 1880 and 1939, are drawn in with bold, broad strokes and in a sober style rare with Zweig.   It combines, in masterly fashion, personal reminiscence with sensitive perception of the true current of events in that cataclysmic era.   For his biographies he had always needed the source materials at hand, and in each case the final product had been the result of the most painstaking research.   When he came to write his own story, in exile in the United States and Brazil and far from the home he had established in Bath, there were almost no aids to his memory--no notes, none of the vast correspondence he had received, and few contemporaries, apart from Friderike, whom he could consult.   The talk he

had prepared for the 1939 P.E.N. Club Congress in Stockholm
--cancelled by the war--was on the theme "Die Geschichte als
Dichterin" ["History as Artist"] and in it he had compared
historical truth with an artichoke, from which successive
layers can be peeled seemingly without ever reaching the
inner core.   Thus history, as he saw it, must always be to
some extent artistic invention, *Gedichtetes*.   The form of
The World of Yesterday shows him a worthy instrument of
history herself as artist; and its success in conveying the
feel and atmosphere of the times lends it an extraordinary
value, beyond that of a mere source book.   "For the third
time what I have built up has collapsed behind me," he
wrote after completing the work in Brazil, "and it was a
small satisfaction to have been able to preserve at least in
written form the life that has gone.   The main thing I could
do for the old Austria was to evoke a picture of what it was
and what it meant for European civilization."[85]   Although it
was not his last work, there is little doubt that the dispatch
of the manuscript to the publishing house of Bermann-Fischer
in Stockholm in November 1941 was for Zweig the end of the
last of his "three lives."   "Choose and speak for me, ye
memories, and give some reflection at least of my life before
it sinks into the dark!":[86] the words of the preface are a
clear prelude to those of his farewell declaration in Petropolis three months later.   In September 1939 "a new world
began, but how many hells, how many purgatories had to be
crossed before it could be reached"[87]--he himself had not the
courage to make the journey.
    There is a revealing poem, dating from his middle
years (1923), that has more significance for an understanding of Zweig's nature than has been realized: the "Ballade
von einem Traum" ["Ballad of a Dream"].   Of unusual length
for him, it portrays, in a galloping, dramatic, Ingoldsby
Legends style a dream of persecution and revelation: a
dream

> . . . des wissender Verrat
> Mein Innen hell nach aussen trat
> Und deutsam quer durch Schein und Schlaf
> Geheimsten Nerv des Lebens traf. . . .

--with the mocking words

> *"Du bist erkannt!   Du bist erkannt!"*

blazoned in fiery letters for all to see and rehearsed again
and again by the victim's pursuers.

> Vergebens dass ich vierzig Jahr
> Der Hüter meines Herzens war--
> Geheimstes Laster, dunkles Tun,
> Die fremden Wände wussten's nun! . . .
> Mein tiefstes Ich, mein Urgeheim
> War nun in aller Schwatz und Schleim . . .

Plunging in despair into the stream of Lethe, the dreamer
escapes to wakefulness:

Oh Dank! Oh Glück! Oh Zuversicht!
Man kennt mich nicht! Man kennt mich nicht!
Mein Urgeheim, mein letztes Sein
Bleibt mir allein, bleibt mir allein . . .

Da - lachte ich in mich hinein,
Tat an mein buntes Kleid von Schein,
Schloss Schweigen um mich als Gewand
Und trat, im tiefsten unbekannt,
Mein Tagwerk an, das wartend stand.[88]

The dream of pursuit, the nightmare of "exposure," is
a commonplace, but its portrayal here seems more than conventional versifying. Zweig strove all his life, against the
demands of fame, loves, and friendships, to preserve his
innermost privacy, what he calls here "Mein tiefstes Ich,
mein Urgeheim." It was this that he meant by "personal freedom," "the finest thing on this earth." "Apostle of the religion of friendship," in Rolland's words, he could be the most
sympathetic and gregarious of men, yet was ever on the move
to escape even the closest of friends and, for all his nobility
in charity, instinctively drew back from any relationship
that threatened to make too great demands on him--*Ungeduld
des Herzens* (literally, "impatience of the heart"), indeed,
"to be rid as quickly as possible of the painful emotion
aroused by the sight of another's unhappiness."[89]   Fritz
Naschitz has pointed out that his deliberate readiness to
help others combined with his shy helplessness in his own
cause could make the perfect illustration of Freud's *Trieb-
lehre.*[90] If Benno Geiger is to be believed, Zweig, in his
younger days in Vienna, had a strong tendency to exhibition-
ism and at one time carried a certificate that he was a
patient of Freud's to avoid any difficulties with the law
over this.[91] Such a trait is not uncommonly associated with
shyness and the desire to keep one's inmost secrets safe.
Zweig's withdrawal, exemplified by his silence in exile, was
certainly often a cloak, even if not the deception implied by
his "coat of false colors." It could be argued that his
cleaving to the middle way was nothing more than fear of
exposure if he took sides and that his humanism was merely
a rationalization of the deep urge to personal freedom. Moreover, those who saw in him a streak of selfishness as the
dominant motive for his suicide may not have been far from
the truth. "Was he not conscious of any responsibility,"
wrote Thomas Mann to Friderike just after his death, "toward
his many brothers in destiny the world over, for whom the
bread of exile is so much harder than it was for him, who
was celebrated and free of material cares? Did he regard
his life as his own private affair, and simply say: 'I suffer
too much. Look. I must go'?"[92]
In his study on Verhaeren, written just before the outbreak of World War I, he had identified the sense of responsibility as the force that decides the effect of a man's work:
to feel this was to look on one's whole life as a vast debt
that one is bound to strive with all one's strength to discharge.[93] His approach to his life's work showed at all

times a clear feeling of responsibility in this sense, a consciousness of the obligation to devote all his effort to promote the moral and intellectual unity of the European community. That it failed him in the end, and that he had not the strength to see the struggle through, detracts in no way from the genuineness of the ideal. But he had tried to meet the obligation without sacrificing his personal freedom, and at the last it was that which counted most. The draught of veronal was the only way he could see to preserve his "last essence": it was a final flight "to the uttermost depths of the being."[94]

Notes

[1]Letter of 21 Feb. 1948, in *Deutsche Literatur im Exil*, ed. Hermann Kesten (Munich: Kurt Desch, 1964), pp. 335-36. (All translations from German in this article, unless stated otherwise, are by me.)

[2]Antonina Vallentin, "Stefan Zweig," *Europe*, 25, No. 22 (Oct. 1947), 58. Cf. Stefan Zweig to Hermann Hesse, 4 April 1905: "I am--as our Grillparzer so neatly puts it in one of his poems--'a wanderer with two other countries and no homeland'" (unpublished letter).

[3]Undated letter to Joseph Roth (end of Jan. 1936?), in *Joseph Roth: Briefe 1911-1939*, ed. Hermann Kesten (Cologne: Kiepenheuer & Witsch, 1970), p. 446.

[4]Arnold Zweig, *Über Schriftsteller* (Berlin: Aufbau-Verlag, 1967), pp. 155-56. Cf. Stefan Zweig to Hermann Hesse, autumn 1922: "I feel . . . we both have been somehow equally shaken by the times we live in, and forced to turn inwards on ourselves--a road that to many may seem a divagation and a flight, though we ourselves know it is an attempt to reach the essence of things" (see note 94 below).

[5]Letter to Sigmund Freud, 23 Sept. 1934, in *Sigmund Freud/Arnold Zweig, Briefwechsel*, ed. Ernst Freud (Frankfurt/M: S. Fischer, 1968), p. 100.

[6]Stefan Zweig to Richard Strauss, 17 May 1934, in *Richard Strauss/Stefan Zweig, Briefwechsel*, ed. Willi Schuh (Frankfurt/M: S. Fischer, 1957), p. 63.

[7]Letter to Franz Servaes, 11 May 1933, City Library, Vienna.

[8]Cf. Hans-Albert Walter, "Der Streit um die *Sammlung*," *Frankfurter Hefte*, 21, No. 12 (Dec. 1966), 852-53.

[9]Letter from Richard Strauss, 2 Aug. 1934, *Briefwechsel*, ed. Schuh, p. 70.

[10]Kurt Kersten, "Vier Jahre Exil," *Das Wort*, 2, No. 4/5 (April/May 1937), 34-37; quoted in *Verbannung: Aufzeichnungen deutscher Schriftsteller im Exil*, ed. Egon Schwarz and Matthias Wegner (Hamburg: Christian Wegner, 1964), pp. 244-46 (cited below as *Verbannung*).

[11]Letter to René Schickele, 27 Aug. 1934, Deutsches Literaturarchiv, Marbach am Neckar (cited below as DLA).

[12]Quoted in Carl Zuckmayer, *Als wär's ein Stück von mir* (Frankfurt/M: S. Fischer, 1966), p. 54.

13 Stefan Zweig to Ewald Balser, 30 Aug. 1933, quoted in catalogue of *Stefan Zweig: Gedächtnisausstellung*, ed. Erich Fitzbauer, Salzburg, 1961, p. 72.

14 Letter to Victor Fleischer, 7 July 1930, DLA.

15 Ibid.

16 Letter of 5 May 1934, quoted in Robert Dumont, *Stefan Zweig et la France* (Paris: Didier, 1967), p. 184.

17 Letter of 10 May 1933, *Stefan Zweig et la France*, pp. 180–81.

18 Emil Ludwig, "Stefan Zweig zum Gedächtnis: Zwei Briefe des Abschieds," *Aufbau* (New York), 8, No. 9, 27 Feb. 1942, p. 15.

19 Alfred Döblin, *Die Zeitlupe* (Freiburg/Olten: Walter-Verlag, 1962); quoted in *Verbannung*, p. 39.

20 Antonina Vallentin, "Stefan Zweig," p. 66.

21 Undated letter (July 1934?), in *Roth: Briefe*, p. 334.

22 Last message, reproduced in Hanns Arens, *Stefan Zweig im Zeugnis seiner Freunde* (Munich: Langen-Müller, 1968), p. 32 (author's italics).

23 Letter of 2 Jan. 1934, in Erich Ebermayer, *Buch der Freunde*, ed. Peer Baedeker and Karl Lemke (Munich: Karl Lemke, 1960), p. 56.

24 Letter of 16 June 1933, in *Deutsche Literatur im Exil*, p. 35.

25 Letter of 26 Oct. 1934, DLA.

26 Undated letter (autumn 1914?), DLA.

27 Letter of 10 April 1933, quoted in Dumont, *Stefan Zweig et la France*, p. 179.

28 Letter of 15 July 1933, in Erich Ebermayer, *Denn heute gehört uns Deutschland. . . . Persönliches und politisches Tagebuch* (Hamburg: Paul Zsolnay, 1959), p. 138.

29 Joseph Roth, *Aus dem Tagebuch eines Schriftstellers*, quoted in *Verbannung*, p. 261.

30 Letter of 6 Aug. 1934, Reed Library, State University College, Fredonia, New York (cited below as Fredonia).

31 Letter to René Schickele, 22 April 1938, DLA.

32 Letter from Felix Braun, 7 June 1938, Fredonia.

33 Quoted in Csokor's reply of 9 June 1938, Fredonia.

34 Undated letter to Ferenc Körmendi (summer 1940), City Library, Vienna.

35 Letters of 21 Nov. and Dec. (?) 1941, DLA.

36 Letter to Wittkowski of 13 Dec. 1941, DLA.

37 Döblin, *Die Zeitlupe*; quoted in *Verbannung*, p. 303.

38 Cf. Döblin to Kesten, 18 May 1943, in *Deutsche Literatur im Exil*, p. 239.

39 *Dichtungen und Dokumente*, ed. Ernst Ginsberg (Munich: Kösel, 1956); quoted in *Verbannung*, p. 278.

40 Undated letter (April 1936?), in *Roth: Briefe*, p. 467.

41 Stefan Zweig to Alfredo Cahn, 19 Sept. 1941, copy in Friderike Zweig *Nachlass* ("literary estate"), 288 Ocean Drive West, Stamford, CT 06902.

42 Stefan Zweig to Felix Braun, 21 Nov. 1941, in *Stefan Zweig: Spiegelungen einer schöpferischen Persönlich-*

keit, ed. Erich Fitzbauer (Vienna: Bergland Verlag, 1959), pp. 92–93 (cited below as *Spiegelungen*).

43Undated letter (early Feb. 1942?), DLA.

44Joseph Leftwich, "Stefan Zweig and the World of Yesterday," *Year Book III of the Leo Baeck Institute* (London: East & West Library, 1958), p. 86.

45Undated letter (summer 1940), City Library, Vienna.

46Stefan Zweig, in English, to Victor Fleischer, undated (1939), DLA.

47Zuckmayer, *Als wär's ein Stück von mir*, p. 53, and Hanns Arens, ed., *Der grosse Europäer Stefan Zweig* (Munich: Kindler, 1956), pp. 245–46.

48Letter to Felix Braun, 21 Nov. 1941, in *Spiegelungen*, pp. 92–93.

49Letter to Wittkowski, 13 Dec. 1941, DLA.

50Letter in English, *Stefan Zweig/Friderike Maria Zweig, Briefwechsel* (Bern: Scherz, 1951), p. 352.

51Letter to Paul Zech, 4 Jan. 1942, in *Stefan Zweig, eine Gedenkschrift* (Buenos Aires: Quadriga Verlag, 1943), p. 38.

52Robert Braun, *Spiegelungen*, pp. 79–80.

53Max Brod, *Streitbares Leben* (Munich: Kindler, 1960), p. 482.

54Letter to Schickele, 22 April 1938, DLA.

55Letter to Guido Fuchs, 8 Oct. 1938, City Library, Vienna.

56Letter to Felix Braun, undated (early July 1939), in *Spiegelungen*, p. 87.

57Letter of 10 Oct. 1938, in *Roth: Briefe*, p. 524.

58Undated letter (April 1936?), in *Roth: Briefe*, p. 467.

59Bertha Zuckerkandl, *Ich erlebte fünfzig Jahre Weltgeschichte* (Stockholm: Bermann-Fischer, 1939), p. 310.

60Franz Theodor Csokor, afterword to A. Sacher-Masoch, *Zeit der Dämonen* (Vienna: Wiener Verlag, 1946), last (unnumbered) page.

61*Stefan Zweig/Friderike Zweig, Briefwechsel*, p. 287.

62Ludwig to Stefan Zweig, 30 May 1940, Fredonia.

63Letter to Gisella Selden-Goth, 12 July 1939, in Gisella Selden-Goth, ed., *Unbekannte Briefe aus der Emigration an eine Freundin* (Vienna: Hans Deutsch, 1964), pp. 60–61.

64Stefan Zweig to Kesten, 12 June 1939, in *Deutsche Literatur im Exil*, pp. 103–104.

65Letter of 6 Aug. 1934, Fredonia.

66Undated letter (ca. 20 Aug. 1934), in *Roth: Briefe*, pp. 372–73.

67Quoted in Leftwich, "Stefan Zweig and the World of Yesterday," pp. 96–97.

68Letter to Alfredo Cahn, 30 Dec. 1933, copy in Friderike Zweig *Nachlass*.

69Zech, *Gedenkschrift*, p. 27.

70Undated letter (end of Jan. 1936?), in *Roth: Briefe*, p. 448.

71Letter of 29 July 1940, Thomas Mann Archive, Zurich.

72Letter to Zech, 4 Jan. 1942, in Zech, *Gedenkschrift*, p. 37.

73Letter of 22 April 1938, in Selden-Goth, *Unbekannte Briefe*, p. 47.

74Letter from Csokor to Stefan Zweig, 2 Dec. 1927, Fredonia.

75Albert Guérard, "Miniature Moments of Crisis History," review of *The Tide of Fortune*, *New York Herald Tribune*, 24 Nov. 1940, Sec. 9, p. 9.

76Robert van Gelder, "The Future of Writing in a World at War--Stefan Zweig Talks on the Plight of the European Artist and the Probable Form of the Literature of the Coming Years," *New York Times*, 28 July 1940, Sec. 6, p. 2. No. 1199 in Randolph J. Klawiter, *Stefan Zweig, a Bibliography* (Chapel Hill: University of North Carolina Press, 1965), cites this interview erroneously as two articles by Zweig; the second date refers only to a reader's letter.

77*Fishermen on the Seine*; *Die spät bezahlte Schuld* [*The Debt*]; *War er es?* [*Jupiter*]; *Schachnovelle* [*The Royal Game*].

78Emanuel ben Gorion, *Ceterum Recenseo* (Tübingen: Alexander Fischer Verlag, 1929), pp. 51, 100.

79Cf. unpublished letter (in French) to his Brazilian publisher, Abrão Koogan, 11 Feb. 1941: "I have written a 40-page *Novelle*, which I think has come off well and which I hope to sell here for a reasonable price."

80*Catholic World*, 151 (Aug. 1940), 599-601; abridged in *Reader's Digest*, 37, No. 220 (Aug. 1940), 26-28.

81I: "What Money Means to Me" and II: "Never Hesitate!" in *Reader's Digest*, 39, No. 231 (July 1941), 39-43. The earlier article was "Anton, Friend of All the World," *Reader's Digest*, 35, No. 210 (Oct. 1939), 69-72.

82*Free World*, New York, 4 (Dec. 1942), 234-35.

83Letter to Thomas Mann, 29 July 1940, Thomas Mann Archive, Zurich.

84Undated letter to Felix Braun (ca. Sept. 1939), in *Spiegelungen*, p. 89.

85Undated letter to Guido Fuchs (Sept. 1941?), City Library, Vienna.

86Stefan Zweig, *The World of Yesterday*, translator unnamed (London: Cassell, 1943), p. 9.

87Zweig, *The World of Yesterday*, p. 327.

88Stefan Zweig, *Die gesammelten Gedichte* (Leipzig: Insel, 1924), p. 143. A translation of the excerpts from Zweig's poem follows: he writes of a dream "whose traitorous insight / laid bare my inner soul / and, cutting clear through semblance and sleep, / touched the most secret nerve of life . . . // *We know you now! We know you now!* // In vain through forty years / had I been the watchful guardian of my heart-- / deep hidden vice and dubious deeds / were plastered now on every wall, / my inmost being and most secret places / were dragged through the mire of common chatter . . . // Thanks be! O fortune! secure again! / *I am not known! I am not known!* / My secret being, my last essence, / is mine alone, is mine alone . . . // . . . I laughed then to myself, / donned once more my coat of false colors, / wrapped silence round me like a cloak, / and turned to the daily work awaiting me--my secrets safe."

89Stefan Zweig, *Ungeduld des Herzens* [*Beware of Pity*] (Stockholm: Bermann-Fischer, 1939), p. 228.

90Fritz Naschitz, "Verwirrung um Stefan Zweig," *Emuna--Horizonte zur Diskussion über Israel und das Judenproblem*, 8, No. 6 (Nov./Dec. 1973), 443.

91Benno Geiger, *Memorie di un veneziano* (Florence: Vallecchi, 1958), p. 423.

92Thomas Mann, *Briefe 1937-1947*, ed. Erika Mann (Frankfurt/M: S. Fischer, 1963), p. 281.

93Stefan Zweig, *Emile Verhaeren* (Leipzig: Insel, 1910), p. 209.

94In *Stefan Zweig - Briefe an Freunde*, ed. Richard Friedenthal (Frankfurt/M: S. Fischer, 1978), p. 139.

German Exile Literature after 1945: The Younger Generation

Sidney Rosenfeld

Professor Walter Berendsohn emphasized in his introductory remarks at the 1969 International Congress in Stockholm on "German Literature of the Exiles from the Third Reich" that investigation of this literature could not be limited to the period from 1933 to 1945. He stressed that literary history must deal with the literary works themselves and that to the present day exile writing had been intrinsically different from nearly everything written by those who had remained in Nazi Germany.[1] Helmut Müssener seconded Berendsohn's views by maintaining that the history of exile literature would not be terminated until its last representative in exile had died or had returned to his native country.[2] It is well known that by far the great majority of those émigrés engaged in some sort of literary activity—an estimate cites 83 percent—did not return to Germany or Austria at war's end, but remained abroad. Even today an appreciable number live and write in other countries, and there are—or, until recently, there were—among them some well-known authors who began to write only after 1945. One thinks first of Paul Celan, Peter Weiss, Erich Fried, and Jakov Lind. But also Nelly Sachs may be considered a member of this new generation of exile writers if one discounts her book *Legenden und Erzählungen* [*Legends and Tales*], which was never republished after its initial appearance in 1921.[3] To name such writers, however, also compels one to ask to what extent, and even whether, they may be considered exile authors. Some West German critics, for instance, do not accept the view put forth by Berendsohn and Müssener and confine the period of exile literature to the years 1933-49. For them the writers mentioned above would not be exile authors, certainly not in the full sense. They would contend that the most compelling reasons for residence abroad were invalidated at the latest in 1949, when the two German states came into existence. Of course, it should not be overlooked that this contention is based primarily on political considerations and does not take into account various psycho-

333

logical factors that for the exiles themselves are of decisive
significance.

Yet even if the most varied circumstances had prevented
a return either in 1945 or in 1949, it might still appear
doubtful, given the gradual but sweeping change of conditions in Germany and Austria, whether exile was still a
necessity that could be transformed into a virtue. In contrast to the older generation of authors, who had lost every
opportunity to write and publish during the Third Reich,
this younger generation was not subjected to restrictions of
any sort--even while living and writing abroad. The works
of Lind, Celan, Weiss, Fried, and Nelly Sachs were published
in Germany by German publishers, as they still are. They
were, and are, reviewed in German newspapers and sold in
German bookstores. Weiss's plays have been performed in
German theaters, Lind's radio plays were broadcast by the
German radio, and Fried's Shakespeare translations have
been used in German stage productions. Visits to Germany
have, from one instance to the other, not been rare, and
frequently the occasion was the award of a literary prize by
a representative German cultural institution. And finally,
the émigré writer is certainly free to return and settle in
Germany (or Austria), thus nullifying the prime condition of
exile status.

At second glance, however, the problem proves to be
more complex. In the case of Celan, for example, new residence in Germany or Austria would not have signified a
return home. To end his exile, Celan would have had to
settle in the Soviet Union, for that is where his hometown,
Czernowitz, is now situated. Furthermore, the intermittent
changes in the cultural climate of his native region were so
radical that Celan had truly become a man without a home,
because the German-speaking Jewish bourgeoisie from which
Celan stemmed no longer exists today. Given such conditions, Celan's exile would appear to have been irreversible
--unless one were to take recourse to the rather overworked
concept of "Old Austria" as a solution. But even though
Celan was known at times to speak nostalgically of Vienna
and on one occasion considered a return there, it is not a
matter of record that he regarded himself as an Austrian,
which, technically speaking, he was not if one recalls that
he was born in 1920 as a citizen of Rumania.

When the writer Jakov Lind, who now resides in London, was asked in an interview why he does not live in
Germany, he replied: "Because I don't have to."[4] The dis-
arming wit of this answer only barely conceals its serious
core, yet one need not assume an unyielding rejection of
Germany from it. One might just as easily conclude that the
Vienna-born Lind, for whom Germany would not have been
the natural country of return in any case, did not mind living abroad and felt no need for still another emigration.
With that, one arrives at the purely personal side of the
problem and could well ask whether in many instances the
decision to remain "abroad" was not motivated by factors
that are intimate and rather prosaic at the same time. One

author may have married in his new country of residence and raised children there whom he did not wish to uproot; another may have chosen residence in Switzerland, for example, simply for tax reasons; perhaps still another might have been prepared to return if the government agencies in his former homeland had been willing to guarantee the material conditions that would make life there possible.

In many instances the reasons for continued residence abroad may well be public knowledge and possibly identical with one or the other of those offered above.   But even at the risk of fostering exile legends in future literary histories, reasons of time perspective, tact, and respect for the privacy of a fate that could not have been happy under any circumstances suggest that one avoid the personal sphere when discussing these specific problems of exile.   Even if residence abroad after 1945 or 1949 could be explained on such strictly private grounds, this still would in no way alter the individual exile experience, which in its entirety became for many writers a permanent inner state of consciousness, nor would it detract from the human or artistic value of the experience as it found expression in literary creation.   If one wishes to come to grips with the problems of exile literature after 1945, its nature and its limits, one must turn to the works themselves.

The exile experience of the dramatist Peter Weiss--who lives in Sweden--is most evident in two early works, the story *Abschied von den Eltern*, 1961 [*Leavetaking*], and the novel *Fluchtpunkt*, 1962 [*Vanishing Point*].   Both are strongly autobiographical and closely combine the theme of exile as a purely personal misfortune with that of liberation from the parental home.   The narrator in *Abschied von den Eltern* sums up his experience of exile with these words: "My defeat was not the defeat of the émigré by the problems of life in exile, but rather that of the person who does not dare to sever all binding ties.   Emigration had taught me nothing.   For me it was merely the confirmation that I belonged nowhere, something I had experienced from early childhood on.   I had never possessed a true home."5 *Fluchtpunkt* contains a similar passage, again emphasizing the personal view of exile: "I did not come as a refugee and seeker of asylum.   I came to Stockholm in order to live here as a painter . . . . For me there was no lost ˌhomeland and no thought of return, since I had never been part of any country."6   A significant variant of this theme of not belonging can be found in the short piece "Meine Ortschaft" ["My Place"], which Weiss wrote for the collection *Atlas* (1965)-- a volume containing contributions by various German authors on the question of which town or place had proven most decisive for their personal psychology.   Weiss specified neither his birthplace, Nowawes in the vicinity of Potsdam, nor any of the many cities in which he had lived after leaving Germany in 1934.   Instead, he named Auschwitz--thus transcending his individual fate and the idea of not belonging: "It is a place for which I was destined and which I escaped."7

The shadow of Auschwitz looms over the work of Nelly Sachs as well as that of Paul Celan and Jakov Lind. The citation accompanying the award of the peace prize of the German Book Trade in 1965 contained the message: "The poetic works of Nelly Sachs represent Jewish fate in an inhuman time . . . ." A similar pronouncement was made a year later when the poetess received the Nobel Prize for literature in her exile homeland, Sweden. To be sure, subsequent studies have criticized the somewhat one-sided emphasis of the early collections of Sachs's poetry on which these and like judgments were based, and take cognizance of broader thematic concerns in her work.[8] One could contend, further, that solely by virtue of her highly sensitive personality and her lonely, closely confined childhood and youth Nelly Sachs had been predestined to portray universal human sorrows and the desire for transformation of everyday reality. But this argument would in no way alter the fact that her work most surely would not have become what it did if she had not experienced the horrors of Nazism and exile.

The same may be said for the work of Paul Celan. To be sure, with each volume of his poetry the splintering and reduction of language to the point where silence itself becomes the central theme grow ever more marked; and yet the theme that dominated his early poems and found its most poignant expression in "Todesfuge," 1945 ["The Fugue of Death"], remained vibrant to the end. The volume *Fadensonnen*, 1968 [*Thread Suns*], contains, for example, the poem "Denk dir" ["Imagine"], in which memories of long past and most recent Jewish catastrophes are interwoven with the thought of survival in a regained homeland:

> Denk dir:
> der Moorsoldat von Massada
> bringt sich Heimat bei, aufs
> unauslöschlichste,
> wider
> allen Dorn im Draht.[9]

Written during the Six-Day War of June 1967, when Israel was threatened with destruction, the poem unites temporal and spatial distances in a way that calls to mind and at the same time transcends the poet's own fate during the Third Reich. If one regards "Denk dir" together with "Du sei wie du" ["You, Be as You"], a poem filled with hope and promise that appeared two years later in *Lichtzwang* [*Light Compulsion*], one becomes aware of the dimensions to which Celan's exile extended and also of the potential the poet saw in his Jewish consciousness to overcome this exile.[10]

The works of Jakov Lind, from the early collection of stories *Eine Seele aus Holz*, 1962 [*Soul of Wood*] to his two-volume autobiography *Counting My Steps*, 1969, and *Numbers*, 1972, both written in English, represent in large measure an attempt to come to grips with the experiences of exile, which in his case often assumed grotesque character, and to portray the barbarism of the Nazi period. A significant result of Lind's exile years would appear to be the loss of the German language, which in a concrete sense was his mother tongue only until his eleventh year, when he was sent to Holland with a children's transport.   He comments on this phenomenon as follows, when describing his personal situation at war's end in *Counting My Steps*: "I had nothing left but my bare skin.   Everything had gone. . . . No love and no hatred and no language.   Worst of all, no language."11   In a note to the German edition, Lind stated that he had written *Counting My Steps* in English in order to achieve a certain distance from his topic.   This leads one to speculate whether a natural relationship to German, which he had "lost" during the war, was no longer possible, whether he had become so basically unsure of his native language that he was ready to risk an experiment in the acquired one, though it be doubly foreign to him.

It has always been the fate of countless emigrants and exiles to become stranded, as it were, between languages, so that in the end they cannot find words to describe adequately even the most common experiences.   And because it is the writer's aim to create a unity of experience and personal vision in language, no one is more severely affected by this situation than he.   Seen from this perspective, one may ask whether there may not even be qualitative variations of the exile phenomenon.   Can one, for example, view the exile of those writers who, sooner or later, found refuge in Switzerland in the same way as the exile of those who escaped from the Third Reich to such distant points as New Zealand, South America, or Palestine, where they were totally deprived of a living German-language environment?   Did not their exile differ in intensity from that of their fellow writers in Switzerland?

It is surely symptomatic of the varying effects of exile on language that Jakov Lind's drama *Die Heiden* [*The Heathens*]--which never appeared in the English original--was translated into German by Erich Fried, who likewise resides in London.12   Such unequal fluency in the old as well as in the new language, to which this somewhat bizarre occurrence points, can of course be the result of rather divergent factors.   Still, it surely makes a difference if one leaves his homeland and his parents at the age of eleven and changes countries five times, as did Lind, and if another, such as Fried, emigrates to England at the age of seventeen and remains there.   A study of Fried's exile experience would not be complete if one did not trace the influence of modern English poetry on his own and did not pay heed to his accomplishments as a Shakespeare translator (just as one may not overlook the influence of emigration on the extensive translation activities of Nelly Sachs and Paul Celan).   But that for Fried, too, exile became an irreversible inner experience is demonstrated very clearly by the long poem "Das fünfte Fenster" ["The Fifth Window"].   The title refers to a living room window familiar to the poet from his Viennese childhood, a window linked with vivid early memories, the same window from which a beloved aunt later plunged to her death when the persecution of the Jews reached new levels of

barbarism.   In the poem this window becomes a symbol of
disaster and alienation.   When the poet visits his former family home after an absence of thirty years, the window is
"more foreign than all the windows of the city."   Standing
at this window he becomes painfully aware of his total alienation, of the permanence of his exile:

> Ich kann
> meine Hirngespinste
> nicht einfach
> wegblasen
>
> wie meine Grossmutter
> die man wegblies
> damals
> im Rauch
>
> Man hat mir Beine gemacht
> ich bin staubig geworden
> auf den Wegen und Rückwegen
> durch die Risse und Löcher der Welt.13

It is no accident that the authors mentioned here are
either Jewish or of partially Jewish origin.   This fact is
inherent in the situation of flight and exile and bears crucial significance.   With the exception of Nelly Sachs, all
were at the time of exile quite young, and it was the par-
ents--as Jews, without choice--who decided on emigration.
Paul Celan, on the other hand, fled to the West only after
the war and the murder of his parents.   Thus it is also not
by chance that certain thematic similarities can be found in
the works of such authors.   This is, in part, a consequence
of common exile experiences, but in much greater degree of
the specifically Jewish experience during the Hitler period.
Certainly, all the exiles--regardless of nationality, religion,
or political persuasion--were united in their unconditional
opposition to Hitler's Germany.   But no group was martyred
in such unparalleled manner by the Nazis as were the Jews.
The traces of the Holocaust can still be felt among Jews
everywhere, not least in the works of this young generation
of exile authors.   The degree to which the Jewish catastrophe
becomes a central theme and the directness of its portrayal
often depend on personal factors that are difficult to ascer-
tain.   In the case of Peter Weiss, his self-identification with
the victims of Auschwitz, as professed in "Meine Ortschaft"
["My Place"], gave way to a general political involvement
of Marxist persuasion.   The poetry of Erich Fried assumed
pronounced political character, but the specific Jewish theme
persists.14   In the works of Celan, Lind, and Nelly Sachs
this theme takes on decisive significance, in each instance
with singular expression, but in a way that clearly shows
its import, if not primacy, for the writer's work.   Of course,
personal isolation in exile, loss of the mother tongue as a
natural element, difficulties of professional and social integration, the overall influence of the new environment and
living conditions on author and work--all these factors and

still others must be considered in the evaluation of exile literature. Nonetheless, one can assume with certainty that for many exile authors, as for most of those mentioned here, the specifically Jewish experience of total victimization during the Third Reich and the trauma of the Holocaust greatly overshadow the particular problems of life in exile and are far more decisive for the author's life and work than the state of exile itself could possibly be. This is a fact that investigators of exile literature may by no means overlook.

Though the period of exile could have been terminated in a formal sense after 1945, it remains true that for many refugees and émigrés exile had become a permanent inner state of being. In this light, it appears at least doubtful whether one can differentiate between authors such as those briefly discussed here who continue to live and write abroad and those (to be sure, very few) who likewise began their literary careers after the war, but have in the meantime returned to Germany. One of them, Hilde Domin, expressed the situation of the returnee in a poem that appeared eight years after she ended her exile:

> Unsere Sprache sprichst du
> sagen sie überall
> mit Verwundern.
> Ich bin der Fremde,
> der ihre Sprache spricht.[15]

Notes

[1] Walter Berendsohn, "Die deutsche Literatur der Flüchtlinge aus dem Dritten Reich und ihre Hintergründe," *Colloquia Germanica*, No. 1/2 (1971), p. 2. All translations in this paper are mine. Also, I am indebted to Frank Steiner of the State University of New York at Albany for helpful suggestions while preparing the English version of this paper, which was originally written and presented in German.

[2] Helmut Müssener, "Aufgaben und Probleme der Grundforschung," lecture presented at the Stockholm Congress in 1969 (mimeographed), pp. 1–2.

[3] In the case of Erich Fried one should note a slim volume of poetry titled *Deutschland [Germany]*, which was published by the Austrian P.E.N. Club in London in 1944. The poetess Rose Ausländer--whose name itself evokes images of exile--has come to the fore only in the past decade. Like Celan, she is a native of Czernowitz and lived through the Holocaust in Europe. In 1946 she emigrated to America, where she wrote in both German and English. She, too, published a single volume of lyrics, *Der Regenbogen [The Rainbow]* (Czernowitz: Literaria, 1939) before the cataclysm overtook her, but it was only after settling in Germany in 1956 that she found her unique lyric voice. That exile is an indelible experience for her is expressed over and over in her writing, for example in such poems from the collection *36 Gerechte [36 Just Men]* (Hamburg: Hoffmann & Campe,

1967) as: "Ein Tag im Exil" ["A Day in Exile"], "Fremde" ["Exile"], "Gespräche mit dem Wind" ["Conversations with the Wind"]; in the title of her 1974 collection *Ohne Visum* [*Without Visa*] (Düsseldorf: Sassafras Verlag); or in the title of the poem "Luftländer" ["Countries in the Air"] from the collection *Noch ist Raum* [*There Is Yet Room*] (Duisburg: Gilles & Francke, 1976).

[4]"Unter Ratten," *Der Spiegel*, 24, No. 46 (9 Nov. 1970), 250.

[5]Peter Weiss, *Abschied von den Eltern* (Frankfurt/M: Suhrkamp, 1961), p. 143.

[6]Weiss, *Abschied von den Eltern*, p. 10.

[7]Peter Weiss, "Meine Ortschaft," *Atlas* (Berlin: Klaus Wagenbach, 1965), p. 32.

[8]See Ehrhard Bahr's article in this volume.

[9]"Imagine: / the peat bog soldier of Massada / learns homeland, in / the most indelible way, / against / every thorn in the wire." Paul Celan, "Denk Dir," *Fadensonnen* (Frankfurt/M: Suhrkamp, 1968), p. 121. Very helpful interpretations of the poems "Denk dir" and "Du sei wie du" can be found in Werner Weber's essay on Celan in his book *Forderungen: Bemerkungen und Aufsätze zur Literatur* (Zurich: Artemis Verlag, 1970), pp. 193-206. My comments on Celan are based in part on these interpretations.

[10]Paul Celan, "Du sei wie du," *Lichtzwang* (Frankfurt/M: Suhrkamp, 1970), p. 101.

[11]Jakov Lind, *Counting My Steps* (London: Macmillan, 1969), p. 177.

[12]Jakov Lind, *Die Heiden*, trans. Erich Fried (Neuwied: Luchterhand, 1965).

[13]"I cannot / simply / blow away // my awful visions / as they blew / away / my grandmother / back then in smoke // They sent me packing / I've become dusty / on the exits and entries / through the world's holes and cracks." Erich Fried, *Anfechtungen: Fünfzig Gedichte* [*Objections: Fifty Poems*] (Berlin: Klaus Wagenbach, 1967), pp. 65-80.

[14]The framework of this paper does not permit discussion of the possible influence of Fried's political views on his later treatment of Jewish themes, especially since the Six-Day War in 1967. Suffice it to say that his New Left orientation has led to controversy, most notably in Israel.

[15]"You speak our language / they say everywhere / with amazement. / I am the stranger, / who speaks their language." Hilde Domin, "Fremder" ("Stranger"), *Rückkehr der Schiffe* [*Return of the Ships*] (Frankfurt/M: S. Fischer, 1962), p. 50. Besides Hilde Domin, two other authors fit into this category: Siegfried Einstein and Edgar Hilsenrath. Einstein was born in 1919 and since his return to Germany from Switzerland in 1953 his life has been almost symbolic for the entire complex of problems touched upon here. In the years from 1946 to 1951 he published six books, among them two volumes of poetry, *Melodien in Dur und Moll* [*Melodies in Major and Minor*] (Zurich: C. Posen, 1946) and *Das Wolkenschiff* [*The Cloud Ship*] (Zurich: Beer & Co., 1950), all of which appeared in Switzerland. From 1954 to

1959 he was the object of some truly sad publicity when he
tried unsuccessfully to defend himself against constant anti-
Semitic harassment in the South Hessian town of Lampertsheim,
where he had settled.   After he had moved in desperation to
Mannheim (a postexilic exile!), he produced a moving documentary, *Eichmann: Chefbuchhalter des Todes* [*Eichmann:
Head Bookkeeper of Death*] (Frankfurt/M: Röderberg, 1961).
After an auspicious literary start, he has published no further books.   It would be difficult to cite a more concrete
instance of an author irrevocably exiled, if a similar fate
were not shared down to the present, the late seventies,
by Edgar Hilsenrath.   Born in Berlin in 1926, he was sent
in 1938 to his grandparents in Rumania.   In 1941 he was
deported to a ghetto in the Ukraine, where he survived three
harrowing years.   At war's end he emigrated first to Palestine and then to New York, where in 1958 he wrote the novel
Nacht.   It was first published by Kindler in Munich in 1964,
but because of its sensitive content--the brutalities of life
among the Jewish ghetto inmates--in a small edition that soon
disappeared from sight.   An American translation, *Night: A
Novel* (New York: Doubleday, 1966), was followed by a re-
issue in Germany in 1978 (Cologne: Literarischer Verlag Helmut Braun).   Fourteen years after its first brief appearance,
the book now stirred considerable controversy among critics.
A second novel by Hilsenrath, *Der Nazi & der Friseur*,
gained an English-reading audience as *The Nazi and the
Barber* (New York: Doubleday, 1971) before it appeared in
Germany (Cologne: Literarischer Verlag Helmut Braun, 1977).
Discussion of the literary qualities of these two novels was
overshadowed from the start by commotion from the extreme
right: readings by Hilsenrath--who resettled in Germany in
1975--were disrupted by bands of Neo-Nazis.   Although he
had returned to the country of his birth and language, it
seemed that the trials of exile had not ended for him.

Index

33, 45, 153, 218, 229; Form als
Protest/Form as Protest 33

Zuckerkandl, Bertha 320, 330

Zuckerkandl, Victor 226, 227

Zuckmayer, Carl 4, 19, 34, 47, 50,
51, 59, 60, 63, 67, 104, 113, 285,
300, 308, 314, 318, 319, 328, 330;
Als wär's ein Stück von mir/Part
of Myself 300; Kleine Sprüche aus
der Sprachverbannung/Little Verses
by One Exiled from His Language
4; Der Seelenbräu/Soul Bridegroom
34; Des Teufels General/The Devil's General 59, 63

Zühlsdorf, Volkmar von 111

Zweig, Arnold 70, 84, 92, 100, 104,
157, 162, 225, 312, 328; Pont und
Anna 84

Zweig, Friderike 266, 314, 319,
325, 327, 330

Zweig, Stefan 30, 40, 47, 70, 77,
86, 100, 103, 162, 225, 226, 263,
311-32; Amerigo 322, 323; Angst/
Fear 312; Balzac 30, 318, 322;
Baumeister der Welt/Master Builders 324; Ballade von einem Traum/
Ballad of a Dream 326-27; Der begrabene Leuchter/The Buried Candelabrum 322; Die Bücher und der
Krieg/Books and the War 323; Castellio gegen Calvin/The Right to
Heresy: Castellio against Calvin
322, 324; Fahrten/Journeys 323;
Fishermen on the Seine 323; Die
Geschichte als Dichterin/History
as Artist 326; Great Lesson from
a Great Man 323; Hartrott and
Hitler 323; Kleine Reise nach Bra-
silien/A Short Journey to Brazil
322, 323; Magellan 322; Maria Stu-
art/The Queen of Scots 315, 322;
Profit from My Experience 323;
Rahel rechtet mit Gott/Rachel Arraigns God 322; Schachnovelle/The
Royal Game 40-41, 318, 323, 324;
Die schweigsame Frau/The Silent
Woman 313; Die spät bezahlte
Schuld/The Debt 323; Sternstunden
der Menschheit/The Tide of Fortune
322, 324; Triumph und Tragik des
Erasmus von Rotterdam/Erasmus of
Rotterdam 312, 315, 320, 322,
324; Ungeduld des Herzens/Beware
of Pity 325; Verwirrung der Ge-
fühle/Confusion of Feelings 325,
327; War er es?/Jupiter 323; Die
Welt von gestern/The World of Yesterday 318, 323, 324, 325, 326

Contributors

ADRIENNE ASH is the Assistant Director of Hay Publications, a division of Hay Associates, a management consulting firm in Philadelphia. She received her Ph. D. from the University of Texas, writing on poetry in exile, and, after several years of teaching at the University of Wyoming, joined John Spalek's staff as Associate Professor for Research at the State University of New York at Albany. Dr. Ash has published and presented papers on a wide variety of topics, from exile to modern American poetry. From 1977 to 1980 she lectured throughout the United States on the historical impact of the emigration. She has also been consultant to the Smithsonian Institution during the Einstein Centennial Year. Currently, Dr. Ash directs a legal consulting service for international corporations.

EHRHARD BAHR is Professor of German at the University of California, Los Angeles. He is the author of books on Goethe, Georg Lukács and Ernst Bloch. Professor Bahr has contributed some thirty articles to journals here and abroad. In addition he has completed a biography of Nelly Sachs, which was published in Germany in 1980. His special interest as far as exile research is concerned has been in German exile politics in the United States, in Thomas Mann, and the German exile novel.

ROBERT BELL is Associate Professor of German at the University of Alabama. He received his Ph. D. degree from the University of Illinois. He has published articles and reviews on German exile literature, as well as other aspects of German literature, and is a co-editor with Joseph Strelka and Eugene Dobson of Protest--Form--Tradition: Essays on German Exile Literature (1979). He was one of the coorganizers of the symposia on German exile literature held at the University of Kentucky (1972) and the University of Alabama (1975). Professor Bell has served as Chairman of the Department of German and Russian at the University of Alabama and as a member of the Executive Committee of the South Atlantic Modern Language Association.

SUSAN E. CERNYAK is Associate Professor of German and German Literature at the University of North Carolina at Charlotte. She has her Ph.D. from the University of Kansas and her dissertation, The Holocaust in German Literature was completed in 1973. Her main interest lies in the literature of the Holocaust. She has also published several articles on German Literature in Exile. She is interested in the literature of the twentieth century, specifically in drama. She is currently preparing a proposal for interdisciplinary Holocaust studies.

LORE BARBARA FOLTIN was at the University of Pittsburgh from 1949 to her untimely death in 1974. She obtained her doctorate from the German University in Prague in 1937. The range of her publications include two books and a number of articles on Franz Werfel, articles on Arthur Schnitzler and other topics in Austrian literature. She is also the author or coeditor of several textbooks, Aus Nah und Fern (1963), and Paths to German Poetry: An Introductory Anthology (1969), and coauthor of "Epochen der deutschen Literatur," in Das Studium der deutschen Literatur, ed. by Wolfgang Ruttkowski and Eberhard Reichmann.

WOLFGANG FREESE received his Ph.D. from the University of Tübingen in 1968. He is Professor of German at the University of Maryland Baltimore County (presently on leave for a guest professorship at the University of Natal, South Africa). Having taught German and Comparative Literature both in Europe and the United States, Professor Freese's main research interests lie in critical methodology and theory, twentieth century literature and philosophy, the modern novel, and the eighteenth century. His publications include books on Musil, Broch, the narrative function of love in the modern novel, articles on high and late medieval literature, and authors like Brecht, Musil, Thomas Mann, Beckett, Kawabata. He is coeditor of Musil-Studien and of the International Robert Musil Society's bi-annual journal Musil Forum.

ERICH A. FREY is Professor of German and Linguistics at Occidental College in Los Angeles where he has served several years as chairman of the Department of Languages and Linguistics. He has also been visiting professor of applied linguistics at the University of Saarbrücken. Thomas Mann's life and work, especially his exile period in America, has been the main subject of Professor Frey's publications and lectures. His work in the area of German literature in exile at the present time deals with the relationship between Thomas Mann and Alfred Döblin.

JOHN FUEGI is Professor of Germanic, Slavic and Comparative Literature at the University of Maryland-College Park. Professor Fuegi's research interests lie in genre theory, Slavic-Western literary relations, the staging of dramatic texts, and the interrelationship of literature and film. He has himself been professionally active in film, having written and directed the documentary The Wall, shown at the 1961 San Francisco International Film Festival. Besides "Shakespeare and the Theatrical Film," which appeared in the Shakespeare Quarterly, he has written over a hundred articles and reviews on various topics. His book, The Essential Brecht, a comparative study of eight Brecht plays, appeared in 1972 in the University of Southern California Series in Comparative Literature. Professor Fuegi was active with Reinhold Grimm in founding the International Brecht Society and is currently managing editor of the annual publication of that Society, Brecht Heute/Brecht Today, 1971-1980. He is currently at work on a book on violence in the drama and is under contract to the Cambridge University Press to do a book on Brecht as a stage director.

HANNO HARDT is Professor of Journalism and Mass Communication at the University of Iowa. His interest in crosscultural communication and the migration of ideas has resulted in a number of publications, most recently in Social Theories of the Press (1979) and Presse im Exil (1979) edited with Hilscher and Lerg. He has been a visiting professor at a number of German universities.

LOTHAR KAHN is Professor of Modern Languages at Central Connecticut State College in New Britain, Connecticut. He has concerned himself in recent years with the Jew in French and German literature, and he is currently completing a history of German Jewish writers. He is the author of Mirrors of the Jewish Mind (1968) and Insight and Action: The Life and Work of Lion Feuchtwanger (1975).

ROBERT KAUF is Professor of German at the University of Illinois at Chicago Circle. He completed his undergraduate studies at the University of Texas and received his M.A. and Ph.D. from the University of Chicago. From 1968-1970 he was review editor of The German Quarterly. He is the recipient of a number of grants for literary research and awards for excellence in teaching. Co-author of the literary reader, Proben deutscher Prosa (1970), his numerous publications are primarily, but not exclusively, devoted to twentieth-century German literature. The principal focus of his interest is on the literature of Austria and on Jewish writers, especially Kafka, and Jewish themes. He was personally well acquainted with the late Ernst Waldinger and is one of the administrators of his literary estate.

HERBERT LEHNERT is Professor of German at the University of California, Irvine. He received his doctorate from the University of Kiel and taught, before coming to Irvine, at the University of Western Ontario in Canada, at Rice University, and at the University of Kansas. As Visiting Professor he taught at Harvard University. He published books on Thomas Mann: Fiktion, Mythos, Religion (1965), on the interpretation of poetry, Struktur und Sprachmagie (1966), on Thomas Mann research, Thomas-Mann-Forschung (1969), and From Jugendstil zum Expressionismus, which appeared as vol. 5 of the Geschichte der deutschen Literatur (Reclam, 1978). Articles on Thomas Mann and other authors have appeared in professional journals.

HENRI R. PAUCKER was Associate Professor of German at the University of Vermont 1970-74 when he moved to Switzerland where he is writing for a variety of newspapers including the Neue Zürcher Zeitung. He combines interest in literature with philosophy, and his publications include studies of Franz Kafka, Günther Anders, existentialism, Heinrich Heine: Mensch und Dichter zwischen Deutschland und Frankreich (1967), and he is the editor of Neue Sachlichkeit, Literatur im "Dritten Reich" und im Exil (1974), which appeared as vol. 15 of the Reclam series Die deutsche Literatur im Text und Darstellung.

CAROL PAUL-MERRITT, Associate Professor at Millikin University in Decatur, Illinois, teaches Humanities Honors courses and all levels of German. She com-

pleted undergraduate work at the University of California at Berkeley and graduate work at Indiana University (Bloomington) and the University of Southern
California, where she received her Ph.D. in 1972. She has presented papers on
aspects of the exile question at the University of Kentucky, several annual
Modern Language Association conferences, the University of Colorado, and most
recently,at the Northeast Modern Language Association conference at Southeast-
ern Massachusetts University. She is coeditor with John M. Spalek of German
Expressionism in the Fine Arts. A Bibliography (1977). Her interests include
the psychology of the culturally displaced artist, particularly the writer,
and myth and fantasy in German literature.

HELMUT F. PFANNER is Professor of German at Purdue University. Before receiving his Ph. D. from Stanford University, he taught in Austrian public schools;
later he held teaching positions at the University of Washington, the University of Virginia, and the University of New Hampshire. His publications include the books Hanns Johnst: Vom Expressionismus zum Nationalsozialismus(1970)
and Oskar Maria Graf: Eine kritische Bibliographie (1976), as well as articles
on nineteenth and twentieth century German literature. He edited a book (together with Wolfgang Dietz) with texts by and about Oskar Maria Graf (Beschrei-
bung eines Volksschriftstellers, 1974), and his exhibit from the Graf literary
estate (catalogue, University of New Hampshire, 1974) has been shown at several institutions. Pfanner has been involved in German exile literature research
since 1969 when he participated in the first international conference on the
exile of the Nazi period in Stockholm.

DONALD PRATER, currently with the European Organization for Nuclear Research,
Geneva,is an M.A. Oxon, where he read German and French between 1936 and 1939.
From 1946 to 1969 he was in the British Foreign Service, his assignments including Germany, Austria and Sweden as well as the Middle and Far East, and
was able to continue his German studies, with a special interest in exile literature. From 1970 to 1973 he was Senior Lecturer in German at the University
of Canterbury, New Zealand. He is the author of a full-scale biography of Stefan Zweig (European of Yesterday, OUP, 1972), an updated version of which is
shortly to appear in German (Peter Lang, Bern), and he is preparing a book on
Zweig for the centenary year 1981 (Leben und Werk im Bild, Insel).

JAMES ROLLESTON is Associate Professor of German and Chairman of the Comparative Literature Program at Duke University. He received his Ph. D. from Yale,
where he taught until 1975. He has published books on Rilke and Kafka and an
article on Werfel's Star of the Unborn as exile literature. His current ambition is to rethink the poetics of the German lyric in the nineteenth and twentieth centuries.

SIDNEY ROSENFELD is Associate Professor of German at Oberlin College. He received his Ph. D. from the University of Illinois (Urbana) with a dissertation
on the novels of Joseph Roth. His interests include early twentieth-century
literature, especially Austrian literature, and lyric poetry. He has published
articles on Joseph Roth and Karl Kraus, and together with Stella Rosenfeld he
has recently translated Jean Améry's Jenseits von Schuld und Sühne for American publication.

CURT SANGER is Associate Professor of German and Swedish at Miami University,
Oxford, Ohio. His research interests pertain to the literature of the Weimar
Republic, Austrian and exile literature. His publications include articles
about Franz Theodor Csokor, Marieluise Fleisser and Joseph Roth.

ERNST SCHÜRER has been Professor and Head of the German Department at Pennsylvania State University since 1978. He studied German language and literature,
history and philosophy at the University of Texas in Austin (B.A.) and did his
graduate work at the Free University of Berlin and Yale University (M.A. and
Ph. D.). A member of Phi Beta Kappa, a Woodrow Wilson Fellow, and Alexander
von Humboldt Fellow, he continued his postdoctoral research with a Morse Fellowship at the Academy of Arts in Berlin. As Instructor, Assistant, and Associate Professor, he taught language and literature courses at Yale University
(1963-73), where he also held the position of Director of Undergraduate Studies from 1969 to 1971, and Director of Graduate Studies from 1971 to 1973.
From 1973 to 1978 he was at the University of Florida as Professor and Chairman (1977-78). His field of research is modern German literature from Naturalism to the present, with special emphasis on Expressionism, drama, and exile
literature.   In addition to numerous articles and reviews in learned journals

and anthologies he has contributed to and edited Lebendige Form. Interpretationen zur deutschen Literatur. Festschrift für Heinrich E. K. Henel, and published a study: Georg Kaiser (1971) as well as a monograph: Georg Kaiser und Bertolt Brecht, Über Leben und Werk (1971).

DIETER SEVIN is Associate Professor of Germanic Languages and Literatures at Vanderbilt University. He completed his undergraduate studies at San Jose State University and received his Master's and Ph. D. degrees from the University of Washington. Besides his work in German Exile Literature, Professor Sevin's research interests range from the prose of the nineteenth century to the literature of the German Democratic Republic. He coauthored several textbooks and is, at present, working on a book about the recent East German novel.

JOHN M. SPALEK is Professor of German at the State University of New York at Albany, where he served as chairman of the department from 1970 to 1979. His areas of research are German literature and culture in exile, German expressionism, and modern drama. His publications include Ernst Toller and His Critics: A Bibliography (1968); Lion Feuchtwanger (1972); Deutsche Exilliteratur seit 1933, Vol. I: Kalifornien (1976); A Guide to the Archival Materials of the German-Speaking Emigration to the United States after 1933 (1979); and he co-edited with Wolfgang Fruhwald Ernst Toller's Gesammelte Schriften, 6 vols. (1978-1979). He is also the recipient of several research grants from the National Endowment for the Humanities and the Deutsche Forschungsgemeinschaft. Work in progress includes Deutsche Exilliteratur seit 1933, Vol. II: New York, a second volume of the Guide to the Archival Materials, and the edition of selected works of Karl Otto Paetel.

GUY STERN is Provost and Vice President of Wayne State University. Prior to this appointment, he served as chairman of the Department of German and Russian at the University of Maryland, and earlier he held the same position at the University of Cincinnati, where he also served as University Dean for several years. He served as President of the American Association of Teachers of German, president of the Lessing Society, and he is on the board of directors of the Leo Baeck Institute. His publications include War, Weimar, and Literature (1971), articles on eighteenth and twentieth-century German literature, and a number of textbooks. He also coedited Erzählungen from the Neue Merkur (1964), and Nelly Sachs' Ausgewählte Gedichte (1968).

JOSEPH P. STRELKA is Professor of German and Comparative Literature at the State University of New York at Albany. His main areas of research and publication are: theory and methodology of literature, modern German and Austrian literature, especially Hermann Broch, Robert Musil, and Alfred Döblin, Renaissance literature, and German literature in Exile. Among his numerous publications are several books on literary theory and criticism, the most recent being Methodologie der Literaturwissenschaft (1978), and other titles ranging from the Renaissance to contemporary literature. He is coeditor with John M. Spalek of Deutsche Exilliteratur seit 1933, Vol. I: Kalifornien; he has edited the works of Margarethe von Oesterreich, Felix Graefe, Gustav Meyrink, and anthologies of modern poetry. He is also editor of the Yearbook of Comparative Criticism. The Penn State Series in German Literature, and most recently he has become editor of Reihe 6: Die Literatur von 1890-1975 of the Lexikon der deutschen Literatur (Peter Lang, 15 vols.).

HANS WAGENER is Professor of German and Chairman of the Department of Germanic Languages at the University of California, Los Angeles. His areas of specialization include Baroque and Modern German literature. Among his book publications are Die Komposition der Romane Christian Friedrich Hunolds (1969); Die Anredeformen in den Dramen des Andreas Gryphius (1970, with Theo Vennemann); The German Baroque Novel (1973); Erich Kästner (1973); Stefan Andres (1974); Frank Wedekind (1979); numerous editions, commentaries and articles.

MICHAEL WINKLER is Professor of German at Rice University in Houston. His scholarly interests include the European literature of aestheticism, modern poetry, the era of Romanticism, and exile literature. He has published on Stefan George, fin-de-siècle plays, various aspects of antifascist literature in exile, Hermann Broch, Paul Celan, and fantastic prose. He is currently preparing a book on the fiction of German Expressionism and continues to read apocalyptic novels and tales of horror and fantasy.

UNIVERSITY OF NORTH CAROLINA
STUDIES IN THE GERMANIC LANGUAGES
AND LITERATURES

45 PHILLIP H. RHEIN. *The Urge to Live. A Comparative Study of Franz Kafka's* Der Prozess *and Albert Camus'* L'Etranger. 2nd printing. 1966. Pp. xii, 124.

50 RANDOLPH J. KLAWITER. *Stefan Zweig. A Bibliography.* 1965. Pp. xxxviii, 191.

52 MARIANA SCOTT. *The Heliand. Translated into English from the Old Saxon.* 1966. Pp. x, 206.

56 RICHARD H. ALLEN. *An Annotated Arthur Schnitzler Bibliography.* 1966. Pp. xiv, 151.

58 *Studies in Historical Linguistics. Festschrift for George S. Lane. Eighteen Essays.* 1967. Pp. xx, 241.

60 J. W. THOMAS. *Medieval German Lyric Verse. In English Translation.* 1968. Pp. x, 252.

67 SIEGFRIED MEWS, ED. *Studies in German Literature of the Nineteenth and Twentieth Centuries. Festschrift for Frederic E. Coenen.* Foreword by Werner P. Friederich. 1970. 2nd ed. 1972. Pp. xx, 251.

68 JOHN NEUBAUER. *Bifocal Vision. Novalis' Philosophy of Nature and Disease.* 1971. Pp. x, 196.

70 DONALD F. NELSON. *Portrait of the Artist as Hermes. A Study of Myth and Psychology in Thomas Mann's* Felix Krull. 1971. Pp. xii, 146.

72 CHRISTINE OERTEL SJÖGREN. *The Marble Statue as Idea: Collected Essays on Adalbert Stifter's* Der Nachsommer. 1972. Pp. xiv, 121.

73 DONALD G. DAVIAU AND JORUN B. JOHNS, EDS. *The Correspondence of Arthur Schnitzler and Raoul Auernheimer with Raoul Auernheimer's Aphorisms.* 1972. Pp. xii, 161.

74 A. MARGARET ARENT MADELUNG. *The Laxdoela Saga: Its Structural Patterns.* 1972. Pp. xiv, 261.

75 JEFFREY L. SAMMONS. *Six Essays on the Young German Novel.* 2nd ed. 1975. Pp. xiv, 187.

76 DONALD H. CROSBY AND GEORGE C. SCHOOLFIELD, EDS. *Studies in the German Drama. A Festschrift in Honor of Walter Silz.* 1974. Pp. xxvi, 255.

77 J. W. THOMAS. *Tannhäuser: Poet and Legend. With Texts and Translation of His Works.* 1974. Pp. x, 202.

78 OLGA MARX AND ERNST MORWITZ, TRANS. *The Works of Stefan George.* 1974. 2nd, rev. and enl. ed. Pp. xxviii, 431.

79 SIEGFRIED MEWS AND HERBERT KNUST, EDS. *Essays on Brecht: Theater and Politics.* 1974. Pp. xiv, 241.

80 DONALD G. DAVIAU AND GEORGE J. BUELOW. *The* Ariadne auf Naxos *of Hugo von Hofmannsthal and Richard Strauss.* 1975. Pp. x, 274.

81 ELAINE E. BONEY. *Rainer Maria Rilke:* Duinesian Elegies. *German Text with English Translation and Commentary.* 2nd ed. 1977. Pp. xii, 153.

82 JANE K. BROWN. *Goethe's Cyclical Narratives:* Die Unterhaltungen deutscher Ausgewanderten *and* Wilhelm Meisters Wanderjahre. 1975. Pp. x, 144.